Arab France

Arab France

Islam and the Making of Modern Europe,
1798–1831

———

Ian Coller

UNIVERSITY OF CALIFORNIA PRESS
Berkeley   Los Angeles   London

University of California Press, one of the most distinguished university presses in the United States, enriches lives around the world by advancing scholarship in the humanities, social sciences, and natural sciences. Its activities are supported by the UC Press Foundation and by philanthropic contributions from individuals and institutions. For more information, visit www.ucpress.edu.

University of California Press
Berkeley and Los Angeles, California

University of California Press, Ltd.
London, England
© 2011 by The Regents of the University of California

Library of Congress Cataloging-in-Publication Data

Coller, Ian, 1968–.
  Arab France : Islam and the making of modern Europe, 1798–1831 / Ian Coller.
      p. cm.
  Includes bibliographical references and index.
  ISBN 978-0-520-26064-1 (cloth, alk. paper) —
  ISBN 978-0-520-26065-8 (pbk., alk. paper)
  1. France—Foreign relations—Arab countries.   2. Arab countries—Arab countries—France.   3. France—Foreign relations— Africa, North.   4. Africa, North—Foreign relations—France.   5. Asianists—France—History—19th century.
  6. Islam and politics.   I. Title.
DC59.8.A4C65   2011
704409034—dc22   2010004922

Manufactured in the United States of America

20   19   18   17   16   15   14   13   12   11
10   9   8   7   6   5   4   3   2   1

This book is printed on Cascades Enviro 100, a 100% post consumer waste, recycled, de-inked fiber. FSC recycled certified and processed chlorine free. It is acid free, Ecologo certified, and manufactured by BioGas energy.

CONTENTS

PREFACE

In late October 2005, as the first draft of this work was completed, two teenagers, Zyed Benna and Bouna Traoré, were killed while under pursuit by police in the outer suburbs of Paris. Protests began in local communities and became more violent as they spread to most major cities in France. In the streets, cars burned, and police fired tear gas into crowds of teenagers from the largely Arab and African populations of overcrowded urban housing estates. Nicolas Sarkozy, then minister of the interior, dismissed the protesters as "racaille" (scum), comments that only fueled the conflagration of anger and protest. After three weeks of inexplicable silence, President Jacques Chirac at last appeared on television to acknowledge that France was confronting "a crisis of meaning, a crisis of values, a crisis of identity." In his speech he declared: "We will construct nothing of lasting value, until we embrace the diversity of French society. That diversity is written in our history: it is our richness and our strength." Since that time, the launch of a national debate on French identity has done nothing to resolve these urgent questions. This book derives in some sense from the deaths of these young men, from the contestation that followed, and from that unwilling recognition wrenched from the French state.

The paradox of French society today is that a nation that so long prided itself on its commitment to freedom and equality, its fearless intellectual critique, and its cosmopolitanism has been unable or unwilling to negotiate the realities of diversity and difference on its own soil. If the "revolt of the suburbs" showed that ethnic and cultural difference is largely confined to the outer zones of the urban agglomerations, it also made clear that such difference has been ghettoized at a distance from the center of French cultural identity. President Chirac spoke of the absence from the media and the government of what would elsewhere be known as "minorities"—in France any terminology that suggests the existence of separate and distinct categories within the Republic is anathema. But this absence can be applied equally to the cultural self-representation of France today, and in particular to the historical identity that underpins this understanding. From Molière to the Revolution, from Napoleon to Jean Moulin, "Frenchness" has been determined above all by an identification with the historical past, a powerful sense of the continuity of French identity over time. In the shock that followed the collapse of the ancien régime, the radical transformation wrought by the Revolution, the glory and suffering of the Napoleonic wars for empire, and the continuing instability of nineteenth-century regimes, a new breed of historians worked to construct a unity that seemed to be unsustainable at the political level, and this unity found its expression at last with the consolidation of the Third Republic at the close of the 1870s. "Our ancestors the Gauls" became the creed of the French history textbooks that taught generations of primary-school pupils to imagine France as an integral and eternal territorial and cultural unit. This "idea" of France inspired many of those who resisted the Nazi occupation after 1940, but also worked to mask the realities of collaboration and anti-Semitism during the Vichy years. In the 1950s it served to legitimate the destructive wars to retain colonial control in Asia and North Africa, and after decolonization and independence it helped erase the memory of those violent struggles.

It is for these and other reasons that France's history of diversity has remained underdeveloped. To ask what role foreigners have played in the development of modern France has often appeared antithetical to what may be called the "republican consensus" of French historiography. Over the last two centuries, millions of immigrants arrived in France. Many came from Italy, Spain, Portugal, Poland, Belgium, Germany, and elsewhere in Europe. The ancestors of Adolphe Thiers and Léon Gambetta, those pillars of the Third Republic, were respectively Greek and Italian. Others came from outside Europe: Charles Aznavour's parents were Armenian; Edith Piaf had an Algerian grandmother. Isabelle Adjani—the face of "Marianne" during the bicentenary of the Revolution in 1989—also came from an Algerian family. But this diversity of individuals is tolerated, even welcomed, because it conforms to the French model—the abandonment of cultural particularity, the irresistible alchemical transformation of the "foreign" into the "French." There is little place in this model for questions about the way French society itself might change in response to the transformation of its population. And this model fails spectacularly in the face of those differences that are not, to use an inimitable French expression, "soluble" into the Republic: race and religion.

It was here that the shock of 2005—and its ongoing sequels—lay. The 1950s saw the populations of French colonies beginning to challenge their subaltern place in a culture imposed upon them by force. The beginning of the twenty-first century is a period in which the expanding diasporic populations across the globe have begun to question the cultural systems into which they have been "inserted," as well as the societies that have signally failed to address persistent conditions of economic and social disadvantage. But the answer to this question cannot lie simply in jobs, black media personalities, and "blind CVs," proposed in order to prevent employers from routinely jettisoning applications headed with Arab-sounding names.

The elephant in the salon of French culture is the glaring fact of ethnic and cultural diversity in contemporary France. Other societies—notably within the anglophone world—have undertaken a sustained investigation of the role of diversity in their national pasts, with rich and surprising consequences. The presence of non-Europeans in French history has remained until very recently little more than a footnote, a handful of exotic anecdotes scattered here and there. But there are signs that this is beginning to change. A growing interest in immigrants, Jews, and slaves, and the reconnection of their histories to the most central debates in French historiography, have been observable for several decades. And in recent years French historians have begun to interest themselves in new questions, such as the lives of people of color in France since the ancien régime, the role of Oriental artisans in the development of French crafts and technologies, and the place of Islam and Muslims in French history.

This book is intended as a contribution to that history of diversity, but not to vaunt the success of one model of coexistence over another, nor to suggest that the problems of racism, prejudice, and ideological inflexibility are in any way restricted to the so-called Franco-French. This is not a question that can be reduced to black and white, French and non-French, Christian and Muslim, or any other radical simplification of social realities. The very concept of diversity is one of plurality rather than binarity: racism and cultural prejudices of all kinds can and do exist between different subaltern groups struggling to find a place in a new society, and bringing with them their own histories and prejudices. And the carving-out of a multiplicity of fragmentary and isolated "communities" segregated by their geographical, linguistic, or religious particularities is not the answer to the frustrations emerging from the suburban fringes of French cities. This is how the putative "Anglo-Saxon" multicultural model is often understood in France. The accuracy of that characterization is the subject for another book; but it is worth emphasizing here that it is not my intention to promote any such program. Many elements of the French republican political culture should be valued and respected, and belong to all of its citizens regardless of their background. The very fact that in three weeks of rioting no lives were lost is in itself significant. Violence was directed against the deteriorating fabric of the suburban housing projects, against the government and the police, despite the best efforts by some in politics and the media to efface the protests with the stigma of racial and religious difference.

The research that underlies this book was carried out in a France still in the throes of a great transformation, and it is irremediably marked by its historical moment. It began with a simple question about the antecedents of the "Arab France"—so evident even to the casual visitor today—that has been so much a part of my own experience of living in cities such as Paris and Marseille. But the investigation of that question gradually revealed a different story—another Arab France that seemed to have disappeared almost without a trace, one that existed even before the "colonial turn" of 1830. Discovering that lost world has been a joyous experience that owes much to my friends, colleagues, and mentors, and to the generosity of many people in many countries.

This book began as a doctoral project and would not have been possible without the wisdom and critical insight of Peter McPhee, who offered me the model of a scholarly rigor and collegial generosity that I will always strive to emulate. I was fortunate to have the inestimable guidance of Carla Hesse in formulating the initial shape of my arguments for publication in *French Historical Studies;* her coeditor Peter Sahlins, and Natalie Davis, Jo B. Margadant, Ted Margadant, Gérard Noiriel, and Daniel Roche, offered insights that have been invaluable in shaping this material. I am grateful to Michael Rapport for his careful advice on the passage from dissertation to book, and to the readers of the manuscript and the editorial team at The University of California Press for their marvelous work. I owe a special intellectual debt to Leora Auslander for opening up new vistas and contexts with her incisive questions and suggestions, some of which I have broached in this book. Many other colleagues have played an important role in the ideas developed here. Chips Sowerwine offered me his vast erudition as well as his friendship; Tim Tackett and Helen Chenut welcomed me very kindly in California and gave me the opportunity to rehearse with two of the finest French historians of recent times some of the ideas emerging in the final revisions. I am grateful to many other colleagues for their helpful comments along the way, including Abdul Samad Abdullah, Samer Akkach, Virginia Aksan, Sunil Amrith, Mark Baker, Christopher Bayly, Nicolas Bourguinat, Michael Broers, Megan Cassidy-Welch, Jocelyne Dakhlia, Joy Damousi, Helen Davies, Laurent Dubois, David Garrioch, Julie Kalman, David Laven, Alain Messaoudi, Sue Peabody, Richard Pennell, Olivier Raveux, Gideon Reuveni, Abdullah Saeed, Emmanuelle Sibeud, Justin Tighe, and Stephen Wheatcroft. My work with Arabic sources would not have been possible without the help of Youssef Alreemawi, as well as Mamadou Diamanka, who has shared with me not only his knowledge but the welcome of his family in Melbourne, Dakar, and Sare Souma. I owe a great deal to my dear friend Krystyna Duszniak for bringing me back to history and for her constant faith in my projects: and to Darek, Julian, Nadja, and Domi Duszniak, who have been a second family to me, giving happiness and respite from my task. My friend and colleague Houari Mired gave many things to this book both personally and intellectually: my understanding of "Arab Paris" and of Algeria would not be possible without him. Many friends in Stidia and Mostaganem, in Luxor, Jerusalem, Delhi, and Colombo, contributed to this book in different ways. In France, Sylvie Boujard and Isabelle de Pierrepont showed me immense kindness and friendship during my time as a graduate student and ever since: this book owes a great debt to their generosity. I have been very lucky to have such wonderful and patient friends—notably, Yesim Aksu, Robert Blum, Amy Brodtmann, Kaushal Bhuta, Nan Canter, Emily Clark, Shadyah Gigis, Khalad Karim, Mounir Kiwan, Sophie Matthiesson, Maher Mughrabi, Moumtaiz Nasser, Thomas Poirié, Nadine Raydan, Halima Taleb, and Zeina Zogheib. None of this could have been done without their abiding friendship. I am deeply grateful for the constant support of my brothers, Ross and Matthew, and my sister, Jen, and their partners Sean, Ruth, and Julius. The incalculable debt is to my parents, Bruce and Mair Coller, without whose unstinting belief and love this book could never have been written.

Introduction

This is a book about a France that never quite existed. It is not a counterfactual or fictitious history. It addresses the making and unmaking of a space that had no name and appears nowhere in the official record. All that remains of that space are mute and hardly decipherable traces scattered here and there across disparate archives and libraries: the unusual consonance of certain names inscribed upon headstones along the grey rows of cemeteries and in the pages of the now largely unread works of early Orientalism; the unnamed turbanned heads looking back at us from the paintings and engravings of postrevolutionary France; police reports and petitions filed away to gather dust in archives; letters written in crabbed nineteenth-century Arabic script recounting quarrels and reconciliations whose resonance is almost lost to us.

These names and faces in themselves constitute a remarkable and forgotten gallery, a crowded proscenium jostling with heteroclite individuals: merchants and rogues, scholars and charlatans, soldiers and slaves. Each of these men and women followed strange and surprising paths that illuminate in different ways the several worlds in which they lived. But this book aspires to be more than simply an "anthology of existences," however surprising or moving those existences may be. Instead, it seeks to examine more fully the space *between* these individuals, and reconstitute the traces of its texture, its significance, its continuities, and its ruptures. That space was primarily constituted by the specificity of the Arabic language—a shared vector, which for all its multifold vernacular differences created a certain commonality. But that vector carried with it another, more complex set of relationships with Islam—an Islam, that is, conceived in the wider sense of a world at once outside and interlaced with Europe. Yet the space we are attempting to describe

1

took its particular form from the France into which it was variously accommodated and constrained, a France that was itself in a period of radical transformation. Only by consciously *imagining* this space that appears nowhere has it been possible to discover so many things otherwise irretrievably scattered and fragmented. It is possible too that this re-imagining may also change in some small way our understanding of France itself and its contribution to the shaping of a modern Europe increasingly distinct from the Islamic world across the Mediterranean.

In this sense "Arab France" is neither hypothetical nor actual: it is an intentional act of seeing, a historical choice, a space of possibility. We should remember that familiar historical ideas have always been in key respects formulated retrospectively to describe and order events already in the past: "revolution," "age," "tradition," even the "nation" itself. Such grids of comprehension are necessary for us to distinguish the significant from the vast ocean of contingency, but other potentialities remain lost below the surface of historical intelligibility. And that necessary historical triage has consequences for the way we make history in the present, just as it shapes the way we write about the past.

In an essay entitled "The Life of Infamous Men" Michel Foucault evoked the intensity, the physicality, of the feelings produced by the fragments of obscure destinies held within the stiff cartons of the archive: "brief lives, chanced upon in books and documents . . . singular lives, which, through some unknown accident, became strange poems." It is a "vibration" like the one Foucault described that lies at the heart of this book, emerging from the curiously appropriate yet quite unexpected surroundings of the Château de Vincennes. In military archives that might well have been imagined barren ground for a social history such as this, fragments of Arab lives in early nineteenth-century France had washed up like piles of driftwood: not just one document, but thousands, in more than twelve cartons, some virtually unread. In petition after petition—written in rounded hand by the public letter-writer, traced in the schoolboy copperplate of a child pressed into service for his elders, scrawled in rough letters by a poor man or woman with only the rudiments of French, and occasionally (out of sheer desperation perhaps) penned in Arabic script—obscure lives were suddenly illuminated by what Foucault memorably called the "lightning-flash" of their momentary collision with power.[1]

And yet I believe it is the historian's task to peer beyond this momentary illumination, this collision with power, and try, however imperfectly, to divine something of the landscape beyond. This is not to say that the historian is not concerned with power, or that there is some more perfect social "reality" to be approached by an empirical path: it is simply to delineate the particular and limited concerns and aims of this form of study of the past. Alain Corbin broached some of these questions in his choice to investigate in detail the life of a randomly chosen individual, an obscure carpenter from a rural village, born at the end of the eighteenth century. Corbin explained that he wanted to resurrect the "spatial and temporal

horizon" of this individual, the invisible center of a description, a kind of cine-
matic point-of-view device that would enable different insights into the political
and social transformations of his world and his age.[2] Neither a microhistory nor a
structural analysis, nor yet a philosophical excavation of the kind Foucault proposed, Corbin's study had the benefit of restoring the significance of event, transformation, and rupture—whether individual, societal, or global—while still giving
weight to the other more persistent rhythms of everyday life. He imagined the possibility of extending this inquiry outward to a whole network of people arising from
their connection with this one individual, a series of "collateral reanimations" that
might provide a new and much greater "understanding" of the nineteenth century.[3]
But in tracing a different network, not defined by *terroir* but by the connections of
Arabic language and culture, quite a different understanding may emerge. The immense and ever-expanding resources of electronic indexing, online texts, and data-
bases have brought the fractal possibilities of Corbin's project closer to the realm of
possibility.[4]

Those tools have made it possible to reconstruct many of the broken links connecting these people, to shed some glimmers onto the landscape briefly illuminated by the archival sources. But other sources make it clear that we should not
imagine these people solely in their relationship to a power defined exclusively in
communication with the state. Indeed, much of the substance of these Arab lives
was particularly opaque to that flash of lightning that Foucault imagined. Among
the documents lie a handful of letters in Arabic, which the authorities were unable
to interpret without assistance. Those orphaned fragments are but the tip of an ice-
berg of Arabic correspondence—thousands of letters, written and exchanged between Paris and Marseille, Damascus, Cairo, Gibraltar, Cyprus, Livorno, and Algiers, to which the authorities had no access at all. Indeed they did not perhaps
even suspect the existence of this highly literate network. Some hundreds of those
letters have been preserved, and the light that they shed is rather different.

These Arabic sources no longer address themselves directly to the organs of state
power but rather chart a whole set of transactions between individuals in a wider
social network, whether relations of friendship or rivalry, alliance or enmity. Their
preservation is not accidental: collections of correspondence were donated to libraries, or published as useful examples of Arab letter-writing by early Orientalist
scholars. But their content is at least no longer structured by the careful articulation of petitions shaped more or less effectively to appeal to the requirements of
the state. Instead, they follow other circuits of power, other norms of greeting,
compliment, and sociability, which can illuminate other aspects of the space in
which they lived. But considered alone, the quarrels and reconciliations they nar-
rate may appear consumingly parochial and barren of historical significance. It is
in the intersections between these two fields of illumination that we may conceive
that space I have called "Arab France."

Thus the sources for this history are diverse both in their form and in their address: among them are petitions, registers, and dossiers; police files and prefectural reports; visual culture, from popular lithographs to caricatures; literary writings, varying from poetry to official speeches; technical works, from linguistic and historical essays to grammatical treatises and dictionaries. The sheer multiplicity of these sources, and the lack of any guiding narrative, even a less than accurate one, upon which to peg an interpretation, have necessitated a relatively hybrid approach, built on a foundation of social-historical analysis based in the archive, but seeking to bring those documents into a productive dialogue with other cultural materials that may help fill the many gaps that those documents reveal. Three examples may serve here by way of introduction to the scope of this book.

In the summer of 1811, an 'Egyptian' named Jirjis Ai'da—in France, Georges Aïdé—wrote to the Ministry of War complaining of an unpleasant incident that had occurred in the course of a stroll through Paris.[5] Aïdé had not been in the capital long: only a few months earlier he had transplanted his large family from Marseille to the rue Saint-Honoré—then a newly constructed quarter, densely packed with apartments and cheap hotels. Shortly after his arrival, he was visited by a young man, Joubran Mehenna Tady, who begged him for financial help, complaining that he was up to his neck in debt. By his own account, Aïdé had been quite generous to his young compatriot. But at some point he grew tired of the continuing requests and refused to advance Joubran any more money. This led to an unfortunate confrontation in one of the alleys of the gardens stretching out in front of the Tuileries Palace. As Aïdé haughtily explained,

> While taking an afternoon walk in the Thuileries [sic], I noticed this young man seated next to Mr C–. When—quite by chance—I happened to pass behind him, he took it upon himself to utter a series of rude and contemptuous expressions, to which Your Servant did not choose to respond for fear of provoking troublesome and unpremeditated extremities.[6]

Later that day, according to the letter, the rambunctious Joubran had an appointment with Elias Pharaon, another compatriot. Pharaon prevailed upon Joubran to explain his insulting behavior toward Aïdé. The young man admitted that the dispute had initially been provoked over money, but dug himself in defiantly, boasting that he would do worse in any future encounter. Aïdé claimed that the young man had already clashed violently with a number of mutual acquaintances, making "malicious remarks" to Mikha'il Sabbagh and Joseph Athaya, abusing another Egyptian, Antoine Siouphi, "with blows as well as words," and striking an unnamed woman. "It is up to you, Monsieur," Aïdé wrote,

> to put an end to the unruly behavior of this young man, using whatever means you think best in order to make this young man take account of his errors and misdemeanors, and send him back to Marseille where his pension is registered.[7]

It is in the interstices of this document—and those others that chase it in a trail leading through the police, the Interior Ministry, and the pensions bureau, through the Tuileries gardens and across the suburbs of Paris, in lines stretching to Marseille and across the Mediterranean—that the "Arab France" of this book situates itself. Such documents gesture casually toward a shared reality too familiar to be explained, a common history constituted from a decade of close and constant interaction, of familial relations and fraternal loyalties, long-standing grudges and conspiratorial schemes, business ventures and common enterprises, religious ties and divisions. That memory is now lost, and in these documents the reality was reshaped for the purpose at hand, to suit the requirements of power. But it is a reality that must therefore be reimagined from fragments, gaps, and silences, because nowhere was it brought to light, given any explicit articulation either by those who lived that reality, in ways perhaps too familiar to be remarked upon, or by those in power who tolerated or even sponsored its existence.

A work by a German engraver (Müller), from that same year, of those same gardens, represents two men in Ottoman clothing standing smoking their pipes amid a scene of leisure, much as Georges Aïdé and Joubran Mehenna and other Egyptians must have done in the same period. The gardens of Paris, freely accessible to the public since the Revolution, along with the urban improvements ushered in by Napoleon, provided a popular subject for engravers who were beginning to use the techniques of lithography to make images much more affordable for consumers across Europe. Collections of "picturesque views" of Paris have never ceased to be a popular purchase since the eighteenth century, and during the Napoleonic years many artists traveled to the French capital, which was the radiating center of power across central and southern Europe. The gardens stretching in shaded avenues from the Tuileries Palace to the Place de la Concorde were a favorite haunt for many: sometimes they might catch a glimpse of imperial carriages arriving or departing, or the well-to-do strolling in from the arcades of the new rue de Rivoli. In a book for the German market titled *Promenades de Paris,* an artist depicted the women in their high-waisted Empire smocks and the men in tailcoats and tight breeches in generic scenes of sociability (fig. 1). Among these typical Parisians, however, he placed another pair of figures conspicuous by the difference of their dress (fig. 2). They sport the turbans and beards typical of Ottoman dress, long dalmatic coats, baggy pantaloons, and curving babouche slippers. One holds a long chibouk pipe to the side as he engages in an intimate conversation with his companion, his scarf wound casually under his arm and over his shoulder. His interlocutor holds up one hand as though to mark a point: their conversation appears somewhat more serious than the gamboling frivolity of the men and women around them.

These men seem quite at home: only the nonconformity of their dress marks them as different. There is no context to explain their presence, and none appears

FIGURE 1. Engraving by Schwartz after Müller, *Allée des Orangers, Jardin des Tuileries,* from R. J. Durdent, *Promenades de Paris* (Paris: Le Normant, 1812). Author's collection.

to be required for the intelligibility of the image, despite the fact that the purpose of the book of engravings was to offer the generic, most typical scenes of Parisian life to those who wanted a souvenir of their journey, or those who could not afford a visit to Paris. The depiction of Ottoman figures in images of Venice or Marseille was quite common in the eighteenth century: the canvases of Canaletto or Vernet often featured the typical turbaned figures to be seen in these important "Gates of the Orient." Paris was a cosmopolitan center, but it was not a port city: to travel there from the Mediterranean took a week or more, an expensive and often uncomfortable journey. Elsewhere we find images of foreign merchants in the bustling European capitals. Among the "Cries of London" of the time, for example, are Turkish rhubarb-sellers and Moroccans hawking leather slippers: their trade is clearly illustrated, since it is the motive for their depiction.[8] The figures in the Tuileries are not marked as itinerant: they have no merchandise to sell, and

FIGURE 2. Engraving by Schwartz after Müller, *Allée des Orangers, Jardin des Tuileries,* from R. J. Durdent, *Promenades de Paris* (Paris: Le Normant, 1812), detail. Author's collection.

they participate here in the generic scenes of Parisian leisure by dint of their tobacco and conversation.

Figures of slaves and Moors frequently appeared in furniture and decoration,
even as architectural ornament, throughout the eighteenth century, to mark the
possession of colonial wealth or simply as a more loosely associated exoticism.
But the "exotic" is marked by its *opposition* to the "generic" or typical elements of
everyday life. In paintings depicting the Napoleonic campaign in Egypt and Syria,
the "exotic" offered the excitement of blood, dust, and steel, dangers domesticated
by the act of representation; distance brought near by the painter's art; the alien
made intelligible by the rules of perspective and composition. But in this engraving there is no perceptible context of threat, no great distance to be traversed between subject and viewer, and no action or composition to give the figures any
narrative intelligibility, just their brute presence. The interpretation of such images as visual evidence poses many dangers for the historian, yet they cannot simply be ignored, particularly given the frequency with which such figures appear in
illustrations of this period. Without corroborating indications, we cannot assume
that they represent a contemporaneous reality. At the same time we should not
make the mistake of asserting a priori that there is no relationship at all between
visual representation and historical reality, however complex that relationship
may be.

The great canvases of Napoleonic military campaigns still overwhelm the viewer
today with their sheer size and color. They were works of political mythmaking, not
historical accuracy. Yet even in these notorious pieces of propaganda, we may look
for the traces of a contemporary reality, since somewhere among the faces, whether
in preparatory sketches, in smaller studies, or in the great tableaux themselves, is
a visual record of some of the men and women of the Arab France of this period.
We know from contemporary accounts that young Egyptians, and particularly
demobilized soldiers like Joubran, could earn a few sous posing in the recreations
of Egypt for painters such as Gros, Girodet, and Delacroix, or even for the ongoing
enterprise of the multivolume *Description de l'Égypte*. Certainly the red-hooded
figure in the great *Sacre de Napoléon* by Jacques-Louis David was a Syrian priest
named Rufa'il Zakhur. But elsewhere the figures remain nameless, only to be
guessed at, or, better still, simply imagined.

The figures in Müller's engraving are silent about their reasons for being there,
about their "Oriental" presence in this pictorial imaginary of Napoleonic Paris. We
would be closer to answering the questions they pose if we had some self-reflexive
voice describing the nature of Arab life in France, or even some contemporary description from an external observer. But no such account exists: even the texts accompanying the images make no remark about these figures. This silence must be
accounted for in some way. It is certainly not the case that these people lacked the
skills to represent themselves, to conceive or present their own story. They were

not passive receptacles of Orientalizing knowledge wielded by Arabist experts; indeed, many were accomplished Orientalists in their own right. Therefore, we must ask whether it was their own self-understanding or external circumstances that prevented them from addressing directly, at least in recorded form, their presence in France as a community rather than as scattered individuals.

In 1820 a young man arrived in the capital from his provincial home in Marseille, hoping to make his way in the cutthroat literary world of romantic Paris. But although he had been raised in Marseille, his origins were more distant: proud of his French language and culture, he nonetheless made a claim to a more particular kind of accomplishment, his fluency in Arabic. In an early letter to a prospective patron, he evoked his childhood in a Marseille surrounded by "the scenery of Oriental life," as he wrote. Joseph Agoub had arrived in France as a six-year-old boy in 1801, along with many other Egyptian families. But he insisted that his childhood was not simply a unilateral adjustment to French society. "Nothing had really changed in my way of life," he wrote.

> And having, so to speak, carried my household gods with me, I felt as though I were still in the land of my birth. Or rather, when I observed around me the mixture of Arab and European customs, when my ear was struck simultaneously by two different idioms, it seemed to me that Egypt had somehow become combined with France, and that the two nations were merged into one.[9]

Agoub became an accomplished writer and a well-known personality in the Orientalist milieux of the 1820s. As this tantalizingly brief passage suggests, he was the most promising candidate to provide us with some description of the "lieu de mémoire" he evoked in his letter. But nothing in his subsequent writings addressed that mixed world directly, beyond a brief note on the contribution his compatriots had made to the study and teaching of Arabic in France. It is perhaps telling that he made no reference at all to the violent events that marked the end both of his childhood and of the mixed Egyptian-French life of Marseille: the murderous assault upon the "Egyptian" community during the transition of power in June 1815. As a result of that great silence, no plaque or memorial stands today to mark this stark episode of racial violence in early nineteenth-century France. That episode did not mark the end of Arab France; instead it proved the surprising vigor of this transplanted community. But it shadowed certain kinds of colonial racial logic that would at last rend asunder the components and conditions of a French Arab identity. It is in this process, this "unmaking" of Arab France, that we may perhaps look for the genealogy of that strange silence.

The period evoked by this book is defined roughly by the beginning of one French conquest in the Muslim world and the consolidation of another. This is not intended to suggest that those dates are constraining in any real sense: they define a particular moment in which a particular population was compelled to develop ways of accommodating a mode of life and identity they brought from the Arab provinces of the Ottoman Empire to a postrevolutionary France still stumbling painfully toward a stable political culture. It is the contention of this book that the Egyptians and Syrians who settled in France during the early part of the nineteenth century created new forms of life that belonged neither to the world that they had left nor wholly to the France where they established their lives—that they built an "Arab France" of their own. This notion of "Arab France" is not intended to suggest that France was an Arab country during this period: to read the formulation in this way would be to assume that there is only one France, a unitary national territory with a distinct and determined self-identity. This book is dedicated to the principle that France, like other spaces and other nations, has always been multiple and plural, a space of possibility to be invented and reinvented, to be lived in many different ways at once. The notion of Arab France contains within itself many possibilities too. Moreover, there is not a single Arab France, but many— this book will seek to trace one of them.

Both Islam and Europe will be central to this book, but neither is determining to the story of Arab France as it evolved over this period. These two great transnational concepts take their place alongside and sometimes against the intensely national ideas emerging out of the revolutionary era—but the very nature of the phenomenon under study here tends to demonstrate their interconnectedness stretching back into a common past characterized by both exchange and conflict. Certainly in this period only the most tangled boundary existed across much of what is today eastern Europe. Only with the rapid improvements in transport and communication in the nineteenth century did the Mediterranean come to seem a natural boundary between two worlds rather than a connecting bridge. And these worlds were interconnected with others, across the Atlantic, the Sahara, the Indian Ocean, and beyond. Thus it is as interlocking spaces rather than as substantive categories that Islam and Europe must figure in this study, which examines these spaces from the perspective of people whose roots lay firmly in the Muslim world, regardless of their religious confession, yet who chose or were forced into a trajectory that brought them to Europe. Behind the commonality of Arabic language and culture lay the structures and traditions of what Marshall Hodgson called an Islamicate society, and it is the accommodation, negotiation, or outright rejection of these cultural differences in postrevolutionary France that forms much of the substance of what is to follow. This was an epoch of enormous change in Europe's idea of itself: over the same period, parallel and interconnected, but nonetheless distinct transformations were taking place in the Muslim world.

The period with which this book is concerned was a critical one for the writing of history in Europe.[10] In important ways these were the years in which modern "national" history was born, providing foundational structures for the national identities that came so strongly into play over the same period. One of the contexts, and indeed the consequences, of this new sense of national unity and purpose was a new kind of expansionism. No longer simply seeking to dominate the European world at France's borders, French men and women looked toward a new imperial space that—in the relative continental stability after the Congress of Vienna— would become the primary arena for the exercise of European national rivalries.

The Ottoman Arab world was not peripheral but rather crucial in this struggle. The weakening of centralized power in Istanbul over the eighteenth century was widely viewed in Europe as a sign that the Ottoman Empire was breaking up, and that its rich provinces were ripe for the picking. In 1798, the Directory, which had come to power after the fall of Robespierre and the radical elements of the Revolution, sent one of its most powerful (and troublesome) generals on a mission to grab Egypt, hoping to fracture Britain's growing imperial power by seizing the trade route from India to Europe. General Bonaparte failed to hold onto his conquest of Egypt and Syria, let alone to fulfill his fantasy of marching on Constantinople, and returned to seize power in France instead. Three decades later the seizure of Algiers set the course to put France into the Arab world, to create a French Arab empire, which, at its height, would extend from Morocco to Lebanon.

The "Arab France," that this book investigates is very different—it emerged in the entr'acte between these two French incursions into the domain of Islam. The world of which Georges Aïdé, Joubran Mehenna, and their associates were a part was in an immediate sense a result of the occupation and subsequent evacuation of Egypt and Syria at the turn of the nineteenth century. But between 1801 and 1830 no European power moved aggressively into the Arab world: indeed, it was rather a period in which the center of Ottoman power was seeking to repair the fabric of its own empire. The year 1798 was once almost universally assumed to be the watershed in the transition to "modernity" in the Middle East and North Africa. This was a vision that imagined modernity to be an exclusive and inevitable result of superior European development, in the Old World and the New. It is a vision that has been almost entirely superseded by contemporary scholarship, which now dates the beginnings of the transformation in the Middle East to the eighteenth century, with the struggles both of local leaders for autonomy and of religious intellectual elites for a renewal of learning—a process that came to fruition in the *nahda,* or "reawakening," of the nineteenth century.[11] Indeed, in a wider sense, the eighteenth century has been reconceived, in the words of the historian C. A. Bayly, as an era of "converging revolutions," from America to Persia, from Portugal to China.[12] This view of Europe as just one part of a world in motion contrasts sharply with the older picture of a "stagnant" Ottoman society suddenly awoken from its torpor by a resurgent "youthful" Europe incarnated in the figure of Napoleon Bonaparte.

This book is focused on that period of transformation, but it examines these events and ideas less from the macropolitical perspective of revolution and imperial expansion, or the economic analysis of industrial production and trade, than from the social perspective of the lives of Arabs in France. It is through the personal trajectories that cross these larger transformations that we can most effectively comprehend some of the larger forces at work, as the works of William Dalrymple, Linda Colley, and Maya Jasanoff have shown.[13] These historians emphasize the neglected "transcultural" dimension within imperial histories, whether through early British officials and their local wives in India, through the lives and writings of Europeans held in captivity in the era of slave trading, or through the extraordinary mania for collecting extra-European culture and antiquities that took hold of so many Enlightenment Europeans. These histories have drawn from relatively unknown lives many important insights into the forms of cultural exchange, hybridity, and connectedness that preceded, and in some important ways persisted through, the period of colonial domination.

What these lives also show in the larger historical sense, however—even by the exception that proves the rule—is the hardening of cultural and national identities in the face of colonial confrontation. Colley's captives found on returning home that their experiences needed to be framed in the conventional terms of "civilized" and "uncivilized." Dalrymple's "white mughals" gave way to a species of colonial administrator no longer willing to engage in any form of intimate cultural exchange with indigenous life. And Jasanoff has traced how the "embracing and tolerant" passion for the other that characterized earlier collectors was transformed by the "violence of collecting empires."[14] These insights are very constructive in giving us a far richer and more complex vision of imperialism as a form of globalization, revealing the potentialities for cosmopolitanism contained within it, as well as the foreclosure of these cosmopolitan possibilities.

At the same time, these accounts of exchange across the imagined limits of cultural systems have tended to approach their subjects exclusively from one side. All of these studies represent *Europeans* negotiating an "other" beyond the bounds of Europe; in none of these books is the reverse experience of non-Europeans in Europe an intrinsic element of the narrative.[15] In part this is because the central concern of these historians has been "empire" itself, and the need to develop a more differentiated, more cosmopolitan, and richer account of the imperial experience. But this experience, and the experience before, across, and within empire, need to be taken back to the metropole so that we may begin to see to what extent the national and colonizing cultures themselves were already engaged in a transcultural exchange, which preceded as much as it accompanied empire, and what happened to these possibilities in the "imperial turn."[16] One key element of my approach in this book is to avoid the a priori assumption of a fundamental or uncrossable divide between Europe and the Muslim world on its borders—I will try to show that these borders were crossable and crossed in both directions. Indeed, as Fernand Braudel memorably observed, "What boundaries can be marked when we are dealing not with plants and animals, relief and climate, but men, whom no barriers or frontiers can stop?"[17] These were often zones of confusion, interlaced with and always involved in the processes that were remaking the world during a period of profound and spectacular political and economic change.

In this sense, the book inevitably engages with Edward Said's influential theses about the close relationship between imperial hegemony and European constructions of the Orient.[18] The passionate and timely polemic of his book *Orientalism* cleared the ground for many of the possibilities contained in this project as well as others. Said's elegant, passionate readings of the Orients of Flaubert and Chateaubriand seem to have offered many critics a golden thread for navigating the difficult questions of power, knowledge, and agency across the putative East/West divide. It has not been my intention to address the larger theoretical questions raised by his work: instead, *Arab France* addresses a space occluded from Said's analysis of East and West, a zone of intermediarity, of "in-betweenness," to which he himself belonged and which played a critical role in forming his own intellectual project. Although my study covers a period that Said insisted was foundational to the enterprise of Orientalism as a project delivering "scientific" knowledge in the service of colonial domination, the cast of characters is very different. None of the Arab Orientalists mentioned in this book appears in Said's panorama, which neglects the possibility of a role for "Orientals" themselves in their own representation: their membership of the "Asiatic Societies," and their considerable literary production in Arabic, Farsi, and Turkish as well as in French, German, and English. I will emphasize the role of French Arabs in what Raymond Schwab called the "Oriental Renaissance" of the early nineteenth century.[19] This is not to contest the entanglement of Orientalist and other knowledges with the structures and strategies of power; indeed, it is rather to explore the multiplicity of those entanglements beyond a Manichaean binary and their transformation by larger forces, including those of an increasingly global imperialism.

In the histories of diversity in France to date, Arabs have rarely appeared as a focus of investigation alongside, for example, French Jewish communities whose lives and struggles have been so richly explored.[20] Nor have Arab lives been brought to light in the increasing attention paid to slavery and its crucial impact upon the metropole in terms of colonial economies and "people of color" living in France.[21] It was only recently that a group of French historians and anthropologists directed their attention for the first time to what they described as "two centuries of Oriental and Maghrebin presence in the [French] capital."[22] A follow-up to *Le Paris noir,* dealing with the black "presence" in Paris, and *Le Paris Asie,* dealing with "one and a half centuries of Asian presence in the capital,"[23] *Le Paris arabe* opened conventional understandings of French history "from the center" to new questions about colonization, decolonization, and postcolonial relationships, making a vital contribution to reimagining the history of a city characterized today more than ever by ethnic and cultural diversity. But the unresolved ambiguity of the word "presence" appearing in all of these works evades the more difficult historical questions about community and identity. In its treatment of the nineteenth century, *Le Paris arabe* relied upon the work of Anouar Louca, an Egyptian historian who settled in France and was for many decades the only historian to manifest any sustained interest in the cultural exchanges between France and Egypt in this period. His monograph on Egyptian "writers and travelers" in France (which dealt with some of the figures mentioned in this book) modeled itself on his mentor Jean-Marie Carré's two-volume work on French "writers and travelers" in Egypt.[24] It is unsurprising, therefore, that the authors of *Le Paris arabe* adopted from Louca a picture of an early nineteenth-century "Arab Paris" defined by high-profile "visitors" from Egypt and other parts of the Arab world— students, writers, merchants, diplomats, and the occasional tourist—and by the French response to these *gens de passage*.[25]

The history of Arab visitors to France is certainly a rich and fascinating story, and one that deserves to be extended considerably further back into French history—there is plenty of evidence that the flow of visitors back and forth between the Arab world and Europe is much older than two centuries, stretching back to the Middle Ages and beyond.[26] But in spite of the significant historical work he carried out, Louca's research has served contemporary historians rather badly. As a Francophile Copt and Egyptian patriot, Louca accepted wholesale many of the commonest Eurocentric assumptions about Arab culture and history and often failed to see the forest for the trees when investigating archives that contained a much larger fund of information about the Arab population of early nineteenth-century France. Instead, he followed a tributary stream of exoticizing fascination with the "Mamelouks," the Orientally attired soldiers of Napoleon, about whom we will have more to say later in this book. What was lost in this divagation was the bulk of early nineteenth-century French Arabs who had not much more connection with the Mamelouks than many French men and women had with the rest of the Imperial Guard.

At the other pole of the "presence" around which the authors of *Le Paris arabe* configure their historical account was Arab mass immigration, beginning at the outset of World War I and accelerating in the years after the decolonization of North Africa. The literature on Algerian migration to France in the twentieth century is considerable, although that on other Arabic-speaking groups is rather less impressive.[27] Mohammed Arkoun directed a project investigating the role of Islam and Muslims across the course of French history, drawing attention to many important and forgotten aspects of that complex multilateral relationship.[28] Still, this work does not significantly challenge an overarching narrative stretching from "influence" through "imperialism" to "immigration." That is to say, the close relationship between France and the Muslim world, developing toward invasion and colonial domination after 1830, eventually gave rise to a late colonial and postcolonial immigration. In the absence of any careful study of Arab populations in France in the nineteenth century, it has been assumed that such movement was an exclusively twentieth-century phenomenon and as such played no part in the larger sweep of French history. The possibility of migratory flows, and even a significant "postcolonial" migration in the aftermath of the occupation of Egypt, have not been considered in this regard.

If extra-European immigration to France has been considered a twentieth-century phenomenon, it has assumed a far greater importance in the twenty-first century, as questions of immigration and integration have become entangled with other notions about "civilizational" clashes, terrorism, social inequality, and religious conflict. It has often been observed that even the second and third generations of Arabs living in France today are spoken of as *immigrés* or, in the more careful phraseology, *issus de l'immigration* (of immigrant background).[29] This may appear to contradict the official doctrine of republican equality: these children of immigration are, after all, French citizens and should surely be referred to as such. But the preservation of any degree of cultural (or religious) distinctiveness, even an Arab name, among those of immigrant origin tends to place these citizens in a category apart from the assimilatory model of the Republic and sometimes provides a blind for other, darker impulses, such as those of racial or religious prejudice. In this ideological structure there is little room for the concept of a distinct "community" existing within French society, yet remaining French—that is, for the kinds of "hyphenated" identities that have formed an important part of the multicultural model in the United States, Canada, and Australia.

Almost any significant group of foreigners in Britain, from Australians to Somalis, has been termed a "community."[30] The literature dealing with the African, Caribbean, South Asian, and other populations of nineteenth-century Britain is relatively rich.[31] In contrast, until quite recently, French historical work on foreign "communities" in France during the nineteenth century or earlier has been relatively rare.[32] The work dealing with the two major "internal" categories, Jews and slaves, has sometimes noted the diversity of those categories, which could on occasion include groups coming from the Middle East, India, and elsewhere. But for migrant populations the historiography is much less rich, in part because migrant life, culture, and identity in France has been considered a phenomenon of recent date and has therefore been the object of sociological rather than historical inquiry. Unlike other dimensions of "French" life, which have been the subject of searching historical questioning, the presence of foreigners prior to the mass migrations after World War I has received comparatively little attention, unless it is in terms of changing attitudes toward foreigners among the French population.[33]

Until very recently, many of the principal interventions into questions of race and ethnic diversity in nineteenth-century French history have come from anglophone scholarship.[34] This difference is in large part an index of divergent responses toward cultural and ethnic diversity: the French model of republican citizenship has tended to overshadow any interest in distinct cultures or communities within the Republic. The collection of statistics on ethnic origin in France is proscribed by law.[35] Thus it is difficult to give an account even of today's "Arab France," due to the resistance of a historical narrative that places the Republic as the center and culmination of French history and strongly discourages the fostering of "alternative" histories and identities, whether Breton, gay, Jewish, or Arab.[36] Both the global climate and recent legal controversies over colonial histories in France have exacerbated this intense reaction against *communautarisme* in a political as well as an intellectual sense.[37]

These questions are complex and have been explored at length elsewhere. They bear on this study in helping explain the paucity of studies of migrant communities in nineteenth-century France. But the problem is wider. While the theoretical literature on "community" in the sociological and anthropological fields is vast, the development of these questions within the historical field is relatively thin.[38] There is no study that deals specifically with the historical question of how we might evaluate whether a given group marked by strong differences from those around them—such as Arabic-speaking migrants and their descendants in France—should be considered a "community" rather than what some historians have termed a "presence." Definitions of community have tended to combine three key concepts: ties of kinship or other social bonds, geographical locality, and the sense of common identification.

In a book on eighteenth-century Paris, David Garrioch noted that "neighbourhood" in eighteenth-century Paris, a highly localized form of community, often outweighed the bonds of *pays* or regional origin for migrants coming to Paris from other parts of France.[39] But he also acknowledged the existence of "non-territorial" communities among minority, migrant, and subcultural groups, whose link to a fixed location might be weak or nonexistent. In the contemporary world we see clearly that such groups of migrants frequently settle across a widely dispersed space, whether across a city, between cities, or even across countries and continents. We may see this as the fragmenting effect of globalization and accelerated mobility. But, as James Clifford has suggested, we may equally see these contemporary communities as a challenge to our understanding of the nature of "community" itself. Clifford argues that in studying these modern "diasporas," we should abandon the "localizing strategies" that lead us to pose questions about social alignments in terms of bounded community, organic culture, and a dynamic of center and periphery. Instead, community may be understood as multilocal, decentered, existing geographically across multiple points, and affectively in a set of "spatially extended relationships."[40]

Clifford suggests that the normative practice of twentieth-century ethnography has, in his words, "privileged relations of dwelling over relations of travel."[41] This is equally true of the practice of historiography, which has, since the nineteenth century concerned itself primarily with "national" histories, privileging territorially defined states and identities over other forms of social and cultural relationship. National histories tend to identify ethnic, cultural, and linguistic differences with the "natural boundaries" defining territorial nations   in the case of France the rough "hexagon" delineated by mountains, rivers, and seas. The dominance of the territorial nation-state in modern Europe has encouraged historians to view history almost exclusively through this paradigm. In particular, the three shores of the Mediterranean—European, Asian, and African—have been separated by a "metageography" of continents, which tends to present cultural differences as natural consequences of the separation of landmasses.[42]

Mobilities come in many forms—forced and free, economic and political, temporary and permanent, gradual trickles and sudden mass dislocations. But historians have recognized that clear distinctions are rarely easy to make in the complex field of human mobility. Paul Gilroy's *Black Atlantic* challenged such assumptions in relation to the "Atlantic system," which was defined by a massive forced mobility of Africans between Africa, the Caribbean and the Americas, and Europe.[43] In a recent book on travel and mobility in Enlightenment Europe, Daniel Roche suggests that societies of the past have been too readily imagined as fixed and immobile before industrial modernity jolted them into sudden and accelerating movement.[44] These understandings of mobility are fundamental to the ways in which I will investigate the Arab community in early nineteenth-century France. If we imagine this community as a relatively fixed and localized set of relationships, we are likely to search for evidence of stable, long-term communal structures: the concentration of residents into a small area, a few streets, or a single quarter of a city; the development of common cultural forms and modes of communication, such as community associations, newspapers, and collective enterprises. At the very least, we would search for raw numbers indicating some kind of critical mass, and the evidence of a self-recognition as a community in some recorded form. In the absence of these elements, we would hesitate to consider it a community of any significance.

If we consider community in a more delocalized sense, we are free to investigate social bonds in an open way, recognizing a far more dispersed and less formalized network of relationships. But such a way of "imagining" community is crucially dependent upon the existence of some common self-understanding, since it is only the strength of common identification that could serve to hold a widely dispersed population together and give the "community" any meaning other than a purely functional category. It is this question of identity that must therefore assert itself in this book, despite the incisive criticisms of the category that have been advanced by, among others, Frederick Cooper and Rogers Brubaker.[45] These critics have observed the confusion that arises when we seek to apply this term to people who do not use it themselves, while we insist, as most scholars of identity have done, that identity is a *construct* and not a fixed substrate of human existence. What is the use of such a term if it is neither a dimension of contemporaneous thought, nor a tool of analysis that can be applied confidently by the historian? Cooper and Brubaker suggested that if the "strong" essentialist conception of identity has been largely repudiated by social scientists, it at least offered a consistency lacking in "weak" constructivist stances. The cases they cite use the category of "identity" to explain the persistence of social conflict, the survival of "tribal identities" or "ethnic identities" into the modern state, or modern "identitarian" political calls for group solidarity in the face of structural discrimination. But it is perhaps possible to conceive of a "strong constructivist" conception—which would treat identity neither as a given to be "discovered" nor as a fluid, multiple, shifting constellation, but as a *project* of configuring cultural practices, group relations, and articulated self-understandings across a particular space. It is a kind of work carried out in particular by minority and diasporic groups in societies in which they are identified as categorically different, and in which their networks may extend very strongly beyond the territorial limits of the social polity.

In 1963 the great British social historian E. P. Thompson wrote a book called *The Making of the English Working Class.* The "making" of this or that phenomenon in history was familiar enough and has enjoyed even greater popularity since that time. In the loosest sense, it implies an interest in process and dynamics rather than static description. But Thompson made it clear why the conception of "making" was fundamental to his approach: he was describing something that existed only as a process and could not be described in any other way.

Rather than simply describing the formation of a social class under specific historical circumstances, Thompson showed how a plurality of heterogeneous individuals and groups with different origins and different interests, different beliefs and regional ties, came together to recognize their commonalities over their differences, partially as a result of the conditions created by those more powerful, but also in part as the result of their own work, even if this was not always explicitly articulated to such an end. Thus he concluded that "in the years between 1780 and 1832 most English working people came to feel an identity of interests as between themselves, and as against their rulers and employers." But Thompson also set out with a passion to rescue the subjects of his study—from poor artisans to deluded utopians—from what he called the "enormous condescension of posterity" by restoring to them their proper role in their own history. Class, Thompson wrote, "is defined by men as they make their history, and in the end this is its only definition."[46] Thus "making" was a process that involved the historian herself or himself in an active role.

In a similar way, albeit on a far smaller scale, the subjects of this study came to conceive of themselves through their commonalities rather than their differences, and equally as a result both of the state's hegemonic role and of their own negotiation of those conditions. To say that these people were Arabs is inaccurate in every way except this one: like Thompson, we must emphasize the longer trajectory in order to perceive the phenomenon at all. The "Arab identity" described here was the result of a multiplicity of choices, of associations, and of reactions to external conditions sometimes conducive and sometimes coercive. It is a crucial difference from Thompson's study, however, that the conditions for the "making" of this Arab identity in France were suddenly and catastrophically altered under dramatically different circumstances, and alongside resurgent categories of race and nation that came to dominate the social world in which these people lived. Hence I have set out to describe both the *making* of this Arab France and its *unmaking,* a trajectory that also helps explain its quasi-total disappearance from the historical record.

In seeking to illuminate at once the participation of the state and the wider society and the active role of these people themselves, I have sought, within the restrictions of this book, to draw upon as wide a range of sources as possible, rather than focusing upon a single archive or source. That search took me from the imposing edifice of the Archives Nationales and the military archives housed in the castle of Vincennes at the edge of Paris to local archives and libraries in Marseille, Melun, Carcassonne, and Aix-en-Provence. In Geneva I was fortunate to discover the existence of a large corpus of letters in Arabic between members of the community that provided quite different insights into their networks, social practices, and modes of address and communication. Without doubt there are many more documents scattered through other archives and libraries in Europe and the Middle East that could be of importance for this research. Although it has been sadly impossible for me to assemble them all, I hope that future scholars who come across such documents by chance or design will be in a better position to interpret them and to evaluate their significance.

The point of departure for this book is therefore a careful work of reconstruction, following itineraries that trace unexpected paths across the Mediterranean to Marseille and Paris. I have sought to explore in as full a context as possible the lives of these French Arabs of the early nineteenth century, to draw a clearer picture of the motives for their displacement, their number, their mode of existence, and their relationship to the social structures that surrounded them. Through the intersections of these itineraries, the conflicts that such further "crossings" could provoke, and their resolution, I have tried to determine what forms of relationship existed between these individuals, how closely they were connected to one another, and whether these connections constituted a form of collective life, a "community" distinct from the larger social context around them.

Further, by tracing the borders and limits of these itineraries, I explore what these "crossings" can tell us about the formation of distinct cultural and national identities across a period of significant transformation on both sides of the Mediterranean. This period culminated in the first long-term colonial incursion into the Arab world by a European power: the French invasion of Algeria in 1830. I have been interested to determine not only how these people lived, but what it meant for them to live these great political and cultural transformations. The first part of the book provides an investigation of the origins of the relatively large emigration of Egyptians and Syrians from Egypt to France, and the experience of these immigrants during the Empire and in the political transition of 1814–15. The second part of the book observes the period from the 1820s to the Revolution of 1830—a crucial moment in the transformation of national identities in Europe, and a turning point for French domination of the Arab world—through the lives and works of a number of Arab intellectuals in Paris. Their itineraries may tell us something about the nature of these transformations themselves, viewed from a rather different perspective, making a small contribution to the project of recovering the "plural or conjoined genealogies" of a shared present.[47] In this sense, I hope, imagining "Arab France" may help us imagine our own history, as well as the fascinating and multiple reality that is France, a little differently.

1

A Rough Crossing

In late August 1801, a fleet of British frigates set out from the port of Aboukir in Egypt. They were carrying the tattered remnants of the French Grande Armée, abandoned two years earlier by their commander, Napoleon Bonaparte, to fight on without much hope in Egypt, and at last given passage back to France by the treaty concluded with England and the Ottoman Porte. One night, just a few days into the crossing, a tragic scene unfolded on board one of these ships, a frigate named the *Pallas*. According to a letter conserved among the papers of the Commission d'Égypte, Ya'qub Hanna, an Egyptian Copt and the first non-French general in the French army, lay dying among the women of his family, watched by a grief-stricken crowd of men, women, and children. Although they had boarded the *Pallas* in Alexandria, they drew their origins from all over the Middle East, from Egypt, Syria, and even farther afield. They came from Georgia and the Caucasus, from Greece and Asia Minor, from southern Egypt and the Sudan, from Palestine and Mount Lebanon, from the Mediterranean cities of North Africa and from the great metropolis of Cairo. Their social origins were just as disparate: merchants and customs officials jumbled together with priests and artisans, soldiers and domestic servants. Most shared little beyond the Arabic language and an origin in the Islamicate society of the Ottoman lands. Their only other commonality was their decision to join the emigration to France led by General Ya'qub, now mortally ill.

"No scene could been more striking for an artist than this tragic tableau," wrote Nemir Effendi, the author of the letter. A painter, he continued,

> would want to capture at once the group as a whole, and the details of the different moral sentiments that animated the onlookers. The variety of feelings can only be

imagined—those of the English, the French, the Turks, the Copts, the Greeks, even a number of Italians. Their prayers opened the vault of the heavens for the dying man. Imagine then the despair of his mother, and his sisters, the tears of the beautiful Circassians and Georgians, the shouts of the Coptic and Turkish women, and the innocent composure of a child, his only daughter, still too young to comprehend her loss. Even heaven seemed to want to play its part in the mournful scene, with its far-off thunder and its flashes of lightning.[1]

General Ya'qub died during the night. His final wish, Nemir wrote, was to be buried alongside his friend General Desaix. Ya'qub was a wealthy man and had contributed generously to Desaix's funeral monument in Paris; now he hoped to share it. Perhaps he hoped too that such a public recognition of French and Egyptian friendship would help assure a welcome in France for the people who had accompanied him. He had every reason to fear for their welfare. Most of them hardly spoke French, and they had little experience of life in Europe and no obvious means to support themselves and their families. But not all of them were unschooled in French manners, as Nemir's letter itself demonstrates. Nemir, who signed himself as the *wakil,* or agent, of the Légation d'Égypte, clearly understood the importance of sensibility and theatricality in postrevolutionary Europe, portraying a terrible and disruptive event as a moment of historic importance, redeeming loss or defeat through symbolism, much as contemporary history painters would do.

Nemir was writing from the lazaret of Marseille, where he and his companions were serving the compulsory forty days of their quarantine. Nemir insisted above all that arrangements should be made quickly for the "more than one hundred young men—Turks, Copts, Greeks, Abyssinians," and their families, who were about to enter the city of Marseille—several hundred people in all. But the political stakes were just as high. The self-styled "Egyptian Legation" on whose behalf Nemir addressed the minister expected an immediate invitation to Paris for discussions about their political project and their status in France. As we will see, they would wait for almost a decade for the permission to travel to the capital.

The "Egyptians" of General Ya'qub were poised to emerge into a different world. But we should take care not to indulge too readily the flights of imagination that this kind of "encounter" has tended to inspire. If French society was different in many ways from the Egypt these people had left behind, we should remember that the contrast between metropolitan and rural life in both France and Egypt was very stark in this period. Both societies contained a patchwork of regional cultures and dialects, with large cities still dependent for subsistence on the countryside, despite the beginnings of the industrial transformations that would have so great an impact later in the century. For an inhabitant of Cairo or Damascus, the city of Marseille would not have seemed so radically different, and, indeed, interconnections between Mediterranean ports had existed for centuries. Paris, to be sure, as both a major metropolis and a cultural capital could perhaps be compared only to

Istanbul among the cities of the Ottoman world. But even in Paris, as we shall see later, a limited Arab milieu was already in existence, in addition to a network of French officials who had served in the occupation of Egypt.

But this brings us to a major difference that these people would have to negotiate: not so much between France and Egypt as between the France they had imagined and the France that greeted them. It was only three years after the revolutionary settlement of 1795 when the Directory sent an army into Egypt to install the French Republic and its radical principles on the farther shore of the Mediterranean. In the same year, they sent an army to Ireland: its failure was immediate, whereas that in Egypt—and largely, to be sure, as a result of its talented commander—took three years to disintegrate. But the principles with which they set out were nonetheless the same: a radical conception of liberty, equality, and fraternity whose echoes had already been felt across the region. In Egypt, and to a lesser extent in Palestine, 1798 brought a great rupture with the deeply corporate and traditional nature of Ottoman society, just as 1789 had done in France. Just as in Europe, these ideas attracted some and repelled others. At least some part of the emigration of 1801 must be attributed to the effects of these ideas. And those who saw France through such a lens must have received a very sharp shock when they arrived in Marseille in 1801. The Revolution was over. Napoleon, it seemed, had departed Egypt eager to seize in France the kind of absolute power he had exercised in Cairo. The "refugees from Egypt" would have to make a swift and radical change of mentality from one system of power to another, just as they had done when the French took power in Cairo in 1798.

The loss of Egypt that gave rise to this emigration was quite a serious shock to the confidence of postrevolutionary France. It was extremely reassuring, then, to insist that France had snatched a cultural and intellectual victory from the jaws of defeat. The principal repository of this national vindication was the nineteen-volume *Description de l'Égypte*, the *grand ouvrage* of scholarship on ancient and modern Egypt published after the French defeat and evacuation: it is as much a substitute for as a description of a lost territory. The images contained in the work themselves filled several volumes in elephant folio: maps, vast panoramas, encyclopedic depictions of dress and ornament, and some individual portraits of important figures and types. One of these portraits shows a young man designated only as "an inhabitant of Damascus" (fig. 3): the revolutionary cockade displayed defiantly on his turban gives us a hint of what these political transformations may have meant for those who chose to join the French. The young man's dark headwear distinguishes him, probably as a Christian, from the exclusively white-turbaned Muslims. His Ottoman clothing is modest and unornamented, yet elegant and voluminous enough to denote at least a middling degree of wealth. The nargileh, or water pipe, he is smoking also draws a certain contrast with the cheaper clay chibouk pipe of most Egyptians: its use was strongly associated with

FIGURE 3. Costumes et Portraits. Habitant de Damas. Dutertre, grav. Morel, Tardieu & Lignon, from *Description de l'Égypte; ou, Recueil de observations et des recherches qui ont été faites en Égypte pendant l'éxpédition de l'armée française.* État Moderne, vol. 2. State Library of Victoria, Melbourne.

the coffeehouses, places of public sociability.[2] He is beardless, in contrast to the other figures appearing in vignettes collected on the same page—ranging from a street violin player to a Muslim *shaykh*—but his bushy moustache nonetheless distinguishes him from the largely clean-shaven French.

The caption informs us that his young man is an "inhabitant of Damascus," so his presence in Egypt is already a matter of change and mobility.[3] In the picture, his raised right knee and left hand suggest a certain tension, a latent movement despite his attitude of repose. His wide gaze is directed at a point in the distance, with the slightly furrowed brow giving a pensiveness to his expression. Whether this portrait was sketched in Egypt, or in the later period when the *Description* was prepared for publication in Paris, it seems probable that the sitter was among those who joined the emigration of 1801. But the meaning of that tricolor cockade is more difficult to gauge—was it merely a marker of opportunistic partisanship, or does it indicate some more substantial ideological connection? Was it imposed, chosen, or merely an invention of the artist? Whatever the case, there is little doubt that the meaning of such symbols had been transformed in the brief span of the French occupation: three years that saw the devastating military defeat of the Mamluks, followed by the first great failure of the French army under Napoleon, two bloody uprisings, and the assassination of Napoleon's successor, General Kléber. These convulsions of violence not only embittered the relationships between French and Egyptian but rent great holes in the fabric of a religious coexistence that had endured over many centuries.

On 1 July 1801, exactly three years after the first arrival of the French army in Alexandria, the Egyptian historian Abd al-Rahman al-Jabarti watched the preparations of the French army evacuating Cairo. Among the crowds of soldiers, he described the "Egyptian" men, women, and children who joined the exodus, leaving behind them homes, possessions, and family:

> There were many Copts, European merchants, interpreters, and some Muslims who had cooperated with the French and were afraid to remain; there were also many Christians—Syrians and Greeks, such as Yanni, Bartholomew, Yusuf al-Hamawi; also 'Abd al-'Al, the agha.[4]

Behind Jabarti's remarks we can detect the complexity of motives implied by the denomination of different factions according to their sectarian belonging, their occupation, or their history of collaboration. Despite the brevity of the occupation, its dynamics transformed the relations of power in Egyptian society, if not at the popular base, then certainly among certain elements of the elite, and above all for the minorities. Jabarti was careful not to suggest that all of these people were traitors and collaborators, an undifferentiated mass of people forced to flee because of their association with the French. It is important to recognize that the end of the French occupation of 1801 did not constitute a "national liberation" but rather the reestablishment of Ottoman imperial authority. In this context, some scores would certainly be settled, but the Ottoman government was anxious above all to ensure an orderly transition of power. In this regard, a general purge of col-laborators would be entirely counterproductive, and the loss of important func-tionaries would only make the new government's task more difficult. Thus, as Jabarti's words suggest, if there were a few individuals among this crowd of emi-grants who feared retribution for their acts under the French, the great majority chose this path for quite other motives. We may recognize two major frames for their choices: the changes wrought by the occupation itself, and the larger dy-namics of change in the Mediterranean region, of which the French occupation was itself a part. In order to understand this moment of 1801, we must look back to the three years that preceded it, and the situation of people such as this young Damascene in 1798, when the French Grande Armée, the largest land army in the world, disembarked on the shores of Alexandria.

In our own era, dominated by a similarly ill-fated Middle Eastern incursion by a world power at the height of its self-confidence, it is perhaps hardly surprising that "Napoleon's Egypt" has reemerged as a favorite subject for historians of many stripes.[5] The year 1798 has been identified by historians as an event of pe-culiar significance in the Middle East and the wider Muslim world, even to the point of marking for some the "watershed" of modernity in the region.[6] The pre-sumption underlying this view is twofold: first, that the society that the French under Napoleon Bonaparte encountered in Egypt was stagnant, characterized by intellectual immobility, social rigidity, and economic paralysis; and second, that the French brought with them previously unknown ideas and social forms drawn from the Enlightenment and the French Revolution, laying the foundations for the transformation that took place in Egypt under the dynasty of Muhammad 'Ali in the 1820s.[7]

This claim regarding 1798 has come to look increasingly threadbare. In Darrell Dykstra's words, "The orientalist image of an unchanging Islamic society being galvanized by western secular energies has lost its persuasive power, and only the staunchest Bonapartist would cling to the old orthodoxy."[8] The benefit of the his-toriographical shift away from this outdated and profoundly Eurocentric concep-tion of the "civilizational encounter" is that more attention has been paid to the ex-periences of the occupied Egyptians and their concrete relations with the French occupiers, as well as to the larger historical transformations taking place in Egypt and the region, within both the dominant Muslim culture and those of religious and ethnic minorities. Henry Laurens has examined the origins of the French "ex-pedition" in detail, connecting it more carefully to the currents of intellectual de-velopment from the Enlightenment to the Revolution.[9] His comprehensive volume on the expedition has demonstrated very clearly the complexities of the French oc-cupation, as a project that attempted to put in place many of the "modernizing" ideas drawn from the Revolution.[10] Among historians of early nineteenth-century Egypt, Khaled Fahmy has provided the most salient riposte to the myth of Muhammad 'Ali as an "Egyptian Bonaparte" taking up where Napoleon left off.[11] Fahmy's work, along with that of other historians, has restored the properly Ottoman and Islamic context of nineteenth-century Egyptian reform.

But the significance of 1798 needs to be revised, not negated. It is the larger narrative frame of the analysis, with the separations and divisions it has imposed, and the corollary fixation on the exoticism of difference, that has been most obfuscating to the historical account of this particular Euro-Ottoman encounter. Fortunately, more recent scholarship has helped dismantle these Manichaean "civilizational" conceptions of the relationship between European and Ottoman societies, investigating in much greater complexity the worlds that were profoundly interconnected by trade, politics, and cultural exchange, and even by political geography, throughout the early modern period.[12] The ease with which Napoleon's army arrived in Egypt was a marker, not of a European miracle of progress, but of a Mediterranean proximity that must have seemed even more immediate to a young general from Corsica. But that very proximity, and its transformation into a perception of cultural distance, are constitutive elements of the story that would unfold from this point—key factors both in the origins of the Egyptian emigration and in its occlusion from the history of the Franco-Egyptian encounter.

In 1798, Egypt was a province of an empire that, over seven centuries, had expanded into a vast domain stretching from Anatolia to the Arabian Peninsula and North Africa and deep into eastern Europe. Ottoman power fascinated and frightened Europeans: in 1517, and again in 1683, the Ottoman army reached the gates of Vienna and was only narrowly defeated on each occasion. After 1700, however, it became clear that Ottoman expansion in Europe had halted; and indeed the Ottoman Empire seemed to be faltering on several fronts.[13] Its population had doubled in the course of two centuries, and the Sublime Porte in Istanbul—both the seat of the Islamic caliphate and the center of Ottoman political power—faced significant challenges in governing by the traditional means that had held the empire together for more than half a millennium. The fundamental role of Islam in cementing the legitimacy of Ottoman rule had provided a constant pressure to expand into the non-Muslim world, but it also served to constrain change within a powerfully theocentric vision of the world. Despite the frequent characterization of the Ottoman regime as despotic and arbitrary, the sultan could by no means ignore the will of his people, and above all the opinions of the religious intellectuals. In the early part of the century, several sultans were deposed in revolts led by populist figures who accused the Porte of neglecting the tasks imposed by Islam, or failing to deliver prosperity to the people. Karen Barkey has compared these political contestations from below to revolutionary events in nineteenth-century Europe: "Set in a different imperial context, 1703 and 1730 were the 1848 of the Ottoman

Empire."[14] This instability at the center created new dynamics in the outlying provinces of Syria, Greece, and North Africa.[15]

In Egypt, as in other regions in the Levant and the Aegean, the eighteenth century fragility of Ottoman suzerainty encouraged what Daniel Crecelius has called the "drift toward autonomy."[16] As both Peter Gran and Afaf Lutfi al-Sayyid Marsot have convincingly argued, Egypt was engaged in an indigenous process of political and intellectual transformation well before the arrival of the French in 1798.[17] Powerful local figures sought to win increasing autonomy from the Ottoman system as Egypt became increasingly integrated into a global economy stretching from Asia into Europe and the Americas.[18] The Ottoman Empire's focus on fighting a war with Russia, its northern neighbor, allowed these developments to proceed unchecked, until the Treaty of Küçük Kaynarca in 1774 gave the Porte a freer hand to impose authority on its fractious provinces.[19] In Egypt, the autonomy asserted by a series of powerful Mamluk beys, particularly Ali-Bey al-Kabir and Muhammad Abu-Dhahab, was ended by an Ottoman reoccupation of Cairo.[20] In Arabic, the term *mamluk* means "owned," and in Egypt it signified an aristocratic class recruited by the purchase and training of slaves rather than by birth. For centuries, the Mamluks ruled Egypt in their own right. Since 1517, despite military submission to the Ottomans, they had retained their position as a ruling class under an Ottoman governor. But the reestablishment of Ottoman authority in 1787 did not put an end to the ongoing struggles between rival Mamluks such as Mourad-Bey and Ibrahim-Bey, whose bases were in the countryside outside Cairo.[21] Ordinary Egyptians, and particularly the merchant class, including the "Franks" (residents of various European origins), bore the brunt of the internecine struggles that continued throughout this period, both through the interruption of trade caravans and the punishing taxes imposed by the warring beys.

Crecelius notes that in this period of dynamic instability, "Egypt assumed a central importance in European strategic planning that it has never lost."[22] As naval power and seaborne trade became globally dominant, Egypt seemed to hold the key to expansion in Africa and Asia. If the Ottoman Empire were to give way like that of the Moguls in India, Egypt would be the richest prize. The importance of the Levant trade to the French, particularly given the severe economic difficulties of the late eighteenth century exacerbated by war and revolution, further accentuated France's interest.[23] Egypt had long played a powerful role in the European imagination: from the Renaissance onward, cultural power in Europe drew increasingly upon the authority of antiquity, challenging the dominance of the medieval church. Most Europeans still saw Egypt as the origin of Greek and Roman culture, and thus as the originating point of a "civilization" that led ineluctably toward their own cultural development.[24] This teleological conception of temporal development became central to European thought in the Enlightenment. In this sense, Egypt was not a distant and unknown land, but rather a key landscape for projecting both the past and the future of Europe. In 1735 the abbé le Mascrier, in his introduction to Maillet's earlier *Description de l'Égypte,* insisted that Egypt was as familiar an idea for the enlightened classes of Europe as Paris itself, a city that for some of his readers might also have remained a site of imagination and projection.[25]

What this suggests is that the Orient/Occident dyad that Edward Said considered fundamental to European self-understanding was, if not absent, far less stable in this period than his argument would imply. Crucially for our understanding of the Egyptian experience of French occupation, some historians have seen in the Egyptian expedition less a capricious attempt to impose an established Western social model on the benighted East than a speculative "laboratory" for attempting many of the ideas of the Enlightenment outside of local European constraints. As Nicole and Jean Dhombres have observed, "The form of government to be established [in Egypt] could prefigure another form of government—that of France itself."[26] In simple chronological terms, Napoleon traveled straight from Egypt—his first experience of direct rule—to Paris, where within a few months the coup d'état of 18 Brumaire would elevate him to the position of First Consul, the prelude to his seizure of absolute power in France. Louis Bergeron has noted that, during the years that followed, the most intimate circle of Napoleon's reforming officials and advisers in France and across his European empire remained those who had served in his first regime—the "Old Boys from Egypt."[27]

Thus, if we must revise our overestimation of the importance of 1798 in the history of Egypt, the reverse is true in regard to the history of France and Europe. A more careful and detailed picture of the French confrontation with the dynamics of Ottoman Egyptian society, and all of its constituent elements, can contribute significantly to our understanding of the shaping of Napoleonic imperialism, and its reconstruction of postrevolutionary Europe. By providing a far more detailed picture of the shifting political, economic, and cultural relations between occupier and occupied, the work of André Raymond on the daily interactions of Egyptians and the French in Cairo strikes chords with studies by historians such as Stuart Woolf and Michael Broers of societies under occupation by Napoleon in Europe.[28] Unfortunately, however, no study has yet sought to bring these different occupations into the same frame of reference—to map exactly how the experience of imperial rule in Egypt was transferred, or transformed, in the occupation of Italian, German, Spanish, or Illyrian provinces.

Egypt was one of the cradles of Napoleonic imperialism, but it should also be considered a critical testing-ground for the Bonapartist system of direct rule in France, as the French regime in Cairo served as the most immediate precursor of direct rule in France. From this vantage point we may view rather differently Napoleon's decision to bring with him to Egypt scores of technicians, scientists, and artists who eventually formed the first Institut d'Égypte. Edward Said's critique of

Orientalism has encouraged historians to see from the very beginning of this intellectual project a European desire to use knowledge as a force for the subjugation
of an "Orient" that it consistently depicted as passive and stagnant, in order to impose its dominating will.[29] We have seen earlier in this chapter that such an analysis
of the *Description de l'Égypte*, for example, loses its persuasive force when confronted with the complexities of the confrontation between the Ottoman system
and the political culture of postrevolutionary France. Indeed, in divorcing the
Napoleonic project in Egypt almost entirely from its material and historical conditions in postrevolutionary France, this analysis tends to reaffirm the ontological
distinction between "Occident" and "Orient" that Said challenged. Daniel Roche
has illuminated the French state's ongoing quest throughout the seventeenth and
eighteenth centuries to order space and time in a new way, through clocks and
roads, urban reconstruction and the management of rivers, assisted by an array of
engineers, bureaucrats, and experts of all kinds.[30] Dissociated from these larger
processes of European modernity, "Orientalism" comes to appear as an ahistori-
cal game of power constituted of pure self-referentiality. In fact, as Marie-Noëlle
Bourguet has noted, if Napoleon failed to convince a single noted Orientalist to
join the expedition, it was largely because his efforts were directed elsewhere, to the
graduates of the École Polytechnique, who were "naturalists, mineralogists, topog-
raphers, mining engineers and civil engineers."[31] Indeed, it was because of this almost total absence of Orientalist expertise that the French were forced to draw
heavily upon local collaborators, particularly among Christians, Jews, and the resident Europeans, or "Franks." These were not, then, European "Orientalists," but
members of long-established local communities with a knowledge of European
languages and customs, perhaps closer to what Carter Findlay in another context
has called the "Ottoman Occidentalist."[32] But even this formulation does not express accurately the nature of these intermediary populations, whose role has
largely been neglected in the history of the relationship between Europe and the
Muslim world. Without them, no French administration could hope to survive
even for a year or raise the necessary tax revenues to finance the military expedition, let alone unroll a modern postrevolutionary administration—complete with
grand schemes of urban renovation, a research institute, a newspaper, a library,
an archaeological museum, and other trappings of modernity. It seems quite certain that the French believed these innovations would so amaze the local population as to easily win their support for the new regime. The reality, of course, was
much more complex.

The unrest within the Ottoman Empire was viewed in a very particular way in
a Europe increasingly dominated by the political perspectives emerging from the
French Revolution. Henry Laurens argued that revolutionary ideologues in general
represented the Ottoman Empire as a bundle of oppressed "nationalities"—Greeks,
Slavs, Armenians, Arabs, and Hebrews—straining under the Ottoman yoke.[33] This

was often imagined as a parallel to the alleged despotism of the deposed French monarchy, and the majority of Ottoman subjects were viewed as kindred peoples themselves on the verge of revolution.[34] Such an analysis of the Ottoman Empire in the late eighteenth century was largely inaccurate: as we have seen, many of the problems in Egypt were the result of the weakening of the central Ottoman power, and not of its despotic grip. But while the analogy between the Ottoman Porte and the French monarchy as forces suppressing the nation was often present in revolutionary rhetoric, we should not be too quick to assume that this view was universally held, or even predominant in French strategic planning. Indeed, Laurens himself emphasizes the significance of Bonaparte's changing "Islamic policy," and this is an aspect of revolutionary thinking that deserves much more attention than it has received. Part of the problem lies in the presumption that whereas ideas about "nation" and "liberty" were sincerely held by revolutionaries, the response to Islam was a purely cynical and preformulated one. Bonaparte himself encouraged this interpretation himself in his words to the Conseil d'État after his return to France from Egypt:

> My policy is to govern men as the majority wish to be governed. That is, I believe, the best way to recognize the sovereignty of the people. It was by making myself a Catholic that I ended the war in Vendée, by making myself a Muslim that I established myself in Egypt, and by making myself an Ultramontanist that I won the hearts of the Italians. If I had to govern a Jewish people, I would rebuild the temple of Solomon.[35]

But these words were only a belated attempt to make the confused and contradictory policy Bonaparte had put in place during his reign in Egypt—dictated by events as much as by decisions—seem logical and planned. At the beginning, Bonaparte sought by every means to win over the population rather than simply to conquer it. A printing press with Arabic type was seized from the Vatican Propaganda and from the very moment of the French landing was used to produce proclamations claiming that the French intention was to "liberate" the Egyptians from the tyranny of the Mamluk regime. Napoleon adopted local dress for a short period and initially encouraged his officers to marry locally and convert to Islam, thus giving substance to his declaration (in the Arabic, though not in the French, proclamation) that the French were "true Muslims."[36] One of his generals, Baron Jacques Menou—later to command Egypt in Napoleon's absence—followed this suggestion, marrying Sitt Zobayda from Rosette, and adopting the name Abdallah-Jacques Menou.[37] Bonaparte soon resumed his customary French uniform, however, and his distrust for Menou—whom he ultimately blamed for Egypt's loss—was well known.

The superficial Islamic pretensions of Bonaparte's occupation were rejected, even ridiculed, by the educated elite of Muslim society, a cross section of the population was inevitably drawn into the ambit of the French regime. In assembling a *diwan* (council) of notables in Cairo, Napoleon appointed a number of important sheikhs and *'ulama* (religious teachers) into the central administration.[38] He showed them considerable deference, attending their festivals and consulting them on matters of law and custom. The one matter upon which Bonaparte insisted, however, was the wearing of tricolor sashes and cockades, which denoted revolutionary partisanship rather than simple pragmatic collaboration. The Egyptian historian Jabarti, a considerable Muslim intellectual in his own right, described the resistance of the sheiks of the *diwan* to Napoleon's vestimentary demands: Jabarti described the sash as a sign of "obedience and submission" and a "token of affection" rather than a symbol of revolutionary equality.[39] The sheikhs tore off these insignia and threw them to the ground the moment they emerged from the chamber of the *diwan*. Dress was an important social and religious signifier in Muslim society, and this visible imposition of French ideological principles was more troublesome to the sheikhs than the pragmatic realities of their collaboration with the French. The French newspaper *Le Courrier de l'Égypte* lamented this failure, invoking the memory of "the unfortunate Camille Desmoulins, who declared on 12 July 1789 that the tricolor cockade would soon make its way around the world."[40] This lament for the symbols of radical equality vanquished by the pragmatics of empire would be echoed in France and Europe in the decade that followed.

The incident of the tricolor sash illustrates the investment of the French in the Muslim elite, upon whom Napoleon drew primarily in the first months of his project of administration. He claimed to have the blessing of the Ottoman Porte for liberating Egypt from the disastrous rule of the warring Mamluks, and an Islamic legitimacy based on what he falsely presumed to be the similarity between rationalist Deism and Islam. When the Egyptians discovered the falsity of the first pretension, having never credited the second, the result was a popular rallying of opposition to the French that created the conditions for a bloody revolt in Cairo during 1799. But the Muslim elite, many of whom were by now closely associated with the French administration, were more troubled by this threat of *fitna* (instability), which menaced their wealth and position and the good order of society, than by the presence of the foreign occupiers. After the uprising of 1799, however, the actions of French troops against mosques and holy places—for example, riding their horses into the revered al-Azhar Mosque and publicly defiling the Qur'an—pushed the Muslim notables toward opposition to the regime.

If Egypt was a "laboratory" for the development of Napoleonic administration and modernizing rationalism, it soon became clear that the experiment had failed. Through the ideological prism of the Revolution, the French imagined that their presence in Egypt would be welcomed by the mass of people, the oppressed peasants and the urban masses, while their superiority in science and the arts would win over the educated elite. In actuality it was from these two sources that the resistance to the occupation finally erupted. André Raymond reminds us that Muslim scholars felt themselves part of a centuries-old world of knowledge and science derived from the Qur'an and the medieval Arabic tradition—an epistemology that was all-encompassing and quite sufficient in itself.[41] The origins of popular hostility were manifold. The French were squeezing the population for tax revenues, and requisitioning all mules and other transport animals—needed for carrying water and food into the city—for the expedition into Syria. The blockade by the British fleet had disastrous effects on the economy, pushing food prices to extreme levels. The urban fabric of the city was altered without regard for custom or religion, mosques desecrated and converted to other uses, gates torn down to enable access of troops. The presence of tens of thousands of foreign men in the city made prostitution rampant, rape not infrequent, and venereal disease epidemic.[42]

Rather than resuscitating some long-buried "national" spirit of popular sovereignty, the French occupation created new divisions between a party of accommodation and a party of resistance and pushed the bulk of the population back toward the Ottoman system, whose impositions they had formerly resented. This division did not occur on strictly sectarian lines, but it quickly took on a sectarian coloring. The reasons for this were various. Egypt was an Ottoman society and thus functioned within the *millet* system, which devolved a certain autonomy to the various "nations" of the empire, defined in ethno-religious terms (Greeks/Orthodox, Armenians, Franks, etc.) as distinct from the *umma*, or community of Muslims. Under the Mamluk beys, certain Christian minorities had achieved an almost total monopoly on the financial dealings of the country, whether as "scribes" or account keepers in the case of the Copts or as customs officials and tax farmers in the case of the Greek Orthodox and particularly the Syrian Catholic minority.[43] The Christians and Jews served an important purpose as groups outside the fabric of the powerful family loyalties and clan-based politics built into Muslim society. In the shifting climate of the late eighteenth century, certain Christian minorities had learned to adjust rapidly to changes in the nature of power and had profited significantly from their intermediary position.

The French were compelled to rely upon these same groups for financial administration, and equally as interpreters and intermediaries. The egalitarian and secular ideology of the French regime meant that the social restrictions on these groups, which had in some sense compensated for their financial power, were lifted, and their privileges were conspicuous to all. This deeply offended many religious Muslim intellectuals, who, like Jabarti, were horrified by what he described as "the elevation of the lowliest Copts, Syrian and Greek Orthodox Christians, and Jews." Jabarti reported that "they rode horses and adorned themselves with swords because of their service to the French; they strutted around haughtily, openly expressed obscenities, and derided the Muslims."[44] There is little documentation of the response of ordinary Muslims, but it is not difficult to imagine their fury at the revelation of the economic power of these minorities, and the loss of their own symbolic ascendancy.[45]

However, while reliant on local Christians to achieve any effective control over the country, the French tended to distrust them as a group. The administration tried to distance itself from an association that would undermine the attempt to present the French as the defenders of Islam and the scourge of Christianity. When Jirgis al-Jawhari, the chief Coptic functionary in Egypt both before and after the occupation, wrote to the French administration in 1798 demanding the full en-franchisement of Copts, as ancient and equal inhabitants of the country, Napoleon refused to grant his request.[46] On his departure, Napoleon left clear instructions to his successor: "Whatever you do, the Christians will always be our friends. You should prevent them from becoming too insolent, so that the Turks should not have the same fanaticism against us as against the Christians, which will make their opposition to us irreconcilable. We have to put fanaticism to sleep until we can root it out."[47] But Jabarti's analysis of the situation suggested the reverse. After the first uprising in Cairo, he reported:

> The Syrian Christians and also a group of Greek Orthodox whose houses had been looted in al-Jawanahiya Quarter joined forces to complain to the chief of the French about the calamity that had afflicted them. They availed themselves of this opportunity to deal the Muslims a heavy blow, showing what was hidden in their hearts, as if they had shared in the vicissitudes of the French. But the Muslims had gone after them only because of their connections with the French.[48]

Jabarti was very careful to distinguish consistently between the various groups of Christians, whether Copts, Syrian Catholics, or Greek Orthodox. The French, on the other hand, tended to lump Muslims into a single category of "Mahometans" or "Turks" and equally to treat Christians as an undifferentiated mass from which a few individuals could emerge on personal merit. The republican discourse of the French, with its modernizing commitment to rational egalitarianism, allowed little space for communitarian subtleties. In contrast, Jabarti, with his Ottoman sensibility, continued to respond to his social environment in terms of vertical groupings of family, lineage, sect, and corporation.[49]

After Bonaparte's successor, General Kléber, was assassinated by a Syrian Muslim in June 1800, it was General Abdallah-Jacques Menou who took command. Fervently espousing the idea of retaining Egypt as a permanent colony of France, Menou intensified Napoleon's policy of co-optation of the Muslims and increasingly disassociated himself from the Christians, for whom he expressed the deepest revulsion:

> I tell you, between you and me, that I have seen for myself since being in Egypt that the Christians are the vilest and most contemptible inhabitants of this country, and

among the Christians the Syrians are in the front rank. Greedy, untrustworthy, cowardly, vindictive, and vile to the last degree—such is their true portrait.[50]

Menou claimed that the Christians, far from adhering in any real way to the French ideology, perceived their new masters as "French Christian Mamluks substituting themselves for the Georgian and Muslim Mamluks."[51] Menou insisted that the Syrian Catholics in particular were cynically working to assure their economic privileges with the new regime. He instituted rigorous surveillance of all their activities at Damietta and expressed equal determination to eliminate the Copts from their control of the country's finances.[52]

Thus any assumption that there was an automatic confluence of interests between French and local Christians should be seriously challenged: cultural and ideological sympathies must be balanced against the unfolding dynamics of power. Moreover, the Christians did not form a single sectarian community: their status varied within Ottoman society, along with their geographic origins and the nature of their social and economic participation. It is worth enumerating some of these differences, because they played an important role, both in the origin of the emigration and in its destinies in France.

The Copts, though a small minority of only 10 to 15 percent of the population, were the oldest Christian group in Egypt—a Monophysite sect long predating the Muslim conquest and living for the most part in Middle and Upper Egypt. While a number of Copts had achieved elite status as scribes and account keepers, the vast majority were poor rural farmers.[53] As an integral part of Egyptian society, they seem to have been little attracted to the French administration: Antoine Galland insisted that "they despise our customs and detest our principles."[54] Bruce Masters suggests that "after almost a millennium of assimilation into the dominant Arabic culture, the Copts were culturally or physically indistinguishable from their Muslim neighbors."[55] They celebrated common festivals and engaged in practices such as abstaining from pork and circumcising their children. But in certain circumstances this cultural proximity only accentuated the limits of social mobility. An ambitious young Copt could enter into the elite as a scribe or a financial administrator, but his dress, his manner of transport, and his deportment were delimited by the prescriptions of law and custom. He could not enter the ranks of the military or the powerful intellectual elite, which was exclusively Muslim in character, unless he chose to convert to Islam and thus effectively leave his own community.

The categories of confession and community were not fixed, particularly in the dynamic environment of late eighteenth-century Egypt. One young Copt, Hibat-Allah Fadlallah, became the protégé of his father's employer, the Mamluk bey Sulayman al-Kashif. Fadlallah entered the prestigious Islamic university of al-Azhar. However, such access was predicated on his conversion to Islam. At al-Azhar,

Fadlallah received the best education available in Egypt, studying with the leading sheikhs, and rose to occupy a chair, and a post as secretary of the supreme council of dignitaries in Ottoman Egypt.[56] By the time of the French conquest, Fadlallah, now Sheikh Muhammad al-Muhdi, was enormously wealthy and influential: he became secretary-general to the *diwan* created by Napoleon, and collaborated closely with the French savants, such as Jean-Joseph Marcel, who later published a collection of al-Muhdi's tales.[57]

This success was only possible after conversion to Islam. Those who remained Christian could rise to positions of great prominence in Egypt, but their social status was considerably more fragile. It was only through his position among the high *'ulama* that al-Muhdi achieved a degree of autonomy, which assured his position through several changes of regime. What al-Muhdi's case suggests is the strict limits on social mobility for those Copts who remained tied to their community and their religion, despite their close cultural ties with Muslim society and their long-established role in Egypt.

In contrast, the "Syrian" Christians traced their origins to the beginning of the eighteenth century in Damascus and Antioch, when they broke away from the Greek Orthodox Church to become "Uniate" with the Roman Catholic Church, becoming known as Melkites or "Greek Catholics."[58] The schism that led to the formation of the community of Melkite Catholics occurred around 1724–25, when the local communities of Damascus elected and appointed their own Arabic-speaking, Catholic prelates in competition with the official Greek appointees of the patriarchate in Istanbul. The *millet* system of the Ottoman Empire guaranteed a certain autonomy for religious minorities: a separatist challenge from within a *millet* was also a challenge to the traditional order.[59] The Uniate Christians looked to Catholic Europe, particularly France, for support. But Thomas Philipp has argued persuasively that the Melkite schism was not the result of missionary influence or trading privileges from European powers, but rather of the movement toward regional autonomy, inflected strongly by Arabic language and culture. The Vatican permitted the Melkites to retain Arabic as a liturgical language almost two centuries before it allowed European Christians to receive sacraments in their own vernacular languages.[60] Their liturgical use of the Arabic language promoted the establishment of the first Arabic printing press in the Ottoman Empire in 1706. Following Benedict Anderson, Masters sees in this a decisive element of the "print revolution" that made possible the "imagining" of a collective identity through "cultural Arabism."[61] Philipp suggests that although "it would, of course, be premature to speak here of a nascent Arab nationalism . . . certainly we can observe the growing strength of local groups, who, just because secular ideologies such as nationalism were still irrelevant, clothed their challenge to the central authorities in the traditional garb of dogmatic deviation."[62]

A sense of cultural distinctiveness expressed through a confessional difference nurtured a strong and tightly knit Melkite community that was well placed to take advantage of the new commercial opportunities emerging through the burgeoning trade in commodities such as coffee and silk between Asia and Europe. At the same time, the decentralizing sympathies of the community brought them into close collaboration with many of the ambitious new political figures across a region that was experiencing a considerable flourishing of local powers, from the Shihabi emirs in Mount Lebanon to Zahir al-'Umar in northern Palestine. The Melkites rapidly expanded their networks across the region. Philipp explains that those who settled successfully in other cities would assist others to establish themselves: "Any Greek Catholic who had established a base for himself in a new place would inevitably draw other Greek Catholics after him and help to set them up."[63]

This was notably the case in Egypt: during the years 1730 to 1780 Philipp estimates that about four thousand Syrian Christians migrated into Egypt.[64] When the French arrived in 1798, they found the Melkites concentrated in the coastal cities, particularly Alexandria and Damietta, with well-established connections to Europe and European culture. They had almost entirely displaced the Jews as the privileged agents of the Mamluk rulers, in trading matters and sometimes in diplomacy between the various rulers they served. Philipp describes a meteoric Melkite rise to positions of wealth and power in Egypt. But the French occupation, rather than favoring the Melkites, in fact sent them into rapid decline. The British blockade interrupted trade almost completely, and the actions of General Menou increasingly stripped the Syrians of their lucrative role in the customs administration.

When Napoleon took his armies from Egypt into Palestine in 1799 in order to forestall an Ottoman advance through the Levant, the French came into contact with much larger populations of Palestinian Melkites. The rule of Zahir al-'Umar in the city of Acre had brought many Melkites to prominence, in particular the family of Ibrahim al-Sabbagh. But Zahir's fall was followed by the reestablishment of Ottoman control under the Bosnian Mamluk Ahmad al-Jazzar, who eliminated all the Catholics from his administration, often by violent means, replacing them with Orthodox Christians and Jews.[65] When Napoleon besieged the city of Acre many Christians from the surrounding region joined the French forces, probably hoping for a reinstatement of the highly favorable regime they had experienced under Zahir. French declarations also made much of "le patriotisme arabe": Napoleon weighed heavily in his later account of his military campaigns on his support for the "Arab nation" against the "Turks."[66] Of course, such Arab nationalism had no base in Ottoman society: "Arab" descendance was a matter of genealogy, not politics, of family rather than nation. But it is nonetheless likely that more fertile soil for such national ideas could be found among the Christian Arabs in Palestine and Syria.

Several entire local communities of Christians joined the French army, particularly in the villages around Shfa ʿAmr in the Nablus mountains.[67] When the siege
was abandoned, these groups had little choice but to depart for Egypt with the
French army. There is every reason to believe that they were fleeing the certain
vengeance of al-Jazzar. The weakness of the Melkite communities in geographical
Syria was due to their lack of strong links with Istanbul—unlike the Jews who retained significant influence and connections in the Ottoman capital.[68] The Melkite
community was thus more at the mercy of its immediate political alliances with
local rulers: in this case, Napoleon.

But politics may not have been the sole motivation for this exodus. In his book
on Acre, Philipp notes that French merchants in Acre consistently expressed their
fears of competition from local Arab merchants, particularly the cotton merchants from Shfa ʿAmr, and blamed them for provoking difficulties with the administration that resulted in the exile of French traders from the city:

> A local commercial class, beginning to compete with the French commercial estab-
> lishment, may have hoped to liberate itself from the foreign merchants. The French
> merchants certainly took this possibility very seriously. They warned in 1786 that
> some "*marchands Arabes d'Acre*" may get ideas and try to establish their own com-
> mercial connections in Marseilles.[69]

Antun Qassis Fir'aun was a member of an influential Melkite family who became
chief customs official, first in Damietta, the base of the Melkite presence in Egypt,
and then in Cairo in 1775. In 1784 he left Egypt for the Tuscan city of Livorno,
probably to avoid the increasing extortions of the warring beys in Egypt.[70] A
Melkite Arab community had begun to establish itself alongside the considerable
Jewish and Greek communities in Italy, with expanding networks across the
Mediterranean.

The key point here is that the Copts and the Melkites represented two significant and different forces of social change in eighteenth-century Egypt: social mobility and geographical mobility. But these two forces remained quite separate,
and in many senses contradictory. For the Copts, mobility remained very much
anchored in the political context of Egypt and Egyptian society, and their struggles were carried out against the vertical limitations placed upon their "corporation." For the Syrian Christians, mobility was an expression of a new cultural
identification and a commercial expansion spreading out across the Mediterranean. The nexus of these two forces would no doubt be a significant point of
change. They met in the figure of the Coptic notable Ya'qub Hanna, when he
broke with tradition to marry the daughter of Syrian Christians.

Ya'qub was a highly respected Copt in Egyptian society: like his father, he was
given the title Mu'allim (learned), an honorific that indicates the high importance
given to intellectual prowess within Muslim society. Born in 1745, Ya'qub occupied

a high position in the town of Assiout before the French conquest. Assiout was a town in Middle Egypt with substantial Muslim and Coptic populations. Its agricultural economy was supplemented by the commission on the large trading caravans that brought goods and slaves twice a year from Darfur.[71] Like Fadlallah/al-Muhdi, Ya'qub was promoted by the provincial governor Suleiman Bey, who encouraged him to learn to ride and wield a sword like a Mamluk. But unless he converted to Islam, he could not expect to rise any higher within the Egyptian elite or to take any active role in the military.

Ya'qub did not take the path of al-Muhdi in leaving his religion and his community. But in 1782, at the age of 37, after the death of his first wife, he married Maryam Ni'mat-Allah Babutshi, a Syrian Catholic. This caused as great, if not greater disturbance in the Coptic community than the conversion of al-Muhdi. The Coptic patriarch refused to bless the marriage, but Ya'qub persevered nonetheless. The Copts certainly feared and distrusted the sensational advance of the Syrian Catholics in Egypt. Through his marriage, Ya'qub allied the force of indigenous Coptic social status to the geographical mobility and commercial dynamism of the Syrian Catholics. His wife, Maryam, though a far less well-documented figure, was clearly a strong and independent woman, as later events would indicate.

For an influential notable like Ya'qub, the French occupation was both an opportunity and a danger. At the behest of Jirjis al-Jawhari, Ya'qub was appointed to accompany General Desaix's advance into Upper Egypt, where for the first time he bore arms in battle, something expressly forbidden to religious minorities by Islamic law. Thus he was far from Cairo at the time of the first uprising in 1799. Ya'qub developed a warm friendship with Desaix during the campaign, but his experience of the French administration on returning to Cairo was profoundly ambivalent. General Kléber's attempts to extort ever greater revenues from all the communities combined with the smoldering anger of the Muslim population to create an explosive situation. In March 1800, a handful of Ottoman troops slipped into Cairo, and their exhortations ignited a second uprising in the city.[72]

This time, the fury of the population turned quickly toward the local Christians, and the Coptic quarter was attacked by armed crowds. Many Coptic notables fled to the Ottoman camp after paying for safe conduct from the besieging forces. But rather than adopting this traditional posture of flight or passivity in the face of persecution, Ya'qub acted to defend the quarter, raising barricades and organizing the young men of the community on military lines during the twenty days of siege. The uprising was finally repressed with violence by the French troops. The result was a hardening of hostility and the elimination of the Copts' role as intermediaries between the French and Egyptian Muslim society. This polarization was as dangerous for the Muslim 'ulama, or religious notables, who were accused of "hypocrisy" by Kléber in having failed to condemn the uprising, as it was for the Christians, who were threatened by an upsurge of violence against them.[73]

Ya'qub was given the task of raising a fine of ten million francs from all classes of the population. To fortify the depleting French ranks, Ya'qub was also instructed to form a Légion Copte within the French forces. According to Jabarti, "A group of Copts was assembled, given French uniforms, and officers were appointed to instruct and train them in the art of warfare."[74] Jabarti expressed an unusually visceral distaste for their physical transformation under Ya'qub's orders:

> Ya'qub . . . assembled young Copts, made them shave their beards, and dressed them in garb like that of the French army but with a different headgear, a hat with a piece of the ugliest black sheepskin fur. Into the bargain they were ugly, swarthy and malodorous.[75]

The vision of the French artist Delpech, who recorded the uniforms of the Grande Armée, seems to have been little different (fig. 4). The Coptic auxiliary is depicted as swarthy and begrimed, seated on rocky ground with a bandaged hand and a sullen expression. His eyes seem to glower at a fixed point, and his body is tense and uncomfortable, as though he has been compelled into this situation against his will. In the distance, two French soldiers are barely visible, as though to mark the Coptic soldier's distance from the action. The artist, who might be expected to celebrate this addition to the French forces, seems to caricature rather cruelly the participation of this unfortunate soldier.

The formation of the Légion Copte was not in itself an innovation: foreign auxiliaries were used by most eighteenth-century armies, and the French enrolled soldiers from other countries under occupation. A number of Muslim Mamluk soldiers and Greek sailors had joined the French early in the campaign, and a unit of around fifty-five Janissaires Syriens was recruited from among those who joined the French during the siege of Acre in 1799.[76] Similarly, a Légion Grecque was created in September 1800. But the Coptic Legion was more significant: it numbered at least a thousand men, drawn from Upper Egypt, under the command of its own Coptic general. This considerable armed force represented a radical alteration to the traditional social balance in Egypt. Thus, when the French finally capitulated to the combined British and Ottoman forces, Ya'qub and his soldiers were faced with a sharp choice.[77]

Under Article XIII of the treaty signed by General Belliard with the British and Ottoman commanders on 27 June 1801, the security of those Egyptians who had cooperated with the French was explicitly guaranteed.[78] Of course, such articles were not always respected, and a number of individuals were persecuted or killed.[79] But there is no evidence at all of generalized retribution. Copts such as al-Jawhari, along with key Muslim officials such as al-Muhdi and Sheikh al-Bacri, were recruited by the new administration and continued to hold high office. However, the treaty contained a new article not included in the cease-fire document of 1800. It provided for any resident of Egypt who chose to leave his or her homeland to be

FIGURE 4. François Séraphin Delpech, *Armée d'Orient: Légion Cophte 1799*, lithograph. Author's collection.

allowed to do so, without prejudice to property or to family members remaining behind. Notices in Arabic and French signed by General Belliard informing the public of these two special provisions were posted in the streets of Cairo.[80]

The second of these provisions seems to have been made at the behest of Ya'qub, now a general in the French army; it is an indication of the transformative effects of the uprising of March 1800. Ya'qub had made the decision to leave Egypt with the French. But he soon faced resistance from his own soldiers, who did not wish to leave their homes and families, as Jabarti recounted:

> That same day, Ibrahim Bey sent a safe-conduct for Copt notables. They came out
> to greet (the Ottomans), and then returned to their homes. But Ya'qub with bag and

baggage crossed to the island of al-Rawda. He also assembled the Copt soldiers but many of them fled and went into hiding. Their women and relatives gathered, and weeping and lamenting, went to the *qa'im maqam* [i.e., General Belliard], pleading that their men be permitted to remain with their families and children, that they were poor, mere craftsmen—carpenters, mason, jewellers, etc. He promised to instruct Ya'qub not to force unwilling Copts to join him on the voyage.[81]

Although Ya'qub had been able to assemble a force of Copts and dress them as a national army, it was impossible to convince the bulk of these soldiers to leave Egypt, where their ties to the land and culture were so strong. Even among those who did leave, many later changed their minds. Jabarti adds that even before the ships departed from Aboukir, "some of the Copt soldiers who had gone with the French lagged behind and returned to Cairo."[82] According to the correspondence of the Armée d'Orient, the first estimates of the population expected to leave for France were "1500 to 1800 Greeks, Copts or Egyptians."[83] But General Belliard's final figures for the emigration were 438 Copts, 221 Greeks, and 93 Mamluks—altogether 752 men—and an uncounted number of women and children.[84] A group numbering only 230 is recorded to have disembarked at the lazaret of Marseille in October of the same year, or 1 Vendémiaire, An IX.[85] The others may have boarded other ships in smaller groups, turned back, or traveled by other routes—through Greece or Italy, for example.

The discovery by Shafiq Ghurbal in the 1920s of the correspondence of Ya'qub with the British and French foreign ministries revealed for the first time the political project that lay behind Ya'qub's decision to leave Egypt for France.[86] With the assistance of Theodore Lascaris de Vintimille, a Piedmontese Italian and a former Knight of Malta who had joined the French and taken a role in the land administration, Ya'qub had drawn up a detailed plan for reinvading Egypt.[87] He was reported to have rejected overtures by the Ottoman governor of Egypt, who sought to retain him in the new administration, making him "the most brilliant offers," according to a French officer who was present at the meeting.[88] The rupture, it seems, was simply too great.

Ya'qub's project involved what George Haddad calls a "chimerical" plan to enlist the support of the Mamluk Mourad Bey and the Arab tribes of the desert to defend Upper Egypt against the Ottoman forces while a force led by Ya'qub, and backed by European naval strength, attacked from the coast.[89] General Menou rejected the plan out of hand, citing his "lack of confidence" in Ya'qub as the motive. We have seen evidence of Menou's prejudicial assessment of the Christians, but it is likely also that he understood that French colonial interests were not the overriding priorities for these Egyptians. Nonetheless, Menou's dream of holding onto a French colony in Egypt could still encourage a willingness to carry a large number of Egyptians on the crowded ships bringing their soldiers back to France.

Of the letters discovered by Ghurbal, one was a letter from Lascaris to the captain of the *Pallas,* the British ship on which Ya'qub and his followers embarked, enclosing the notes of the "principal articles of our political meetings on board his ship"; these notes set out the basis for requesting Great Britain to agree should the Legation succeed in convincing France to support an independent Egypt. To the ship's captain, Ya'qub had made it clear that his alliance with the French stemmed from his commitment to his own political purposes. Captain Edmonds wrote to the Admiralty:

> The Pallas under my Command received on board in Egypt a Copte—a man of excellent character and great weight as one of the Chiefs of that Sect in Egypt—he was made General of brigade in the French service to secure his assistance to them, some little attention of mine to this unfortunate exile induced him in conversation to speak of his Country—he declared (in his mind) any Government was preferable to that of the Turkish, that he had joined the French from a patriotic wish of ameliorating the hardships of his countrymen, the French had deceived them and at that time the Egyptians despised the French as they did before the Turks.[90]

Ya'qub and his followers, who styled themselves the "Egyptian Legation," insisted that an independent Egyptian nation would benefit the European powers by preventing the unceasing competition for such a prized military and commercial interest. In the same document, they quoted the words of the Mamluk Murad Bey: "Because everyone wants to possess it, [Egypt] will be the object of their eternal discord."[91] Although they appealed to a common European ideological opposition to "Turkish despotism," their references were resolutely indigenous. They continued with a call for a government that would be "just, severe, and *national*"[92]—quoting not France or Britain, but the reign of Sheikh Humam, a famous Arab leader of Upper Egypt who had struggled against the Mamluks during the eighteenth century. Michael Winter has identified the rule of Humam as "the zenith of Arab power" in Egypt.[93] Building on this indigenous vision, they emphasized in particular that the national government would not be simply a sectarian one:

> We should not forget to say here that Egypt, divided as it is into several sects, disposes of simple ways to oppose them to one another in order to balance them, and that the Egyptian Legation keeps in touch with them all *without partiality*, through ramifications that are so extensive that they are and will be completely unknown to the Turkish government in Egypt, which is a necessary precaution towards the permanently suspicious despotism which would not hesitate to sacrifice even the last of the *independent brothers* if it could identify them. Those who came with the army defy its rage, but such is not the same with our brothers in Egypt; they are under the sword and the stick; they have to dissimulate and appear as the most zealous slaves of the Sublime Porte.[94]

Ya'qub's letter was submitted to Lord Keith, commander in chief of the British navy, by way of the ship's captain, Joseph Edmonds. A similar submission was dispatched to Talleyrand, the minister of foreign relations under the Consulate. The Legation was seeking support from both France and Britain, with a sophisticated awareness of the relations between the two powers, and the differences in their political repertoire. To the British, they emphasized the notions of utility and pragmatism in trade and administration, insisting that "it will not be in this case a revolution made by the spirit of enlightenment or by the fermentation of opposing political principles, but a change occasioned by absolute necessity in a community of peaceful and ignorant men."[95] This practical, utilitarian language stood in stark contrast to the florid rhetoric of their petition to the French:

> In the past ages of the world, in those uncertain and distant epochs when France, hardly emerging from the hands of nature, presented perhaps nothing but ice and forests, Egypt, already flourishing and civilized gave lessons to the first Greek legislators. But such is the natural cycle of events that those same Egyptians, who were so enlightened, are coming to France under your immortal consulate to be informed about the customs of a people they love, and to know by what unknown device one could consolidate the military triumphs of a newly born Republic through new political triumphs.[96]

The Legation was playing a skillful game to gain their independence, employing the appropriate rhetoric to win the support of both major European powers. It is clear from the first that the Egyptians did not consider their own interests as identical with those of the French. Despite an obvious recognition of the political realities of their situation, the Egyptians clearly opposed the imperial projects of both sides, except insofar as such projects might shelter their own movement toward independence.

The sophistication of the political vocabulary in these letters has led a number of historians to question who really wrote them. Henry Laurens insists that they could have been written only by Lascaris:

> The range of themes discussed show that they were written by the former Knight of Malta. Their vocabulary is that of the political economy of the end of the eighteenth century, the concept of civilization [that] was the ideological justification of Bonaparte's action in Egypt. It is very difficult to know what Ya'qub really thought. The important thing is that for the first time here one can attribute an Occidental political vocabulary to an Oriental. It will take two decades before Muhammad Ali uses in turn the concept of civilization.[97]

I believe Laurens is wrong to attribute this discourse so readily to the only "European" among Ya'qub's Legation. A clear distinction can be observed between Lascaris's correspondence and the ideas of Ya'qub: the Knight of Malta consistently drew not on the concept of *civilization,* but on that of *colonization.*[98] He reminded

Menou—a fervent partisan of *l'Égypte française*—of the benefits that would accrue to France in retaining a foothold in Egypt. Nowhere did such an idea appear
in the letters of the Egyptian Legation; at no point did they raise the idea of retaining or restoring Egypt as a French *colony*. Instead, they drew upon the Enlightenment model of civilization in order to remind the French of what they owed to
Egypt in a cultural and historical sense.[99] Above all, their project was framed in
terms that invoked the libertarian-revolutionary conception of the nation.

In assuming that the vocabulary of these documents must be "Occidental,"
Laurens perpetuates the assumption that the ideas that characterize modernity
were born in the West and were transferred outward through European expansion, an assumption that has been challenged by Dipesh Chakrabarty among others.[100] Some postcolonial critics have also interpreted the occupation in similar
ways, suggesting that the indigenous adoption of a modernizing vocabulary must
be interpreted as either "mimicry" or, as Laurens implies, ventriloquism. It is pre-
cisely this assumption that a better understanding of Ya'qub and the emigration allows us to challenge. The documents of the "Egyptian Legation" were signed, not by
Lascaris, but by Nemir Effendi. We must take seriously the possibility that the os-
tensibly subaltern voices of the occupied—albeit drawn from among the wealthiest
and best-educated Cairene elite—could speak articulately of their own national aspirations. If they drew upon the ideas of "civilization" in their correspondence with
the French, and on commercial pragmatism in their dealings with the British,
these responses should be recognized as tactical rhetorical moves rather than
mimicry or wholesale adoption of "Occidental" models.

Ya'qub was a powerful political figure who had developed his own idea of national unity and the struggle for independence, in a dialogue with the French
model, but drawn equally from the experience of local semiautonomous leaders
such as Sheikh Humam, during the period of relaxation of Ottoman control over
Egypt. He drew together the vital forces of social and geographical mobility that
characterized this period of change across the Ottoman world, and provided a
central focal point for the aspirations of Syrian Catholics, Egyptian Copts, and
those elements of the Muslim elite who sought independence from Ottoman imperial control.

But only a few days into the crossing, Ya'qub became ill and died. What did
this tragic event mean for the hundreds of Egyptians and Syrians on board the
Pallas en route for Marseille? The chief unifying factor of the emigration was suddenly removed, and those who were left behind might well be expected to disintegrate into their quite disparate group identities: sectarian, regional, economic,
linguistic, ethnic. Nemir, in his description, reminds us of just how various these
identities were: Turk, Copt, Circassian, Italian, Greek. The emigration had lost its
most effective claim to French support as a national movement in exile. Nemir
chose to present the moment of Ya'qub's death in his letter, but his manner of

presenting that moment sought to turn loss into plenitude. Christopher Prender-gast, in his discussion of Napoleonic history painting, emphasizes the importance of the choice of narrative moment in the construction of the "great man" as part of a patriotic narrative of the nation.[101] In his tableau, Nemir did not seek simply to report a singular event, but to convey its *meaning*, its "before" and "after," in a single frame. He projected a common "patriotic" feeling that could unify not only the disparate populations of the emigration, but even the natural world of the sea, the thunder and the lightning. These elements were intended to accentuate the "historical" nature of the moment, with its intense convergence of feeling, like a moment of sacrifice that gives birth to a national unity. He seemed to address his words to some future moment in which this loss would find its fulfillment in the completion of a national project, a project whose ultimate collapse we must explore in the next chapter.

This moment of ostensible emotional unity, if such indeed took place on board the *Pallas,* would prove ephemeral, if not altogether false. The boat was sailing away from the land where the national ambitions of its passengers were anchored, taking them into an uncertain exile. The figure of the dying Ya'qub, at the center of Nemir's tableau, had little to offer in the way of positive political meaning: his words did not set out any future trajectory beyond the immediate arrangements for his burial, and even these small hopes would be disappointed. The only other individual figure who appears in this tableau of types is Ya'qub's daughter, a child who was still "too young to feel all the significance of her loss." If her innocent confusion about this event provides a dissonant element in the scene, it is one that characterizes more accurately its underlying meaning. In a patriarchal society, the presence of an only daughter also signified the absence of male heirs to carry on Ya'qub's dynastic heritage. In reality, then, Ya'qub's death was an absolutely un-foreseen disaster that left the emigration confused and vulnerable. When these people emerged from the quarantine in Marseille a few weeks later, they would confront a postrevolutionary France on the brink of an equally surprising lurch toward authoritarianism and empire.

2

Ports of Call

On their release from quarantine in Marseille, the first act of the Egyptian exiles was to organize the funeral of their leader, General Ya'qub, which attracted a crowd of onlookers as they carried his body to its sepulchre. The body had not been buried at sea: his widow had insisted on its preservation during the journey in a barrel of rum. The burial of Ya'qub was an important ritual for the heterogeneous population now arrived in France: their unifying figure was now gone, and something new would have to bring together the various and contradictory currents of the emigration. According to a French observer, "The Coptic Legion accompanied the convoy, along with detachments from every corps, officers of all kinds, and the military and civilian authorities. They were followed by the aga of Janissaries from Cairo, the brother of General Jacob [Ya'qub], his nephew, and his slaves."[1]

The leadership that remained was composed of vastly different individuals. There were those who had exercised—and on occasions abused—the authority given to them under the French administration, including Muslims such as Abd el-Al, the aga of Janissaries, and Orthodox Greeks, like Bartolemeo Serra, the former police chief. According to Georges Spillmann, Serra's wife had also played an active role, "skillfully wielding a sabre" during the uprising in Cairo.[2] Ya'qub's brother, Henin (Hunain) Hanna, was expected to lead the Copts, who had been reduced to a relative minority due to the return of large numbers to Egypt; and his nephew, Gabriel Sidarious, was appointed to command the remainder of the Légion Copte.[3] Ya'qub's widow, Maryam Ni'mat Allah, remained the wealthiest and most important figure among the large group of Melkite Catholics. This group also included a number of important traders and customs officials from Egypt, in addition to a more substantial and poorer population from the villages of Palestine.

Among the rest were various former Mamluk soldiers who had joined the French army, along with slaves and servants, sailors, priests, and many others.

The conditions that these emigrants confronted on their emergence from quarantine were radically different from those they had anticipated when they set out from Egypt. France was no longer a republic living out, however peripatetically, the legacy of the Revolution. Since the coup of 18 Brumaire 1799, a three-member Consulate had been installed, and only the fiction of a rotating presidency masked the growing power of Napoleon Bonaparte. The loss of Ya'qub left the emigration deprived of its leader, whose unimpeachable dignity as a general in the French army might alone have helped them to negotiate this new post-Brumaire reality. Within a year, Napoleon would declare himself First Consul for life, the first step to his coronation as emperor. But that year would bring even greater changes to the fabric of republican isonomy that the radical phase of the Revolution had installed. The reestablishment of slavery, the amnesty and return of émigrés, and the Concordat with the Vatican to place the Catholic church back at the center of French life all served to mark a fundamental rupture with the ideals of liberty and equality that had limped on, however miserably, under the Directory. The Peace of Amiens, concluded between France, Britain, and the Ottoman Empire in March 1802, would make no reference at all to the project of Egyptian independence so fundamental to the departure of these emigrants from Egypt. But if the political ambitions of the Legation were left in disarray, the status of the hundreds of emigrants arriving in Marseille was an even more profoundly troubling question. What provisions could be made for these people, from wildly diverse origins, hardly speaking French, and with no immediate means of subsistence, in a city itself wracked by the conflicts and contradictions of the Revolution and its aftermath? It hardly seemed possible to constitute even the most fictive identity for this fragmented population, let alone to find a meaning and a foundation even for their temporary settlement in France. And yet, over the course of a decade, through struggles waged both among themselves and with the structures of the state and the wider society around them, the emergence of an incipient mode of community can nonetheless be recognized. This chapter will trace that rather surprising trajectory and the dynamics, both internal and external, in the first decade of the nineteenth century that laid the conditions for what I have called an Arab France.

At first, the surviving members of the Legation thought they could take Ya'qub's place, at least in presenting the political aspirations of the emigration. They wrote to Talleyrand, the minister of the interior, to insist on this point:

> The Egyptian legation, which is the representation of the Egyptians to the French government, concentrates in itself alone the public spirit, the aspirations, the policy, the influence, and the means of its numerous participants, who are united under the same goals. . . . The Legation makes so bold as to inform you, Citizen Minister, that

you will find in it the convenient means of repairing the important losses which your government has suffered in the East, and that if you would invite it to Paris before the preliminaries of peace with England have been agreed upon, France would always preserve her political influence in the East.[4]

The Legation thus expected to be invited to Paris and to be given a voice in the peace conference. It was still possible to imagine that the motley population that had disembarked from the British ships might be the basis for a future Egyptian army of independence. They asked to appear in their customary dress, explaining that "our Muslims" considered such dress a religious obligation. It is notable that this request is the only direct reference to the Muslims of the emigration in all of the correspondence of the Legation. We may find hints of this presence in the various propositions of the Legation, but these remained coded rather than overt. As we have seen, dress had played a very prominent role in Bonaparte's "Islamic policy" in Egypt: here, however, this concern was already in transformation into an appeal to the European fascination with the exotic, an interest the Legation hoped to co-opt to its own ends. In their letter to Napoleon, the Egyptian representatives spoke of "an Oriental spectacle" that would remind the French of their conquest, and substitute a new independent Egypt for the loss of a French territory.[5] But this was a fatal misreading of the new political context of 1801. Toward the end of their quarantine, the members of the Legation wrote again to the First Consul with a proposition for the "absolute or modified independence" of Egypt, under an Ottoman suzerainty that would recognize Egyptian autonomy and eliminate the power of the Mamluk class, anticipating the arrangements that would be implemented in Egypt with the rise of Muhammad 'Ali a few years later.

None of the organs of the French state responded to the numerous requests of the Legation, effectively failing to recognize it as representative of any "national" entity whatsoever. Nemir received a brief reply from General Berthier, who informed him simply that "measures had been taken to provide for those of your compatriots who have arrived in France."[6] Nemir wrote to the general requesting that they be allowed at least a symbolic presence in Paris. Berthier explained to the Ministry of War : "They ask for nothing. . . . They could look after themselves, but they seem to want the government to show them some mark of deference in order that they might retain something of the esteem they held in Egypt. This might be useful to us should we ever be in a position to return and make use of them."[7]

In the absence of any Egyptian representation, the Peace of Amiens signed in 1802 left Egypt unstable: an Albanian Janissary would eventually prove the "strong arm" that would remove Egypt from superpower contention for several decades. The disorientation of the Egyptians arriving in France must have been profound. At the time of the French arrival in Egypt in 1798, less than a decade after the beginning of the Revolution, the ideal of independent "sister republics" under French tutelage had remained the model for France's relationship with other peoples, offering refuge to "defenders of liberty" from across Europe.[8] But that situation changed irrevocably with the coup d'état of Brumaire in 1799. The idea of a *Grande Nation* of universal liberty had been replaced with an expansionist militarism that would soon take on an imperial cast.[9]

Napoleon's ambitions for aggressive expansion in Europe made the reforging of ties with the Ottoman Porte an immediate priority for the First Consul.[10] The overt presence of a group of Egyptians in the capital could provoke unwelcome publicity and irritate the Porte at an untimely moment. But, as Berthier recognized, a future reconquest of Egypt was certainly not out of the question, so the Egyptian exiles could potentially be of value, so long as they stayed out of sight in Marseille. They would be furnished quite generously with the means of survival, according to their services. But the term "Legation" would never again be mentioned; any question of political independence was definitively at an end. Lascaris alone was summoned to Paris, where he initially sought to promote Ya'qub's plan. But he soon recognized that the project was unwelcome and moved on.[11] The other members of the Egyptian Legation were consistently refused permission to travel to Paris for the next decade.[12]

It was not only these immediate political considerations that had changed, but the very nature of what it meant to be a citizen in France. Nemir's letters addressed the ministers as "Citizen"—the term conventionally decreed by republican isonomy, which placed all individuals in equality before the law. The letters invoked "despotism" as an evil characterizing both Louis XIV's regime and that of the Ottomans from whom they hoped to achieve a "liberation." But the foundations of that democratic isonomy were already shifting: only months earlier, Napoleon had concluded the Concordat with Pope Pius VII, reconciling church and state, thus closing the parenthesis of the Revolution, which had radically rejected the role of organized religion in structuring the social world. Napoleon would henceforth use religion strategically as a tool to organize and administer a subject population, creating Protestant and Jewish consistories to ensure the loyalty of minorities to the state. Even more radically, a decree of 1802 reestablished slavery in the colonies returned to France by the British—perhaps the greatest symbolic rupture with the principles of the Revolution.[13] In the war to impose slavery on the island of Saint Domingue, a population of slaves and free people of color would win by force of arms the independence that the Egyptians had failed to achieve through negotiation. Those events, and the racialized violence that accompanied them, would cast a long shadow over the lives and destinies of the "Egyptian refugees" in France.

Thus the burial of Ya'qub in Marseille was effectively the burial of the political identity of the Egyptian Legation. The first difficulties arose in articulating the relationship between these people and the central state. In his important study of citizenship in revolutionary France, Michael Rapport cites a letter from the same Georges Aïdé whom we encountered in the introduction to this book, addressed to Napoleon Bonaparte in person soon after Aïdé's arrival in Marseille in 1801. Rapport was surprised to note the apparent political astuteness of this "Egyptian" in addressing his letter directly to the First Consul, given the highly centralized and personalized nature of the newly installed Napoleonic administration. Even more surprising was a scribbled note in the margin of the document, where the First Consul himself had written: "As this individual has rendered great services to me, the Minister of the Interior will let me know what I might do for him, when he presents his report on the Copts and other individuals who have arrived from Egypt."[14] For Rapport, this response was paradigmatic of a shift in the nature of citizenship in Napoleonic France, as the right of citizenship ceased to be primarily determined by *ideological proximity* to revolutionary and republican principles and became a function of *usefulness* to a state increasingly personified in the figure of Bonaparte himself.

Understandably, in the absence of other information, Rapport attributed Aïdé's action to political naïveté or unawareness of the customary channels of approach to power in France.[15] But if these "refugees," as they would henceforth be designated, had to make some hasty recalibrations in the political values they invoked, they could benefit from a far closer experience of the First Consul's own modus operandi. In Egypt they had learned the lessons of Napoleon's identification of service to himself as service to the state, and his willingness to use rewards and gratifications to build the institutions of privilege and interest that would sustain his rule.

In the postrevolutionary period of shifting borders and political systems, of competing universalist, imperialist, and nationalist conceptions of citizenship, the concept of "refugee" was equally a shifting one, with a multiplicity of meanings.[16] Where the Revolution had given rise to waves of political "refugees"—whether *émigré* aristocrats leaving France for London, Koblenz, or New Orleans, foreign *patriotes* flocking to France after 1789, or *colons* from Saint Domingue fleeing the slave revolution in 1791—the changes in the political direction of the Revolution under the Directory, and under the leadership of Napoleon Bonaparte, transformed the nature of these movements.[17] Just as the Bonapartist state synthesized elements of absolutism with those of the political order of the Revolution in its refiguration of citizenship, so too the expansionist conception of the *Grande Nation* altered the nature of political asylum, basing it on criteria of "usefulness" and proximity to the central power, rather than on any universal category of rights.

Many Italian refugees had arrived in France in successive regional groups— Cisalpins, Piedmontese, Neapolitans, Romans—after the counterrevolutions of 1799. At first they were accorded a warm welcome by the state and provided with a central sum administered by a specially appointed commission.[18] However, this welcome turned rapidly to hostility: the presence of Italians connected through Buonarotti to Babeuf and his "Conspiracy of Equals" led the Directory to suspect all Italians as radicals or anarchists.[19] Fragmented by regional differences, divided between partisans of unification and those seeking French tutelage, most Italians ultimately returned to their homeland.[20]

The fate of Spanish exiles under the Empire was more varied: as Jean-René Aymes has shown, the occupation of Spain produced a mixed group of several thousand deportees, auxiliary troops, prisoners of war, priests, hostages, and *ralliés*. Some of these categories were granted temporary financial assistance, but no overall system was put in place. The destinies of these expatriates was altogether more complex, and largely based on individual background, the experience of exile, and the shifting political climate in Spain.[21] Some individuals who had married in France, and others who mistrusted the consequences of return, chose to remain in exile, but the vast majority returned to Spain as rapidly as they could.

The term "refugee," so often used to describe these populations, hardly begins to map the complexity of political affiliation and fear of persecution, of direct relationship with the state and collective consciousness. The Italians, united by political proximity to the Revolution, found themselves divided by the realpolitik of the Directory and Consulate. The Spaniards, lacking any real unity of political allegiance either for or against the French regime, tended to disperse in the Franco-Spanish borderlands. The "Egyptians," however, were a different case. Their choice to embark for France was not a decision that could quickly be reversed. While Marseille was certainly a hub of the Levant trade, with a few Arabic-speakers already residing among its population,[22] and many other families who had long divided their life across the Mediterranean, this was not a boundary zone like that described by Peter Sahlins.[23] There were few possibilities for a large group marked by differences of dress, color, language, and culture to blend into their surroundings.

The differences between the new arrivals and the other inhabitants of Marseille were so marked as to give the former a single identity in the eyes of local authorities. During the early period, it was common to utilize the term *réfugiés d'Égypte*, which implied only the act of fleeing Egypt, without conferring any particular identification; insensibly, however, this soon devolved into *réfugiés égyptiens*, in line with other usages, such as those pertaining to Italians and Spaniards, implicitly assuming a common ethnocultural identity rather than a geographical origin. These "refugees" were allocated pensions, not in a single, centrally administered sum like the Italians, but rather in a sliding scale of four classes, allocated individually and administered through a pay office in Marseille. The pensions were not allocated according to need, but rather according to the services of the individual to the French army, and their estimated losses occasioned by their support for the

French. In this sense, we should not imagine the administrative category of "refugee" as approximating the humanitarian conceptions of today, but rather as a more general classification for displaced persons within the state who had some political claim other than that of citizen.

However, the manner in which these "refugees" were administered by the state does not tell us how they imagined themselves. Georges Aïdé is a perfect example: he was not in fact either "Egyptian" or a "refugee": his family came from Aleppo in Syria, and he himself was born in Beirut.[24] As the former chief of customs in Damietta, he certainly brought some wealth with him, and he later emphasized that he remained in France by choice. Other "refugees" also had considerable resources, although the richest of them, such as Ya'qub's widow, were not enrolled on the refugee lists. Aïdé was trading between Marseille and Paris and had considerable trade connections throughout the Mediterranean. When he wrote to Napoleon he certainly presented himself as completely penniless, and he received a substantial pension in compensation. It is very likely that he had lost a great deal through the British embargo and his decision to leave Egypt. He felt that he deserved recompense—not charity—from the French state. And the First Consul, it seems, agreed.

Moreover, after Ya'qub's death, Aïdé was one of the three most prominent figures in the Egyptian Legation, alongside Ya'qub's brother, Henin Hanna, and 'Abd el-Al, the former aga, or chief, of the Janissary police in Cairo. The three notables came from quite disparate religious and regional backgrounds. Aïdé was a Melkite Catholic from Syria, Henin was a Copt from Upper Egypt, and 'Abd el-Al was a Muslim from Cairo. Still, in the provisional space of the lazaret, the triangulated Legation seemed to remain relatively unified despite the loss of their leader. Their *wakil* (agent), Nemir Effendi, penned the Legation's eloquent petitions to the various organs of the French state and continued to sound the tone of an "Egyptian" identification in an active, *national* sense. This is clear in the petitions written to the First Consul, the minister of foreign affairs (Talleyrand), and the minister of war, which were published by Auriant and George Haddad.[25] But a further letter from the Legation, signed by Nemir Effendi and addressed to the minister of the interior, has remained unexamined among the papers of the Commission d'Égypte at the Archives Nationales in Paris.[26] This petition is particularly useful in tracing the transformation of the idea of national emigration into an acceptance of permanent refuge in France.

In this letter, the Legation proposed a series of measures that the French administration should apply in order to deal with this sudden influx of refugees from Egypt. Nemir helpfully provided the text for a ready-made decree he hoped might be promulgated by the Consulate:

In one of the largest national edifices of the city of Marseille or its environs, by choice of the Egyptian Legation (the Convent of the Capucins has been mentioned as appropriate to our object), will be established an *Oriental Harem-Hospice* to lodge and educate the refugees from Egypt, men and women arriving along with the Army of the Orient. The printing press and the national library of Egypt will be assigned to this establishment; the individuals who shelter there will be allocated military rations and allowance like soldiers. This *Oriental Harem-Hospice* will be directed and administered by *Mallam Henen,* brother of General Yacoub, commandant of the Egyptian auxiliaries, who died during the voyage. . . . The Egyptian Legation is charged with the presentation of a project of regulation for the interior of this establishment, useful to the meridional departments of the Republic.[27]

The members of the Legation were sufficiently aware of the consequences of the Revolution to suggest shrewdly the use of *biens nationaux* seized from the church. The "Harem-Hospice" they proposed was clearly intended to function as a temporary substitute for the project of Egyptian independence. It would be a kind of "nation in embryo" in the Midi of France, which could serve as the basis for a cultural nationalism now that the prospect of armed struggle for independence seemed more and more remote. In proposing the creation of an independent and self-governed community, the Egyptian Legation clearly sought to accrue to it many of the classic accessories of national identity, in particular those connected with language—such as the printing press used during the French occupation in Egypt (and the first to produce a newspaper in Arabic) and the "national library" drawn from the Institut d'Égypte.

But the inherent contradictions within this national idea were evident even in this fanciful proposition. At no point did this letter use the word "Egyptian" to describe the emigration as a whole. Even the "Harem-Hospice" was identified as "Oriental" rather than "Egyptian." If the Legation still subscribed to a national project in a *political* sense, the regional, sectarian, and ethnic diversity of the emigrants made it virtually impossible to use the name "Egyptian" to describe their commonality. Thus it seemed that the Legation's project to resuscitate an Egyptian national identity as a focal point for the emigration was doomed from the very beginning, both from within and from without.

However, we may read in this project a discreet allusion to the Muslims of the emigration who no longer appeared overtly in descriptions of the population to be settled in France. The "Islamic policy" that Bonaparte had employed in Egypt was definitively at an end, replaced with a new Ottoman policy bearing all the hallmarks of the old Franco-Ottoman alliance pursued under the ancien régime. That politics had been based on reciprocal treaties assuring French subjects of full rights of residence and religious freedom in the Ottoman domains: conversely, the subjects of the sultan were assured of these rights in France. One of the provisions of the older treaties had been the allocation of a space to be used as a mosque and cemetery in Marseille. As Regis Bertrand has noted, in 1770 a group of Muslim merchants from North Africa wrote to the Chamber of Commerce in Marseille to request the placement of a plaque written in Arabic on the door of the compound designated for their use. They declared that "they would be very satisfied to be able to announce to their masters . . . that the Muslims have a hospice here as the Christians do in their own [the Muslims'] lands."[28] Thus, we may read in the choice of "hospice" as a term for the institutional provisions to be made for the emigration some echo of this earlier structure of reciprocal privileges pertaining specifically to Muslims.

But this reciprocality could not serve them now either as a privilege or as a right. The Egyptian and Syrian Muslims could no longer count themselves the subjects of a foreign sovereign power—however ambivalently, they were now subjects of France on French soil. At the same time, these privileges were caught up in the tangle of postrevolutionary politics, between republican versions of isonomy and the restoration of corporate structures and privileges. The application of the Concordat in Provence was particularly fraught with struggles, and on occasion these struggles drew in the Jews and Muslims of Marseille. Permission to celebrate Catholic ceremonies in public spaces had been granted by the new law, except in places with substantial non-Catholic populations. But the newly reestablished archbishop, Monseigneur de Cicé, pushed rapidly to extend these prerogatives into all parts of his archdiocese, and Marseille in particular, claiming that the town's Protestants had spontaneously supported his request. The prefect of the Bouches-du-Rhône, Charles Delacroix, requested a report from the commissioner of police in Marseille, who responded that in his opinion such a move would be dangerous: although the Catholic religion was now "tolerant in principle," long-established custom demanded exterior signs of respect. "The Turk, the Arab, the African, and the Jew," the commissioner wrote, "not presenting such homage and respect . . . might well cause a great deal of trouble in the present circumstances."[29] In his report to Jean-Étienne-Marie Portalis, the minister in charge of religious affairs, Delacroix insisted that the archbishop's claim of Protestant support was largely fabricated. In any case, he argued, Protestants were not the only non-Catholics living in Marseille: the town had a substantial Jewish community and synagogue. Furthermore, Delacroix added, "in Marseille, before the war, there was a mosque that the prosperity of our trade with the Levant may permit to be reestablished."[30] Here then, the presence of Jews and Muslims could still be seen to counterbalance the claims of Catholics, even of Christians in general, within a republican structure of equal rights. Within a few months, however, and with the personal prodding of Bonaparte, Portalis gave way in almost everything the archbishop demanded: Catholic religious processions, obligatory rest on Sunday, and the sound of church bells announced the church's triumphant return to the public space, protected by the government's indulgence. Delacroix was transferred to the Gironde, his term as prefect in Aix cut short under pressure from the archbishop and his supporters.

Beyond these few, scattered hints, however, we simply do not know what arrangements were made for Muslim religious practice in Marseille. It is clear from the bulletins of the secret police that there were also a number of North African Muslims in Marseille, although it has not yet been possible to locate any substantial documentation about their residence in France—nor are they mentioned in the correspondence of the "Egyptians." A secret police report of 1807 mentioned a fight in Marseille "between Africans, Tunisians and Moroccans, provoked by Mohamet Berberi, Algerian."[31] After the assassination of the dey of Algiers in 1808, it was observed by the secret police that "the Algerians of Marseille are celebrating."[32] We may suspect, therefore, that the Muslim elements of the population might have formed connections with these North Africans. It appears, however, that the Algerians were considered by the regime as tolerated aliens, standing hostage to the treatment of the French citizens in Algiers, and not as residents of any permanent status. The "Egyptians," as partisans of the French, could certainly not be considered in this light, so some other administrative structure altogether had to be found to accommodate them.

The French classification of the new arrivals in Marseille as "Egyptian refugees" provided them with an administrative Egyptian identity yet simultaneously rejected any Egyptian national or political claim on their part. Like other populations fleeing the consequences of collaboration, they were to be compensated and sustained on French soil on a temporary basis. Although they might still be useful in some future project in Egypt, they were to be maintained at a distance from the capital in order to ensure that their presence did not give rise to unfortunate political consequences in future relations with the Ottoman Empire. The most immediate consequence of this policy was the disintegration of the emigration into contradictory and conflictual groups. Some former members of the Egyptian Legation followed their own individual trajectories toward personal advancement. Lascaris and Colonel Papas Oglou, the head of the Greek Legion, made their way to Paris, on the condition of renouncing any larger political claim to represent the Egyptian project.[33] For those who remained in Marseille, sectarian and class differences began to reemerge. These differences first surfaced in the conflict over the legacy of General Ya'qub.

The Egyptian historian Jabarti reported that the news of the death of Ya'qub reached Cairo in 1803, and he gave an account of the problems that ensued. The general had brought with him to France a considerable fortune, and on his death his widow claimed her rights under French inheritance law. But Ya'qub's brother, Henin Hanna, denied the legitimacy of her marriage, since it had not been carried out under the auspices of the Coptic church to which Ya'qub belonged.[34] The French authorities wrote to the Copts of Cairo, who supported Henin's claim. Jabarti assumed that this settled the matter. But this religious argument could not hold under French law. It seems clear that Ya'qub's widow received the inheritance, since in 1805 she purchased for 26,500 francs a property of five hectares in the Madrague, slightly north of the old port.[35] This struggle between the two most important figures of Ya'qub's legacy, underpinned as it was by older sectarian conflicts between Christian communities, indicates how deep the divisions within the emigration remained.

In a letter to the Ministry of War, Nemir described the divisions in the emigration not in terms of religion or ethnicity, but according to socioeconomic differences. Nemir outlined three distinct components of the population based on their social position: affluent merchants, the destitute poor, and soldiers. The first sector in Nemir's classification comprised "the families of merchants," whom he described as "affluent people, who ask for an asylum in France only in order to conduct their business in peace."[36] Some of these people, like Georges Aïdé, received substantial pensions from the government. The presence of these affluent families in Marseille attracted other relations and friends to join them—the Homsy family is one example, arriving in Marseille much later, marrying into the family of General Ya'qub, and eventually inheriting the properties of Ya'qub's widow, which were later named *Les Mamelucks* and *La Jacobe* in memory of the "first generation" of the Arab emigration [37]

The second sector of the population, described by Nemir as the *infortunés,* or impoverished, were totally dependent upon the government for the provision of means of survival. Divided into four classes, not according to need, but rather according to their grades of "service" to the French, they seem to have formed their own, relatively tightly knit community on what were then the edges of the town. More than sixty years later, the writer Léon Gozlan, a child of Algerian Jews who had grown up among the "Egyptian refugees," described them in an article for the *Revue contemporaine:*

> Not wanting to separate, because to separate is to be destroyed, and they wanted to remain Egyptians of Alexandria, Egyptians of Cairo, Syrians of Jaffa and Aleppo, they searched for, and found, in this admirable city of Marseille, a spot predestined for them. It was a stretch of plain, half green, half browned, which recalled for them at once the banks of the Nile and the sands of Giza. There they constructed small white houses on the left and right, reaching two stories at most, as many of the houses had no upper story at all. The habitations opened on one side to the street—a charming promenade called the Cours Gouffé—and on the other to their gardens, where they soon planted the vegetables of their country: beans, onions of Tanis as big as melons, zucchinis, watermelons, corn, and above all okra (gombo).[38]

Gozlan's portrait may be idealized by time and memory and by the profoundly different conditions in which he was writing. But the general impression at least is confirmed by an earlier and far more hostile writer, Laurent Lautard, who described these inhabitants of the town as "refugees from Egypt who vegetated in hovels abutting the Place Castellane."[39]

It is clear that a considerable group was quite densely concentrated in a small area. However, from his researches in the état civil and cadastral registers of Marseille, the archivist Georges Reynaud concluded that this group in fact represented only 25 percent—"the most impoverished fraction"—of the population.[40] But it seems certain that this concentration tended to encourage the maintenance of many cultural practices, including diet and clothing. Gozlan describes "their Egyptian merchants, their Egyptian tailors . . . [who] would wind their wide turbans of airy muslin or make their long dalmatic coats out of dark fabrics, to their wishes."[41] Such practices maintained a degree of cultural continuity, adding to the group's visibility as an unassimilated "foreign" population. In fact, according to their own correspondence, they cultivated *molokhiyya,* a favorite green vegetable of the Middle East, which they dried and sent to their compatriots in Melun and Paris. Their letters are filled with details of other foods they were sending from Marseille—dried fish (*batarekh*) and coconuts, olives, and dates. They speak also of the *tarabeesh,* or turbans, they were sending. From Paris, in return, they received books, ink, and, most valuable of all, *appui*—personal influence and powerful contacts in the capital.

The third group that Nemir Effendi described was the most visible of all. He divided the soldiers who had served as auxiliaries in Egypt and Syria into four corps— "the Mamelouks, the Syrians, the Greek and Coptic legions"—that were differentiated variously by ethnic, regional, class, and sectarian commonalities. Thus, he continued, "at most two or three hundred men will be arriving in France, who, although mostly footsoldiers, are more suited to become good Arab cavalry than soldiers trained in the handling of arms and various other French drills."[42] The letter went on to outline the reasons for this unfitness to join the ordinary ranks of the French army: "Not knowing French to follow orders, short, ugly, dark-skinned, and completely without what the French call *la tournure,* they would be ridiculous and certainly very unhappy to be the constant butt of the other soldiers, with whom, furthermore, they would not be able to communicate." Nemir drew on a combination of linguistic, cultural, and physiological differences as an argument for the creation of a distinct Arab regiment, for which he proposed the name "Tribu arabe de Cavaliers Égyptiens ou Cavaliers Errants," (Arab Tribe of Egyptian Cavaliers or Wandering Cavaliers) and which, in his words, "more richly fitted out than the Mamluks, but in an Egyptian uniform, could bring about a useful revolution in the light cavalry of the Republic and entertain France with all the drills of the Arabs of the desert."[43] This was a delicate tracing of the lines linking Egyptian particularism with Arab commonality—"an Arab tribe of Egyptian horsemen"—although his second suggestion dropped the Egyptian inflection altogether for an identification that emphasized mobility itself as the defining commonality. The term "Arab," in contrast, seemed to present a more stable counterbalance to these shifting identifications. We must return to this crucial question in greater detail later in this chapter.

In the event, this suggestion coincided very effectively with the desires of the French authorities. A squadron was chosen from the pick of the military men. But it was called neither "Egyptian" nor "Arab"; instead Napoleon insisted upon a corps of "Mamelouks."[44] This was an unhappy designation indeed. In 1798, Bonaparte had declared to the people of Egypt that he had come to liberate them from the greedy and oppressive rule of the real Mamluk class. Yet it was this name that he now chose to represent his "Oriental" soldiers, investing them with the allure of exoticism and more than a hint of cruelty. The uniform of these soldiers was adorned with a green turban and Muslim crescent, despite the fact that many of them were Christian.[45] This islamicizing adornment continued long after the ranks of the Mamelouks were filled with Frenchmen. By associating the conventional "terror" of Islam with the power of the emperor, the "Mamelouks" served an important role in the semiotics of Napoleonic propaganda, one which justified their considerable cost. Their Oriental dress was elaborate and extremely expensive and was specified down to the smallest detail in the military orders: red *tarbouche* or green *cahouk* surrounded by a white turban, loose-sleeved *béniche* under a Greek vest, voluminous *charouals,* drawstring trousers of crimson, purple, or white, and grey cloak held by a blue or maroon belt.[46] Where the members of the Egyptian Legation were ordered to remain in Marseille, the military contingent was brought to Paris and Fontainebleau, to be quartered in the town of Melun. They soon played an important role in official spectacle in the capital: on the celebration of 14 July 1802 the *Journal des débats* reported: "At today's grand parade . . . the Mamelouks excited the regard of the public no less by the novelty of the spectacle that their costume and their unusual uniform presented. They numbered one hundred, and all on horseback."[47] Two years later, this festival celebrating the Revolution would be effaced in favour of 15 August, the emperor's birthday.

It is as "Mamelouks" that the Arab population of early nineteenth-century France have been marked down in history, as exotic and fabulously attired incarnations of Napoleonic glory or as cruel Oriental auxiliaries carrying out the most dreadful repressions. In his decision to adapt into his own symbolic repertoire the figures he had once vilified, Napoleon placed the Arab population under his rule in a characteristically unequal and irregular relationship to the state. *Mamluk* literally means "owned," as we have noted: the regime cultivated the conception of the Mamelouk as the perfect, slavish, and devoted servant of the emperor, a role implicitly to be followed by others. Napoleon was constantly attended by a Mamelouk servant and was frequently represented with this slave at his side. It was not a portrayal that explained anything of the origins of these people, their

FIGURE 5. Charles Abraham Chasselat, grav. Godefroy, "Habaïby Daoud, Capitaine des Mameloucks," from *Les fastes de la gloire ou les braves recommandés à la postérité: Monument élevé aux défenseurs de la patrie,* vol. 1 (Paris: L'Advocat, 1819). Author's collection.

motivations for coming to France, or their own sense of their destiny. As a rule they remained anonymous, their uniform more important than their identity; on rare occasions extraordinary acts of courage became subjects of individual iconography, such as the image of Daoud Habaïby, a Palestinian Melkite notable, who rode forward into the ranks of the Prussian infantry despite receiving three bayonet wounds (fig. 5).

The exotic representations should not distract us from the recognition that these men were soldiers like any others of the time, and their experiences of war, conscription, injury, death, and retirement resemble those of other soldiers studied comprehensively by historians from Alan Forrest to Natalie Petiteau.[48] They played an important role in providing income and social mobility for their families in Marseille. But they did not represent the bulk of the population at any point. Given the dominance of this group in the representation of the "Egyptians" in France, it is worth reviewing a few statistics compiled from the work of earlier historians. Analyzing Jean Savant's list of the Mamelouks of the Imperial Guard, it is possible to determine that only 44 out of 221 (20 percent) of the "Oriental" Mamelouks died while in active military service.[49] Of these almost half disappeared during the retreat from Russia, and it is conceivable that part of that number may have taken the opportunity to desert. The average length of service for those who enrolled before 1812 (a total of 211) was around six and a half years, but more than a quarter of these men served only three years or less.

These numbers are important in dispelling the idea that this was a military population whose fate was to serve and die under arms. The average "Mamelouk" spent less than half of the period 1801–15 in military service. Further, the reduction in numbers of "Oriental" soldiers in the Napoleonic armies was due largely to retirements rather than casualties. Hundreds of ex-soldiers went into retirement; but rather than receiving the ordinary *retraite* of a French soldier, they were reclassified along with the other "refugees" on a pension scale varying from thirty-three francs per day for the most privileged down to fifty to sixty centimes along with a ration of bread for the last among the "Fourth Class" of refugees (including wives and children).[50] For the average retired Mamelouk, the pension amounted to 1 franc 25 per day—although some received double and others half this amount.[51] In addition, their wives and children received approximately half of the pension accorded to the man of the family, bringing the family income, in some cases, to a reasonable level of sustainability, and encouraging the "Egyptians" to marry among themselves and to produce larger families in order to increase their entitlements.

The correspondence contained at Vincennes is primarily concerned with the question of this pension: applications for increases, the hope of admitting children born in France, or even relatives arriving from Egypt and Syria. But it is also the case that the refugees' own private correspondence in Arabic raised this question repeatedly. The correspondents described their pension as a *jamakiya*, meaning "pay," rather than as a pension or a form of charity. Later, one correspondent distinguished between the payment he would receive for his work in giving Arabic classes, and the *rafujiya*, transcribing the French term *réfugié* and adapting it to Arabic grammatical form. His need to specify the difference emphasizes that *jamakiya* did not in itself carry the meaning of "pension," but rather of "salary." The importance of this pension in shaping the Arab community in France cannot be overestimated: it offered a consistent incentive to maintain a communal identification and reinforced bonds between individuals even as it created conflicts and jealousies.

The sectarian issues (both within and between groups) continued to exist and were exacerbated by these economic divisions. The majority of those "wealthy merchants" Nemir described, who sent their children to the Lycée of Marseille and conducted business with the Orient, were from the Melkite families of Egypt and Palestine, a highly mobile and well-connected Mediterranean community. In contrast, many of those in the poorer class of the community, living in shacks near the Place Castellane, were Copts and Muslims—soldiers of Ya'qub's legion; peasants from Upper Egypt, illiterate and without resources; a few former Mamluk soldiers; domestic servants; and soldiers recruited into other units in Egypt. There were also a number of women of various origins, including some who prostituted themselves openly.

The two economically distinct sectors of the community could simply have taken separate paths. But this did not happen, and in this the role of the Legation is crucial. If their political projects for independence, and the "Harem-Hospice," were decisively rejected by the French government, the legacy of the communal project remained. Marseille was officially recognized as the *dépôt* for Egyptian refugees, with an appointed council comprising members of the Legation and officers of the military corps. This council was responsible for making recommendations to the Ministry of War regarding the numerous applications for admission to the register of refugees. The council would also provide support for certain applications for increases in the pension and for permission to travel to other places. One of the council's officers was appointed to distribute a daily bread ration to the poorest class of refugees. Beyond these administrative tasks, however, the role of the council was hazy during these early years in Marseille. The population was in flux: as a result of ongoing instability in Egypt after the departure of the British and Ottoman armies, new arrivals continued to land in Marseille. The reform of the Corps of Mamelouks also resulted in a large number of former soldiers swelling the "Egyptian village" near the Place Castellane. This increase in the visible population created tensions with local authorities.

In July 1806, things came to a head. The mayor of Marseille, Antoine-Ignace Anthoine, wrote to the prefect of the Département des Bouches-du-Rhone, Antoine Thibaudeau, to complain about what he claimed was a growing racial problem in the city. A detachment of seventy-four Egyptians had just arrived in the city, after their release from the army. Now, he wrote,

> the city of Marseille, already full of refugee Jews from Algiers and Egyptian negresses—this last the worst species of all—watches with alarm these foreigners collecting here in ever greater number. I have acted with rigour several times, above all against the women of colour, but within the limits of the police, by making them suffer a detention of several days. That is all the severity I can use against them.[52]

These "negresses" were mostly former slaves brought by the Egyptian families as domestic servants or purchased by French officers in Egypt. Enrolled in the registers of "Nègres et Gens de Couleur," compiled in 1807 at the behest of the authorities, are a number of women from Cairo and others from places such as "d'Alfort," and "Cy Narry" or "Seinard." Erick Noël has suggested plausibly that

d'Alfort is a transcription of Darfour, in Sudan, and Cy Narry/Seinard is probably
Sennar, also in Sudan.[53] It is notable that these women identified these places of
origin, despite their double displacement. Some of the women must have recognized that they were no longer slaves in France; many certainly enrolled their
names on the list of refugees and received a small pension. Some took the surname Alimé or Halimé—a French version of the Arabic term '*alima* (learned),
meaning "courtesan" or "entertainer." Others were simply known as Fatoumé, Ga-
didgé, or Victoire. But the titular freedom they received as a consequence of arriving on French soil did little to erase the status connected with their color. Their
identification by the authorities as *négresses* rather than *noires* carried an implicit
connection with slavery.

Some of the notables among the "Egyptians" exploited this confusion to exert
power over others. Such a case was reported by the grandmother of the great
nineteenth-century statesman Adolphe Thiers, who was born in Istanbul and
made close connections with the families arriving from Egypt and Syria while living in Marseille. In a letter to her brother, Mme Amie recounted that she was
awoken in the night by the frantic knocking of a young black woman, Fatima. The
girl had been viciously beaten by her mistress, the redoutable wife of Bartholomeo
Serra, former aga of police in Cairo. Bartholomeo claimed that Fatima was his
property, a slave returned to him by General Menou.[54]

This story points to the importance of women in the story of the emigration.
As in this case, they could be victim, perpetrator, or protector. Women's lives are
far less frequently illuminated by the archival record, but it is clear that their role
was more than domestic: these women were not confined to the "harem" but able
to play a political and contestatory role. Several Egyptian women who had traveled to France after marrying French citizens fought in court to defend their inheritance rights after the death of their husbands.[55] A Persian traveler returning
from Britain in 1803 shared a carriage with a young Egyptian woman who defended herself courageously against harassment by two male passengers.[56] Another Egyptian woman was immortalized in the iconography of Napoleonic power
when she intervened directly with the emperor during the Prussian campaign in
1806 and was awarded a pension of 1,200 francs: according to General Rapp, "She
was a young Egyptian woman who displayed that religious reverence toward
[Napoleon] that the Arabs always accorded him."[57] The image of her supplication
was produced in dozens of different versions: one shows the *Égyptienne* enclosed
in swirling draperies topped with a turban, guiding her small son toward Napoleon
(fig. 6). She stands between an empty chair crowned with laurels and the man
who seems destined to occupy it. The composition reflects other images of the
emperor's acts of "generosity," many involving women or families. It suggests
equally an older iconography of the continents, of tributary nations hailing their
civilizing benefactors. It is a far cry indeed from the revolutionary incarnation of

NAPOLÉON LE GRAND,
au Château du Grand Veneur de Saxe, 24.Oct^{bre}. 1806.

FIGURE 6. Louis Lafitte, grav. Delvaux, *Napoléon le Grand au château du Grand Veneur de Saxe, 24. Oct^{bre} 1806.* Author's collection.

the Republic as a powerful, warlike female figure, "Marianne": here it is the very helplessness and depoliticization of this foreign woman that makes her an ideal figure to articulate the new relationship of power proposed by Napoleon's regime.

But real Egyptian and Syrian women were not always so compliant with the patriarchal structures into which they were inserted, insofar as we can ascertain from the few fragments that remain of their voices. A certain "Maryam" wrote in Arabic to Mikha'il Sabbagh, a key figure in the small Arab presence in Paris, angrily refuting accusations that had been made about her private life and declaring her intention to remarry. The legalization of her status, she insisted, would "cut the tongues of all those who slander me." Her letter continued: "As for the food and other items you received," she wrote angrily, "it was I who paid for them. Ask Joubran Takhakh who the perfume is from; ask the wife of M. Naydorff who bought the *tarabeesh;* ask Girgis Hamawi who bought the dried *molokhiyya.* They are all a gift from me." She closed her letter with defiance: "My livelihood and my life are not in your hands, they are in Allah's hands."[58]

At the intersection between the questions of gender and race we can observe a particularly virulent response that would have extremely dangerous implications for the whole population of Egyptian refugees and serve as a potent and sometimes violent force shaping their identifications in the years that followed. In the years of 1806–7, the black women of Marseille were singled out for particular opprobrium within a generalized "racial threat" and pursued with extraordinary aggressiveness by the authorities. In his letter to the prefect cited earlier, the mayor of Marseille linked Egyptians, Algerian Jews, and black women together to suggest a general racial danger, adding that black women were "the worst species of all." His description of these women as "negresses" rather than "noires" (blacks) assimilated them to the centuries-old structures of chattel slavery and the triangular trade in slaves between Europe, West Africa, and the Americas. This terminology carried very serious ramifications for the women and for others among the Egyptian refugees whose skin was perceptibly darker than the population around them. With the reestablishment of slavery in 1802, the residence of *gens de couleur* in France was no longer legal; the renewal of the force of decrees of 1777 removing their rights to residence in France had been explicitly confirmed by the administration. Sue Peabody has described the "Police des Noirs," which operated under the ancien régime, and the establishment of places of incarceration—which were also called *dépôts*—to house slaves brought to France, preventing them from asserting the automatic right to liberty they could claim as a result of arriving on metropolitan French soil.[59] Thus the act of 1802 transformed the status of people of color living in France as well as those in the colonies. But in the case of "Egyptians" of color, this status was extremely ambiguous. Jennifer Heuer has noted the confusion regarding the definition of "blacks" when the authorities attempted to apply to Egyptians the prohibition on interracial marriages reintroduced in France in 1803.[60] In 1802, when local authorities were instructed to provide a register of the "people of color" in each of the *arrondissements* of Marseille, one of the police commissioners complained that he could not, since "almost all the Egyptians have *nègres* with them who do not appear on any census."[61]

In 1806, the reformation of the Imperial Guard reduced the number of Mamelouks serving in it to 109. The decree of the "New Organization of the Guard" contained a provision stating that "the refugee Mamelouks, who are at Melun, will be sent to Marseille, where they will enjoy the same advantages, and will be paid in the same way as in the past."[62] The arrival of these men, with the strong Muslim associations that, as we have noted, were encouraged by Napoleonic propaganda, brought a religious as well as a racial difference to bear in the hostility that the mayor sought to invoke. At the same time, an uprising against the dey, the governor of Algiers, led to reprisals against the Jewish minority, which had been closely associated with the regime, and this led a stream of Algerian Jews to take refuge in Marseille. The municipality of Marseille had only quite recently been unified into a single administration, after its punitive division into three sections during the Revolution. The mayor was particularly eager to assert his own influence over that of the prefect, Thibaudeau, a functionary from the days of Jacobin ascendancy. The "racial threat" he invoked was intensified by political and religious overtones: it offered an opportunity to test the limits of his power by taking radical steps, but steps fully in line with the trajectory of imperial dispositions.

The mayor's claim was supported with police reports that retailed a series of violent acts, disorder, and defiance of police by these black women and the soldiers who allegedly frequented their company; the infractions reported involved the nonpayment of rent, domestic arguments, drunkenness, public brawling, and resisting arrest. Accusations against these women also included child abuse, and in one instance cross-dressing as a man and fighting in public.[63] Using these intersecting anxieties about gender, family, and public disorder as leverage, and leaning also on the legal interdiction of *gens de couleur* in France, the mayor began to press the prefect to sanction the creation of a physical *dépôt* for the confinement of these women, along with all the other Egyptians, "forcing them, without too much rigor, to return home at an appropriate hour."[64] The prefect demurred, perhaps out of sheer dislike of Anthoine:

> It is not in my authority, M. le Maire, to place the Citadel of St. Nicolas at your disposal to serve as a depot for the Egyptian and Algerian refugees and others who were the subject of your letter of the 5th. I suggest, however, that you keep these refugees under close surveillance.[65]

The threat, however, remained very real. At first the chief notables of the depot seemed hardly able to respond to the mayor's threats, writing in extremely irregular French to explain that they had done their best to collect information on the "naigresse et fames blanche" (negresses and white women) who were causing the trouble, but insisting that it was impossible to know where they lived, as they were always changing their lodgings. By the following year, the notables had come to understand the genuine threat to their liberty and the statute of their residence in France that this crisis entailed. In September, Abd el-Al, Georges Aïdé, and Henin Hanna, along with Hassan Odabachi and the captains Salloum and Ibrahim from the Corps of Mamelouks—now designating themselves the "Principal Egyptian Refugees Ex-Members of the Commission"—wrote officially to the mayor (this time in more accurate French) and offered him a list of the "troublemakers, men and women, of our depot":

> We thought we should anticipate the measures that your wisdom will order, M. le Maire, to act against them with severity, in the most effective way, through a permanent detention in one of the forts of Marseille.[66]

It was in response to this crisis, then, that the most influential individuals from the various fractions of the refugees came together at last to defend and define their status in France. In accepting the demand to draw up this list, they assumed responsibility for people about whom they had previously claimed to know nothing. In response to the question of the Algerian Jews, the mayor had summoned the representatives of the Jewish community in Marseille and demanded that they take responsibility for ensuring the passage of their fellow Jews to Livorno. Such a demand was fully in line with the "Jewish policy" emanating from Paris, where a national council of Jews, improbably named the "Great Sanhedrin" was soon to be assembled. Protestants, too, had been reorganized in the form of a consistory rather than simply as citizens of France. The creation of the "Council of Egyptian Refugees" represented the reformation of the "Egyptian" community in a consistorial status along the lines of the Jews, in order to avoid finding themselves incarcerated in a physical depot like that decreed for people of color.[67] Further, they proposed the creation of a second depot that would stabilize the status of their own. But the twenty-six individuals they nominated in their list were almost all young men, between the ages of sixteen and thirty. The letter offered to provide another list of the "black and white Egyptian women who lead a licentious and depraved existence," but proposed instead the creation of a "hospice" where they would be gainfully occupied and learn a trade, returning to the language of the Legation in 1801.[68]

It is evident that the racialized nature of the threat meant little in itself to these "principal Egyptians"; yet they had little choice but to respond, and they agreed implicitly to take on a function of social control over those designated as belonging to their community. At the same time they attempted to turn this exercise of power to their own advantage by denouncing a number of young men who had been children or adolescents at the time of the emigration, and who had now begun to challenge the authority of their elders.

A flurry of private letters exchanged between Marseille and Paris in 1807 describes the events that followed the denunciation of the shabab, or young men: an affair involving further denunciations, forged letters, arrests, and a trial that split the population in two. Gabriel Taouïl reported to Sabbagh: "The trial lasted for twelve days, and for six hours each day. The debate between the witnesses of the two parties was very heated, and they nearly fought." Taouïl reported that one participant was called "a kidnapping wolf" and reduced to tears; another was insulted as "Abu Tabeeq" (father of meals) because he would sell his own father for a plate of lentil soup.[69] The question of color seemed to have been forgotten, perhaps because it policed only the edges of their community, and these struggles were taking place at its center. Those racialized questions would return with violence, as we will see, in the turbulent days of 1815. But the struggles within the community continued: in early 1808, the Marseille police reported "Five Egyptian troublemakers, of whom four were arrested at the request of the aga, and then freed on his recommendation, and one at liberty but placed under surveillance."[70] The municipal authorities evidently had recourse to notables such as Abd el-'Al in controlling the Egyptians of the town.

The focus of the community centered instead on the single element common to all of them—the Arabic language. As a result of lobbying by the noted Orientalist Sylvestry de Sacy on behalf of his protégé, Gabriel Taouïl, a chair of Arabic language was created in Marseille by the emperor on 31 May 1807. According to a report,

> The Emperor, in placing [Taouïl] in Marseille, judged that his skills would be more useful there than in any other city, and if [His Majesty] had him give his courses at the Lycée, that is simply because it brings together the largest number of youngsters who are capable of profiting from Arabic lessons—a knowledge which will be indispensable to most of them, since, as Marseillais, they will certainly have direct relations with Orientals later on, because of the nature of commerce in the city.[71]

Taouïl was appointed to provide free Arabic lessons to the public at state expense in the precincts of the Lycée of Marseille, established in 1803 in the former Bernardine convent. The appointment was met with considerable resistance from the local municipality: the councillors consistently blocked the release of funds to cover Taouïl's emoluments, even after the Ministry of Education agreed to pay half of the salary from central coffers. Their argument rested upon the "lack of usefulness" of such training in the light of the blockade of trade on the Mediterranean.

In fact, the real "usefulness" of the classes, as certain notables of the town frequently complained, was for the Arabic-speaking families of the town, allowing their sons to study Arabic every school day at 2:30 p.m. Eusèbe de Salle, a bilious competitor for Taouïl's position, claimed that Taouïl alienated local students by teaching in Arabic from the first day. If this was true, it was not because Taouïl did not speak French; whether it was an attempt at "education by immersion" or simply because Taouïl oriented his role as teacher toward his own community is difficult to determine. Out of these classes would emerge a second generation carrying a new synthesis of French and Arab cultural identifications that will be explored in the second part of this book.

As a consequence of occupying this crucial role in a community emerging around the primary commonality of the Arabic language, Taouïl found himself thrust to the center of both internal and external struggles. In a report addressed to the Ministry of Education, Taouïl answered accusations that he was the instigator of a denunciation signed by eleven refugees against Abd el-Al, the former aga of the Janissary police in Cairo and a member of the "Council of Refugees." Three of the chief signatories of this denunciation were arrested and taken to prison, where they were interrogated with the assistance of a Coptic interpreter, Ellious Bocthor. According to Taouïl (although his testimony cannot be taken as reliable), they were told they would be released only if they admitted that Taouïl was the author of the petition. In the trial of the *shabab,* Taouïl claimed to Sabbagh that he had intervened to defend the truth, and that he had been praised by Ellious and Shukr'allah, another Copt, as well as by the lawyers and judges "for what I did to make the truth win out."[72] He insisted that Sabbagh would one day see that he was working only for the good of his community "unlike what you've been told by these sons of whores."[73]

The local authorities viewed these conflicts as reflecting the bad character of the "refugees." In 1811, the commissioner of police complained to his superiors:

> Generally, and with few exceptions, the refugees are troublesome, grasping, jealous, prone to quarrel ceaselessly among themselves and to hold deep grudges against one another, often for very little reason whatsoever.[74]

Beyond a liberal dash of xenophobia, this comment suggests how opaque these struggles within the community were to those outside. But these grudges, quarrels, and reconciliations were equally an index, and a consequence, of the emergence of strong ties binding these people closer together. The very viciousness of the infighting, particularly the ways in which the groups involved tended to shift and reconfigure across the period, was an indication of the emergence of tight (even claustrophobic) bonds of community among the heterogeneous Arabic-speakers of Marseille, a community constituted by circumstance as much as by choice, and constrained quite artificially within the bounds of this provincial city. If, with few exceptions, the conflicts took place within the community rather than with outsiders, this was because these people lived in much closer contact with one another than with the wider French society around them. As Georges Aïdé wrote to the minister of war, explaining comments he had made about Abd el-Al, "I have never done anything against your wishes, or written anything against the Government. *I was speaking only against an Egyptian like myself.*"[75] Aïdé clearly considered internal and external relationships as of quite different kinds. Taouïl reported that Abd el-Al returned to Marseille and gleefully recited an Arabic poem written by Sabbagh that criticized Aïdé.[76] At the same time Ellious Bocthor wrote that "Antun Hamawi invited Jerjes [Georges] Aïdé, and no one could believe it after everything that happened between them. Some said it is just politics from Hamawi, some said it is fear, and other people said Hamawi wants Aïdé to mediate between him and Jebreel [Gabriel] Taouil and Jerjes [Georges] Hamawi."[77]

A document reproduced in Gaston Homsy's book about his family suggests that after the crisis of 1806–7 some of the earlier conflicts among the elite were resolved. In 1801, Henin, the brother of General Ya'qub, had come into conflict with his sister-in-law over the control of Ya'qub's fortune. But now he was listed as signing the "act of notoriety" by which Ya'qub's death was officially recognized, ensuring the ability of his widow Maryam (now known as Marie Namé) to remarry.[78]

These bonds of friendship and enmity, these exchanges of presents and vitriol, letters and secrets, the arrangement of marriages and consignment of goods, quarrels and reconciliations, traced the lines of an incipient Arab France, which had begun to emerge over the decade from 1801 to 1811. It was a landscape of mobility and exchange, a flow of people as well as goods—*molokhiyya* and *tarabeesh*, books and tobacco, ink and olives. To take an example from the myriad details of everyday life, in late 1809, Mikha'il Sabbagh wrote from Paris to his friends in Marseille, asking for coconuts. He wanted to mark the new year of 1810 with a party to impress influential people in Paris. The continental blockade made such items extremely difficult to procure, but one suspects it was this fact that made Sabbagh all the more keen to have them. The coconuts were the subject of an intense correspondence between Sabbagh and his friend Ellious Bocthor, the Sakakini brothers, Maryam Chébib, François Naydorff, and others. These people were all of disparate origins: Melkite Syrians, Egyptian Copts, Franks. In return, they hoped Sabbagh might use his influence in the capital to advance their cause. But the coconuts also pointed up a growing gap between those at the center of imperial power and those on its fringes. They were a symbol of ambition and aspiration. François Naydorff wrote to Sabbagh that he had cracked one open to test it, finding it a little yellow, but still satisfactory. He added: "I left the other eight coconuts whole because in France people consider the flesh inside less valuable than the shell, which they use for hunting goblets."[79] Naydorff, like the other correspondents, understood that the value of these exotic fruits was calibrated in relation to French, not Arab, customs. Their exorbitant cost (ten francs each) was an investment in the circuits of power ever more intensely concentrated in Paris. The appearance of coconuts on Sabbagh's table in Paris was thus in a real sense the result of the binding together of these ties of mutual interest, friendship, family, and culture. They were the product of an Arab social network that had emerged over the course of a decade.

Naydorff, an Egyptian of European origin married to an Arab woman with four children (two from a previous marriage), wrote numerous letters to Sabbagh in Paris in both French and Arabic. In one of them he complained:

> I promise you that the only thing that has prevented me from making greater claims has been the fear of making myself unwelcome and abusing the generosity of our august sovereign toward the Egyptians . . . but the example they have set in their continual petitions, with very positive results for some of them, along with my most pressing needs . . . imposes a Law upon me, being in the greatest distress.[80]

This "law" was not imposed from outside; it was a way of expressing the requirements Naydorff felt were dictated by his social position within the community.

He protested against the provisions of the state "that assimilate us to the lowest of the refugees." Even the small increase in his pension, he wrote Sabbagh, from fifty sous to seventy sous per day was "not worth all the effort."[81] But the only way to change this status was by access to the capital. As Joseph Hawadier complained to the Ministry of War in 1810, "Numerous Egyptian *Messieurs et Dames* have gone from Marseille to Paris and have succeeded in increasing their pensions."[82] Hawadier's use of these polite titles may have been ironic or merely conventional, but it suggests that Paris was associated with the acquisition of status. And it was toward Paris that Naydorff, along with the other refugees, looked in the second decade of their residence in France.

There were many reasons why the Arabs of Marseille, like so many other French people, and others across Europe and beyond, should be attracted to Paris, a city of entertainments and intellectual exchange, a place for ambition and the making of fortunes, the administrative center of an imperial superpower. But, as Naydorff remarks here, it was not only as individuals that Arabs looked toward Paris, but as a community. Indeed, the capital would prove to be a central ground of contestation over the formation of practices of identity that might offer a possibility for the creation of a new space. An "Arab Marseille" had emerged from the intersection between the political projects of the Legation—transformed ultimately into communal authority and institutions—and the categories sponsored by the authorities, including those threats that policed the boundaries of these categories, and new models that might serve to integrate the community into a fabric of social privilege under reconstruction by the Bonapartist state.

In 1806 the notables of the emigration had discovered that their fate in France was inescapably joined to that of others equally defined by the French state as "Egyptian refugees," regardless of their sectarian, regional, and class differences. But it would be a mistake to view the reconstruction of their identifications as a purely passive process dictated by reactions to external forces. This period of war, invasion, and revolt threw up other miscellaneous displaced groups without any obvious national category, and on occasion these were simply joined to the "Egyptian" *dépôt* regardless of their origin. But other Arabic-speakers who had been living in France long before the arrivals of 1801, and without the remotest connection to Egypt, also gained admission to the "refugee" pension, through their personal connections with members of the newly constituted council in Marseille. Some were Uniate Catholic priests, such as Joseph Behennam, an Iraqi Chaldean living in France during the Revolution, and Isa Carus, a Palestinian Melkite who had come from Italy in 1799.[83]

Joseph Chammas, a merchant born in Diyarbakir, a town in Anatolia, is a useful example. He was awarded a *certificat de civisme* as a "Mesopotamian" by the revolutionary authorities in 1790 and remained in France after the Revolution. Yet he was added to the list of "Egyptian refugees" along with his wife and children. Later he wrote to the Ministry of War, complaining that he was being blackmailed by a character named Mansour Saad, who claimed falsely to be the "Inspector of Refugees" in Paris. Saad extorted money from Chammas by threatening to reveal just how long he had been living in France, the fact that his wife was French, and the real names of his sons Jean and Antoine, who had now taken the Arabic names Ya'qub and Ibraïm.[84] Chammas complained to the Ministry of War, clearly seeing nothing wrong in his claiming membership of this group, despite his having, by his own admission, "lost everything in the Revolution" in France, rather than ever having served in Egypt. The classification of "Egyptian refugee" had become a space harboring a far broader category defined by the solidarities and sociabilities of Arabic language and culture.

In this sense, the state unwittingly sponsored the formation of an Arab space that only named itself as such by default, and in the interstices of the structures articulated by the authorities. For many of the "Egyptians," an Arab self-definition was the only one possible when attempting to identify themselves with this impossibly diverse population. This necessitated a shift from the genealogical conception of "Arab" to a much looser associative and cultural configuration. Georges Aïdé, writing to Mikha'il Sabbagh about the struggle for the pensions he called *jamakiya*, assured him "Khawaja Juber tawakkal bi-jamakiyat abna-l-'arab" (Monsieur Joubert will be responsible for the pensions of the Arabs).[85] *Ibn*, "son of," is a genealogical expression, but here, in the plural form, it was used to designate a much broader population, those receiving the pension as "Egyptian refugees." Aïdé did not use the term "Egyptian"—and why would he, since he was born in Beirut? This gesture is one of the few clues to how these people "represented themselves to themselves," to use the phrase of Clifford Geertz.[86]

The roots of this gesture can be traced back to the early letters of 1801: Nemir explained, in requesting permission to come in person to Paris, that "Arabs like us talk as much as you want, but write little."[87] This comment hardly seems accurate given the voluminous Arabic correspondence we have observed. But this can be read as the kind of gesture that another anthropologist, Michael Herzfeld, has called "cultural intimacy," a gesture of "rueful self-recognition," which, Herzfeld argues, provides an "assurance of common sociality."[88] Where some scholars have seen this kind of self-stereotyping as an interiorization of structures of domination,[89] Herzfeld sees it as a "comfortable" mode through which individuals accommodate the power structures and determining conditions in which they live. He suggests that it is the resonance of these forms of identification that provides important conditions for the "imagined communities" of nationalisms, in Benedict Anderson's formulation in his seminal work on national identity.[90]

But this "cultural intimacy" should be distinguished from a formal and unitary "identity": it did not exist in *contradiction* to other identifications such as "Egyptian," "Coptic," or "Muslim." It was, rather, a lived mode of commonality, based on shared cultural practices, and a set of common interests and identifications. Rashid Khalidi noted in his study of Palestinian identity how several overlapping identities could function at the same time in the ways that the Palestinians he studied defined themselves. They "identified with the Ottoman Empire, their religion, Arabism, their homeland Palestine, their city or region, and their family, without feeling any contradiction or sense of conflicting loyalties."[91] Gilles Veinstein suggests that even the words used to signify a particular identification could shift and mix together religious, ethnic, and regional significations: for example, the term *Rum* (a word derived from "Rome" and denoting in particular the Eastern Roman/Byzantine Empire), which could refer to all the inhabitants of the central Anatolian provinces, the whole Ottoman Empire, Greek Orthodox Christians, or ethnic "Turks."[92]

It was in a moment of difficulty that Nemir used the characterization of "Arab" as the most comfortable common identification: he was making the Legation's first formal request for asylum. This was the only phrase in all the letters that was expressed in Arabic. He asked Talleyrand "to give us, as the Arabs of the desert say, your *fiardac* of hospitality."[93] Rather than requesting asylum in a conventional European language, Nemir invoked a custom deeply related to Arab concepts of honor or '*ird*, closely related to the safety of women and children, and often opposed to *ard*, or land.[94] The gesture cannot have been meant to communicate something to Talleyrand, who is highly unlikely to have been aware of this phrase or its customary basis in Bedouin culture. Instead, it seemed to suggest that something in the structures of feeling of this population was untranslatable: it was a gesture of honor and shame.

The resort to this untranslatable Arabic concept points to something that is central to this study: the vital role of the Arabic language and the Islamicate cultures it carried in any account of the destinies of those who boarded the ships from Egypt. Yasir Suleiman has pointed out the incontestable importance of the Arabic language in any understanding of Arab identity. Unlike the "heritage" of European civilization, which needed to be translated from ancient Greek and Latin, the past "golden age" of Arab civilization was directly connected to the present through the medium of high Arabic.[95] Thus the unifying conceptions of Arab identity have almost always been based on *high* culture, rather than the *vernacular* languages and cultures that Benedict Anderson and Ernest Gellner identified as the key building blocks of European nationalisms.[96]

The Arabic language was the only commonality that could provide a point of unity after the loss of Ya'qub. We can recognize the struggles between Ellious Bocthor, Gabriel Taouïl, and others involving the teaching of Arabic in Marseille as symptomatic of the importance of this vital point of convergence. Where the inarticulate practices of culture served to unite the poorer refugees in closely concentrated "village" life, the elite of the emigration, living in more dispersed conditions, maintained their cultural continuity by sending their children to study Arabic at the Lycée. But this growing centrality of the Arabic language carried an unresolved relationship to the other aspects of the emigration, in particular its origins in an Islamicate society whose structures and customs were distinct from the French context in which these people had settled. These contradictions would pose a particular problem for the second generation of Arabs born or raised in France, as we shall see later in this book.

By 1811, the Arab commonalities of the "Egyptian refugees" in Marseille had begun to replace the political project with which the emigrants had started out from Egypt. From a heterogeneous group of exiles, they had become a relatively settled and permanent, if small, community whose internal struggles for power may be seen to indicate a certain solidity. But this "Arab Marseille" was still little more than an entrepôt at the edge of the Mediterranean. It had little connection as yet to the wider France of which it was nominally a part. That is to say, there was as yet no "Arab France" that might articulate something more than an ephemeral Arab presence within this national territory. It was this larger ambition, in addition to the more immediate attractions of the metropole, that drew many of the notables of the emigration to undertake another journey in the second decade of the nineteenth century.

A set of transformations in 1810 and 1811 simultaneously opened a route back to Egypt and a route toward Paris. After ten years of living in France, the question of identity was now practical and immediate. Did these people belong in the France they had adopted? Was their residence still temporary, or were they sufficiently settled to have a permanent role? While they remained as refugees in Marseille, on the edge of the Mediterranean, they could not really consider themselves French. On a practical level, power in France was concentrated in Paris, and without access to the capital no advancement would be possible either within the community or outside. Only an "Arab Paris" could answer the question of the future of these people as a community in France and not simply in Marseille.

After 1810, the notables of the small community that had formed in Marseille began a second emigration, this time across the territory of France. But when these notables arrived in Paris it was already an Arab city, if in a more furtive and clandestine way; it had its own quite different modes of sociability and dependence among its smaller and more scattered Arab population. This set the scene for the conflict between disparate formations of Arab identity in France that the next chapter will explore: one intensely communal, forged in the parochial and often xenophobic environs of Marseille; the other distinctively individualist, a wily opportunism conditioned by the demands of survival in a cosmopolitan metropolis.

3

The Making of Arab Paris

The most ancient monument in today's Paris is not French but Egyptian. The obelisk of the place de la Concorde stands at one end of the "golden road" stretching through the Jardin des Tuileries, past the empty site of the Tuileries palace favored by Napoleon, and the triumphal arch celebrating his victories, to meet the Egyptianizing glass pyramid of the Louvre at its farthest point. Thus the axis of an Egypt part real and part imagined plays a central role in imagining modern Paris and its history. The glass pyramid of the Louvre stands today in an open square. In the early nineteenth century, that square was still a disreputable warren of streets where cheap lodgings crowded upon one another. One of the streets of this quarter took its name from a church disaffected during the Revolution, Saint-Thomas du Louvre. In this street, opposite the imperial stables at number 36, was a cheap lodging-house called the Hôtel de Bretagne.

In the early years of Napoleon's rule, the authorities in Paris kept a record of the foreigners arriving in the capital, classified into various ethnonational categories. In the miscellaneous file marked "Russes, Turcs, Africains et colons," the address of this hotel—36, rue Saint-Thomas du Louvre—can be noted again and again as the place of residence given by a certain group of foreign arrivals. Their names included Abdallah and Azaria, Joseph Hamawi, Antoine Gibril, Lutfi Nemr, and Charles Vitallis.[1] All of these names were linked in one way or another with the "Egyptian refugees," but otherwise they were quite heterogeneous. Among them were Muslims, Christians, Franks, and Armenians; interpreters, soldiers, and merchants from Cairo, Aleppo, Damascus, and Istanbul. Their immediate ports of departure for the capital, however, were much closer at hand: Marseille, Melun, Lyon, or occasionally Strasbourg. Ironically, then, the Egyptianizing gesture of the pyramid conceals another, forgotten history, a hub of the itinerant and shifting Arab milieu of postrevolutionary Paris. In the register, alongside the names of these guests of the Hôtel de Bretagne, are others who may have belonged to this milieu: Hamed, a merchant from Algiers; Moyse Rabi Isaï of Jerusalem; Boulos Bachera and his daughter, coming from Melun; Ahmed Kachef de Soliman from Egypt; Assa-Ossman ben Mabrouk and his son Mahomet from Tunis; al-Haggi Mohamed Arzara from Morocco.

Unfortunately, however, the register is silent about the relationship between these people, and whether their jostling against one another in the official record is no more than a stroke of the bureaucratic pen, or whether this categorization in fact might contain some more intimate proximity, some encounter, exchange, or even sociability. In 1807, when Jean-François Champollion arrived in Paris as a young and avid student of Oriental languages, he wrote to his brother with excitement at his discovery of a milieu he had doubtless never experienced in his provincial hometown of Grenoble. The lodgings of Rufa'il, according to one biographer, "constituted, with the Persian embassy, the principal rallying point of the Egypto-Oriental colony."[2] These spaces were also those of a Muslim cosmopolitanism: in a letter to his brother, Champollion reported with pride that a Muslim acquaintance, Ibn Saoua, "mistook me yesterday for an Arab, and began to give me his *salamat*—when I replied with the suitable responses he quite overwhelmed me with his expressions of friendship until I thought he would never stop!"[3] Champollion studied Arabic with Rufa'il Zakhur, and Coptic with another Egyptian émigré, Youhanna Chiftichi, studies that ultimately proved crucial to his success in solving the riddle of hieroglyphic writing. But these classes were interrupted when he was forced to return to his provincial Grenoble, too soon to offer anything more than these few glimpses.

Another young Orientalist, Maximilian Habicht, from the town of Breslau (Wroclaw), who arrived in Paris as an attaché at the Prussian embassy at this time, immersed himself more fully in this milieu. Keen to learn Arabic, he found lodgings with Arabic-speakers and formed a very close friendship with a Tunisian Jewish writer, Mordechai al-Najjar. He later published a selection of the correspondence he had received from his friends among the Arabic-speaking milieu of Paris, including al-Najjar, an Algerian Muslim named Muhammad, Gabriel Taouïl, Mikha'il Sabbagh, Aid-el Bajaly, Rufa'il Zakur, Youhanna Chiftichi, and many others.[4] In fact, the dozen or so letters Habicht included as examples in his book belonged to a collection of 220 held in Wroclaw, which were destroyed during World War II, according to Paul Fenton.[5] What these letters confirm without any doubt is the strong connection among Arabic-speakers in Paris, across the bounds of region and religion: Muslims, Christians, and Jews; from Egypt, Syria, Algeria, Morocco, Tunis, Tripoli, and sometimes farther afield; and moving back and forth between Paris, Trieste, Livorno, Aleppo, Madrid, Tunis, and other cities in the Mediterranean basin.

As we noted in chapter 2, a handful of Arabs were living in Paris before and during the Revolution, and others had arrived prior to the evacuation of Egypt. Joseph Chammas was one of the rare merchants in a group who were for the most part Uniate Catholic priests from the Arab world, such as the Chaldean priest Joseph Behennam and the Syrian Michel Abeid.[6] Chammas had enthusiastically embraced the Revolution in 1789 but was forced to leave Paris in 1792, when foreigners were banished from the city.[7] The Palestinian priest Isa Carus had sufficient connections in Paris to publish a pamphlet in 1804 describing his services to the French and his losses in the troubles and expressing his eternal gratitude to his friend Dom Raphaël de Monachis (Rufa'il Zakhur).[8] Isa Carus had known this influential Syrian priest during his time in Rome; Rufa'il had subsequently served as interpreter to Bonaparte in Egypt and maintained a close personal correspondence with him in Italian. In 1803, the First Consul appointed Rufa'il to a chair of colloquial Arabic (*arabe vulgaire*) at the École des Langues Orientales, much to the disgust of Sylvestre de Sacy.[9] In 1802, another former interpreter, Elias Fir'aun (Pharaon, in France), decided to bring his young family from Egypt to Paris, and his strong connections found him various functions, including acting as Parisian consul for the Ionian islands. Mikha'il Sabbagh was given the important post of curator of Arabic manuscripts at the Bibliothèque Impériale after his return from accompanying General Sébastiani's diplomatic mission to Cairo and Istanbul.

This plurality of origins and experiences was the key difference between the Parisian milieu and that of Marseille. Where the Marseillais Arab population had arrived in a large convoy, attracting further immigrants in subsequent years, the Arab population of Paris had accrued more gradually, bringing together long-established residents with those arriving from other parts of Europe, as well as a few individuals who had come directly to Paris in 1801. In the middle years of the decade, and particularly after the retirement of so many Arab soldiers in 1804, a trickle of new arrivals flowed in from Melun and Marseille. Where the Arab population in Marseille was concentrated in clusters, and structured by institutions such as the Council of Refugees, religious services, and the Arabic-language course, the Parisian milieu was far more scattered, in a way that was typical of the metropolis itself. It may be that some of the new arrivals were seeking a certain anonymity: a case of adultery lay behind the arrival of at least one couple.

Other such foreign "colonies"—such as the Irish, the Americans, and the Poles—also existed in Paris; in the authoritarian atmosphere of the Consulate and Empire, they were supervised with care, and tolerated where they served to enhance the cosmopolitan and civilized image of the regime. Others were considered dangerous: the association of Italians with radical conspiracies made them particularly suspect. The space that these foreigners occupied in postrevolutionary France was an ambivalent one. Stuart Woolf draws attention to the contradiction between, on the one hand, the cosmopolitan "cultural pluralism" of Enlightenment thought and, on the other, the increasingly influential Voltairean conception of civilization as a progress from barbarism toward refinement, accompanied by the triumphs of reason, science, and technology.[10] Though deeply infused with a hardening sense of the superiority of European manners and achievements, the latter was primarily an elite conception that still defined the "civilized" primarily by its distinction from the barbarous French lower classes rather than in contrast with extra-European peoples. The presence of a non-European intellectual elite, particularly one associated with Egypt—still often invoked as the "cradle of science"—could still be considered as adding an exotic glow to the lustre of Paris, the "Capital of the Enlightenment." And those Arab intellectuals residing in Paris also gained prestige from their association with this powerful cultural politics.

There were important differences between the "Egypto-Oriental colony" in Paris that Champollion encountered and the increasingly "Arab" village in Marseille that go beyond a simple question of numbers. They represented, in a sense, two different directions for articulating the common Arab identity of the emigrants from Egypt at this critical juncture. In Marseille, as we have seen, the population tended to congregate, whether in the crowded environs of the Place Castellane or through such institutions as the Council of the Dépôt of Refugees and the Arabic classes at the Lycée. They had developed their own subeconomy, producing, selling, and consuming food and clothing among themselves. The very closeness of the community, and its intensification of collective action in response to pressure from the authorities, gave rise to a series of conflicts, quite opaque to outsiders, that demonstrated how internally focused the relations of this now quite substantial population had become. In Paris, by contrast, intellectuals such as Rufa'il offered a rallying point for a scattered population that lived in relatively close interaction with the wider society. Of course, these relations are difficult to trace because of the almost total lack of personal documentation in the archives of official correspondence. We have seen, however, how Orientalists such as Sacy, Champollion, and Habicht mixed closely with the Arabic cultural milieu. Beyond these Orientalist circles, we can draw a suggestive hint from personal communications Joseph Chammas included in a letter to the Ministry of War to prove that he had not been defrauding the pensions bureau but had been collecting a pension on a friend's behalf.

This friend, Ahmed, a former member of the Mamluk elite born in Tiflis, Georgia, and raised as a Muslim in Egypt, had served the same *kachef*, or governor—Suleiman Bey of Asyut—who had fostered the aspirations of Ya'qub.[11] In 1805, when Muhammad 'Ali became governor, Ahmed left Egypt and traveled from Marseille to Paris, watched throughout his journey by police spies.[12] But he seems to have settled quite easily in Paris, with a generous pension granted directly from the Tuileries. Ahmed wrote to Chammas from Lyon on 8 June 1816:

> My Friend, I received the hundred francs you had the goodness to send me. They didn't reimburse me until today, and I leave tomorrow. Don't be worried for me. I'm doing very well. Give my best to the stablemaster and his wife as well as to his children. And to M. and Mme de Fernéx and to their children. Above all don't forget Mademoiselle Besinard. Give my respects to your wife and hug Tonin for me.[13]

This rare personal note suggests the close affective relations that could exist between Arabs and other Parisians. Chammas had lived in Paris for most of his life, so it is not surprising that he would have many friends and contacts. This evidently allowed newer arrivals such as Ahmed to establish themselves in these networks of sociability, both French and Arab. It also suggests that Lyon, on the route between Marseille and Paris, played an important role for these clandestine travelers. Taouïl wrote to Sabbagh in 1808: "Antun Hamawi is currently in Lyon—I hear he is in Paris to plot with his friend Rufa'il against his enemies. If it's true, it means he traveled without a passport, which is against the law." Be careful, Taouïl warned Sabbagh. "This man is as sneaky as smoke."[14] Taouïl was combating rumors spread by Rufa'il that he had been sent to Marseille in disgrace: this was not true, but a sense of "exile" from Paris was expressed more than once by Taouïl, and others seemed to miss the forms of sociability and cosmopolitanism they had experienced, as well as the friendships they had forged in the capital.

When the "Egypto-Oriental colony" met at the house of Rufa'il, it did not do so in order to deal with a large and fractious community, as in Marseille. Instead, it was free to articulate its role in the cultural capital of the empire. This did not mean that there was no conflict: the dominant role of figures such as Rufa'il gave rise to both clientelism and jealousy. In Jacques-Louis David's monumental painting of Napoleon's coronation, Rufa'il appears among a group of Italian clergy in the foreground, adding an element of mystery to the proceedings with his red hood pulled over his head, probably to bolster Catholic legitimacy by reference to the Eastern Uniate churches. In a France where proximity to the emperor was power, Rufa'il wielded significant social influence both in his own milieu and in the wider society of Paris. Life in Paris was expensive and difficult, and the patronage of such privileged individuals as Dom Raphaël was the key to success. Isa Carus's publication of 1804 was largely given over to a sycophantic encomium of Rufa'il's virtues and endless expressions of gratitude toward his compatriot. In contrast, Joseph Chammas wrote to the School of Oriental Languages to protest the behavior of this "ex-priest and monk" who "dishonors by the most atrocious scandals the government which so favors him," accusing Rufa'il of becoming drunk every night, insulting all and sundry, alternately beating and fondling his servants, and occasioning the intervention of the local police commissioner, often making "such a racket in the houses where he lives, he has been forced to leave precipitately several apartments."[15] Isa Carus was later accused of similar debaucheries and exiled to Marseille. He wrote to Habicht in Arabic:

> I was one the highest priests of Jerusalem. I left my country and my family for the sake of the holy beliefs and for the purity of my soul, and my reliability. Thanks to the strength of God I did many good deeds for countless confessions [tawa'if] in the East and West, as the almighty God knows. And after that my good deeds were rewarded by evil. And you my beloved son, I ask for your mercy and your friendship, so that you can bring us back to Paris, back to the people you know who respect their word. [16]

Isa Carus was at pains to insist that his role went beyond the confessional differences between the various tawa'if, and he appended a petition from Mamelouks of various origins—Catholic, Orthodox, and Muslim. Indeed, it is true that his problems arose from within his own confession, and in the tension between the intellectual elite in Paris and the military elite in Melun.

Before 1811, among the many visitors arriving from the Ottoman Empire, and the merchants from North Africa, there is evidence of a trickle of individuals coming from the Arab community in Marseille. In 1806, "Lotfi, Egyptian interpreter" was among these names; so too was "Gabriel Joubram, 37, Egyptian refugee coming from Lyon."[17] The latter was none other than Joubran Mehenna Tadi, the same obstreperous character of whom Georges Aïdé complained in the document we cited earlier. That conflict might seem no more than a petty squabble, and it is not my intention to suggest that it was in any sense a determining moment in this history. But it does reveal something about the identity of these people—or rather the plurality of identities in play, and the dynamics of the contestations that shaped them. The documents that it left scattered through so many archives are so many traces of the intersections with power, both internal and external, which was supplicated, stonewalled, or co-opted in so many different ways by these two enterprising and quarrelsome individuals, on the basis of their quite different and conflicting understandings and practices of what I have called "Arab Paris." The city itself became a central question in the conflict as it unfolded. Yet the struggle took place only because these two men identified themselves with their Arab commonalities despite the difference in their origins and their experiences in France. This struggle was just one of many occurring at the time: indeed, the Ministry of War was so bombarded with these quarrels that an instruction was sent out forbidding the "refugees" to submit any more petitions and complaints of this kind. Aïdé referred to this order in the opening of his letter, only to ignore it completely, arguing that the refusal of intervention encouraged a sense of impunity among "troublemakers" like Joubran.

Like so many of the entries in the police register of 1806–11, the entry for "Gabriel Joubram" already shows the difficulties faced by the French authorities in sorting into a single given name and surname the complex patronymics, nicknames, regional appellations, titles, and honorifics of the Ottoman Arab world.[18] In negotiating with the authorities, Joubran chose, or was given, an identity that was closer to a French consonance, more familiar and comprehensible.[19] In early letters (written by a public letter-writer) he signed his name in Arabic. What did it mean for Joubran to become Gabriel? Was there a meaning in that transition? One thing we may note from this official registry in Paris is that he cited his point of departure as Lyon rather than Marseille. This may have been for purely practical reasons, but it already suggests a certain willed separation from the settled community in Marseille.

Joubran was not a member of the wealthier Melkite families who had come to dominate the community in Marseille. Nor did he remain long among the officers of the Armée d'Orient, which he joined as a cavalry lieutenant in Egypt, according to his own words, "at the behest of Seigneurs Pharaon and Ventura, the interpreters."[20] He stated that he had joined "the company of Homar Mograbi," which would date his entry into French service very early in the French occupation, with the formation of a company of "Guides" in September 1798, commanded by the Janissary Omar el Koladi, whose familiar designation "Mograbi" suggests he was North African in origin, as were many of his soldiers. Thus, unlike the members of the Coptic and Syrian legions, Joubran had served in a largely Muslim unit, some of whose soldiers were executed on Bonaparte's orders after they turned their arms against the French during the uprising in Cairo in 1799.[21] There is nothing to indicate that he was himself Muslim, and his name would suggest otherwise. But these circumstances may help to explain the quite different trajectory followed by this young man, and his distaste for the parochial bounds of the community in Marseille. In this he may stand for other, less troublesome members of this diverse population, whose stories did not leave so marked a trace in the archives. At any rate, it is important to note that Joubran portrayed himself as a free agent making an individual choice, rather than a victim of circumstances or a "refugee." He emphasized the part played in this decision by another Arab Parisian, Elias Pharaon, rather than referring his claim for the support of the notables at Marseille and Melun, as had become customary in such cases.

The early part of Joubran's life after his arrival in France remains obscure. He was entered simply as "Gobran" in the list of arrivals in Marseille in 1801 as one of the "individuals in the suite of 'Abd el-Al, aga of Janissaries in Cairo," alongside Yossef Tedi and "the wife of Tedi."[22] These were probably relations, perhaps his parents, but there is no further indication of their status. Joubran is listed in the register of refugees in 1804, with a pension of 2 francs 50 per day.[23] The military corps created from the Egyptian auxiliaries was restructured in 1804, and many former soldiers were allocated a refugee pension instead of the retirement pay French soldiers might receive. Joubran could have lived a quiet life in Marseille on this pension, but it certainly did not offer any hope of advancement.

It was at this time, he explained later, that he was asked to accompany to Melun the mother of one of the officers serving in the Mamelouks:

> My first arrival in Paris was with the aim of accompanying from Marseille Madame Rennot [Renno], who had come from Acre to see her son, and that was by the order of the Inspector and Commandant Valliant. Invited by our officers, as stated in the certificates that I had the honor of transmitting to you, I accompanied her to Melun and from there returned to Marseille, where I stayed for a short time.[24]

The journey to Paris seems to have confirmed for Joubran that his future lay in the capital. In 1806 he was living in the Hôtel de Normandie in the rue des Boucheries Saint-Honoré, near the new Marché des Jacobins, which had been built in place of the former convent. These *hôtels garnis* were the most common lodgment for new arrivals and foreigners in the city.[25] One contemporary description of such a hotel described long corridors of single rooms at nine francs per month, reached by climbing ninety-seven steps from the street.[26] On the other hand, Joubran may have shared his quarters with others: at the same hotel lived at least two of his compatriots, Mikhaïl Koubroussi and Gabriel Manna Daty.

Where the notables of the emigration were denied permission to travel to Paris, Joubran's lesser notoriety allowed him to move with greater ease. But in doing so, he lost the ability to collect his pension. In 1807, he wrote to the Ministry requesting to receive his pension in Paris, and was asked to account for his presence there. He replied:

> I received the letter that Your Highness did me the honor of addressing me and in which he asked the reason for my stay in Paris. . . . Wanting to learn the French language, and not at all desirous of acquiring either the language or the accent of Marseille, I was forced to come to Paris to continue my instruction. Every month I send my *certificat de vie* and another [certificate] to my language teacher at Marseille, following the orders given to me so that I should be in accordance with the laws of this country.[27]

It is tempting to see Joubran's arguments about the civilizing influence of Paris as purely opportunistic. Though never officially mandated, it is clear from the correspondence that one of the few acceptable motivations for those registered at Marseille to shift their residence to Paris was the need to acquire an education. The assumption of the authorities seems to have been that such an education was not possible in Marseille. A *lycée* had been established there in 1803, but Joubran skillfully invoked the Parisian disdain for regional languages such as Provençal or

Occitan, as well as for provincial accents and manners, from which the metropolitan elite dissociated themselves.[28]

The "civilizing" dispensation to the refugees that allowed them to move to the capital for their education was in line with the wider cultural politics of Napoleonic imperialism. The notion of "civilization" so central to Napoleon's postrevolutionary synthesis underpinned French cultural imperialism in Europe, mandating the education of dominated populations as a way of creating a new local administrative elite on the French model.[29] A similar principle seems to have been applied as a general response to this displaced foreign population within France itself, which was equally conceived in terms of a separate "nation" within the French cultural ambit.

Thus, where the notables of the Egyptian Legation were prevented for political reasons from reaching the capital, others could take advantage of this "civilizing" path to gain their freedom of mobility toward the capital. Some managed to reside in Paris while still receiving their pensions in Marseille if they could provide a monthly certificate of their educational activities. Youhanna Chiftichi moved directly to Paris soon after his arrival in 1801, serving as a Coptic minister at the church of Saint-Roch, and collaborating on the grand *Description de l'Égypte*. In 1807, he briefly ceased to receive his pension because he had failed to send the certificates to Marseille.[30] Chiftichi's residence in Paris was never officially approved: it was justified ex post facto by his "usefulness" to the projects of the Commission d'Égypte. Nevertheless, although Chiftichi could demonstrate his cultural value to the state, other refugees were not able to take this risky path. The former interpreter Joseph Messabki, for example, "having come to Paris fruitlessly to search for means of support," asked to be permitted to return to the depot.[31] Isa Carus mentioned Messabki along with others seeking to enter the Orientalist milieux of the capital; Carus wrote from Melun: "Send regards to the family of Fart al-Rumman, and to our son Betros, and to *mua'llim* Jubran Mehanna, and tell him we prayed for him, and to *mu'allim* Mikha'il, and Yousef Messabki, and Yousef Ataia, and Marcus, and all the people who asked about us."[32] The term *mu'allim* means "learned"; it is also a general title of respect.

Joubran's correspondence shows that he did not find employment as an interpreter or linguist. But he was determined not to return to Marseille. He gained permission to follow the army to Spain as a *vivandier*. Returning in 1810, after the failure of the Spanish campaign, it seems likely that he was at a loss for work, and he was compelled to seek readmission to the pension. By this time, the authorities had begun to allow the refugees to reside in Paris, and a special pay-office was appointed in the Place Vendôme. Joubran was compelled to seek the support of his compatriots: Aïdé insists that he quarreled with Mikha'il Sabbagh, although Gabriel Taouïl mentioned sending him money in a letter to Sabbagh a few years earlier. Others in Paris also seemed to be in difficulties: Mikhaïl Koubroussi wrote several times to Sabbagh about goods he was trying with difficulty to sell, and he seemed to be consigning personal effects for others in financial transactions that also involved the Arab Jews of the capital, such as Ben Soussan and Mordechai al-Najjar, as both Sabbagh's correspondence and the letters published by Habicht indicate. This was a period of war, invasion, and revolt, and the vicissitudes of the times served often to push closer together those who found some commonality, above all in the rough and tumble of city life. Al-Najjar's letters often referred to others, whether Muslim, Christian, or Jewish, as *min baladina,* "of our country," if they came from a common Arabic-speaking and Islamic culture.

Antoine Siouphi was an Egyptian armorer who had left Egypt some time after the French evacuation. In France he was awarded a pension but was compelled to collect it in Marseille. His dossier contains his petition against this decision, due to an illness that forced him to remain in Paris, where he stayed at the Persian embassy in the rue de Fréjus:

> At this moment I am gravely ill, lying on a miserable mattress in a corner at the house of H.E. the Ambassador of Persia, who has kindly given me asylum, but without sheets, without succour, having no one to help me, my arms swollen, and my legs swollen halfway up to the thighs. I am deprived of all pecuniary means. . . . My situation at any rate requires that I stay in Paris, as when I am in full health, it is I who takes care of the *damas* [steel for swords] that the French generals and the Mamelouk officers carry, something no other armorer in France is able to do.[33]

It is worth nothing here how, even in his extreme suffering, Siouphi seemed to anticipate the possibility that he might be dispatched to Marseille, and therefore insisted upon his need to remain in Paris. Some of the poorest "refugees" lived in the "Cours des Miracles" of the rue du Bac, a notorious haunt of criminals and beggars, yet they insisted on remaining in the capital.

But Joubran was compelled to seek work where he could find it, in the train of the military expedition to Spain, on which so many of the Arab soldiers departed in 1808. The Peninsular War was a painful and disillusioning campaign, characterized by guerrilla violence, repression, and atrocity.[34] The Mamelouks were particularly hated by the Spaniards, who recalled the Muslims who had ruled Spain for centuries. Francisco Goya depicted them as ambivalent figures, their ostentatious presence making them the principal victims of the crowd, in his painting of the Dos de Mayo, the uprising of 2 May 1808 in Madrid, now in the Museo del Prado.[35]

When Joubran returned to the capital after the Spanish campaign, he found an Arab Paris that had already begun to change. More of the retired officers from Melun had begun to establish connections in or to move to the capital. By 1814, the Syrian Catholic priest Joseph Sabba could claim that "almost all his compatriots having come to reside in the capital, he finds himself obliged as their chaplain to establish himself close to them."[36] Even if Sabba's statement was an exaggeration (as the Ministry noted in its response), it indicates nonetheless that there was a perceptible movement toward the capital. There was now a new Arab elite living in Paris, including the families of Youssef and Daoud Habaïby, for example, who took up lodgings in the rich avenue of the Chaussée d'Antin.

We can derive a very rough picture of the pattern of settlement in Paris by tabulating the hundreds of addresses given in correspondence with the pensions bureau. These addresses can give no more than the most approximate indication, as some represented the same individual in different locations, and others were the abode of large families. Still, in the absence of any real statistical information, the addresses can give us some idea of where the "refugees" were living. By dividing them according to *quartiers* it is possible to identify three general areas of concentration in the later years of the Empire. It is clear that the addresses remained scattered, but focal points emerge around the Palais Royal and the Tuileries, in the area of the Pont Saint-Michel on the Left Bank, and close to the Hôtel des Invalides.

The last of these concentrations is probably explained by the number of wounded soldiers who took up residence in or near the Invalides itself after the campaigns in the Iberian Peninsula, Germany, and Russia.[37] From the penury described in many of the letters, it appears that the concentration near the rue de la Harpe and along the Seine close to the Pont Saint-Michel was composed of poor refugees, who often changed address and frequently remained in Paris for only a short time. Among them were a number of young women whose common surname Halimé gave an indication of their status as former slaves in Egypt.[38] Others among this group were ex-soldiers, who managed to find work as domestic servants or even as manual laborers in the city markets.[39] These groups of poorer refugees were more likely to mix together. By July 1809, Antoine Siouphi had found lodgings near the Invalides, at 9, rue des Brodeurs. Other Egyptians lived in the same street, including a young "négresse" from Egypt named Louise Virginie, who would play a role in Joubran's story.[40]

Joubran's Arab Paris was not "Arab" in the same sense as the community in Marseille. The scattered nature of the population over such a vast and expanding metropolis meant there were few opportunities to foster modes of Arab identification, language, or everyday life. And it seems that this was not what Joubran was searching for; indeed, he seemed to have sacrificed quite a lot to escape the bounds of the close community in Marseille.

In a rough sense, then, the population of this Arab Paris was composed of two distinct segments: a relatively small and settled group of Arab intellectuals who continued a presence established in Paris even before the Revolution, and a growing heterogeneous *population flottante* whose presence was not subsidized by pensions or a bread ration like the poorer "Egyptians" in Marseille. But that situation changed suddenly in 1810, when a pay office was established in the Place Vendôme. Suddenly it was possible for "refugees" like Joubran to reapply for the payment of their pensions, and Joubran did in fact begin to receive a pension of 3 francs 50 from December 1810. But like Naydorff, whose comments we noted in chapter 2, Joubran resented the implication that he belonged to the lowest category of "refugees": only some weeks after receiving his pension, he wrote the Ministry to request that it be increased to 7 francs, in line with the pensions of other former officers.

After 1810 Joubran found himself in a slightly better financial situation, but he found that the networks of Arab sociability were changing as the elite from both Melun and Marseille converged upon the capital. He sought to change his status, declaring himself eligible as an "ex-lieutenant," for the same retirement pay as other officers, although he had served for only a brief time in the army. Having provided a number of certificates and recommendations, he expected to be treated similarly to the other officers. It is painfully clear, however, that such decisions rested in most cases on the power of *appui,* or connections: the official system of meritocracy was underpinned by a traditional politics of notables reinstituted by Napoleon.

In 1811, it suddenly became possible for the Arab notables from Marseille to consider moving to Paris. 'Abd el-Al with his wife, servants, and children arrived in 1811, the same year as Georges Aïdé with his large family, and several other important figures. The reasons for this were various. By 1811, the political situation in Egypt had changed radically. In the chaotic aftermath of the French evacuation, a former Ottoman soldier named Muhammad 'Ali had gradually developed a power base that allowed him to claim the governorship from the Ottoman authorities in 1805, and to expel the British from the country in 1807.[41] The problem of the warring Mamluk leaders, which had troubled Egypt since the mid-eighteenth century, still persisted. Then, on 1 March 1811, Muhammad 'Ali called the remaining Mamluks together in the Citadel of Cairo; his troops ambushed and massacred those who had the misfortune to accept the invitation. This bloody dénouement was only the most spectacular demonstration of Muhammad 'Ali's monopoly on power, which served to end the instability that had been the pretext for British and French interventions.[42] His dynasty would rule Egypt for the next 140 years. In Palestine, the governor of Acre, Ahmad al-Jazzar, had died several years earlier and had been replaced by a more tolerant Ottoman administration. It therefore seemed possible that the "Egyptians" and "Syrians" might return home. Yet the vast majority did not.

The stabilization of Egypt removed—for the moment, at least—its valency in the European balance of power. Henceforth the presence of the "Egyptians" in Paris was no longer unwelcome. The regime's imperial ambitions were now focused on European expansion, particularly in eastern Europe. On occasion, the

Muslim associations of these Egyptians (regardless of their actual confession) and their linguistic abilities could be useful in forging new alliances, against the Russians in central Asia, for example. The euphoria of Napoleonic victories made all sorts of possibilities conceivable. In March 1811 Napoleon's second wife, the empress Marie-Louise, gave birth to a healthy son. The future of the Empire now seemed assured: Napoleon had an heir, linked through his mother to one of the old royal families of Europe. This meant that the emperor himself was no longer so vulnerable to conspiracy: an attack on his person would no longer ensure the destruction of the imperial line.[43] Napoleon spent more time in Paris than ever before during 1810, supervising the intense activity of building and urban transformation he had set in train.[44] Napoleon's empire stretched from the Iberian Peninsula into the Balkans, with an unparalleled system of bureaucratic centralization, both for France and for the conquered territories. Paris was the "New Rome," the flourishing heart of this vast empire. The city was crowded by "new" Frenchmen drawn from the annexed and satellite provinces of the Empire— Italians, Germans, Dutch, Swiss, Belgians—whose presence, Stuart Woolf suggests, "was a deliberate political gesture, a consecration of the reality of the expanding Empire, for which Napoleon was directly responsible."[45]

For the "Egyptians," Paris exerted just as magnetic an attraction. Their presence in the capital, however, was rather more ambivalent than that of the other imperial functionaries, in that they could represent only their small community of "refugees" in Marseille. Any further reference to the East, to Egypt or Syria, was entirely symbolic. But what kind of space did this cosmopolitan capital of Napoleonic Europe offer for Arab Frenchmen? After 1810, more and more of those living in Marseille or Melun would seek their fortune in the "New Rome." In the next chapter we will look at the cultural dimensions of that cosmopolitanism; for the moment we will examine more closely the paths that brought Joubran Mehenna and Georges Aïdé to the brink of violence.

In the ten years before 1811, Georges Aïdé had established a relatively prosperous and successful life in Marseille, surrounded by hundreds of his compatriots, who shared his Arabic language and culture and maintained many of the "comfortable" cultural practices to which he had been accustomed in Syria and Egypt, even if that proximity sometimes erupted in communal conflicts. His children could attend Arabic lessons at the Lycée, and he could purchase from Egyptian merchants the bread, vegetables, and fruits to which he was accustomed, order from the tailor the Ottoman clothes he had always worn, and carry on a brisk commerce from the port. Why then did he suddenly decide to uproot his large family and move them lock, stock, and barrel to Paris, some eight hundred kilometers away, more than a week's travel by coach?

Some recent changes facilitated this choice. In a sudden act of largesse, the pensions administration now permitted the "refugees" to register their children born in France for a small daily allowance. This was quite a windfall for those, like Aïdé, who had large families, and the result, according to Ellious Bocthor, of lobbying by his compatriots in Paris. This sudden alteration in the status of some must have had a significant impact on the economics of the community in Marseille. Large and influential families, like Aïdé's, became even more affluent, particularly if they were sufficiently educated and well-connected to ensure the smooth passage of their requests. The family of the Muslim notable 'Abd el-Al also benefited from new arrangements: the records indicate that he had three children added to the pension in 1811.[46] Fatal Riskallah, who came to Paris at this time, had five daughters; Gabriel Choukrallah had two; and Joseph Hamaouy (married to a Frenchwoman in Marseille) had six, though he left them behind in Marseille on his departure for Paris. Meanwhile the poorest refugees, who received only a ration of bread, could not benefit in the same way from these changes, regardless of the size of their families.

Georges Aïdé himself had five children by 1811, in addition to the three children of his brother Elias, who had been killed by Ahmed Djezzar in Acre. In a document of 1816, Aïdé outlines the pensions his family received under the Empire:

The petitioner	per day	15,28
Anne Aydé	idem	2,50
Rose Aydé	id.	1,25
Joseph Aydé	id.	-,75
Josephine Aydé	id.	-,75
Alexandre Aydé	id.	-,75
Michel Aydé	id.	2,—
Miette Aydé	id.	2,—
Hélène Kair	id.	2,50
Nassera négresse	id.	-,75
Total per year	10	413,45[47]

Between Georges, his wife Hélène, their seven children, and a servant, the family was receiving well over ten thousand francs per year. This was a remarkably ample income: in addition, Aïdé's Arabic correspondence reveals that he was engaged in quite profitable business activities, which were never declared to the Ministry of War. It is this prosperity that made it possible for Georges to bring the family to Paris. But the fact that this income was divided across the family meant that Georges needed to keep his family together in order to aggregate their income. His nephew Michel later took a lawsuit against him because of excessive control of the young man's finances.[48]

When Aïdé arrived in Paris, he moved immediately with his family into a house at 355, rue Saint-Honoré with other Arabs of similar background. One of them was Lotfi Nemr, who had once signed his name "Nemir Effendi."[49] But others citing this address in the same period were Joseph Ataïa, Isa Carus, and Gabriel Sakakini. Joseph Ataïa was listed in 1815 as an "employee of the crown treasury." [50] He was a sufficiently eligible bridegroom for Nicolas Sakakini, one of the successful Sakakini brothers, merchants from Marseille, to accompany his daughter Wardé to Paris for her marriage to Ataïa in 1813.[51] As often in these cases, an alliance with a successful young man in the capital was extremely desirable for the family's fortunes.

Georges Aïdé's journey to Paris in 1811 was very different from Joubran's tentative and ultimately unauthorized displacement of 1806. After a decade in Marseille, Aïdé had a strong sense both of his community and of his own place in it. The problems that had arisen in Marseille were primarily conflicts among the elite in which the bulk of the community seem to have played a relatively instrumental role. If their complaints against members of the Council of Refugees were real, they had neither the education nor the resources to express them without assistance. It was Aïdé's prominence as a member of this community that had prevented him from reaching the capital earlier; but others, like Lotfi Nemr and Elias Pharaon, who dissociated themselves from any political or communal project, were already established in the capital. The leaders of the Arab military units in the French army, quartered at Melun, also had increasing access to the nearby capital. The center of power in the Arab community was shifting toward Paris.

Aïdé was at pains to insist to the French authorities that he was well suited to occupy his position as an Arab notable in France. In a petition to the Ministry, he included three letters written to him in 1805 by his relations and associates, including the sons of the Emir Bechir, ruler of Mount Lebanon. They wrote to inform him that since the death of Ahmad al-Jazzar in 1803, calm had been restored in the region:

> As you are one of our dearest friends, it is not right that you should remain the sole *émigré* from our country, all the more because so many of your relatives are attached to our service. You should now return to your country, since it enjoys a perfect tranquillity. There is no longer any reason for your exile, and all the more so because the climate of the country where you are living is so unsuitable for the health of Levantines. We demand therefore that you make your way here without the slightest delay.... We have need of you for essential matters that cannot be effected by letter, which is why you should return with your family and why we insist upon it so strongly.[52]

Aïdé included this letter in a petition of 1816 in order to demonstrate that his decision to remain in France had been a voluntary one. Whatever the circumstances of his departure in 1801, he now wished to indicate to the authorities that his motivation for remaining in France was his devotion to his life there, and not merely the result of circumstances. The letters are strong indications that Aïdé might indeed have returned had he chosen to, although the guarantee of such a generous pension paid to himself and all his dependents was certainly an extra incentive to remain in France.

While acknowledging the role that al-Jazzar's oppression had played in his departure, Aïdé's compatriots address him in these letters as an "expatriate" and an "émigré" rather than as a "refugee" (at least in the translation that Aïdé provided for the benefit of the Ministry) and call him home on the basis of his importance in the business and social affairs of their administration, in addition to ties of family and loyalty. The maintenance of these ties was a vital dimension of Aïdé's existence in Marseille, as they were for many other families that belonged to the highly mobile Mediterranean diaspora of Melkite Arabs, such as the Sakakini, the Hamaouy, and the Homsy families. It is crucial to recognize that these wider links to the Arab world existed and were maintained without contradiction alongside their growing sense of "Frenchness," above all in its inflection by Napoleonic imperialism, which was similar in so many ways to the Ottoman system by which their lives had been structured.

In 1809, Aïdé wrote to the Ministry to request the payment of arrears on his pension. He had been absent for his monthly payments for three months, during which time he had been in Tuscany. In explaining his unauthorized absence, Aïdé claimed that he had traveled to Tuscany to visit famous surgeons who might help him with his eye ailments (and this was certainly a very common problem among the Egyptians in Marseille).[53] Having been caught in Livorno during an epidemic, Aïdé claimed, he was obliged to remain in the city until the road was open again. In fact it is clear from Aïdé's letters to Sabbagh that he was engaged in importing various products into France from Italy and the Arab world. In 1807, he had written: "I want to travel to Livorno. I have to apply for a travel permit so they don't put my *jamakiya* on hold like the last time."[54] Livorno was home to a significant Melkite population of merchants and traders who had settled there in the last quarter of the eighteenth century. When Constantin Volney passed through the city in 1783, he met Antoun Faraoun (Pharaon), the former controller of customs in Egypt, who had left for Italy in 1784 with a large fortune.[55] Thomas Philipp has identified this wealthy merchant's departure as "a serious blow to the Greek Catholic community" in Egypt, the beginning of the crisis that affected them for the last decades of the century.[56] In 1801, the Egyptian Legation had requested that dispatches from England be addressed to them via Faraoun, who was at that time in Trieste. These trans-Mediterranean commercial and political networks provided an incentive for a figure such as Aïdé to remain in France, particularly given the devastating impact of the French occupation on the previously rich trade out of Egypt.

But Aïdé's decision to remain in Marseille in 1805 was surely also a commitment to the French Arab community in which he now played a key role. It was this sense of established, settled community that he brought with him to Paris, one that was quite foreign to the Arab milieu that existed in the capital on his arrival. Characteristically, Aïdé began to arrange for others in his retinue to join him in Paris. In November, he wrote to the Ministry of War to request that his associate, Joseph Joubarra, be allowed to join them. In fact, the young man had already arrived in the capital, accompanying Maryam, the widow of General Ya'qub, on a visit. Aïdé certainly had economic interests in the capital: he had traded through the intermediary of Sabbagh and others in previous times, and there is little doubt that he would be more successful conducting his own business than entrusting it to Sabbagh, who was far more interested in language and literature than in commerce. It seems very likely that Aïdé might have had commercial motives for setting himself up at the heart of a booming empire. But cultural power and prestige certainly also exerted its attractions.

Indeed, according to another "refugee," Jean-Louis Clément, born in Syria of French origin and married to an Egyptian, Rose Chébib, such "privileged" individuals did little better than waste their money on living in a grand style. Clément expressed in 1812 the bitter frustration of those who had come to Paris at an earlier stage, as migrants attempting to achieve assimilation and social mobility, but finding little hope of prospering in the huge city:

> In truth, Your Excellence can rest assured that since we have been in France we have not had any enjoyments, whether those of the theaters big or small, public balls, caffés [sic], going out in a carriage, or other pleasures that one permits oneself from time to time for recreation. And all through an economy of the most severe kind, unlike that of a certain preferred refugee who enjoys between himself and his wife and two very young children around ten thousand francs, and since being here in France he owes more than ten thousand and is always pursued from one tribunal to the next for his debts—claims occasioned by his misconduct in crazy spending that exceeds his means.[57]

If this "preferred refugee" was Aïdé—and the description seems to fit only too well—we can perhaps read here in Clément's frustration some of the anger that Joubran Mehenna would display toward this Arab notable from Marseille who enjoyed all the privileges of Paris. "In the end," Clément continued, "we do not think ourselves in Paris, but in the depths of an uninhabited and deserted forest or on the summit of a mountain."[58] The cosmopolitan possibilities of Paris were cold comfort to those who found themselves excluded from the powerful relations of sociability, clientship, and mobility that characterized the new Arab elite in Paris.

It was for similar reasons, perhaps, that soon after Aïdé's arrival in Paris, Joubran approached him with a request for money. In his complaint to the Ministry of War, Aïdé claimed that he had been "very generous" on several occasions.[59] To demonstrate this, Aïdé appended the "translation" of a receipt for 100 francs that he had given as a "gift" to Joubran through Joseph Sabba. The receipt was evidently written originally in Arabic. Aïdé clearly felt some responsibility to fulfill a request from another member of his "community" and did so through the intercession of others in the social group. However, not long afterward, Joubran made a further request for 160 francs, which Aïdé refused. Joubran's response to this refusal was very hostile: according to Aïdé, he wrote a series of abusive letters and promised to do him bodily harm. The conflict came to a head one afternoon, when Aïdé was taking a walk in the Tuileries gardens. When Joubran saw him passing by, he abused him thoroughly. Aïdé did not respond, he later claimed, because he was afraid the encounter would become violent.

That evening, Joubran spoke with another important member of the community, Elias Pharaon, his former sponsor in entering into French service, who had been employed by the government in Paris for many years. Pharaon attempted to intervene with the young man and call him to account for his insulting behavior. But Joubran seems only to have become more incensed and swore he would do physical violence to Aïdé the next time he saw him. According to the letter, this was not his first infraction against the community. Aïdé reported a litany of other offenses committed by Joubran against his fellow Arabs: his insults to Mikha'il Sabbagh and Joseph Ataïa and physical violence against Antoine Siouphi and an unnamed woman.

In his letter Aïdé insisted that Joubran suffered from an "inflamed imagination" (*une imagination exaltée*), and described the young man as being *très emporté*, an expression that could refer as much to the passions of love as to those of anger and violence. This language can tell us something about the emotional currents that underlay the respective behaviors of these two men, and their very different reactions to the crisis. Aïdé's outrage at Joubran's "inflamed imagination" suggests that he saw the younger man's antisocial behavior as resulting from Joubran's rejection of a certain way of seeing the world, a perspective framed by custom, communal norms, and propriety. What Aïdé was suggesting here was that Joubran imagined himself to be something he was not, and it is this conflict of identities that is, I believe, crucial to understanding the violence of this encounter.

I have argued that Aïdé brought from Marseille a sense of community that was foreign to the Parisian Arab milieu. In speaking of this "community," we need to be precise about what this term means. The amorphous nature of the concept has been observed many times, and one scholar compiled ninety-four different social-scientific definitions of the term.[60] Most of these definitions in some way involved a human group exhibiting social connections, in relation to a defined locality or territory. But other studies have suggested that this link with a fixed "place" is not an unvarying element of community, above all as pertains to migrant or diasporic communities. James Clifford has criticized the "localizing strategies" that have tended to make us imagine mobility as a force fundamentally destructive to community.[61] Thus, when people migrate, their social bonds are attenuated or broken, their communications reduced, their link to place and custom weakened.

Accordingly, when Georges Aïdé left Marseille for Paris, we might imagine this act as the abandonment of community, seeking to rupture the "parochial" bonds of the provinces and join the more fluid and scattered milieux of the metropolis. But this is not what Aïdé's correspondence suggests at all. Instead, this act of mobility was what he felt to be appropriate to his principal role in this community. In this sense, as Clifford suggests, it is a mistake to look solely to spatial cohesiveness as an answer to the difficult questions of community. In his work on eighteenth-century Paris, David Garrioch identified three factors that may help define community structures that might not be associated with particular "neighbourhoods": the existence of social bonds; the quality of human interaction; and, most importantly, the existence of a particular set of norms that do not apply outside the group.[62]

Those dimensions of community can be recognized quite clearly from the first enunciative "We" with which Aïdé began his letter. In doing so, Aïdé presented the Arabs living in Paris as equal members of his community with those in Marseille. And indeed, it is evident that constant mobility between the two cities, passing by the military barracks at Melun, and the exchange of letters and goods—like the coconuts we discussed earlier—had maintained vital links between Paris and Marseille. In asking for money from his compatriot, Joubran had implicitly acknowledged his membership of these networks of clientship. Yet the help he demanded had been refused, perhaps because the demand itself was based less on the acknowledgment of Aïdé's position in the community as on Joubran's sense of entitlement and equality.

The social bonds Aïdé described in this letter were not the simple product of geographical proximity: he pointed out that Joubran lived on the other side of the Seine, in the Faubourg Saint-Germain, whereas Aïdé was living in the rue Saint-Honoré on the Right Bank, some half hour's walk away. An extract from the birth certificate of Aïdé's daughter Césarine Alexandrine, included in his dossier, lists the witnesses present as "Messieurs Elias Pharaon, interpreter of His Majesty the Emperor in Egypt, aged thirty-eight years, residing in Passy, near Paris, and Lotfi Nemr, interpreter of Oriental languages, pensioner of the state, aged thirty-two years, residing at 355, rue Saint-Honoré."[63] Thus the individuals described in Aïdé's letter, such as Elias Pharaon, could travel a significant distance from the outskirts of Paris in order to carry out social responsibilities toward their compatriots, while others shared the same address.

Yet despite these distances, membership of the community was defined, as Garrioch suggests, by the existence of a set of norms distinct from those outside. It was the enforcement of these norms that seemed to set off the conflict. Aïdé attempted in his letter to co-opt the Ministry into enforcing the norms of the community by exiling Joubran to Marseille. Thus he did not argue that Joubran had committed any offense with which he might be charged under French law—and this was confirmed by the subsequent police reports. Instead, Aïdé was invoking (whether reasonably or not) the will of the group to which he belonged, which he called the "Egyptian refugees," although as we have seen, he was neither Egyptian nor in any real sense a refugee. Instead, I think we must see here that Aïdé had brought with him from Marseille a sense that the Arab community was a group with collective norms and a collective will, which had been offended by Joubran's actions. This was in no way out of line with the consistorial function that the elite in Marseille had been called upon to take a few years earlier. Aïdé invoked the protection of the minister in the name of the community's order and tranquillity, which consequently also served the interest also of the state.

But this "community" on whose behalf Aïdé felt empowered to speak was clearly not that of a settled or bounded Parisian social unit. Nor, however, was he speaking purely as a member of the "community" in Marseille, which he had recently left as a result of the sectarian friction and political infighting there leading to denunciations and arrests. Indeed, he declared that he had left because of his wife's insistence that "it would be impossible for her to live any longer among these mischief makers."[64] Instead, Aïdé seemed to feel that his arrival in Paris now gave him the platform to speak in a larger capacity, as a representative of the Arab community in France. In his Arabic correspondence, as we noted previously, he used the term *abna-l'arab* to refer to those he called in French the "Egyptian refugees"; as a Beiruti Catholic, this was the only definition of the community in which his role could be intelligible. And his displacement from the province to the capital was not so much the disintegration as the expression of a sense of community.

Joubran, on the other hand, seems to have imagined himself as an Arab in terms of a French, and particularly a Parisian, identity that he had chosen quite consciously in 1806, rejecting the provincialism of Marseille like many other French men and women of his time. In 1811, he claimed to have been living in Paris for seven years; this was not entirely accurate, but it seems that he considered himself as belonging to the city from the moment he arrived in 1804. In this sense, we should not read Joubran's insistence on his wish to acquire Parisian accents and manners as an opportunistic and retrospective justification of his presence. It was something he had struggled for since his first arrival seven years earlier.

When Georges Aïdé arrived in Paris, it was not only his wealth that excited the resentment of the young Arab Parisian, but his attempt to impose his authority on an individual he considered to be an "unruly" member of his own community. Although Joubran had proudly cited his connection to Elias Pharaon in his request to be recognized as a former French officer, when Pharaon chose to intervene on the side of Aïdé and the community, Joubran's fury was only intensified. His previous infractions against the community can be better understood in this context. Mikha'il Sabbagh was employed at the Bibliothèque Impériale as a copyist of Arabic, a salaried member of the small group of Arab Orientalists around Rufa'il. Joseph Ataïa was a successful government employee who married into the affluent Sakakini merchant family, just as Georges Aïdé's daughter would do later in the decade.[65] Sabbagh and Ataïa represented the successful members of an Arab "colony" that was suddenly tightening its long-established connections with the community in Marseille. Thus the arrival of Georges Aïdé marked a moment in which Arab Paris was taking on a new complexion, one in which its connections to the community in Marseille were strengthened by a new kind of mobility, by new familial, social, and commercial connections that would articulate a different, more multilocal mode of existence for Arabs in early nineteenth-century France.

But Joubran's identity was very different. He had come to Paris not to extend the networks of Arab community, but to escape them. He wanted to become a new kind of cosmopolitan citizen. But in the Paris of 1811, this was not easy. Without financial resources, and without the background or connections to find himself a niche in the milieux of Parisian Orientalism, it was not clear that this promise could be fulfilled. His circuits of sociability remained Arab; if he mixed more widely in Parisian society, we have no evidence of it. Perhaps the strongest indication of this is his romantic attachment. A letter to the Ministry of War from Louise Virginie, a young and independent black woman who had been working in Soissonne and returned to Paris at this time, suggests that she had suddenly moved in with Joubran—so rapidly that her address needed to be corrected by hand on her letter.[66] Her previous address was in the same street, rue des Brodeurs, as another refugee, Antoine Siouphi, whom Aïdé claimed Joubran had violently attacked. Aïdé suggested that Siouphi was Joubran's "dupe" as well as receiving a beating from him, and this may suggest that there was a prior relationship between Siouphi and Louise. Aïdé clearly felt that his role allowed him to intervene in such personal quarrels among those he considered as members of his own community.

But Joubran did not take Georges Aïdé's denunciation lying down. At first it seemed as though the notable from Marseille would win out in this confrontation Not only did Aïdé denounce Joubran to the Ministry of War, but he had another Egyptian, Mansour Saad, make a similar denunciation to the police. Joubran was arrested and held for three days, at the end of which he was provided with a passport and instructed to leave Paris for Marseille. But Joubran did not leave Paris.

Instead he took to his pen and wrote a scathing denunciation of those who had conspired to exclude him from the city. First he attacked the pretensions of his accusers: he called Mansour Saad "un homme sans état et sans aveu"—in other words, a good-for-nothing vagabond. Less convincingly he cast doubt on Aïdé's claims as a "so-called controller of customs," challenging Aïdé's credentials as a natural representative of the community. He skillfully drew the attention of the authorities to the fact that he had done nothing under French law that could incur the penalty applied, declaring his possession of certificates testifying to his good conduct, and the wounds he had received under the French flag. Most importantly, he identified himself as a legitimate inhabitant of the city:

> Having acquired knowledge, habits of life, and even a few debts, which he cannot allow himself to dishonor, during the seven years that he has lived peacefully in Paris, it would now be impossible for him if a forced departure should send him away from Paris.[67]

This claim to a local attachment to Paris and the "impossibility" of leaving the city is almost unique among the letters of the "refugees." The other "Egyptians" based their claims on rights accrued from service to the state, intensified by penury, with the help of testaments of good conduct from powerful acquaintances. Joubran insisted instead, not on his poverty, but on the importance of his "debts," whose repayment was a question of honor, and, most importantly, on the knowledge and habits of life he had acquired in Paris. He cited his lack of resources, which made it impossible for him to afford the costs of the journey, "along with the negress, also a refugee, who is with him." Joubran was concerned for their survival if he was forced to leave Paris, and asked for enough money to make the difficult journey.

Even if we take Joubran's claims as partly rhetorical in nature, we must see across his correspondence a consistent return to the idea that his life in Paris was central to his identity. Unlike Aïdé, who had willingly chosen to leave Marseille for the capital, Joubran was invoking a very local belonging, an attachment to the city, an experiential relationship that made him feel like a legitimate and settled Parisian. Of course, Joubran did not rely wholly on this appeal to prevent his exile: he suggested pragmatically that the authorities make inquiries at Marseille concerning the "conduct and morality" of Aïdé. The recent problems there may have strengthened Joubran's case. In the event, the order to leave was rescinded a few days later, and Joubran was permitted to remain in Paris.

The credibility of Joubran's claim to be a Parisian was reinforced by the direction he took after this crisis. In 1812 he wrote to the Ministry of War to request permanent residence in Paris, since he was now married to a Frenchwoman, Anne Victoire Précieux.[68] Joubran had obviously broken from Louise Virginie, and—we may speculate—from the Arab networks of family and social relationships that he had rejected. Whatever the personal circumstances of this choice, it was one that decisively separated him from the endogamous connections central to Arab social relationships. The "community" represented by Aïdé could no longer exert any direct influence over him. Joubran now received his pension in Paris rather than Marseille and could look forward to a future as a Parisian.

Thus, in the last years of the Empire, at least two distinct modes of Arab identity were in construction and in conflict in Paris. Joubran, arriving in the capital at the beginning of the Empire, took on much of the spirit of a city only a decade away from the Revolution and assumed some of those values as his own. He insisted upon his rights to be treated equally on merit. He tried to acquire the language and accent of the capital rather than remain a "mere" provincial. Finally, he chose a path that gave him permanency in the city, even if this permanency was as much a hostage to circumstance as that of any other Parisian.[69] Aïdé, on the other hand, truly a product of the Napoleonic system, in Egypt and France, adjusted himself to the ruling structures of the society, with its return to corporatism and privilege, and turned them to his own purposes wherever he could.

Each man took a different path toward constructing an Arab identity in the capital. Joubran sought to become a full Arab Parisian, seeking a difficult path of assimilation on his own terms in a cosmopolitan city. Georges Aïdé brought to Paris a more hierarchical model of French Arab identity that had developed over a decade spent in Marseille, a close set of connections that was *in* Paris, but not *of* it. His identity was more Arab than Parisian, although Paris was certainly included in an important way in the circuits of his Franco-Arab existence. What the stories of Joubran and Georges can tell us is that there was more than one "Arab Paris" in 1811. Indeed there were many: the Paris of Louise Virginie, the young black woman from Egypt; the Paris of Antoine Siouphi, living out a miserable existence in a hovel near the Invalides; the Paris of the successful merchant Joseph Ataïa; and the Paris of Arab intellectuals like Mikha'il Sabbagh.

But the very nature of the conflict suggests that something else was emerging at this time, a larger sense of Arab life in France that traced these circuits between Marseille, Melun, and Paris, lines of mobility built up over the course of a decade. The long-delayed arrival of the Marseille notables of the "Egyptian refugees" in the more cosmopolitan Arabic-speaking milieux of the capital was a necessary moment in the making of an Arab France, and as such it is hardly surprising that it was attended by conflict and contestation. But those conflicts were not only internal. Arab life and identity in France was not free to articulate its own trajectory independently of the larger political and cultural framework of a society increasingly tightly controlled by networks of spies and secret police, by an authoritarian ruler and a burgeoning bureaucracy, many of whom were accorded more power through ennoblement, laying down those "masses of granite" that Napoleon believed would sustain his empire. For the independent intellectual, this was not a propitious moment for free and liberal thought, indeed for any project that did not serve the ambitions of the emperor. The arrival in Paris of a young Arab intellectual, eager to make his contribution to the Orientalist milieux of the capital, revealed a different face of cosmopolitanism in the imperial capital. His particular trajectory, and those of other Arab intellectuals of this period, can tell us a great deal more about the contradictory place of racial and cultural difference in imperial Paris and Napoleonic Europe, and the transformations of cultural politics as that empire hurtled toward a period of violent political transition.

4

Policing Orientalism

At almost the same moment that Georges Aïdé arrived in Paris, trailing behind him the controversies of the community in Marseille, another of his fellow notables from the Council of Refugees also arrived in the capital, albeit at an address some distance further along the rue Saint-Honoré. 'Abd el-Al, the former aga, or chief, of police under the occupation in Cairo, clearly saw this as a propitious moment for extending his own networks of sociability into the capital of the Empire. 'Abd el-Al brought with him a young Copt, Ellious Bocthor, as his assistant and translator. But Bocthor would experience great difficulties in finding a place in the capital. Bocthor was looking for more than subsistence and sociability within the Parisian Arab milieu. He was seeking the opportunity promised by the ideals of the Revolution that had brought him to France, ideals of universalism and opportunity, which were bound to be disappointed in the Napoleonic police state. But the more curious aspect of this story was the interest that the police took in this Arab Orientalist, which contributed to the problems that forced him to leave Paris and return to Marseille. Bocthor's trajectory tested the limits of cosmopolitanism in Napoleonic France, and the space that it created for Arab self-expression. The boundaries of Orientalism, on this occasion, were literally policed by the intervention of the state and its agents. There are wider questions to be asked here about Napoleonic cultural politics. The nature of intellectual practice and its relation to the state had changed with the transformation of political structures. Certainly, Bocthor had to learn a new way of positioning himself within a cultural politics of an Orientalism that was itself in conflict over the response to modernizing intellectual practice. But most of all Bocthor had to adjust himself to the structures of the Napoleonic imperial state. It is very much the argument of this chapter that the bounds of cosmopolitanism were *not* simply enforced through a set of internal regularities proper to Orientalist representations, but by a more complex field of ideas and practices in the wider context of Napoleonic Europe.

In August 1811, the duc de Feltre, the French minister of war, wrote to the duc de Rovigo, minister of police, to inform him of the arrival in Paris of the "Coptic refugee from Egypt" Ellious Bocthor, accompanying the aga 'Abd el-Al as an interpreter:

> [He] has informed me that he wishes to take up residence here, in order to perfect his knowledge of French, to translate several Arabic works held at the Imperial Library into our language, and to put together a dictionary of Common Arabic— something France does not yet possess, and which answers the need both of literature and of public utility.[1]

The minister of war had provisionally approved Bocthor's residency in Paris. "The comments I have received concerning this refugee are very favorable," he wrote, requesting the minister of police to "prescribe such arrangements as Your Excellence considers appropriate."[2] However, Rovigo (about whom we will have more to say later in this book) responded with an order to place "this foreigner" under surveillance, dispatching a note to that effect to the prefect of police in the Fourth Arrondissement.[3] In the *Bulletin of Secret Police* on 17 August, it was duly noted that "the minister has ordered that this foreigner be observed with circumspection."[4]

It is impossible to tell from Bocthor's carefully worded observations a few months later exactly what role this police notoriety played in his decision to return to Marseille, but his heavy disappointment was only too evident. Bocthor hoped to present his petition to the director of public education, in the hope of finding employment at the Imperial Library, like his friend Mikha'il Sabbagh:

> But the author of this letter, who was then in Paris, given that his health (which was in a poor state, as it is still today) could only be made worse by remaining in the capital where the climate is so different from that of his country, and having observed furthermore that his presence upset a number of people in his profession, was forced to give up his project and return to Marseille.[5]

So Bocthor returned to Marseille, after spending only a few unhappy months in Paris. It may be true that his poor health made him wary of a winter in the capital without employment, but that seems to have been little more than a polite excuse to cover the ignominy of his departure.

Why would the police interest themselves in this apparently innocuous, bookish—and, according to his own description, prematurely infirm—Egyptian? A decade earlier, the members of the Legation had been denied access to Paris because of the potential ramifications of their political projects. Now those restrictions had been lifted, not through a change of policy, but from a change of interests. Bocthor's sponsor, 'Abd el-Al, applied at this time for the admission of his son on a full scholarship to the Lycée in Marseille: Rovigo noted on this request that he should be be sent back to Marseille "unless he has been called here by the minister of war."[6] The Muslim notable, however, managed to remain in Paris throughout the remainder of the Empire: instead, it was Bocthor who was compelled, most reluctantly, to leave the capital, where so many of his hopes for advancement lay.

It seems therefore that it was the intellectual rather than the notable who was now to be treated with the greatest suspicion. This change suggests something important about the transformation of imperial culture in France, and the role that it created for the Orientalist project of knowledge about the Muslim world. Egypt, the Middle East, and North Africa remained of critical importance to France, as the rest of the century would demonstrate. The Napoleonic moment was a crucible for the changing representations of that relationship: it was characterized by the restoration of a corporatist and privilege-based society, and an attempt to find an accommodation with the transformations wrought by the Revolution. Universalism and nationalism, imperialism and patriotism, cosmopolitanism and civilization—all of these ideas were in the balance. The Napoleonic system exerted tight controls on intellectual activity and sought to bring it under a regime of social and imperial utility. This chapter will explore what role Arabs who had become to a greater or lesser degree "French" after a decade of life in France could and did play in this cultural politics: the ways in which they sought to adopt and adapt this cultural politics, and the ways in which that activity was tolerated or policed.

Few explorations have been made into the nature of cosmopolitanism in the Napoleonic empire. While a series of excellent studies have examined Napoleonic Europe and the dynamics of occupation, this analysis has not yet extended to the "new Frenchmen" within the limits of France itself.[7] It is clear from the registers of foreigners arriving in Paris that this presence was considerable.[8] The difference for the "new Frenchmen" who had left Egypt and Syria for Marseille and Paris was that they did not come from an occupied, annexed, or satellite state of the Empire. Their position was ambiguous; their *ralliement* to the French had occurred under French rule, but at a very different moment—the occupation of Egypt was a revolutionary rather than an imperial phenomenon (although of course the two cannot be entirely dissociated). The presence of the "Egyptians" in Marseille was a political counterweight with regard to Britain and the Ottomans, and an indication that the question of Egypt remained open. The presence of Egyptians in Paris was the result of a depoliticization, a changed set of geopolitical and local circumstances that rendered their presence no longer dangerous. Egypt's loss had been transformed ideologically into a victory, but a *cultural* victory. The presence of

Egyptians alongside other *nouveaux Français* in Paris tended to confirm this propaganda: they were consistently figured (and sought to figure themselves) as passionate partisans of Napoleon.

Napoleonic Paris has conventionally been viewed as the ne plus ultra of "Egyptomania," the high point of a fervor for Egyptianesque architecture, design, and imagery that had spread across Europe and even across the Atlantic from the eighteenth century onward.[9] Certainly, the Egyptian campaign was the subject of several imposing works of history painting in the Consulate and the early years of the Empire, which depicted Napoleon as a great military and civilian leader. The studies carried out by the many scientists, artists, and scholars who had been invited to join the French army in the invasion of Egypt were formalized into a single project that would provide a full picture of both ancient and modern Egyptian life. The *Description de l'Égypte* resulting from this project has been understood, notably by Edward Said, as the originating point for modern Orientalist discourse, effacing Egypt's Arab and Muslim present for the ruins of its ancient past.[10]

Scholarship has challenged the idea that Egyptomania was such a dominant element in the self-representation of Napoleon's empire. It is perhaps the sheer size and grandiosity of the paintings that took Egypt as their theme during the Consulate that has led many critics to suppose that Egypt was a frequent and popular subject for artistic production under the Empire. But the huge canvases that now hang in the Louvre were painted as official commissions and served specific political purposes of shoring up the fragility of Napoleon's regime in its earliest years. Egypt represented both his most glamorous victory and his most significant defeat, and thus it was vital to the structuring of the propaganda narrative. There is little doubt that the fabled exoticism of Egypt was an attractive subject for artists. But as Anna Piussi has shown in her study of the salons from 1801, Egypt *"did not constitute a significant 'trend' in early nineteenth-century French painting."*[11] Even in 1801 and 1802, only 7 works depicted "Oriental" subjects each year, out of 384 and 650 works respectively. In 1804, the number was 16 out of 560. In 1806, Piussi reports, only 2 of 18 commissioned war paintings depicted Egyptian subjects. She concludes that "the few memorable canvases were a minority of what was already a minor trend in painting at the time."[12] Public response was often unfavorable: critics sometimes complained that the extravagant clothing of the Egyptian soldiers distracted attention from the less exotic (but more pictorially important) French soldiers.[13] It is perhaps for this reason that so often in later paintings of Napoleonic campaigns the Arab soldiers in their colorful attire were pushed to the background and often constituted little more than a turban poking out from behind someone's elbow.

The sharp decline in representations of Egypt after 1804 was in part the result of an official ban placed on the public exhibition of preparatory drawings for the

Description. In 1808, Napoleon declared the map of Egypt that had been prepared by the Commission d'Égypte to be a state secret. This map was to have been the centerpiece of the first volume of the *Description,* on topography; the publication of this volume was consequently delayed indefinitely, leaving only the volume on antiquities to be published in 1809. As Marie-Noëlle Bourguet observes, "The original objective was obscured—to compose a portrait of Egypt in the form of an inventory based on a topographical map—whereas antiquity found itself, in fact, placed in the foreground."[14]

Thus we should not be led into thinking that Napoleonic Paris was in any hurry to embrace all things Egyptian. Opportunities for "Egyptians" themselves were in fact quite limited. The intellectual milieu of Arab Paris was a crowded and competitive place by 1811. Rufa'il Zakhur occupied a personal chair in colloquial Arabic at the École des Langues Orientales; Mikha'il Sabbagh was employed at the Bibliothèque Impériale, copying Arabic manuscripts and giving private lessons; Youhanna Chiftichi, in addition to his sacerdotal function at the church of Saint-Roch, was employed by the Commission d'Égypte (at a salary of 2,000 francs) on the production of the multivolume *Description de l'Égypte.*[15] Other Arabs, including Mansour Saad, were also occasionally employed on this work.[16] There were others who tried unsuccessfully to find a position in the highly competitive world of Paris. Gabriel Taouïl had managed instead to gain a chair at Marseille, but Michel Abeid, Joseph Chammas, Lotfi Nemr, and Mansour Saad had tried and failed to find public employment for their Arabic skills and turned to commercial employment or some other trade altogether.[17]

Nonetheless, the presence of so many Arab intellectuals in Paris suggests that Paris under the Empire offered certain cosmopolitan possibilities. If opportunities were limited and competition fierce, there seems to have been no insurmountable obstacle to intellectual success for Egyptians and Syrians in the imperial capital. Postrevolutionary Paris certainly seemed to provide opportunities for these intellectuals from which they were excluded in Egypt. This is almost certainly what drew Ellious Bocthor, like so many other intellectuals before and since, to the *capitale des lumières.*

As we saw in chapter 1, an ambitious young Copt in Egypt might receive a classical Arabic education and participate in the considerable intellectual developments of the late eighteenth century. But the traditional restrictions on the *dhimmi* – the approved religious minorities—limited them in two ways. The most important intellectual positions at the university of al-Azhar remained restricted to Muslims; a Christian could not become a sheikh or a member of the *'ulama,* in whose hands rested the major intellectual developments of the society. Secondly, the nature of the *millet* system meant that Christians were subject to the authority of their own community, which could be parochial and restrictive, particularly for a relatively small and regionally contained minority such as the Copts. This created stark choices for Copts with aspirations to rise higher: whether to convert or to accept a position as a dependent state functionary.

Only fourteen years old when the French arrived in Egypt, Ellious Bocthor was influenced during his formative years by the French occupation and had begun studying French language and literature from this young age. The certificates he presented in Paris included one from General Davout, who had written in 1803: "This Copt has skills, knows the two languages perfectly, and might be usefully employed."[18] Edmé-François Jomard confirmed this later, writing that Bocthor, "by dint of work and study, had attained a degree of perfection in French language and literature. . . . He could express himself with ease and clarity, in both French and Arabic."[19] Bocthor later came into conflict with Gabriel Taouïl, who accused him of abusing the access he had been given to Taouïl's papers; Bocthor wrote to his friend Sabbagh to explain that he was only trying to learn French. One suspects that it was Bocthor's application and ambition that irritated Taouïl.

The situation was very different for the Syrian Christians. Gabriel Taouïl and Mikha'il Sabbagh readily found paths to educational advancement through the wider networks of the Arab Catholic diaspora. Sabbagh's family had held a powerful position in the Palestinian city of Acre, and he was sent to Damascus for his early education. After the downfall of their protector Zaher al-'Umar, Sabbagh was taken to Constantinople, where his father was killed on the whim of an official in 1775.[20] The family fled to Egypt, where Sabbagh's uncle found an influential position as a customs official. There too, among the large Syrian Christian population of Damietta, were many opportunities. The Lebanese historian Mikha'il Mishaqa reported that his own uncle had studied with the most renowned Muslim scholars and translated French books into Arabic during the occupation.[21] When the French arrived in Egypt, Mikha'il Sabbagh (then known by his paternal name of Ibrahim) already possessed the skills to be appointed librarian to the Institut d'Égypte. [22]

Such multilocal connections, and the paths of mobility and education they offered, were not freely available to Copts, particularly those from Upper Egypt like Bocthor. Thus, for Bocthor, the French occupation offered an opening for intellectual advancement that did not mean conversion or functionary status. By careful study of the French language, he became the only member of what he called the "Coptic nation" to serve as an interpreter for the French.[23] But the nature of the French administration in Egypt was very different from what Bocthor discovered on his arrival in France.

Bocthor had expected to follow General Ya'qub to Paris. Instead, he found himself stranded in Marseille, and classified as a "refugee" on a meager pension of 2 francs 50 per day, accorded by the Ministry of War. At first, as he wrote in a letter, he had anticipated that his pension would be increased once his services were recognized, but instead it was further reduced in 1804 to only 2 francs.[24] Much higher sums, and the social power that accompanied this relative affluence, were granted to those retiring from military service. Thus Bocthor was downgraded in relation to those in the community whose military services could promote them in official favor. More sharply, this gesture reflected a shift away from universalizing and civilizing values toward military and imperial priorities.

Bocthor was effectively confined in Marseille, working on the elaboration of his dictionary, and in the business transactions of his patron, 'Abd el-Al and other notables in the town. In 1807, he watched with considerable frustration as the Syrian priest Gabriel Taouïl went to Paris and succeeded in establishing himself in a new chair of Arabic created for him by the emperor at the Lycée de Marseille. The crucial distinction was not strictly a regional or sectarian one. Taouïl possessed strong connections in France from well before the Revolution; he had studied as a Catholic priest in Lyon during the 1780s. Indeed, according to his obituary notice by the abbé Bargès (a former pupil), he "spoke French like a true Lyonnais."[25] In Egypt, Taouïl was appointed as chief interpreter for the French army after the promotion of Rufa'il to the Institut, and he returned to France with the other emigrants in 1801. Taouïl's fortunes in France were secured by his journey to Paris, where—as we have seen—he was able to use his personal acquaintance with the influential Orientalist Sylvestre de Sacy to obtain a chair of Arabic in Marseille. But many in Marseille, including Bocthor, felt that Taouïl did not merit an appointment made purely as the result of influence.

In a wider sense, Taouïl's appointment, mandated personally by the emperor, can be seen to coincide with the imperial policy of fostering national elites under French tutelage, which was being instituted across French-occupied Europe.[26] This policy does not appear to have been entirely assimilatory in intent: while acknowledging the natural superiority of French "civilization," the cultural priority of a French education was to be tempered by the commercial and diplomatic "utility" of preserving the students' Arabic skills. Stuart Woolf has noted that in the later years of the Empire local vernacular language skills were increasingly required for public office in the non-French territories in Europe.[27] In the same way, Arabic could be seen as a useful tool, not only for commerce but also for the cultural politics of the *Grande Nation*.

As early as 1784, Constantin de Volney had been promoting the benefits of establishing Arabic classes in Marseille, the city known as the "gate to the Orient." In a later text he proposed the establishment of a new Collège de Drogmans, which

> should be placed in the town of Marseille or as near as possible in the vicinity: since it is intended to serve in the practical instruction of the languages of the Levant, it must be in the place where this practice is greatest, the residence or boarding place for those of our countrymen who spend years in the Levant, and for the natives of the Levant who come to trade in Marseille.[28]

Volney's ideas exercised a powerful influence upon the young Napoleon Bonaparte, who had met him briefly in Corsica. Volney's works took an important place in the library Bonaparte carried with him to Egypt: the notes Bonaparte made on Volney's works during his journey to Egypt have survived. A similar proposal was made by the Egyptian Legation in 1801, but it languished along with the Legation's other "national" propositions.[29] But these precedents proved a fertile ground for Taouïl's propositions. The founding professor of Arabic at the École des Langues Orientales, Antoine-Isaac Sylvestre de Sacy, visited the minister of education to press his protégé's case, describing Taouïl as "a man whom it would certainly be useful to retain in France ... who speaks and writes Arabic very well, both literary and colloquial, and writes perfectly in French."[30] But Sacy read correctly the pragmatic nature of the administration: despite these intellectual attainments, Taouïl's *utilité* was measured in more concretely political terms. Sacy continued:

> I should also add that Don Gabriel has been involved in collaborating on the Arabic translation of the bulletins of the army; at my request he has taken on the translation of the present campaign, and I have in my hands already a good part of this work.[31]

The aim of these translations was not simply to update the archives, but also to distribute propaganda. Taouïl worked alongside Sacy and other Orientalists on the production of a pamphlet in Arabic and Turkish entitled "The Ottoman Muezzin to His Brothers, the True Believers," which was destined, along with the Arabic translations of the bulletins of the Grande Armée, for distribution to the Muslim populations of eastern Europe, Turkey, and the Levant, exhorting them to rise against Russia, France's enemy.[32]

The teaching of Arabic in Marseille was valuable for its commercial and "civilizing" benefit. As the prefect of the Bouches-du-Rhône declared: "The emperor wishes to restore the capital of the Midi to the place it once occupied among the trading cities, and the aim of the Arabic course is to improve relations with the Levant and the two northern ports of Africa."[33] The policy was resisted strongly by members of the local administration, who protested against the establishment of the course, until the École des Langues Orientales in Paris agreed to pay half of the salary.[34] This tension was accompanied by conflicts within the Arab community itself. Taouïl's position as professor had not been won by merit, but by the established personal connections of a particular member of the community. For Ellious Bocthor, this was particularly galling, and he wrote to Mikha'il Sabbagh, complaining that Taouïl had plagiarized the teaching materials of Sylvestre de Sacy.[35] Taouïl complained to the Ministry of War:

> This Ellious has a particular interest in causing me as much harm as he can. He has long desired to take my position as professor of Arabic at the Lycée and has made incessant denunciations against me and caused me all sorts of trouble. . . . Moreover, I have irrefutable proof of these evil intentions that these two, the said Ellious

said Boctor *[sic]* and the said Abd el-Al Agha, have always had against me. Your Excellency would certainly be convinced of this on reading an attestation provided to me last November by several Egyptian refugees living in Paris, translated by M. Sylvestre de Sacy, member of the Institut . . . from which it is clear that [these people] have done everything in their power to cause problems for me, and to find a way to make me lose my position and have it given to the said Ellious.[36]

Taouïl insisted that the fundamental conflict between himself and ʿAbd el-Al was religious: "We differ completely in character and religion. I am a Catholic priest; he is a Muslim, and that is the only reason I have ever found for his hatred toward me."[37] Bocthor wrote in a letter to Sabbagh: "This man is a liar, and I don't understand how a person in his position can lie! De Sacy should have investigated it before he got so angry."[38] Taouïl doubtless presented this clash to Sacy, himself a devout Christian, as a sectarian conflict in order to bolster his own position; however, this does indicate the persistence of an undercurrent of hostility toward Islam that might well coexist with more utilitarian uses of religious difference.

In a more general sense, the clash seems to have been less religious than ideological. At stake were different conceptions of the role of an Arab intellectual in France, a conflict that was reflected in the divisions within Orientalist knowledge in its response to the modernizing project. Despite his Coptic background, Bocthor expressed his own intellectual and cultural practice through modern Arabic, and not through Coptic language, religion, or history, or the ancient Egyptian past. The heritage upon which he drew was very much an Arab cultural heritage deeply inflected by the culture and history of Islam. But Bocthor had adapted this in an important sense as his own heritage, independent of any Coptic specificity. This relationship to Arab identity distinguished Bocthor from a figure like Youhanna Chiftichi, who was a Coptic intellectual, was directly involved in Coptic Catholic ritual at the church of Saint-Roch and gave private lessons in the Coptic language to students such as Jean-François Champollion.[39] Even in his work as a consultant on the *Description de l'Égypte,* Chiftichi was referred to under his religious titles Abouna (Father) or Kassis (Priest), often in preference to his full name.

Bocthor, by contrast, was an Arabist intellectual who showed no interest at all in religion. After a visit from the highly religious Isa Carus, he wrote to Mikha'il Sabbagh: "I told him that it has been a long time since I last prayed and that I am not involved in religious matters, and he left. I thought he was visiting me to buy some books. Frankly speaking, I am so glad I left the church."[40] Most of his correspondence is filled with the competition over intellectual merit, the exchange of ink, pens, and books, particularly those necessary to the completion of his dictionary, and attempts to forge closer alliances with the Orientalist milieux in Paris. His driving force was the urge to modernize, simplify, and organize the Arabic language as a vernacular rather than a sacred language. This project is cognate with the "lexicographical revolution" that, in the words of Benedict Anderson, was central to the vast transformation of "imagined communities" that Anderson traces across the eighteenth and nineteenth centuries.[41] There is little doubt that Bocthor's ideas were deeply influenced by his encounter with the French at a critical point in his development. He expressed this in a letter:

> A boundless devotion to the French, and services rendered to the Army of the Orient in Egypt, compelled me to share forever the fate of a Great Nation, and so I followed the army in its retreat to France, abandoning at a young age my country, my family, my friends, my possessions, and a brilliant career.[42]

Of course, these professions of eternal devotion to France were *de rigueur* in any such petition, but the nature of Bocthor's formulation, I would suggest, may lead us to see his commitment as more than a florid rhetorical gesture. The capitalization of *Grande Nation* associates this phrase with a specific political project of early Napoleonic imperialism, more closely linked to the ideals of the Revolution: the inclusion of sovereign national republics under a French aegis.[43] The "brilliant career" he abandoned to leave for France suggests—as we saw with Georges Aïdé—that Bocthor understood his expatriation as voluntary, rather than as a forced exile.

A contemporaneous autobiographical text by the Muslim scholar Hassan al-'Attar may help us understand better the impact of the sudden arrival of a large group of foreign intellectuals—who represented an avant-garde even in their own culture—on a young intellectual in eighteenth-century Egypt. Al-'Attar wrote, in a short work called the *Maqamat al-'Attar* (Recitations of al-'Attar), of the "dizziness" he experienced in this contact with people he had heard about from travelers, and heard reputed as cruel "only to those who make war on them," and full of a love for "secular philosophy," which remained something of a forbidden fruit in the religious context of al-Azhar.[44] But it was the fluent Arabic of one of the young men among them, "free from ungrammatical usages and from barren phraseology and other defects," which impressed him most, reviving his own love of Arabic language and poetry, and his pride in explaining to them the riches of his cultural heritage. Shaden Tageldin, in analyzing this piece of writing, has described al-'Attar as a "colonized intellectual" and interpreted his responses, using the work of Frantz Fanon, as a cultural seduction by a hegemonic power.[45] We should be wary of oversimplifying the complex relations of the occupation, particularly the intellectual interactions of indigenous modernizers and French "experts." These dynamics, and their sequels in France, are much more accurately comprehended within the dynamics of the postrevolutionary situation than within the framework of later nineteenth-century colonial empire. Al-'Attar left Egypt around the same time as Bocthor, also as a result of his encounter with the French. He traveled to the center of Ottoman power in Constantinople, where he searched for and found his own secular, modernizing, and cosmopolitan milieu within the Islamic ecumene.[46] Bocthor, in contrast, followed the path of his Coptic compatriot, General Ya'qub, to France.

Bocthor's point here was that in abandoning a potentially "brilliant career" in Egypt—which one might nonetheless imagine as confined within the traditional Coptic role as an economic functionary—he had chosen to pursue an intellectual project from which he would be barred by his religion in Egypt. But this project was a modernizing one. As he explained,

> Since my childhood I have been devoted to my studies, pushed by nature toward serious and substantial things. Hoping to make myself useful to my new homeland, I set myself to produce a classic work for the promotion of politics and commerce throughout the Orient, a true modern Arabic and French dictionary. No other nation possesses any work comparable to this, and only an interpreter who knows the two languages not just through theory, but also through practice, could undertake it.[47]

The word *modern* in the phrase "un vrai dictionnaire français et arabe moderne" has an ambiguous position in referring either to the dictionary itself or to the kind of Arabic language it would contain. The positioning of the adjective suggests that it was intended to refer to the language. However, the ambiguity itself suggests a certain "double consciousness," which may be opposed to Tageldin's (Freudian-Fanonian) "double bind." Modernity here may be understood either as *technical* in the European sense or as *linguistic* in an Arabic sense. It is in the intersection of these two senses that Bocthor's project is best understood.

The beginnings of "linguistic modernism" in the Arab world predated the arrival of the French in Egypt. The lexicographical ambitions that Bocthor expresses here, as Peter Gran observes, were a key feature of the eighteenth-century Egyptian intellectual revival that, Gran suggests, formed part of a general local response to modernity, to the increasing integration of Egypt into global trade and capitalism. This integration brought with it new ideas and concepts that needed to be translated into Arabic.[48] At the same time, the language sciences retained an intense religious and cultural prestige that acted as a powerful barrier against the kind of rationalistic ordering of knowledge in which language could become a transparent, practical tool for the exercise of science. The religious elite tended to preserve the hermetic, "perfected" structure of the language, particularly in terms of grammar, where "certain areas of substantive change were virtually closed," according to Gran.[49] Thus it is quite natural that Bocthor, emerging from this educational tradition, yet restricted by his religious identity to its periphery, should have been inspired to enter this work of lexicography from the reforming and rationalist perspective.[50] At the same time, Bocthor's work was devoted primarily toward translation: the rendering of French words through Arabic equivalents. His dictionary was equally an extension of the modernizing project in which he had first begun to participate under the French occupation in Egypt.

But Bocthor discovered on his arrival in Paris in 1811 that struggles over the control and application of knowledge analogous to those that were occurring in Egypt were also being played out within French Orientalism. The pointed remarks that he made in his letter about the need for both "theory" and, crucially, "practice" in Arabic help explain difficulties to which he alluded in his letter of 1811. What was at stake in these struggles was the modernization of the study of Oriental languages, and Arabic in particular; the conflict ranged on one side hermeticists such as Sacy, who were committed to the ideal nature of Arabic as a language, and on the other pragmatists like Volney and Jomard, who viewed the study of Arabic, Turkish, and Persian as serving national interests (particularly commerce and diplomacy) as well as a universalist conception of "civilization."

This conflict over the role of Oriental languages had begun with the Revolution, which had fostered the universalizing and modernizing vision of the Enlightenment while registering France's pragmatic needs in commerce and diplomacy. The École des Langues Orientales, founded in 1795, represented an important step toward the inclusion of Arabic studies in the modernizing frame of postrevolutionary science; however, in effect this was not exactly what happened. Sylvestre de Sacy, the first president of this new school, had been trained in a Jansenist monastic environment, within which Oriental languages had only recently emerged as a discipline independent from biblical study. Christian Décobert has pointed out that Sacy strongly resisted applying the "modernizing" philosophical tradition of the Enlightenment to the study of Arabic. The new school was officially dedicated to "the public utility of politics and commerce" and was intended to train interpreters and diplomats. But Sacy completely altered its orientation, "directing it toward research and not simply language training, which seems to have been decisive in the shaping of Orientalism in French universities."[51]

This more careful examination of Sacy and his place in the history of Orientalism challenges the widespread view that the cultural politics of Orientalism in the first decades of the nineteenth century was connected in any simple way to the colonial project. In Edward Said's interpretation, Sylvestre de Sacy had a special place as "a man standing at the beginning of an important revisionist project . . . a self-aware inaugurator," whose work formed a kind of "Benthamite Panopticon"— in other words, a modern, rationalizing technology of domination.[52] Décobert strongly challenges Said's insistence that Sacy and Volney shared some fundamental continuity of thought about the "Orient," suggesting rather that their relationship to the Arab-Muslim world was radically different. Sacy's vision of Arabic language and culture was a hermetic one, a project to "make visible" a truth Sacy considered to be inherent in the texts that he simply collected, organized, and commented upon. Décobert insists that this contemplation of a revealed truth implied a subordination of the knowledge of the Orientalist to the ideal authority of the Arabic language and the Arab authors themselves. The Arabic language was conceived in terms of an originally perfect system, and any defects in this perfection could be restored by the research and commentary of the Orientalist. Said was right to suggest that in Sacy's project the Arabic authors would be brought to comprehension, corrected where they strayed from the ideal, and re-presented by Sacy himself. But Décobert aligns this intellectual position with that of the monks of Port-Royal: "an erudition which tended in the direction of reproducing an autonomous Arabic discourse, independent of the intervention of the philosopher-expert."[53] Sacy was, in this epistemological sense, extremely conservative. In Décobert's words, he "turned his back on the *spirit* of the Revolution and the Enlightenment . . . concerned with problems such as the origin of nations, the legitimacy of power, the foundations of social relationships."[54] For Décobert, Sacy was fundamentally an antimodern thinker, anchored firmly in an older structure of thought.

It is probably for this reason that Sacy, and other leading Orientalists such as Louis Langlès, declined flatly when called upon in 1798 to participate in a military intervention and modernizing project in Egypt.[55] The Egyptian expedition, as we have noted, was almost entirely lacking in qualified Orientalists.[56] This did not overly concern Napoleon, whose ideas , as we have noted, were based on those of the modernizing Enlightenment intellectual Volney. The latter proposed a radically new system for the transcription of Oriental languages in the Roman alphabet.[57] This system, he suggested, "being innovative, could not but find itself under attack from *antiquated habits of mind*."[58] But Sacy's Orientalism could not possibly countenance such a radically profane approach to a sacred language. The conflict came to a head when the members of the Egyptian expedition returned to Paris and began to compile the map of Egypt for the *Description*. Should the names on the map be printed in Arabic script as well as French, or in a transliteration following Volney's system? The conflict divided new Orientalists from old. "Not wanting to subject the honor of a public monument to a personal vanity," Volney wrote, "I requested that the scientific quarrel be resolved by a jury in a closed session."[59]

Volney's jury included a Syrian Arab, Michel Abeid, who had come to Paris from Italy, "having served French merchants and agents voluntarily in the three languages [Arabic, French, and Italian] for over twenty years."[60] The inclusion of Arab intellectuals was necessary because leading Orientalists such as Sacy had never traveled outside Europe and therefore had virtually no idea of Arabic pronunciation. As Rifa'a al-Tahtawi observed of Sacy in 1831, "When he reads, he has a foreign accent and he cannot speak Arabic unless he has a book in his hands. If he wants to explain an expression he uses strange words, which he is unable to pronounce properly."[61] Thus it seems hardly surprising that Sacy should have greeted with some ambivalence the arrival in France of a series of native Arabic-speaking intellectuals, particularly those associating themselves with a modernizing program.

Sacy's discomfort quickly turned to outrage in 1803, when the Syrian priest Rufa'il Zakhur was appointed as adjunct professor of colloquial Arabic at the École des Langues Orientales Vivantes. "I cannot constrain my surprise," Sacy protested to the minister of education.

> Giving me an adjunct for the Arabic chair is like giving me a certificate of useless-ness or incompetence. . . . The government is hardly lacking in opportunities to use the talents of D. Raphaël in the field of Oriental literature or even in some sort of work for which he would be more suited than in public education, without in some sense working to paralyze my position by appointing an adjunct professor.[62]

But Rufa'il was appointed in spite of Sacy's outright protests and remained in his position at the École throughout the Empire. In 1816 he returned to Egypt to become an important figure in the printing and translation movement at Boulaq under Muhammad 'Ali.[63]

In decisive ways, Rufa'il conformed closely to the ideal model of the Napoleonic scholar. Born in Cairo to a Syrian Melkite family in 1759, from the age of fifteen he had studied for seven years in Rome, where in addition to religious study he trained in medicine.[64] After a period in Sidon (in present-day Lebanon), he accompanied two Syrian bishops to Rome as an interpreter, and then returned to Egypt before the arrival of the French.[65] Under the French occupation he worked at first as personal interpreter for Napoleon, and then was appointed as a member of the Institut d'Égypte. This appointment was not simple tokenism. The expedition lacked real expertise in Arabic and Turkish, and experts familiar with the administration and society of Egypt. According to Joseph Fourier, "It was the recognition of his zeal, his talents, and his morals that determined the choice to make him a member of the Institute, a distinction accorded to no other inhabitant of the country."[66]

While carrying out his essential duties as a translator, Rufa'il did not primarily concern himself with linguistic and literary projects but turned his capacities to the characteristically scientific projects of the Institut. He was commissioned by Napoleon to collaborate on the creation of a popular almanac for Egypt based on the model of the *Connaissance des temps pour l'an VII*, which had been produced in Paris.[67] Drawing upon his medical and scientific knowledge, he translated into Arabic Desgenettes' treatise on smallpox and Macquer's on silk dyeing, for the use of the *diwân*. We can see here the revolutionary-Napoleonic model of "rational conquest" through the application of modernizing knowledge, actively promulgated by an Egyptian savant. Rufa'il helped Jacques-Denis Delaporte translate an Arabic manuscript into French,[68] and assisted in ethnographic studies carried out by members of the Institut. In his unpublished writings in Arabic, Rufa'il identified himself as "secretary and interpreter of the General Administration of Finances in Egypt, member of the National Institute of Egypt and of the Commission of Sciences, and First Interpreter of the Diwan of Cairo during the French Occupation in Egypt."[69] It is significant that Rufa'il conceived his participation with the French in terms of an Egyptian national project, suggesting a close alignment with the ideas of the Egyptian Legation in 1801.

Rufa'il's unpublished manuscripts included another text, the *Marj al-azhar wa bustan al-hawadith al-akhbar,* which may be translated as "The Hubbub of al-Azhar and the Garden of New Events." Rufa'il contrasted the rationalist, ordered idea of science and education—the "garden"—with the apparent disorder of the individual teaching method used at the great university of al-Azhar, the chief Islamic educational institution in the world at that time, where hundreds of students studied individually with the *'ulama* in the great courtyard. This system had developed over many centuries of unbroken continuity, but it was increasingly under question in Egypt as a result of social and political changes.[70]

This wide-ranging collection of manuscripts—which also included an incomplete work on the Jabal Druze of Lebanon, notes on the Bedouin peoples of Egypt and Syria, and a variety of other notes on subjects from astronomy to Arabic botanical names—suggests that Rufa'il felt a real intellectual proximity to the new configurations of knowledge.[71] Intellectual practice in the Enlightenment, as described by Daniel Roche in his work on eighteenth-century France, was no longer directed to hermetic pursuits, to illuminating the design of a relatively fixed universe, but instead as a spatially and temporally ordering force, actively engaged in projects to shape reality, from rivers and roads to clocks and machines.[72] In 1803, probably as a result of the continuing instability in Egypt, Rufa'il arrived in France. He traveled directly to Grenoble to stay with his close friend, the mathematician Joseph Fourier, now prefect of the Isère. According to a letter he wrote to Talleyrand, he claimed to be the "bearer of important letters to the French government," perhaps from those supporters of Egyptian independence who had remained behind in Egypt.[73] He requested a private audience with the First Consul, and his nomination for the prestigious teaching post followed a few days later.

But if Rufa'il and other Arab intellectuals had expected to find in Paris the opportunity to engage in a modernizing and universalist culture, which would favor their own linguistic and cultural projects, they were to be sorely disappointed. Instead, they found themselves in an environment that was tightly controlled both politically and intellectually. The dominant scholars, such as Sacy, who enjoyed considerable cultural prestige, made only rhetorical gestures toward the values of "civilization," without engaging in the modernizing project at all. The great work of classification and description of modern Egypt, which had been initiated largely by Kléber after Bonaparte's departure, was halted in its tracks by Napoleon's ban on publishing the map that was to be its centerpiece. Volney's success in the transliteration of Arabic names turned out to be a Pyrrhic victory: such questions of a grand and speculative nature were placed indefinitely on the back burner.

Indeed, Bonaparte broke violently with his mentor over the Concordat, which Volney viewed as a foolish and reactionary misstep. When the First Consul responded that 88 percent of the French people wanted the pope, Volney asked ironically what Bonaparte would do if the same proportion wanted the return of the Bourbon monarchy. Bonaparte was reported to have kicked Volney in the stomach and knocked him to the ground. This story—which had wide currency at the time—whether it is true or not, gives some suggestion of the violence associated with these intellectual conflicts, and the coercive regulation of opinions and ideas.[74]

What the regime increasingly required of intellectuals was legitimation, propaganda, and statistics. Stuart Woolf has observed how ethnographic forms of knowledge, which had been so privileged by the Enlightenment and Revolution, were marginalized in the course of the Empire, replaced by an increasing stress on the statistical and quantifiable: the emphasis shifted "from curiosity about the science of man to culturally less ambitious and in practice more immediate concerns." Woolf noted that "police surveillance offered more effective control than anthropological descriptions over a society which itself was more disciplined than in 1789."[75] Marie-Noëlle Bourguet has further suggested that this emphasis on the statistical emerged within an understanding of the national that remained tied at an administrative level to the "mosaic" of revolutionary departments rather than the "vertical, sectorial, and centralized perspective" that characterized administrative inquiry from the 1830s.[76] This prefectoral "mosaic" of France was certainly connected also to the fluid nature of its borders, which continued to expand and contract as a result of military vicissitudes.

These contexts are key to understanding the role of the intellectual in Napoleonic France. The "mosaic" of empire left open the possibility of adding or subtracting: its borders were constituted by changing political realities, and not by a national ideology. This created a space in which Arab intellectuals could function in Paris, at the center of a cosmopolitan Empire, adding themselves agglutinatively to the "national" without being compelled to articulate their exact relationship to the nation, whether in terms of linguistic, cultural, or ethnic identity. But they had to demonstrate very clearly their relationship to the *state*. Rather than becoming free and modernizing intellectuals, they found themselves transformed into an accepted, sometimes even favored minority, whose privileges rested upon their total disengagement from political self-representation. This position, then, was not radically different from that which they had occupied within the Ottoman system. Worse still, they found that their intellectual opportunities were caught between the instrumentalism of the state and the hostility of Orientalists such as Sacy toward anything that smacked in the slightest of modernization, vulgarization, or the dilution of the "perfection" of the Arabic language.

In this environment, Arab intellectuals in Paris had become in some sense the victims of their own preferment. In his long career, Taouïl seems to have produced only an Arabic manuscript translation of Aesop's fables.[77] Despite the feverish intellectual activity that we have noted, Rufa'il published nothing at all during the thirteen years of his employment at the École des Langues Orientales. Yet on his return to Egypt in 1816 Rufa'il rapidly published a series of important works, including an Arabic-Italian dictionary and numerous translations.[78] If Rufa'il had found his place in Paris through his association with the technical rationalism of Napoleonic administration, there is almost no indication at all that he was able to implement any of his projects. The distracted and even debauched behavior of which he was accused by Joseph Chammas might well be the result of this enforced paralysis. In the ultimate irony, he appeared in the official painting by Jacques-Louis David of Napoleon's coronation as emperor, dressed in a monkishly hooded red cape. It is evident that his role here was one of legitimation, as a Catholic priest.

The apparent exception to this rule was Bocthor's close friend Mikha'il Sabbagh, who, like Taouïl, found a niche as a protégé of Sacy. Sabbagh published a number of short works in Arabic throughout the Empire. Mikha'il was the son of Ibrahim al-Sabbagh of Acre, a highly influential counselor to Zahir al-'Umar, one of the regional governors in the Levant who had claimed greater regional autonomy from the Ottoman Porte during the late eighteenth century. Sabbagh had received a strong and traditional Arabic education with Coptic monks in Upper Egypt, and later with important figures from the Muslim 'ulama in Cairo and Damascus. This unusually broad apprenticeship across an Arabic cultural space made him a very unusual figure even among the educated members of the emigration. He was a favorite of Fourier and General Caffarelli during the French occupation and was made librarian to the Institut in Cairo.[79] Mikha'il Sabbagh's accomplishments in Arabic were of considerable utility to the growing collection of manuscripts in the Imperial Library. But, as his student Jean Humbert wrote later,

> M. Sabbagh, like so many other scholars, died in poverty, and without leaving enough even to pay for his own funeral. Had he been rich, he would have published several valuable works that he had written, such as a history of the Arab tribes of the desert, a history of Syria and Egypt, and a host of lovely poems. [80]

Sabbagh did publish several works, beginning with a poem about messenger pigeons, which was translated into French by Sylvestre de Sacy.[81] But after this promising start the rest of Mikha'il Sabbagh's published works were propaganda poems celebrating the key events that seemed to assure the legitimacy and longevity of the regime: the Concordat, the marriage of Napoleon and Marie-Louise, and the birth of their son, the king of Rome.[82]

This handful of works was rightly judged to be miserably below his real potential: they remained entirely trapped within the structures of clientelism from which he benefited. Humbert insisted that "he had so great a knowledge that our most erudite Orientalists often turned to him for enlightenment."[83] Silvestre de Sacy acknowledged a debt to Sabbagh on several occasions in his *Chrestomathie arabe*.[84] But for Sabbagh the Arabic language was not just an intellectual tableau; it was a living culture and an identity. In fact, the "valuable works" that Humbert mentions still exist in manuscript form: one work was a history of the events during Sabbagh's grandfather's time in Acre, entitled *Tarikh Zahir al-'Umar al-Zaidani*. Thomas Philipp has identified this work as a new development of historical consciousness with considerable significance for the development of modern Arab cultural identity, an intellectual orientation that aligns Sabbagh with other contemporaneous Arab writers, particularly among the Melkite community of Syria and Egypt.[85] For Philipp, Sabbagh's text presents a "new view of the world and the self" that abandoned the traditional annalistic form of history (still found, for example, in the histories of Jabarti) for a new style focusing on particular themes, communities, and sets of events conceived as historical topoi. This focus was even clearer in Sabbagh's other manuscript, *Tarikh Ibrahim*, which treated the history of his own family in relation to the events in Acre. Philipp suggests that Sabbagh had begun collecting oral histories, and developing a manuscript written by his uncle, even before his emigration to France.

But Sabbagh clearly found no place to advance such new styles of thought or such ideas about his own Arab history within the "cosmopolitan" environment of imperial Paris. Instead he became little more than a creator of propaganda. His ambitions were effectively crushed between the authoritarian instrumentalism of the Napoleonic state and the conservative establishment of French Orientalism. While his mobility had brought him to synthesize many of the indigenous developments of an Arabic culture with the modernizing impulses he had encountered under the French occupation of Egypt, the reality of intellectual life in the French empire was scarcely less constrictive than that which he had experienced under the Ottomans.

During his first decade in France, Ellious Bocthor wrote repeatedly to Sabbagh expressing his fervent desire to join him in the capital, begging for books and other materials to which Sabbagh had access, and complaining of the infighting and jealousies of the parochial community in Marseille. It seems likely that Bocthor had projected onto Paris ideas that he had formed in Egypt, of the value placed on modernizing knowledge, the freedom of expression and thought, the equality of citizens. When he arrived in the capital he found a vastly different city from the one he had imagined. He collided with the limits of Napoleonic cosmopolitanism, or rather, I would suggest, with its very *structure*. The police response, however, was not simply a "xenophobic" reaction of distrust toward foreigners. Indeed, on the whole, the administration had showed itself very ready to prefer and promote these "foreigners" under the right conditions.

Bocthor's reception highlighted a phenomenon we may call "repressive cosmopolitanism." Imperial Paris quite openly fostered cultural difference where this embellished and did not challenge the ruling order. Cosmopolitanism, in this context, reflected an imperial politics aligned with other major multiethnic continental empires of the period, the Ottoman and Austro-Hungarian, rather than assimilable to the colonial model of the British Empire, for example. This form of cosmopolitanism was, to echo Pamela Ballinger's observation on Habsburg Trieste, "a validation of an imperial context that favored the fortunes of . . . [the] elite, rather than the universalistic outlook and celebration of diversity often implied by the term."[86]

The difference in Paris, however, was that this "imperial context" also carried the legacy of the Enlightenment and Revolution, with their powerful ideological claims. It was these universalist and modernizing claims that drew Bocthor and other intellectuals to France. Like others, Bocthor soon found that the reality of power, and the instrumentalization of knowledge, in imperial Paris were very different from what he had seen in Egypt. What these exiles hoped to do in Paris (as exiled intellectuals from other lands would do after them) was to "modernize" the culture and teaching of their own language, in the intersection between their own cultural politics and that of postrevolutionary France. What they encountered instead was the entrenched resistance of elites and a pronounced lack of interest from a government they had expected to be modern and enlightened, but that was more concerned with the pragmatic realities of running an empire.

Bocthor returned to Marseille in 1811, disappointed by his discovery of the real workings of Napoleonic cosmopolitanism. The following year, he returned to Paris, where he remained until his death in 1820. This time, however, he sought a position as a state functionary, translating correspondence of the Egyptian campaign from Arabic into French: a far more acceptable and "useful" role. He also served on occasion to provide translation and advice to various ministries, particularly where there were questions as to the origins of Arabic-speaking individuals. There is no indication that he experienced any further vexations from the police; his role in the capital was henceforth assured by his official "utility." During the remaining years of the Empire, he continued to work in the Depot as an inconspicuous clerk—a rather disappointing finale, it would seem, after the grand ambitions with which he had set out.

But the success and the opportunity that Bocthor craved would come to him from a very unexpected quarter. The end of the Napoleonic system in Europe might have been expected to bring nothing but calamity to these Egyptians so closely associated with the emperor. But this was not quite the case, for reasons we will seek to understand in the subsequent chapters of this book. In 1816, when the pensions of the refugees were reduced across the board by the Restoration authorities, Rufa'il was furious to discover that his salary had also been lowered. In a fit of pique he resigned from the École des Langues Orientales and returned to Egypt. There, however, he became a highly influential figure in the translation movement sponsored by Muhammad 'Ali. In Egypt he found the opportunity he had lost in France to develop and publish some of his modernizing ideas, at least those that were favored by the Egyptian regime. In Paris, his post in colloquial Arabic remained empty, and the death of Mikha'il Sabbagh soon afterward removed the most obvious candidate for the position.

In 1819, an official from the Ministry of the Interior met Bocthor by chance at the home of Edmé-François Jomard and wrote to Langlès expressing his surprise that this talented Egyptian had been so ignored:

> This morning at M. Jomard's I met an Arab, Elious Bouctour *[sic]*, who has made applications at various points but has received nothing here in France but a small allowance that he is paid at the Ministry of War. The Ministry of the Interior could usefully employ him if he were to give a course in colloquial Arabic—which is rather under a cloud with the Arabists, but which is eminently suitable for our plans to improve relations in the Levant. This seems to me very worthy of attention. If you speak to M. Jomard about M. Bouctour, you will see much better how capable this foreigner is. He is full of ardor and courage. It is my duty to bring such men and such ideas to your attention; you will best know how to follow up this matter. [87]

On seeking an opinion from Jomard, Langlès received a surprisingly personal encomium:

> He is of even greater interest through his devotion and his troubles than through his learning. The work that he has recently finished would do honor to a member of an academy: it is a French-Arabic and Arabic-French dictionary on the model of that of the Académie Française.[88]

If Bocthor was now "this foreigner" rather than a "new Frenchman," the embrace of his talents *as a foreigner* indicates the shift toward a different kind of cultural politics in Restoration France, whose ambivalences we must explore in the chapters that follow.

On 8 December 1819, Ellious Bocthor, now identified as "Égyptien, professeur," stood on the stage of the auditorium in the École des Langues Orientales, in front of an audience filled with the intellectual luminaries of Paris. He delivered a grand address inaugurating his course in colloquial Arabic, and despite the conventional rhetoric of such a discourse, he took careful aim at the cultural politics that had so constrained his career. While weaving his praise of the Egyptian expedition together delicately with appropriate admiration for the restored monarch, he did not fail to mention the "spirit of denigration" that, he suggested, had attacked the universalist civilizational conception of the expedition. His chief target was the teaching of Arabic as a "dead language." Certain members of the audience must have shifted in their seats as he weighed forcefully upon the relation between Frenchmen and *real* Arabs, in a reciprocal bond of respect that demanded communication and mutual knowledge: "It is such knowledge," he declared, "that determines, at least in part, whether the nation to which a merchant or agent belongs is held in admiration or contempt in a foreign land." In suggesting that Frenchmen might be held in contempt for their lack of cultural expertise, Bocthor was confidently presenting his own relationship to Orientalism as a reciprocal one. He continued:

> In the Orient, as in the Occident, the world reasons the same way, judging a whole people by a single individual. And are they wrong to think thus, when we know that it often takes just one man to found or to topple empires—and sometimes to do both together—to enslave or liberate a people, to bring them happiness or misfortune?[89]

This philosophical question could only have brought to mind the figure of Napoleon. Bocthor's words suggest his profound ambivalence toward the emperor—Bonaparte had promised liberation and the toppling of empires, only to restore slavery and found an empire of his own in which Bocthor's ambitions had been so heavily disappointed.

But this question perhaps also implicated Bocthor's own individual path and tied it to the destiny of a whole population of "Egyptians," a people who, as he insisted in his speech, "through the vivacity of their imagination and the generosity of their sentiments seem born rather on the banks of the Rhône or the Seine, than on those of the Nile."[90] This conception of a population uniting elements of both Egypt and France—crucially, in their "imagination" and their "sentiments"— seems to come close to the articulation of a space he had been unable to find in Napoleonic Paris, between the unwelcome attentions of the police and the cold shoulder of the Orientalist establishment. Strangely, this articulation seemed possible in the changed atmosphere of the Restoration. Bocthor made a delicate allusion to Marseille *and* Paris, through the rivers that served as routes of travel as well as axes of cities, although he made no direct reference to the hundreds of Egyptians and Syrians who had settled in France after 1801. As we will see, there were very good reasons for him not to do so.

Bocthor closed his oration with an appropriate encomium for the government that had promoted him:

> Which government, besieged by the most terrible troubles, has better succeeded in defending national dignity and independence? It is said that the Roman Senate awarded triumphant honors to one of its generals who did not despair of the Republic even after the loss of a great battle. What homages and what gratitude do we not owe to a monarch who has brought the ship of state safely into port through so many storms?[91]

If Bocthor's praise seems effusive, these closing words of his speech still contained a strong echo of the revolutionary and republican sympathies that had first inspired his decision to come to France. The "Rome" of which he spoke was very different from that repeatedly invoked to legitimate the Napoleonic system —the Rome of the Republic rather than that of the Empire. That he could do so without fear suggests the rapid repoliticization of French society in these early years of the government of Louis XVIII, who sought very much to steer a course between liberals and ultras.

But Bocthor's words also evoked trouble and loss, and the "storms" that had beset France over a period of wrenching changes of regime, wars, and invasion. His anecdote described a kind of "victory" that consisted only in keeping faith despite terrible loss and defeat. The years that intervened between 1811 and 1819 brought with them a shattering political transition for all French men and women. For Ellious Bocthor, as for other Arabs living in France, these events had a very particular and violent meaning, one that transformed forever their relationship to the state, to the wider society, and among themselves. It is to that dark chapter that we must now turn.

5

Massacre and Restoration

On the night of 25 June 1815, an angry mob surged through the streets of Marseille baying for Egyptian blood. The pogrom had begun as a settling of political scores with the Bonapartists, who had dominated this royalist stronghold under the Empire, and again during the Hundred Days of Napoleon's return to power from his exile on Elba. But it rapidly took on a racial cast. Intoxicated by violence, the crowd accompanying the royalist militias began to focus their fury upon easier targets, those whose color or dress marked them out as guilty. Within hours, dozens lay butchered in the streets and in the sea at the edge of the town. The killing lasted for more than a day, taking on the rhythm of systematic destruction. The Egyptian village of the cours Gouffé was burned to the ground, never to be rebuilt. If events seemed to be moving too fast for the authorities to control, this pogrom, like so many others throughout modern history, could not have unfolded without their collaboration, passive or active. When Marseille fell quiet at last, the new regime sought to efface the nasty memory of its violent beginnings by blaming the victims. The town authorities incarcerated hundreds "for their own protection," while leaving the murderers to walk free in the streets. If, in the years that followed, the events of the massacre gained some notoriety as a political weapon used by Bonapartists against the restored Bourbon monarchy, when the opposition acceded to power once again this uncomfortable memory of racial violence in France passed into silence, becoming nothing more than a footnote in official history.

The period that unfolded from the beginning of 1814 was an extraordinarily difficult one for many people in France. In April, the military failure of the Napoleonic regime became evident, and the emperor abdicated, leaving the way open for a British-backed restoration of the Bourbon monarchy. The later months of 1814 saw the initial *mise en place* of the new Restoration regime under Louis XVIII, governed by a relatively hastily assembled charter whose status— whether it was a true constitution or a benevolent dispensation by the monarch— was never fully clear for the next decade and a half.[1] But the exile of Napoleon to the island of Elba, intended to minimize the divisions in France, left him in a position to exploit the failure of the monarchy to consolidate its support across the country. Napoleon's landing on the Mediterranean coast in March 1815 led to a period of one hundred days that would destabilize the political structure of the nation. Many of those who had initially pledged themselves to the reestablished "legitimacy" of the Bourbons, including many of the liberals who were seduced by Napoleon's apparent enthusiasm for ideas he had previously proscribed, now changed camps for the second time.[2] But the "liberal Empire" turned out to be a short-lived illusion, and the defeat at Waterloo saw Bonaparte the "usurper" exiled more securely to Saint Helena, where he died in 1821.

The problem of the Restoration, as many historians have observed, was primarily one of forgetting. The Charter of 1814 forbade all "investigation into opinions or votes given prior to the Restoration."[3] But the rapid changes of allegiance over the months that followed made such mandated forgetting impossible and opened just the space of recriminatory violence the first Restoration had hoped to forestall. As Alan Spitzer has observed, "In no era in modern French history, save possibly the post-Vichy era, have past political commitments been recollected with such ferocious intensity."[4] Those who changed allegiance with dizzying rapidity were satirized as *girouettes*, or weathervanes, that pointed wherever the prevailing wind was blowing. In the frontispiece of César Proisy d'Eppe's *Dictionnaire des girouettes,* a figure decorated with the Légion d'Honneur and the Croix Saint-Louis, the tricolor rosette and the Bourbon insignia, was shown signing up to a rotating windmill of political commitments. Below this figure, a proverb from a Persian poet, Saahdi, declared cynically: "If the plague gave pensions, the plague too would have its toadies and flatterers."[5] This piece of "Oriental" wisdom could not have been more applicable to the position of the Arab population in France. Relying on state pensions for their survival, they were indissolubly bound to the center of power as its "toadies and flatterers." At the same time, the Arab presence in France was inevitably connected to a single regime, even to a single man, Napoleon Bonaparte. The privileged relation of Arabs to the state became almost overnight the most dangerous liability, one that would destabilize every element of their existence.

The responses of the populations in Marseille, Melun, and Paris to the First Restoration in 1814 were at first sight very different. In Melun, the active military elite of the Arab population was divided between a majority who embraced the new Bourbon regime and a minority who held stalwartly to their commitment to

Bonaparte. There was nothing surprising in this: as Natalie Petiteau has shown, such a response was common among French soldiers as a whole. As she argues, "If it is incontestable that some veterans maintained an unwavering support for the dynasty of the Bonapartes, the group was not unanimous in its attitude: its members were undoubtedly much more caught up in communitarian conflicts where their identity as former soldiers was not necessarily to the fore, although it might well be a source of solidarity."[6] These "communitarian conflicts," as we have seen, were very strongly in evidence among the Arab population, and Petiteaus's observation can be applied for our purposes with equal accuracy. The figure of the "Mamelouk" suggested a fanatical partisan of Napoleon (which persisted as a proverbial description into the Second Empire),[7] but real Arab soldiers, like other soldiers, tended to follow the loyalties of their community.

In January 1814, Joseph Ibrahim wrote from 355, rue Saint-Honoré that "all the soldiers who were retired have been called to take up service again in their former corps."[8] Like him, many of the soldiers dispatched into retirement at Marseille had now been summoned back to Paris. Accordingly, many of those who had taken the road to Marseille retraced their path to the capital. Stationed close to Fontainebleau, they were naturally more closely tied to the emperor than were soldiers in Bordeaux and Paris, where the royalist agitators were working hard to convince the population that the Empire was a dead letter. There were those among the Mamelouks who felt an undying personal loyalty to the emperor: some even followed Napoleon into exile on Elba, including Pietro Ruggieri and Séraphine Bagdoune, and these men were later kept under surveillance by the Restoration authorities for their "troublesome views."[9] Others, however, refused to accompany Napoleon to the island: the famous Roustam Raza, the emperor's personal Mameluke, preferred instead to move to Paris and open a lottery bureau, something that appeared "quite extraordinary" to the new royalist chief of police.[10]

If Roustam was found unexpectedly to prefer his own family and interests over the "cult of Napoleon," others more definitively turned their coats. Youssef Hamaouy in particular arrived in Paris with dispatch on 4 April, before Napoleon had left Fontainebleau. According to the comte de Semallé, he swore the oath of allegiance to the king and offered not only to bring over the entire Mamelouk corps, but to deliver Napoleon's head "in a sack." He based this possibility on the unlimited trust placed in the Mamelouk soldiers who guarded the emperor's personal rooms; it would seem that even Napoleon himself had been convinced by the maxim that these soldiers were devoted and fanatical partisans, rather than individuals with their own shifting political commitments, their own ties of family and community.

Semallé indicated that he rejected Hamaouy's proposition, "which had so little in common with our Christian ideas and our mode of understanding of royal power."[11] He noted that Hamaouy was not a Muslim, but still interpreted his actions as representing "Oriental" ideas of royal absolutism, which held the king as beyond criminal reproach, having the right of life and death over his subjects, and to whom the life of a "usurper" was forfeit. It is difficult to determine the real meaning of this private conversation, which may have had no more concrete reality than Marshall Ney's famous promise to bring Napoleon back to Paris in an "iron cage." Despite the aspersions cast on his character, Hamaouy, unlike Ney, remained loyal to his word and after Napoleon's return from Elba fled to the Spanish border to avoid the pursuit of the civil and military police.[12] Hamaouy was rewarded for his services with the rank of colonel, the Legion of Honor, and the Cross of Saint-Louis, partly as a result of his involvement in the shady "affaire Maubreuil," which involved the hijacking of the carriage of Queen Catherine of Westphalia, wife of Jérôme Bonaparte, in order to seize her valuable jewels for the new regime.[13]

Hamaouy sought in the transition of power a redress of his grievances in regard to his changed position in the community. In the expatriation from Egypt, Hamaouy was mentioned alongside the other notable figures by Jabarti: he was the commander of the "Syrian Janissaries" during the French occupation.[14] In France, however, he found his position very different. Six officers of the Mamelouk corps had written to Rapp, the chief of brigade, in June 1802, declaring that they would refuse to serve under the command of "Egyptian leaders who understand nothing of military practice in France."[15] They threatened to resign their commissions if forced to serve their former leaders, Ya'qub Habaïby and Youssef Hamaouy. The rebellious officers were drawn from different auxiliary corps during the Egyptian campaign, and from very different origins: for example, Lieutenant Chahine was originally Georgian, drawn from the *mamluk* elite in Cairo; Captain Ibrahim was a Christian who originated from Deir-el-Qamr in Mount Lebanon. Neither had previously served under these commanders, and the imposition of such figures upon these men seems to have promoted considerable resistance. Habaïby and Hamaouy were kept in retirement with generous pensions: four thousand francs annually for Habaïby and three thousand for Hamaouy.[16] Habaïby settled at Melun and maintained his ties there. He reentered military service in 1818 and finally moved to the affluent Chaussée d'Antin quarter of Paris.

Habaïby could weather the storm because of his close links to the military establishment. Hamaouy's relations, in contrast, were merchants in Marseille; his brother Antun Hamaouy later bought a five-hectare property in the town.[17] Youssef Hamaouy himself had married a French woman and had six children, in addition to a son from a previous marriage. Leaving this large family behind in Marseille, however, he continued to live officially in Paris. Jean Savant notes that he changed address a dozen times between 1814 and 1825; given his situation, it seems probable that he traveled back and forth between the two cities.[18] Hamaouy's chief object was to seek compensation from the government for the losses he had sustained in joining the French in Syria, which could also restore his position in the community at a time when that status was so bitterly contested. His early decision to defect to the royalist camp was thus largely based on the internal politics of the community, and indeed, he did succeed in bringing a considerable number of the Mamelouk officers to swear allegiance to the Bourbons, which restored his influence for a short time.

But the return of Napoleon, and the hundred days that followed, threw these choices into confusion. Several of the Mamelouks rejoined the emperor's party. Others, however, were forced to take refuge. Moussa Istoui was part of the royalist army that resisted Napoleon's return as he marched through Sisteron toward Grenoble. In a petition to the Ministry of War, Moussa wrote that he had "suffered as a fugitive during all the time the Usurper was in France."[19] These choices were probably as much economic as ideological: Moussa complained of the high cost of subsistence in the Midi and in 1816 "walked one hundred leagues on foot from Marseille to Paris . . . reduced to misery and almost naked."[20] In an atmosphere of economic crisis and dissatisfaction, many such deserters looked to the new regime to provide for them. They provided the main support for the royalist hopes of seizing and maintaining power.

But if economic difficulties could play a role in the political choices of members of the Arab community, they were not always determining factors. There was undoubtedly a significant core of political allegiance to the Empire and the figure of the emperor himself, particularly in Marseille. According to many contemporary accounts, the Egyptians played a prominent role in the ceremonies that followed the retaking of the city by Bonapartists after Napoleon's landing. But even the most sympathetic observers tended not to view this allegiance as a political demonstration, but rather as a show of "Oriental" fanaticism, an idea that was always ready at hand. Joseph Méry pleaded on behalf of the "ardor of their Oriental enthusiasm for Napoleon their father," a childlike simplicity that failed to understand the political complexities of the inveterate Marseillais hatred toward Bonaparte. Méry continued:

> During the Hundred Days, in every revue, at the head of every civic march, on the doorstep of every Bonapartist café, in the public square where the military bands played national songs, there were always a dozen or so Mamelouks who mingled menacing gestures, and a refrain of Oriental insults against royalists listening nearby, with their patriotic songs.[21]

But these "Orientals" were certainly no strangers to the intricacies of communal politics, and it is likely that they understood the Marseillais context in which they had lived for a decade and a half. Indeed, it is quite possible that these manifestations by the retired veterans, surviving on a fraction of the pensions of the notables, were aimed as much at their own community leaders—leaders, we should recall, who had collaborated with the authorities to have just such rowdy "troublemakers" arrested in 1807. In the absence of testimony by any witness who could understand what they were shouting in Arabic, it is impossible to discern fully the political and social motives behind their aggressive partisanship toward the emperor.

What is clear, however, is that these demonstrations played an important role in hardening Marseillais hostility toward these "fanatical Egyptians." The withdrawal of General Verdier's troops from Marseille on 25 June 1815 left the city undefended against attacks by the royalist gangs that had already entered the previous day. A hastily composed town committee had at its disposal only seven hundred National Guard and less than one hundred police.[22] Verdier's sudden and inexplicable withdrawal left the partisans of the emperor exposed to violence. The "Egyptians" visible in the town, whatever their individual role had been in the previous months, became the most immediate target for the royalist gangs, and the angry crowds who gathered alongside them. None of those who had participated in the festivities of the Hundred Days were identified or targeted by name; they were referred to only as "Egyptians" or "Mamelouks."

But the first to be attacked were two women identified as "négresses." As we saw in chapter 2, color, and in particular these women of color, had played an important role in defining the status of the Egyptian refugees, and their assumption of a kind of consistorial responsibility in line with other accepted minorities in Napoleonic France. The privileges associated with that status, such as the pension accorded them as refugees, the appointment of an Arabic professor, and other provisions such as medical services, served as an easy focus for resentment about unequal conditions under the Empire. But the question of color at the edges of the population assumed a more threatening complexion, associated with the violent reimposition of slavery and its failure in Saint Domingue. The authorities had been very clear that the restoration of slavery also entailed a new prohibition on the residence of "people of color" in France. The decree of 1802 returned to force the law of 1777, which declared:

> The Negroes are multiplying every day in France. They marry Europeans, the houses of prostitution are infected by them; the colors mix, the blood is changing . . . these slaves, if they return to America, bring with them the spirit of freedom, independence, and equality, which they communicate to others.[23]

It was this intersection between race and politics that fostered the excesses of violence visited against this minority in Marseille in 1815: a violent rejection of racial difference, conceived through color, combined with a political proscription visited on these putative "fanatical Bonapartists" by the transitional authorities. Laurent Lautard, a royalist recruited to the National Guard, reflected something of this explosive mixture of racial, sexual, and political vilification in his description, which remained aggressively racist thirty years later:

Two Ethiopian negresses, disgusting and almost nude, disturbed the public square with unintelligible vociferations, mixed with the name of Bonaparte, their Providence and their God. The wildest of these women, the dregs of the Egyptian colony, as of the human race, howled after the deposed idol like the she-wolf after her cubs, provoking murder in her stupid frenzy, murder incarnate. Driven to the edge of the quay, she fell into the water, struggled convulsively, still crying out; a bullet struck her forehead, and she disappeared.[24]

Lautard's account reduced the cries of the woman to inarticulate, inhuman screams and then blamed this very abjectness as a "provocation" to the crowd. In another account, by Charles Durand, the confrontation was far more politically explicit. According to Durand, the crowd insisted that the woman cry "Vive le Roi!" but she refused, trying instead to utter a different cry ("Vive . . .") , which was cut short by the thrusts of a bayonet.[25] Joseph Méry completed the woman's foreshortened cry, reporting that the persecuted woman threw herself into the water to escape, while crying "Vive l'Empereur!" As a convinced Bonapartist, Méry instinctively transformed the scene into one of heroic martyrdom. "When she disappeared under the water," he wrote, "she held her hand raised above, as though to complete with her signs the cry that she had begun."[26] The evidence of that political belonging and agency among these people should not be downplayed; it appears across a number of accounts with different political colorings. It may be that these political frames helped make this racial violence more intelligible on both sides. But it is true that these women displayed a great deal of independence in their conduct, and such intense partisanship is by no means impossible.[27]

Soon afterward, an elderly black man was murdered on the rue Lancerie. Léon Gozlan reported later that the black population of the city went into hiding, afraid to show themselves in public; those whose skin was dark began to wear signs reading in the Provençal dialect *Siou pa négré*—"I am not black."[28] Gozlan read this as a "burlesque" reflection of their helpless confusion, their failure to comprehend the real motives of the violence against them. Of course, the signs, if they existed, were hardly likely to have any efficacity in protecting their wearers. But it is also possible to read these signs as a frantic response to the entanglement of racial and political violence. The signs did not so much address *color* as *juridical statute*: they were a desperate attempt to insist on the individuals' status as "Egyptian" people of color, rather than *nègres*, a category intimately linked to slavery, and completely denuded of rights.

Political violence and murders were carried out against a number of individuals. Charles Durand wrote that he was warned that he had been seen too often at the home of the Bonapartist General Brune.[29] According to Gozlan, once that purge had been carried out, the next target for the crowd was the highly visible "village" near the cours Gouffé where a large number of Syrians and Egyptians had built their dwellings and planted their gardens. This time there was no attempt to identify individuals accused of specific crimes: the target was the population itself. It was reported later that the attack was too rapid for the "forces of order" to intervene. By the time they returned, Durand wrote, "the massacre of the Mamelouks had been general; a large number of soldiers had been killed, several houses looted, corpses lay here and there in the streets and in the squares."[30] But there is evidence from the authorities themselves that they participated, at least in a symbolic way, in the preliminaries to this violence. An unsigned author (very likely a member of the unofficial Comité Royale Provisoire) wrote in an account of the events to the interior minister:

> Later that night, the capitulation of General Verdier was announced to the people by the light of flaming torches, and the mayor in person ordered the townspeople, in the name of the king, to respect property and not to raise a finger against any soldier who had not been able to follow his commanders.[31]

The explicit orders given to protect property and to respect the soldiers under arms—but not the population—suggest an implicit legitimation of the murders carried out in the purge. The authorities were frightened by popular fury—one official wrote later: "I am sitting on a volcano here"—but their strategic silence and the official presence at the torchlight assembly clearly gave the violence a symbolic legitimacy.

Two days of looting and destruction followed. Joseph Méry, a member of the National Guard, wrote that "the gutters were red with blood . . . our feet stumbled against corpses . . . [and] the sight of the graveyard of Mamelouks, slaughtered in the oasis of their village, met our eyes."[32] For those who survived among the poor inhabitants on the outskirts of the city, the burning of their houses, the destruction of their gardens, and the pillage of their small businesses were devastating. Saad Chaate, a former domestic servant to General Ya'qub, found the two tobacconists' shops that he had rented "entirely looted by an uprising of the population."[33] He estimated his losses at 21,000 francs. He "owed his salvation only to the rapidity of his flight into the mountains." His wife, Hamia, an African woman, had given birth only a few months earlier and must have fled with the child in her arms.[34]

According to Gozlan's account, the Egyptian community was that day celebrating the marriage of Ibrahim-el-Mansour and Maria Damanhoury when the news reached them of these killings at the port; they fled in a convoy toward the mountains a few miles away. Méry confirmed their flight: "The majority of the Mamelouks who composed the colony," he reported, "very luckily escaped into the woods near Mazargues; they left in a caravan, men, women, children, led by a majestic old man with a long white beard."[35] Gozlan described more evocatively the testimonies he collected later: "The peasants who saw them passing, at sunset, fleeing in such a procession, most in their Oriental clothing, turbans, cloaks, their Turkish slippers dragging, have recounted to me the desolation of these poor people—their fervent prayers, their tears, and their signs of the cross."[36] Another band of royalists, according to Gozlan, continued to persecute those escaping, murdering anyone who fell behind the main group, throwing them from the rocks or hanging them from branches. A few days later, he wrote, "the beach at Montredon was choked with corpses."[37]

Joseph Méry was among those who brought "these unfortunate creatures camped on the hills, awaiting death from starvation," back to the city. He described the scene he witnessed:

A company of the Garde Urbaine left at ten in the evening to offer them asylum and protection. I had the honor to take part in this expedition, as it was one of the few consolations that refreshed our spirits during these days of grief. These poor people, surprised in the middle of the night, let out cries of terror at our approach and threw themselves at our knees, begging for their lives. They were soon reassured by seeing the respect we showed toward the old men and the care we took with their children.[38]

Lautard described a different scene on the beach at Montredon, where the company of M. Lazare Estien arrived with bayonets, terrifying the Egyptians who had fled there; finally, they were convinced to accompany the soldiers back to the town, where they were imprisoned in the Fort Saint-Jean "for their safety."[39] Joseph Nakacly confirmed these arrests, reporting that "in 1815, because of his opinions, he was detained for several months at the Palais de Justice in Marseille with 3,500 other unfortunates of different classes and in the same situation as him."[40] In August the prefect claimed that the people threatened to punish the prisoners themselves, and maintained them in detention.[41]

It is difficult to estimate with any accuracy the numbers killed in the Arab community in Marseille during these days. From the police bulletins, Daniel Resnick has found evidence that at least twelve were killed on 25 June[42]—though perhaps many more victims went unrecorded. Edouard Saman, himself a descendant of the Melkite community in Marseille, has suggested plausibly that only those victims who belonged to the more respectable families were officially reported.[43] Gozlan insisted that the total population was reduced by two-thirds. But he could not explain what had happened to most of them—always inclined to the picturesque, he imagined them escaping to Genoa, or washed out to sea, back to Egypt.[44] Lautard insisted that "the honorable and civilized portion of the Egyptian emigration, which lived in the *quartier* of la Plaine, were not disturbed in any way. Afterward, this esteemed class of the refugees melted into the commercial population of Marseille."[45]

Lautard insisted on the distinction between this group, the "Copts who carried on an honorable commerce in the town," and another group, "the horde of miserable negros and Moors, the scum of the human species, who had lived from Bonaparte's crumbs."[46] Lautard's relentless conflation of political opprobrium with racial and religious vilification demonstrates just how dangerous were the edges of the "Egyptian" identity in Marseille even years after the events of 1815. The reports of the time concurred in Lautard's attempt to separate an acceptable fraction of the population from a mass who were utterly undeserving of rights: "Among the refugees who make up the *dépôt*," one official wrote, "there a few respectable individuals who never shared in the evil done by the others, and who continue in their good character, but in general these foreigners have made themselves detested by the population of this city, and it would be better to send them away in order to calm the anxieties their presence causes."[47]

Given the strength of the divisions among the "Egyptians" of Marseille, and the bitter conflicts they had created, we might well have expected to see in these days of 1815 the final dissolution of whatever little remained of the "community." This is how Lautard saw the meaning and resolution of the violence: the "redeemable" group among the immigrants was absorbed into the surrounding society, while the "dangerous classes" were killed or fled the city. Gozlan did not disagree in substance with this conclusion. Yet instead of confirming the separation between the different classes of "refugee," the violence seems to have given rise to a much greater solidarity across these divisions, as we shall see.

There is little evidence for Gozlan's claim of the virtual destruction of the "Egyptian" population in the massacres of 1815. According to the refugee register of 1834, almost twenty years later, 317 refugees remained on the list at Marseille and elsewhere.[48] After 1815 no more children were admitted to the register, and for boys admitted after 1810, their entitlements ended at the age of eighteen.[49] Since no new names were added to the list, and others had died or lost their entitlement, it would seem that a large group of those on the original refugee lists survived and continued to collect their pensions over the next two decades. Their many children increased the population considerably, and many young men continued to study the language of their parents at the Lycée, under the tutelage of Gabriel Taouïl. Why then did Gozlan imagine that they had been destroyed? It seems certain that it was rather the *visible* presence of the "Egyptians" in Marseille that disappeared after 1815; instead, they found new modes of accommodation in the city.

Political transition was not the only change to affect the Arab population of Marseille during this period. The collapse of the Empire sent tremors across most of Europe, and its effects were felt beyond the shores of the European continent. The tensions between the Greek Orthodox and the breakaway Uniate Catholic Melkites became even greater in Syria and Lebanon. With the loss of the prestige and influence that the French formerly wielded, Catholics were more exposed to persecution from the Orthodox Church. The restoration of Mediterranean trade now revealed the significant shift of economic power from Asia to Europe that had taken place over the preceding decades.[50] Persecutions of Catholics in Syria produced a stream of new Arab immigrants who "came to Marseille to increase the colony that commerce had already formed there," according to Polycarpe Kayata.[51] By 1821, the community of Melkites had reached sufficient numbers for them to apply to build their own church of Saint Nicolas de Myre in the city. The deliberations of the municipal council of Marseille in January 1821 reported that there were around 450 Greek Catholics in Marseille at the time, and that this number "may increase considerably by the necessity of emigration from various trading *échelles* in the Levant due to the persecution of which the Catholics of this rite have recently become the object. It is also generally true that commerce attracts many Greeks into our town for short periods, many of whom are Catholic."[52] The building of the church was approved by the government; its funding was raised by the Arab families of the town. The Sakakini, Hamaouy, Homsy, and Zidan families provided almost 15,000 francs between them, while Marie Namé herself provided 2,000 francs, and the remainder of the Arab families almost 4,000.[53]

In the revivalist Catholic atmosphere of the Restoration, the Melkite church served to shelter the Arab population from the hostilities they had experienced in 1815. A number of Muslim Arabs, most notably 'Abd el-Al, were converted to Christianity by the patriarch Maximos Mazloum, who took up residence there in 1821. This united the elite of the emigration, old and new, into a single community defined by its common adherence to the Arab liturgy practiced in the church. Melkite religious services in Marseille had been provided previously by Gabriel Taouïl, who was now free to concentrate his energies on the teaching of Arabic language to the children of these families. Was this then a sign of the contraction of this mobile and multilocal community to the environs of Marseille, to the limits of its sectarian identity, and to the comfortable, depoliticized circle of family and social connections?

The edification of this church during the Restoration should not be seen purely as an act of religious faith; it was also a political act of negotiation with the new regime, one that reformulated an identity placed in immediate danger by the visible difference of the "Egyptians" of Bonaparte. Where the civilizing narrative and personal connections to the Egyptian expedition had been the key to political negotiation with the imperial regime, now the connections with Catholicism, and in particular the Holy Land, had a new political and cultural valency—from the Catholic revival missions described by Sheryl Kroen to Chateaubriand's journey to Jerusalem.[54]

We can see the potency of these reidentifications on 28 July 1816, only a year after royalist crowds were slaughtering "Egyptians" in Marseille, when Abdallah

Hasboune (see fig. 13 in chapter 6) was received by Louis XVIII in a personal audience. According to the *Journal de Savoie,* Abdallah had previously presented a verse to the king:

> Très-éloigné de ma patrie
> C'est sur cette terre chérie
> Qu'heureux pour la première fois
> Je vois enfin mon Roi
>
> [So far away from my country
> It is in this beloved land
> That filled with joy for the first time
> I see my King at last]

If not great poetry, this was excellent politics. Abdallah cleverly drew attention to his Palestinian origins, and by inference, as the *Journal de Savoie* kindly pointed out, he "made reference to the title of 'King of Jerusalem' that our sovereigns have borne since Charles I."[55] The king was reported to have discussed with him the French campaign in the Holy Land and waxed lyrical on the "great and pious memories that this land evokes."[56] Abdallah had married a Frenchwoman and altered his name to D'Asbonne to evoke an aristocratic lineage. However, despite his sycophantic poem, he clearly held on to some subterranean opinions: they were signaled as "troublesome" according to a police report of 1820.[57] Youssef Hamaouy, too, sought to have himself recognized as "the nephew of Agabius, patriarch of Antioch, and Athanasius, patriarch of the Orient," allying himself with a Christian heritage in the Levant.[58]

Others, too, saw the change of regime as an opportunity to alter their circumstances: Mikha'il Sabbagh, the Arab scholar working at the Bibliothèque Impériale (now Royale) wrote to "His Most Christian Majesty," seeking to be granted the Cross of Saint-Louis, because "with this signal honor I will be able to seek through the Porte the restitution of a part of my property."[59] He provided proofs that he was from "one of the first families of Syria" certified by the Orientalist Sylvestre de Sacy and signed by Rufa'il, Georges Aïdé, Captain Ibrahim, Youhanna Chiftichi, Elias Pharaon, and Youssef Hamaouy.[60] This list of signatories tells us something about the consolidation of the elite that had occurred since 1811: it drew together Copts and Melkites, intellectuals, merchants, and military personnel. Such common subscriptions to the petitions of other members of the community would become increasingly common after 1815. By 1820, the "Depot of Egyptian Refugees" in the Midi had its own council, its church, its Arabic language course, and even its own doctor, Barthélemy-Joseph-Pierre Méffre, who identified himself as their "official physician" in the dissertation on the effects of coffee that he published in Montpellier that year.[61] It seemed in certain ways as though the "Arab France" of the late Empire, defined by cosmopolitanism, mobility, and the search for a

Franco-Arab identity, had been replaced by a small, settled migrant community in the provincial surroundings of Marseille.

But Léon Gozlan wondered in 1866 what had happened to the rest of the population. That had disappeared from Marseille in 1815. He conjectured that they had dispersed from Marseille back across the Mediterranean. In fact, the evidence indicates that the main response of flight was to the north, in the direction of Paris. Many of those whom Gozlan considered to have been lost in the violent days of 25–26 June in fact fled to the capital, where they found an easier invisibility in a crowded city, and some support while they considered their future. Ibrahim Saleh, for example, left Marseille at this time. He wrote that "the circumstances fallen upon us in the last few months forced me against my will to leave in order to avoid by my flight a horrible end."[62] Madame Chamin-Abdallah fled to Melun with three children "at the time when the attack occurred in Marseille."[63] Elias Barouty wrote on 20 June that "the current events make him desire to leave his residence in Marseille to fix it at Paris."[64] Many others, such as Hanna Samanne, Mikha'il Barbary, Issa Amouth, and Abou Saoud, also arrived in Paris at this time. And these names, of course, represent only those whose standing in regard to the Restoration regime was sufficient for them to hope for some assistance through their petitions. Many more must have left little trace of their displacements.

It certainly seems to have been easier to avoid problems in Paris than in Marseille: George Angeli was condemned in 1815 to a fine of 1,000 francs and twenty years forced labor as "the leader or instigator of seditious meetings in a *guingette* at Marseille."[65] He remained in the *bagne* at Toulon until 1831, when he was freed by royal decree under the July Monarchy. Thérèse Tutongi lost her twin brother in the massacre and claimed that her husband, who had accompanied Napoleon to Elba, died suddenly on his return "from a violent tetanus infection caused by fright at the spontaneous changeover of power."[66] Despite this tragedy, she was imprisoned for a year in the forts of Saint-Jean and Saint-Nicolas.

What is critical here is to recognize that the paths of mobility between Marseille and Paris that we have explored in earlier chapters now became not simply paths to community and social mobility, but also paths of survival. The reconstitution of the Arab community in Marseille was more than ever dependent upon the Arab presence in Paris for its physical as well as its political survival. If the Restoration was a massive transformation in certain ways, it did not touch the centralized nature of the French state, which Napoleon had intensified with his prefectoral system of government. For the "Egyptian refugees," this centralization was even more immediate because their pensions remained in the hands of the Ministry of War in the capital. Although reduced, these pensions were maintained along with most other existing entitlements. The respectability conferred by the "Catholic" identity of the community certainly helped sustain this decision. But pecuniary advantages were not the only important factor in the centrality of Paris for the Arab community.

The political importance of Paris was very clear to the Restoration government, which became rapidly worried by the presence of so many Egyptians and Syrians. In 1817, it was decided that the conglomeration of these dangerous foreigners in and around the capital was not to be tolerated, and a list of forty-eight individuals "whose presence close to Paris is unsuitable" was drawn up.[67] These *mauvais sujets* were to be deported to the Île Sainte-Marguerite, off the coast of Toulon. The reasons for appearing on this list were most often political, but they were expressed as questions of moral order, since such political purges were not official policy (excepting those who had betrayed their oaths to the king during the Hundred Days). Hanna Samanne, for example, who fled to Paris in 1815, was recommended for deportation because, "by his turbulent conduct, he compromises the public tranquillity and gives rise to disturbing scenes. It is said also that he has already been arrested twice for misconduct, that he is a drunkard and a brawler, and dangerous in his liquor."[68]

Certainly a number of deportees did end up on the island. Some took their wives and children; other families remained behind to petition the government to release their husband or son.[69] But the deportation orders quickly led to a frenzy of evasive action by those on the list. In previous years it had occasionally been the practice to award lump sums to those who wanted to return to their countries of origin, renouncing any further right to the pension.[70] The new Ministry of War had seized upon this expedient to encourage these "foreign Bonapartists" to leave for good. From mid-1816, French officials were willing to agree readily that those who wished to return to their *patrie* should receive one year's pension in advance.[71] For many, like Hanna Samanne, this was—according to his file—merely a "pretext to avoid being directed to the Île Sainte-Marguerite."[72] In fact, he fled and enrolled himself as a bodyguard at Le Havre, before being rearrested and taken back to Melun, where he apparently left for Genoa. Others, however, chose to take the option of repatriation rather than face deportation to the depressing confines of the tiny island.

The results of this policy were, however, quite surprising. A large number of applications were made by individuals and even families to receive a year's pension and "return to their *patrie*." But within a few years the majority of these people had returned to France. Some made immediate claims for assistance or even for readmission to the pensions they had renounced. Others simply used the sum they had received as capital and remained inconspicuously in Marseille or Paris. Their names would not have reappeared had they not reapplied for the pension after the change of regime in 1830. According to Joseph Nakacly, who spent six years in Syria after his losses in Marseille, but returned to France in 1822:

Numerous Egyptian refugees have at different times left French soil, and on their return they have always been readmitted to the pension of sixty-five centimes: if you will allow him to observe, M. le Ministre, there are even some negresses among these individuals.[73]

If Nakacly showed his own manipulation of racist assumptions in this comment, he was nonetheless correct in his statement. Women such as Halimé (identified only as n° 129, her name betraying her slave origins) were readmitted to the pension without great demur.[74] Some claimed their conversion to Christianity as a watertight justification of their need to return to France, an argument that the pro-Catholic regime was unlikely to refuse.[75] Salem Youdi (Charles-Louis Salem) was sent first to Sainte-Marguerite, and then left for Egypt in 1816. However, he reported that on his arrival in Malta he "heard stories" of ill treatment in Egypt, and returned immediately to Europe via Genoa. He then traveled to Germany, where he entered the service of Prince Charles of Bavaria as a Mamelouk for three years, before finally returning to France in 1820 to tell his story of persecution.[76] His conversion to Christianity in 1824 brought him into great favor and allowed his full readmission to the pension.

Intended as a way of ridding France of its unwanted foreigners, by the mid-1820s this strategy of repatriation had become a loosely enforced policy that allowed many on the refugee list to leave for their countries of origin (and sometimes other places) with a considerable sum of capital, and return to France. It seems likely that this promoted their fortunes and allowed them to establish trading or business possibilities in the new economic boom across the Mediterranean. Thus the poorer among the "refugees" found quite sophisticated ways to adapt the administration's assumptions to their own needs, and primarily to enjoy a level of mobility that had previously been accessible only to those wealthy and independent merchants in Marseille and Paris. This too must have drawn the different elements of the community together. Now more of them traveled back to Egypt and Syria, reestablishing connections, and perhaps improving their circumstances. Through mobility, then, many of the divisions that had produced bitter conflicts in the community were broken down. Where, in 1811, the chief instigation of the perturbations in Marseille was the complaint by the poorest class of refugees against abuses by the notables of the council, now the most important members of the community sought to protect the most vulnerable.

The events of 1815 and the decisions of 1816 thus served paradoxically to promote an increase in geographical and social mobility that helped allay divisions in the population caused by social and economic differences. Yet these events and decisions also served to highlight the serious problems faced by a visible foreign minority in France, above all one coded as "Oriental." Thus, as the community itself drew closer together, the dangers posed by conspicuous difference were all too evident. The "Egyptian" identity that they had adopted, at least in an official sense, had very clearly played a central role in their political and racial targeting in 1815. This official identity had never represented the actual heterogeneity of the population: with the influx of more Melkite Catholics from Syria and Palestine, this category was less and less sustainable.

If the church had become a central communal institution in Marseille, this only represented one point in an increasingly multilocal existence characterized by mobility. It was the Arabic language that provided the distinguishing difference of this congregation, and that was the focus of the other chief institution of Arab life in Marseille. Language was a difference that could be controlled within the private space, not a visible difference of dress or cultural practices like those of the "Egyptian village" before 1815. When the Egyptian cleric Rifa'a al-Tahtawi passed through Marseille in 1826, he wrote that none of the Arab Christians continued to wear their traditional dress.[77] Did this mean that they had given up their Egyptian and Arab identity in order to assimilate without trace into Restoration France?

Let us take one final journey. In February 1818, Marie Namé and her nephew George Sakakini made the long trip from Marseille to Paris, perhaps taking the easier course along the river from Avignon to Lyon, and then following the road as far as Melun, where they must certainly have stopped for a period. They cannot have stayed long, however, as they had a very precise objective to accomplish in the capital. Marie was the widow of General Ya'qub; she had mourned his death on that tragic crossing of the Mediterranean. She was a wealthy woman: clearly an astute manager of her husband's fortune, she was the owner of a sizable property on the outskirts of Marseille. Her name had appeared only rarely in the correspondence of the "refugees" seeking to plead their situations of penury or to request permission to change their residence. Nor had she featured among the members of the Council of Refugees who acted to quell the disturbances among their compatriots, or signed testimonials to attest the services of other Arabs toward the French.

She was was heading toward Paris with a document to present to the minister of war. It was written in a careful hand by her nephew, who had studied at the Lycée in Marseille and occupied a bench in Gabriel Taouïl's Arabic classes alongside the other children of the Arabic-speaking families in the town. It was signed by him on behalf of "the widow of General Jacob, my Aunt, Delegate of the Dépôt of Egyptian Refugees."[78] In accompanying his aunt as "secretary and interpreter," without receiving prior permission, George infringed the rules of the pensions administration and was struck off the list, losing his pension of two francs per day. He was only readmitted two years later, with no restitution of the sum he had lost. For a young man about to be married—to Georges Aïdé's daughter Rose—

this must have been quite a blow. But he chose to take the risk regardless of the consequences.

The petition Marie and her nephew were carrying did not bear on their own circumstances. Instead, it pleaded with the new government of the Restoration on behalf of the poorest class of "refugee." Soon after the Bourbon return to power, the pensions of the refugees had been reduced across the board. The pensions of the widows and their children, previously entitled through the services of their husbands, had been abolished altogether, leaving them in a dire position. George Sakakini wrote in the petition:

> All the Egyptian refugees have the honor to present humbly to Your Excellence that they have sacrificed their tranquillity and their sometimes very substantial property in the service of the French government and are still ready to lay down their lives for it. If the small pension accorded to their widows is taken away, these women will no longer be able to live in France, not knowing the French language, and having no trade to support them.[79]

His opening phrase expressed the wishes of "*all* the Egyptian refugees." But George, unlike Aïdé in 1811, used the third person—"they" rather than "us"—to describe those on whose behalf he spoke; he was not pleading on his own account, but on behalf of a group to which he did not belong. Why did he feel solidarity toward these unfortunates? It is unlikely that he was tied directly to the poor widows and their families by kinship or social connections. His life would have remained physically, socially, and culturally distinct from theirs. But he felt a commonality with these people strong enough for him to take the very significant risk of losing his own means of support. There are echoes here of the petitions of the Egyptian Legation in 1801 and Georges Aïdé in 1811. But the collective voice was different. It was not that of an individual or a small political elite, but of a single community whose concern was to "be able to live in France."

Sakakini's own voice demonstrated just how French he had become. Appealing to the notion of the lowest class of refugees as the "widows and children" of "men covered with glory, who devoted themselves to France, and are so strongly connected to its prosperity," the petition made sophisticated use of French stereotypes about the devoted service of the "Egyptians." But Sakakini went further to employ the conventional picture of Oriental cruelty. If the refugees returned to their countries, he insisted, "the zeal of their husbands for the French cause is enough to expose them to the fate of *having their heads cut off.*"[80] The underlining of this sentence in the original document perhaps betrays a certain bad faith in exploiting a set of crude stereotypes that he had no reason to believe.

Sakakini would certainly know how many "Egyptians" had already returned to Egypt without any difficulty. His own cousin Auguste was one of them and was already a significant figure in the new translation movement emerging at Bulaq.[81] The key Arab intellectual in Paris, Rufa'il Zakhur, as we saw in chapter 4, left for Egypt, where he was appointed as a personal translator to Muhammad 'Ali, and as a teacher in the newly established technical school. If Rufa'il—who, we must recall, had served the *diwan* under the French occupation—could return so easily, it seems highly unlikely that the widows of ordinary soldiers would be immediately decapitated. But to define the refugees as the *victims* of "Oriental tyranny" was to remove them in some way from the category of "Oriental" in the eyes of the French bureaucrats, and thus to strengthen their rights. The choice may appear cynical, but it was dictated by circumstances. These ambivalent terms would have larger consequences, however, for the second generation of Arabs seeking to make their lives in France.

In 1801, the Egyptian Legation had used the word "Oriental" to describe its project for a communal "Harem-Hospice" in France. It saw nothing dangerous in this terminology, which served, as it did later for Ellious Bocthor in his inaugural address of 1819, on the "Egypto-Oriental colony," as a convenient way to designate the common extra-European origins of an otherwise heterogeneous population. The designation of "Egyptian" had come to replace this, at least in the administrative categorization of the "refugees." But in the wake of the stabilization of Egypt under the rule of Muhammad 'Ali, and the influx of Syro-Palestinian migrants in the early years of the Restoration, such a category was an administrative fiction. Few of these people intended seriously to return to Egypt: many were not considered "Egyptian" in origin, and others had no connection there at all. If this "Egyptian" identity was the key to receiving a pension from the government, it was also the rubric under which the crowds had attacked the Arab population in Marseille. As Tahtawi noted, by 1826 most of the "Egyptians" in Marseille had ceased to identify themselves in any visible way with this origin. But they had not ceased to function as a community: indeed, in the aftermath of violence it appears that divisions between groups were increasingly weakened in favor of a stronger communal identification.

The petition written by George Sakakini emphasized the common history of the emigrants from Egypt, their sacrifices in French service, and their inability to return to their countries of origin. If there was an element of administrative and Orientalist rhetoric in this argument, it also demonstrated a sense that the community was permanently settled in France. It is here that we may identify the significance of the journey of General Ya'qub's widow, almost two decades after his death at sea. This journey was an act of political representation, the declaration of the community's permanence in France. George ended his petition with a grand gesture:

France, which rejoices in the brilliance of your great virtues, admires along with the rest of Europe the great project of French generosity [*le grand œuvre de la générosité française*], confirmed by the immense resources of a spirit such as your own.[82]

Here, George spoke not only in the name of "all the Egyptian refugees," but also in the name of "France" and the cosmopolitan project of "French generosity." It is across these two ideas that he was seeking to articulate an identity deriving both from the common history of the sacrifices made by his compatriots and from the common future they held in France. It was a difficult task, and one carried out in the shadow of violence. The next chapter will explore the Egyptians' struggle to find a new place at the heart of France, in a Paris now reconceived as "the modern Athens," a new Orientalist cultural politics that would take them to its heart in an ambivalent embrace.

6

Cosmopolitanism
and Confusion

By the third decade of the nineteenth century a significant population of Arabs was living in France, chiefly in Marseille and Paris, with a presence in the town of Melun, and a few scattered souls in other towns and villages. These people had survived the catastrophic collapse of a political system, the upheavals of transition, and the installation of another, more hostile administration, despite the murderous violence that targeted them. The mobility that had come to characterize their lives in France served them well during this tumultuous period. But they also showed considerable political acumen and the political skills for survival at a time when so many lost their way, their property, and even their lives. And yet this fascinating history was left in silence by those who lived it. They left nothing, beyond a few scattered phrases, that might serve to record the memory of the shifts and transformations they had collectively lived; they left no account of what they experienced during those terrible days of June 1815.

As Jean-René Aymes showed for Spanish exiles in France, and Anna-Maria Rao for the Italians, other refugee groups left a rich record both in their own publications and private manuscripts and in the responses of others to their presence.[1] But this is not the case with the Arab population of France. In Paris, above all, one might expect to find such public inscriptions of presence, but one looks in vain to the numerous publications of both first and second generations of the population to find any statement of self-recognition or any description of the community, and its practices and modes of accommodation with French culture. Nor, conversely, did any French writer during this period of fascination with the city and its denizens, of romantic exoticism and the birth of modern Orientalism, give us any account whatsoever of this group living among the French. This was the era of Balzac and Delacroix, both of whom had indirect connections with the Arabic-speaking milieux of Paris. Balzac's secretary was Léon Gozlan, the Jewish writer of Algerian origin who later published the only account of the "Egyptian refugees" of Marseille. Delacroix's father was prefect of the Bouches-du-Rhône when the Egyptians arrived in Marseille, and his close friend Théodore Géricault's domestic servant Mustapha Sussen was a Tunisian Arab, apparently the survivor of a shipwreck, who was depicted in portraits by Girodet, Vernet, and Géricault himself. Mustapha was a disconsolate mourner at Géricault's funeral, although his "eccentric manners" were said to have disturbed Théodore's father. Afterward Mustapha apparently established a successful business selling Turkish confectionery in Paris.[2]

Hundreds, even thousands of other French men and women must have come into contact with this population in their daily life. The banker Jacques Lafitte wrote a note on behalf of Elias Barouty, the Egyptian husband of his servant.[3] The Destaing family were engaged in a lawsuit over a marriage between their son and an "Egyptian" woman, Anne Nazo.[4] Aly Hamid was living "chez M. Robin, pharmacien." Joseph Aboudalker was a member of the Garde Nationale in Paris. Ibrahim Abdel Malek and Mikha'il Barbary were engaged in bringing horses to Paris for the duc de Clermont-Tonnère and other notables. Joan Habaïby was a supernumerary in tax collection for the prefecture of Seine-et-Marne. Adelle, the daughter of Pierre Kiardel and Madeleine Sèmeka, was studying to be a midwife at l'Hospice de la Maternité. Aboutidjé Badiri was living "chez Michel Invalide" in a cul-de-sac of the rue Grenelle near the Gros Caillou, the large military hospital near the Champ de Mars. People of all walks of life—from the most desperately poor to the most fabulously wealthy—might interact with Egyptians, Syrians, or North Africans in most parts of the city, from the prison of Sainte-Pélagie to the Faubourg Saint-Germain, from the rue Saint-Honoré to—heartbreakingly—"chez l'écrivain public sur le Trottoir près le Palais Bourbon."[5]

Yet nowhere were these names recorded, their stories told, except in their fulsome petitions to the Bureau of Pensions for a small increase in their daily allowance, to be readmitted, or to be allowed to collect their pension henceforth in Paris. In these documents they parceled out small fragments of their daily grind, liberally mixed with conventional expressions and more than a few fabrications, to the only ears that were occasionally prepared to listen. Otherwise their silence, and that of those around them, was almost total.

The events of 1815 in Marseille must surely have played a principal role in this silence. Certainly the visibility of the "Egyptian village" at the edge of the town helped attract the murderous violence of political retribution, and the ambivalent ways in which color and race contributed to this violence only accentuated the value of "melting away" into the surrounding population. The trauma surrounding such events can certainly make it difficult for survivors to speak of them later on. Yet violence has often been the inspiration for discourses of identity, a focal point of common suffering that could become a kind of communal myth. This never happened with the massacre of Marseille; it passed into history almost unrecorded by those who lived through it. This was certainly not because the survivors lacked the capacity to render an account; indeed, this population seems to have included a disproportionate number of intellectuals and writers of all descriptions. Throughout the decade that followed, there must have been opportunities to speak, above all in opposition circles hostile to the Restoration government. And indeed, some of the young French Arabs joined these circles and even criticized the government of the day. Yet they never joined to this criticism any account of the violence visited against them. We must consider further the reasons for this silence.

In 1819, as we saw in chapter 4, Ellious Bocthor suddenly found his skills in Arabic recognized, and his intellectual contribution welcomed in Paris. It seemed a remarkable shift from the cultural politics that had so frustrated and stifled his aspirations in Napoleon's "New Rome." In the *Revue encyclopédique,* his great champion, Edmé-François Jomard, wrote in enthusiastic response to the inaugural lecture:

> Who would have said, twenty-five years ago, before the French expedition to the banks of the Nile, that an inhabitant of Sioût would come to give lessons on the banks of the Seine, at the heart of the modern Athens, among the most learned professors? Who could have believed that a semibarbarian, simply through application and insight, would come at last to a profound knowledge of general grammar, and to produce an almost academic work?[6]

The shift is a crucial one. For Jomard, the "New Rome" had become a "New Athens," but a "modern" Athens, conceived in relation to a civilizing discourse that could bring the "semibarbarian" to join its groves of academe—or *almost,* as the fatal qualifier declares. This cultural politics could embrace the foreign *as foreign,* no longer as a tributary element of an expanding empire. Further, this concern with ancient Greece reflected a new European cultural politics that would be reflected in the widespread liberal support for philhellenism, and a willingness to fight for "Greek" independence from Ottoman rule.[7] The idea of "Egypt" was ambivalently situated between these two forces, one side increasingly idealized as European and patriotic, and the other disparaged as Oriental and despotic.

Ellious Bocthor did not live long enough to test the boundaries of this new cultural politics: he died within a year of his appointment. But in the early 1820s a second generation of Arab intellectuals, born or raised in France, arrived in the capital, eager to make their mark in the expanding Orientalist milieux. They soon found a place there and played a significant role that has hardly been recognized either in the history of Orientalism or in the history of Paris. But that space was a very particular one, whose outlines Jomard's hesitations and qualifications may help sketch. It was a space determined once again by a cultural politics that was badly matched to the lives and identities of these young men, and of the population from which they had come. It is in those malformed trajectories, in those contradictory and misleading successes and the sudden and unexplained failures, in the gap between "Egyptian" representations and "Arab" realities, that we may find an answer to that puzzling and disappointing silence.

We may see the ambivalence of this new "Arab France" reflected in some of the popular imagery of the period. During these years the figure of the "Oriental" with turban and dalmatic coat, pantaloons and slippers, became quite a common feature in the burgeoning visual culture of the metropolis. Views of Paris had always been a popular subject for prints, and the cheaper techniques of engraving and lithography now made them more available to a wider public. Perspectives of the public spaces of Paris were designed to be framed and consumed in the private space of the home: they usually included figures engaged in generic everyday activities appropriate to the scene. In the introduction, we noted the figures of Arabs smoking their chibouks in the Tuileries gardens in an engraving from 1812 (figs. 1 and 2). But in the period after 1815 these images seem only to have become more common.

In 1817 a spectacular new roller coaster called the Promenades Aeriennes opened in the Jardin Baujon. A popular engraving made to commemorate the visit of King Louis XVIII to the park was carefully captioned "Drawn after nature by L. Garneray" (fig. 7). Naturally, the chief subject, a roller coaster drawn in meticulous detail, dominates the pictorial space, against a cloudless sky. In the foreground gambol the figures that enliven the subject with miniature scenes of sociability: a father chasing a runaway child, a gentleman bowing to two ladies, carriages arriving and leaving. But at the center of this scene, with no obvious explanation for their presence, are two figures wearing entirely different clothing from the tight leggings and tailcoats of the other men (fig. 8). In this image, the two men, one with a white beard, the other younger, stand apart from the other figures and their scenes of sociability, gazing out at the viewer as though conscious that their presence is being recorded. We can say no more about them than that they are "Oriental": their dress is not military, their presence not threatening, nor does it attract the attention of those around them. Indeed, they appear to be almost invisible, except to the viewer.

Other visual images from the same period confirm that Garneray's image was not just an anomaly. Similar figures in Oriental dress appear frequently, whether conversing in the gardens of the Tuileries or simply crossing the courtyard at the Palais Royal in one of Henri Courvoisier-Voisin's scenes depicting the architectural attractions of Paris. In an image by Angelo Garbizza (fig. 9), two turbaned young men cross the large vaulted space of the arcades at the same Palais Royal, a

FIGURE 7. Engraving after Louis Ambroise Garneray, *Promenades Aériennes, Jardin Beaujon, Honoured by the Presence of Her Majesty, 2nd August 1817*, c. 1817. Anne S. K. Brown Military Collection, Brown University Library.

space of sociability and vice. Here, although they are crossing the scene once again with a vector that seems quite distinct from their surroundings, one of them turns, distracted by a tall woman who is lifting her dress slightly from her petticoat, signifying her status as a prostitute (fig. 10).

What is particularly striking in these images is the lack of any marked exoticism, threat, or sense of unease with the presence of these "foreigners." This seems to confirm Victoria Thompson's analysis of literary "panoramas" of Paris during the Restoration, which, she argues, tended "to emphasize distinctions among the urban population and in the urban landscape while at the same time presenting these distinctions as part of a stable and harmonious whole."[8] We may draw a contrast here with an earlier image by Louis Léopold Boilly that placed an Arab figure at the edge of a similar scene of depravity at the Palais Royal under the Consulate (fig. 11): his glowering look staring in from the shadows suggests an unease with the role of this foreign figure, inside an enclosure of vice fenced off almost like a cage.[9] It is notable too that in Boilly's image the immediate object of the lustful gaze of the turbaned figure is a black prostitute, suggesting that racial dyad of "négresse" and "Mamelouk" that preoccupied the authorities in Marseille around this same period.

FIGURE 8. Engraving after Louis Ambroise Garneray, *Promenades Aériennes, Jardin Beaujon, Honoured by the Presence of Her Majesty, 2nd August 1817*, c. 1817, detail. Anne S. K. Brown Military Collection, Brown University Library.

Nothing of this racialized danger seems to intrude upon the scenes of the early 1820s, in which color does not appear to play a role. Thompson suggests that writers on Paris during the later Empire and Restoration saw the urban fabric as a patchwork of diverse districts with their own customs, trades, and distinct modes of behavior, dress, and comportment. She quotes Victor-Joseph-Etienne de Jouy

FIGURE 9. Angelo Garbizza, *Vue des galeries du Palais Royal prise du côté de la rue des Bons Enfants*, watercolor. © RMN / Agence Bulloz.

in 1813: "Each neighborhood is in some sense a separate nation, all of which come together to form the general character of Parisians and the particular physiognomy of this great city."[10] But here too we should note the hesitation expressed by the words "in some sense"—Jouy did not specify in what sense these "different nations" should be understood, nor what it might mean for those whose difference within the nation was literal rather than figurative. But the primary concern of many intellectuals in the early Restoration was political rather than cultural or racial: the question of rebuilding society in the tempestuous aftermath of revolution and empire.

Jouy belonged to the opposition circles hostile to the Restoration government, circles that also included Louis Garneray (with whom he collaborated) and Eugène Isabey (his next-door neighbor), who produced a watercolour of the Louvre featuring a "Mamelouk officer" at its center (fig. 12).[11] The series of works Jouy wrote under the pseudonym "Hermit" well expressed both a new sense of the urban environment and the bitterness of those who felt France had been betrayed

FIGURE 10. Angelo Garbizza, *Vue des galeries du Palais Royal prise du côté de la rue des Bons Enfants,* watercolor, detail. © RMN / Agence Bulloz.

by the restoration of a monarchy it had rejected. In his account of his journey across the country, entitled *L'hermite en province,* Jouy mapped out this oppositional terrain, praising those who had proven themselves during the terrible events of the preceding decade, and expressing a barely hidden nostalgia for the Empire. On his way from Paris to Provence in 1818, he reported his interrogation of a fellow passenger who dismissed the violence in Marseille as "almost nothing . . . 168 people [killed] all in all, including men, women, children, French, Arabs, etc., etc." Jouy was astounded. "What do you mean, Monsieur?" he expostulated. "Women were killed? What—unfortunate Orientals, not knowing our customs, our opinions, our language?"[12] It is telling that in his empathetic response Jouy presented the fate of both women and "Orientals" as purely a passive one—their political significance derives only from their *innocence* of any participation in French culture and politics. It was their extraneousness to political events that rendered their murder a political scandal. Jouy's comments suggest how the space of the "Oriental" in Restoration culture—here in its oppositional

FIGURE 11. Louis Léopold Boilly, *Les galeries du Palais Royal*, oil on panel. © RMN / Droits réservés.

forms—projected the figure of the Arab as naturally distinct from its French context, while nonetheless uneasily registering an Arab presence at the very heart of political events.[13]

Garneray's image of the roller coaster carries some hints of a similar political reference: the king, whose visit is the ostensible subject of the scene, is invisible amid a jumble of figures around a golden carriage in the background, greeted only by desultory salutations by Parisians who seem spectacularly uninterested. Only the Egyptians turn their faces to the viewer, and seem to raise by this direct gaze some undefined question about the "arrival" of the king (indeed, this undignified arrival might recall the king's notorious scramble out of Paris on the news of Napoleon's return). In a period in which images were frequently read as coded with political meanings—for example, violets signifying Bonaparte's return from Elba—there is reason to find such interpretations plausible. If other images, such as those of Courvoisier and Garbizza, seem to hold no easily identifiable political implications, they may still reflect some nostalgia for a Napoleonic cosmopolitanism, recalling the grandeur of the Empire through these figures of conspicuous

FIGURE 12. Louis Eugene Gabriel Isabey, *Grand Escalier du Louvre*, 1817, watercolor. Bridgeman Art Library.

difference. It is notable that many of these artists were themselves foreigners, from countries like Switzerland and Italy, which were deeply touched by the transformations of Napoleonic empire.

These representations cannot tell us much about Arabs themselves, but they do say something about the spaces that Arabs might occupy in the larger conception of the urban fabric. If their presence appears unremarked and unremarkable in these generic scenes of metropolitan life, it is also unexplained. It is a space marked off from others—there is rarely any interaction with the larger scene, save in those instances where the interaction is with a prostitute, at the very margins of bourgeois society. In this sense the space seems both central and marginal, marked and unmarked; in a word, unresolved. From the perspective of those who actually moved and interacted in these urban spaces, these images of conspicuous difference raise another question. What place was there for these Orientals once simply reclothed in French dress? This question is raised by a much later image of Abdallah d'Asbonne, the "last of the Mamelouks" (fig. 13), wearing his stiffly respectable suit adorned with *both* the Legion of Honor and the Cross of Saint-Louis. We may remember that Abdallah was the author of the poem expressing his rapid conversion to the cause of the Bourbons. By the time of this portrait he had lived through the July Monarchy and the Second Republic into the new Bonapartist Empire of Napoléon III. He had changed his name from Hasboun to d'Asbonne, apparently at the urging of a socially ambitious wife. Here the sense of Abdallah's Arab origins required an explicit visual cue: his hand resting ostentatiously on a book marked "L'Expédition d'Égypte."

These representations are important because they offer a few clues to the context in which a second generation of Arabs struggled to find their place in the France they had known since their childhood. We should not read these images as holding any keys to the identity of this generation of Arabs, but rather as indicating some of the limits and contradictions of the space that was offered to them. They themselves were agents: they had choices to make that would be based on their own family experiences, their origins and education, their skills and proclivities. But those choices would never be made in a vacuum. In a general sense we can observe that a large number of those Arabs born in France did not abandon their cultural particularity to seek success wholly in the field of Parisian literary achievement. Instead, they tended to draw upon their Arab particularities, and the Arabic language that had drawn their community together, as the basis for their aspirations in the capital. It may be helpful to take one major example, the most successful of all these young French Arabs, and follow his journey through the landscape glimpsed in those curious and inarticulate images.

In 1820, Joseph Agoub arrived in Paris from the provinces, one of a generation of young men in a hurry, fired with ambition for literary and social success in the

M. Abdalla d'Asbonne, dernier officier des mameluks, mort récemment à
Melun, d'après le portrait peint par M. Barrias et copié par lui.

FIGURE 13. Engraving after Barrias, *M. Abdalla d'Asbonne, Last Officer of the
Mamelouks, Recently Deceased at Melun,* 1860. Author's collection.

capital. A letter he wrote to a patron in 1821 emphasized the Arab dimension of his childhood, describing the "mélange d'habits Arabes et Européen" that characterized his young life.[14] Joseph wrote:

> Ever since my arrival in Marseille, along with my family and a large number of other Egyptians, the scenery of Oriental life has been constantly before my eyes. Given that nothing had really changed in my way of life—having, so to speak, carried my household gods with me—I felt as though I were still in the land of my birth. Or rather, when I observed around me the mixture of Arab and European customs, when my ear was struck simultaneously by two different idioms, it seemed to me that Egypt had somehow become combined with France, and that the two nations were confused into one.[15]

"Deux nations s'étaient confondues": Joseph used here a verb that signified at once "merged into one another," "mistaken for each other," and "confused" in the conventional sense of being mixed-up, troubled, uncertain. But he seemed to have found a way of reconciling these disparate threads. If like Joubran Mehenna before him he sought to slough off his provincial upbringing, he saw himself as distinguished primarily by his command of the Arabic language:

> Having spoken Arabic all my life, I could not but show a predilection for this language because it is my mother tongue, and because it always brings back to me the memories from my cradle.[16]

But at the same time, and like George Sakakini, he also claimed a direct and unmediated relationship to France and French culture, expressed through a devotion to the literary heritage of the French language, which was also the currency of ambition in the salons of the Restoration:

> For me, French literature has always exerted an irresistible fascination. Destiny having thrown me suddenly outside the circle of my earliest affinities, I could not find in any other literature of the peoples of Europe either the same pleasures or the same advantages I have already acquired through twenty years of living in France and by the direction I have so far taken in my studies. From an early age I was filled with the ambition to educate myself in the tongue of my new homeland. For the first time, an Arab understood Virgil, admired Racine, meditated upon Montesquieu. Carried away by my enthusiasm, I ventured to take up the lyre myself.[17]

Joseph saw himself as a new kind of Arab, a *French* Arab, through a painstaking cultural synthesis between his "earliest affinities" and an elective association with France. His "lyre" represented in this sense his own poetic representation of this identity, his self-expression as a French Arab. Unlike Ellious Bocthor, he was seeking to occupy the ground of cultural expression in French, *outside* the cultural politics of Orientalism. But he was seeking an Arab space within this French cultural milieu. In moving from one continent to another, he insisted that he had carried with him the lived expression of his cultural identity, which he poetically termed his *Pénates,* his "household gods." But that elegant and classicizing reference concealed a more ambivalent configuration of identities .

Joseph-Élie Agoub was born in 1795, in the cosmopolitan world of late Ottoman Cairo. His father, Elias Agoub, was Armenian by origin and a jeweler by profession; his mother was a Syrian Melkite Catholic, Rose (Warda) Chébib, from Damascus.[18] Joseph was only a small child when the French marched into Cairo in 1798, and still only six years old when the French army finally departed from the shores of Egypt in 1801, carrying with it the diverse population that would form the core of the Arab community of nineteenth-century France. Among them was Joseph's mother; in the intervening period she had been widowed and had married a French-Egyptian merchant, François Naydorff, who left for France with most of the French population of the *échelle,* as these French enclaves in the Ottoman world were known. Naturally she took along her two sons from her first marriage: Gaspard-Joseph and Joseph-Élie. The family arrived with hundreds of others in Marseille in October 1801.

There is little to tell us how Joseph's parents managed to survive in the first months of their arrival in Marseille, but they were able to place him in a small private school, where his precocious ability won him a scholarship to the Lycée de Marseille. From 1807 Gabriel Taouïl was appointed by imperial decree to a chair as professor of Arabic at the Lycée. Léon Gozlan reported:

> It was at this royal institution that we came to know the sons of the best families of Cairo and Alexandria, excellent schoolmates whose memory remains indelibly with us, and where we received our first lessons in Arabic language from the erudite priest Gabriel, Abouna Gibraïm, and from Joseph Agoub, who was professor of Arabic at the Collège Louis-le-Grand until his death.[19]

Thus Agoub evidently began to assist his teacher in providing Arabic lessons to the children of the community, between the completion of his schooling in the last years of the Empire and his arrival in Paris in 1820. Joseph lived in Marseille through the political transition of 1814–15, and he could not have remained untouched by these events. He had every reason to be anxious—his brother Gaspard was still serving in the Corps des Mamelouks, which he had joined in 1808 at the age of seventeen along with dozens of other young men from the community in Marseille. By 1814, Gaspard had been promoted to *maréchal de logis chef,* the highest noncommissioned grade; he took a wound to the head from a lance at the battle of Moscow. In June 1815, Gaspard was still quartered in Melun, leaving Joseph to experience the violent events in Marseille alone, but closely associated with those "Mamelouks" who figured so prominently in the popular hostility in Marseille. Yet in his later writings, and even in those letters that are extant, he makes no reference at all to the events of this terrible time.

In Marseille, Joseph was categorized as an "Egyptian refugee," and in 1815 he must have felt himself in danger along with the other Egyptians. But, as Anouar Louca pointed out in a biographical sketch written in the 1950s, although Joseph Agoub was born in Egypt, he could not be considered "Egyptian" in any straightforward sense. Louca—himself a Coptic Egyptian—remarked rather acidly that "[Agoub] never stopped repeating, with a kind of clinging incredulity, that he was Egyptian and a poet."[20] The name Agoub was very recognizably Armenian in origin, although Joseph had no direct connection to Armenian language or culture. For the Egyptian society into which he was born, a nonindigenous origin was often retained as a marker for many generations, and this was all the more evident for non-Muslims.[21] Whether as an Armenian, on his father's side, or as a Melkite Catholic originating from Syria through his mother, Joseph would never have been identified as "Egyptian" within the Arab community, despite his being labeled this way by the surrounding French society. In his earliest letters, Joseph did not refer to himself as "Egyptian" but as "Arab." Yet success was offered to him as an "Egyptian": when he arrived in Paris, he was quickly and warmly embraced in this role, as someone who could provide a direct link to the exotic Orient. Like Ellious Bocthor before him, his "Egyptianness" was considered to give added luster to his abilities in French, lifting him out of the crowd of young, ambitious intellectuals. But what began as a glamorous fabric soon became a *peau de chagrin*.

Joseph Agoub arrived in Paris in the midst of a burgeoning cultural preoccupation with Egypt. I have suggested in earlier chapters that Egyptomania waned considerably within Napoleonic cultural politics, outside the few prominent campaign paintings devoted to the emperor's personal cult. For much of the Empire, Egypt retained too much political valency to become an open and popular cultural theme. All of this changed with the removal of Egypt from the European strategic contest, and the end of the Napoleonic wars. The "cultural victory" that had assuaged the defeat in Egypt became a subject of passion in a vanquished postimperial France, a subject in which liberals and conservatives could share. Even the grand *Description de l'Égypte* was more a product of the Restoration than the Empire: only its first few volumes appeared after 1809, restricted by Napoleon's refusal to disseminate sensitive material. The first edition was huge and expensive and sold very poorly. In 1819, Louis XVIII authorized a cheaper version to be produced by Panckoucke, inscribed with a personal dedication to the king.[22] The first Egyptian galleries of the Louvre were constructed at this time and finally opened in 1827.

Todd Porterfield, in his study of Egyptian themes during the Empire and Restoration, has suggested that this fascination with Egypt and the "Orient" was a coded urge toward the restoration of France's colonial empire, and a redirection of energies associated with the Revolution.[23] This conception of Egyptomania as a protocolonial "surrogate" of revolutionary politics insists upon a fundamental continuity of expansionist nationalism across the postrevolutionary period. In this schema, the Restoration appears only as a momentary distraction from the underlying continuities running from the revolutionary wars through Napoleon's invasion of Egypt to French expansion in North Africa. But there is very little evidence that the regime of Louis XVIII harbored such expansionist ambitions.

Despite the intervention to save the Bourbon monarchy in Spain, the government under Louis XVIII was more preoccupied with internal consolidation and the "struggles within the bourgeois and noble elite."[24] Sheryl Kroen has described the ways in which the reestablishment of the monarchy was based on a politics of *oubli*, forgetting the bitter conflicts that had divided revolutionary from royalist, Bonapartist from Legitimist.[25] It was in this atmosphere that the cultural politics of the Restoration was free to expand and flower into all sorts of exotic blooms. The cultural complexities and contradictions of the early currents of Orientalism have been explored by Douglas McGetchin: he has described the bitter conflict that pitted the "Florists," who gloried in the beauties of Arabic poetry, against those who sought to draw upon other, more rationalist currents in Arabic thought as a source for new ideas about analytical history.[26] The Restoration also saw a vogue for novels that imagined the experiences of non-Europeans in Paris.[27] The cultural politics of Restoration cosmopolitanism is a topic that deserves far more detailed study. It must suffice here to sketch some broader outlines of the "modern Athens" that Joseph discovered in Restoration Paris.

The defeat of the expansionist *Grande Nation* of the Napoleonic empire had not in the long term dented Paris's prestige as the "Capital of Europe." But it had perhaps wearied a younger generation of that very Europe that had invaded French soil in the form of allied armies. Now the younger generation looked to farther horizons for its cultural imaginary, where an atmospheric distance cast a haze over the rather humiliating collapse of the French occupation of Egypt and bathed it in a comforting glow. At least this is what Victor Hugo suggested in his poetic cycle *Orientales*, which burst onto the Parisian literary scene in 1829: "The Orient, whether as image or as idea, has become a kind of general preoccupation, for the intelligence as much as for the imagination."[28] Egypt played a central role in Hugo's imaginary Orient (he had never been there); as it did throughout the Restoration, which saw the completion of the massive eighteen-volume *Description de l'Égypte*, Champollion's decipherment of hieroglyphic writing in 1822, the opening of the Egyptian rooms in pride of place in the new Musée Charles X in the Louvre, and even the popular Tombeau Égyptien and the Montagnes Égyptiennes among the many cheap entertainments of the Paris streets.[29]

Joseph Agoub enjoyed a meteoric success in Paris: within only a few years he was being fêted in the Parisian salon of Madame Dufrénoy, mixing with the intellectual celebrities of the Restoration, such as Constant, Tissot, and Lamartine, delivering papers at learned societies, writing articles for *Le Mercure,* and teaching

Arabic at the prestigious Collège Louis-le-Grand.[30] His works of poetry, linguistics, translation, and criticism, and even a popular song appeared in print regularly throughout the 1820s[31]—no small achievement in the cynical and cutthroat world of Parisian publishing.[32] By 1830, he looked to have conquered literary and intellectual Paris and seemed set to climb even higher—an extraordinary achievement for a young immigrant with no wealth or influence.

Then, quite unexpectedly, this success seems to have deserted him in a headlong rush. In 1831, he lost his position at the Collège and failed to find a publisher interested in his last work, a translation of the fables of Bidpaï; these misfortunes seem to have cost him the remains of his health. In 1832, reduced to his refugee pension of two francs per day, he took his wife and child back to Marseille, his childhood home. A few months later he died, at the age of only thirty-seven, disappointed and forgotten, except by a few loyal supporters.[33] As the *Biographical Dictionary* of the period put it, "Of this professorship he was unexpectedly deprived in 1831, by the then minister for foreign affairs, General Sebastiani, and, being unable to bear up against the destruction of his prospects, he died on the 3rd of October, 1832, of a broken heart, at Marseille, at the house of his brother."[34] Despite his service to the nation, his wife, Esther, was forced to write repeatedly to the government to plead for a pension for herself and her young baby, who died only a few months later.[35]

Joseph Agoub's disappearance from the Parisian literary world was as meteoric as the éclat of his early successes. One might easily be tempted to read this story as a Balzacian fable of provincial illusions lost in the cynical world of Paris: talent seduced by bright lights, salons, society ladies, and success on a silver platter, mistaking the caprices of fashion for hard-won recognition. And, in many ways, Joseph Agoub did enter this very world. In fact, his friend and former student Léon Gozlan, whom, as an assistant to Gabriel Taouïl, he had tutored in the Arabic course in Marseille, was a close associate of Balzac, and the model for the character of Nathan in *Lost Illusions*.[36] Gozlan, the child of Algerian and Egyptian Jews, shed this "Oriental" and Jewish identity for much of his life, achieving the lasting literary success in Paris that Joseph never had, and finally chronicling Balzac's last years at his home Les Jardies, in his popular book *Balzac in Slippers*.[37]

Gozlan had chosen to leave his identity as an Arabic-speaking provincial Jew behind, to the point that it was discovered after his death that he appeared to have been baptized.[38] Joseph, in contrast, never ceased the struggle to reconcile the different categories to which he belonged. Raised in the Collège at Marseille, speaking perfect French, extremely talented, and with the social graces to succeed in the fashionable world of the salons, Joseph might well have sought to create an entirely new identity as a French *homme de lettres* like his friend Gozlan. This was a very different world from that of the "repressive cosmopolitanism" under the

Empire. The intellectual was no longer expected to be an instrument of the state. Nor were the "modernizers" shut out of the closely guarded bastions of academic Orientalism. Cosmopolitanism was defined largely by the liberal impulses taking hold in the public sphere: it embraced, even celebrated difference. Balzac, however, saw this embrace as a deceitful one, catering to the vanity and foolishness of young men.

Twenty years later, Edmé-François Jomard gave an account of Agoub that re flected very closely Balzac's parable of the provincial consumed by a false and flattering Parisian cosmopolitanism. Some thirty years later, forwarding Agoub's letter of 1821 to a certain M. Grille (who would appear to be the same official of the Interior Ministry who had taken such an interest in Ellious Bocthor), Jomard appended a brief sketch of his protégé's fall:

> He had style, imagination, color. I pushed him, helped him, established him. . . . He wrote some beautiful verses, and some fine, if rather emphatic prose. The salons petted him and spoiled him: he sinned in various directions. I arranged an appointment for him at the Egyptian School with an enormous salary. Unfortunately for him, he didn't enjoy it for very long.[39]

This could almost be a description of Lucien de Rubempré, the flawed hero of Balzac's *Lost Illusions*, who came to Paris at almost the same moment as Joseph, assumed an identity that was not really his own, and finally came to grief through a success that came too easily and at the expense of sincerity. But Jomard's description was shaped by his own cultural politics, and perhaps too by this ready-made moral fable. As we shall see in the next chapter, he was not an entirely objective observer of the Arab protégés whom he sought to educate.

There were many things that Joseph Agoub shared with other young Frenchmen of his generation. Alan Spitzer has argued persuasively that the generation born between the approximate dates of 1792 and 1803, the "cohort" of young Frenchmen that included Thierry, Delacroix, de Vigny, and Hugo, formed a relatively coherent intellectual and social network. This generation can be distinguished in its political allegiances, its artistic styles, and its modes of sensibility from those that preceded and followed it.[40] This was a perception very much in evidence at the time, whether in positive judgments by Constant and Lafayette or negative ones from Lammenais and Chateaubriand; the generation was generally characterized as one reared on revolutionary passions and Napoleonic victories, but subsequently stifled by the established elites and political frustrations of the Restoration, and denied the vote (even if they could reach the prohibitive financial threshold) until the age of thirty.[41] The previous generation, which had earned power, wealth, and influence under the Empire, remained by and large in power, despite the *épurations* of the Second Restoration, now padded out with returned émigrés. The youth emerging from the lycées entered a world stripped of the rapid avenues of advancement promised by Napoleonic meritocracy, and offering only the excitements of the political sphere opened by the provisions of the Charter.

Agoub certainly belonged to this cohort by virtue of his birth in 1795, and more so through his characteristic education in a Napoleonic lycée and his arrival in the capital amid the political ferment of the early 1820s through the failed republican-Bonapartist conspiracies of the Charbonnerie, which climaxed in 1822. The atmosphere of the Restoration, which combined a relaxation of the stringent limits on thought and culture under the Empire with a progressive narrowing of the actual possibilities for political participation, fostered dense social networks among the *jeunesse du siècle*, for which the resurgent salons of the Faubourg Saint-Germain provided the theater, a place where the "aristocracy of talent" could mix with traditional elites. Steven Kale has pointed out that many observers remembered this period as one of remarkable tolerance, a kind of balance point between the old regime and the Revolution, which lived with its own contradictions—whether out of exhaustion and fear of a return to instability or through a more stable consensus on the role of the Charter and the constitutional monarchy, which would be ruptured under Charles X at the end of the decade.[42] In this atmosphere, Joseph could participate directly in the social and political networks of Restoration Paris.

But if in many ways Agoub belonged to this "French generation of 1820," he was undeniably a member of another "generation"—the second generation of the Arab emigration to France. And for many of his contemporaries, even those most sympathetic to his work, he remained primarily marked by this difference, a difference that was often perceived to create a subtle dissonance with the "French" identity that had been so generously accorded to him.

Thus the founder of *Le Constitutionnel*, Pierre-François Tissot, wrote of him in 1825: "In celebrating the marvels of the ancient country that was his cradle, M. Agoub showed himself to be both French and Egyptian at once."[43] But while contemporaries considered him French by virtue of his talent and acquisition of the French language, they did not forget that he was foreign-born, and that his status as French remained an honorary one. Indeed, Joseph drew upon this "foreignness" himself as a quality that made him stand out from others in the highly competitive literary atmosphere of the Restoration.

But Agoub did not seek to present himself as an exotic and miraculous exception. He drew attention to the Arab intellectual heritage in France—a remarkable flowering of Arabic literary and intellectual culture that continued through the Restoration and had its climax in the mid-1820s. In a footnote to a work published in the late 1820s, Joseph described the arrival of the "Egyptians" in France and drew attention to the many among them who had served their new country "either with the sword or with their talents." In an explanatory note, he added:

Those Egyptians who came to Paris have been very useful through their skills in the Arabic language. Michel Sabbagh, who was attached for a long period to the Royal Library, which he enriched with many manuscripts he copied in his own hand, himself composed several pieces of Arabic literature. Don Raphaël and Ellious Bocthor both taught Arabic at the School of Oriental Languages, the latter, who was stolen from among from the muses of the Orient by a premature death, left behind him an Arabic-French dictionary that is still unpublished, and a number of beautiful calligraphic models. I should mention in addition M. Gabriel Taouïl, who today occupies the chair in Arabic at the Royal College of Marseille, and who has discharged his functions there for more than sixteen years with a zeal that does as much honor to his erudition as to his devotion.[44]

At an intellectual level, at least, Agoub acknowledged his belonging to a common Arab milieu in Paris: for convenience, he called these Arabists "Egyptians" despite the fact that few of them could actually be considered Egyptian in origin.

The considerable literary and linguistic output of these Arab intellectuals has never been considered as a common project, or understood in the light of the wider history of an Arab community in France.[45] Their works are numerous, varied, and rich—a whole series of published books and pamphlets, in addition to unpublished sources in Arabic and French, and significant contributions to works such as the *Description de l'Égypte* and to a variety of educational, religious, and scholarly institutions. Thus, in the early 1820s one might have heard Mass celebrated in Arabic at Saint-Roch by Joseph Sabba, attended the Arabic courses at the École des Langues Orientales Vivantes taught by Ellious Bocthor, or encountered Joseph Agoub tête-à-tête with Tissot or Constant at the salon of Mme Dufrénoy or teaching at the interpreters' school at the Lycée Louis-le-Grand. Nearby, one could have passed Joanny Pharaon returning from his teaching duties at the Collège Sainte-Barbe or picked up a copy of Mikha'il Sabbagh's *Cantique de félicitation à Sa Majesté très-chrestienne Louis le Désiré, Roi de France et de Navarre* or Joseph Agoub's recent and very popular *Dithyrambe sur l'Égypte,* originally published in the *Revue encyclopédique.* By the end of the decade, these slight volumes would have been crowded on the shelf by more than twenty other texts published or containing significant work by Arab intellectuals living in Paris, including Ellious Bocthor's dictionary, an Arabic translation of Joseph Agoub's French poetry, and Joanny Pharaon's political writings, including his history of the Revolution of 1830. Nor was Agoub the only member of the second generation to dedicate himself to the acquisition of Arabic; this was the case equally for Pharaon and George Sakakini, who later took important teaching positions in the language; others such as Joseph Habaïby, Nicolas Siouffi, and Georges Bullad, who became noted interpreters; and Louis Abdelal, later a French general in the Franco-Prussian War.[46] Many other lesser-known young Arabs studied Arabic with Gabriel Taouïl at the Lycée de Marseille.

In his letter of 1821, Joseph seemed to speak for this second generation in insisting on the ties that held him in France, no longer just "service" or political loyalty, but intimate experience:

> To leave France would be a second expatriation for me; even if it were to return to Egypt. I am now drawn to France by all the feelings of my heart, all the bonds of duty, all the affection of my memories: my family, my habits, my interests, my affections, are all here. Anywhere else I would have to begin my existence over again. [47]

The skill with which Joseph employed the rhetoric of the moment was itself an indication of his "Frenchness." He called adroitly upon terms such as "civilization" and "utility," the legacy of the Revolution and Empire, which continued to form the underlying basis for bureaucratic governance. Emphasizing his loyalty as a citizen of the French *patrie,* he credited the Baron, a former imperial prefect, with the enlightened view that the "prosperity of letters is a chief source of the prosperity of nations," and proceeded to build from this to the importance of foreign languages for commerce and diplomacy. It was a far more polished performance than that of George Sakakini or Ellious Bocthor. The latter, in his address to the École des Langues Orientales, had emphasized the differences between the "Oriental" and the "European," to the advantage of the former in the question of Arabic language, writing, and pronunciation. In contrast, Agoub emphasized his bonds to France, at once those of gratitude, duty, and affinity, while subtly suggesting that his aspirations might lead him away from France unless he was given protective patronage by this high official. Although it did not result immediately in the offer of a position, the letter did seem to secure the protection of this notable and certainly seems to have resulted in an entrée to the salons of the capital.

In his letter Joseph described those with whom he had grown up as Egyptians, but referred to himself as an "Arab." He did mention that he had written a "poem entitled *Egypt*" in addition to an article on Arabic philology. This poem, *L'Égypte: Dithyrambe,* was published in October 1820 in the *Revue encyclopédique,* with a byline that emphasized the origin of the author: "by M. Joseph Agoub, a young Egyptian." A note explained that although the editors had been compelled to refuse much of the poetry sent to them,

> the *Dithyrambe sur l'Égypte* seemed to us, for two reasons, to deserve an exception. Firstly, the author, M. Joseph Agoub, is a young Egyptian, a native of Cairo, who came to Marseille with his family in the wake of the French expedition; his brother is one of the brave young men who served in our armies, and the penchant that draws him to cultivate our literature deserves encouragement. [48]

Thus the editors identified Agoub as deserving of attention primarily *because he was an Egyptian,* although "en second lieu" they added some praise for the work itself. Their approval of its "noble inspirations" was surely a coded reference to the military exploits of Napoleon.

Agoub's poem itself suggested a much less certain identification. Beginning with classicizing evocations of the Greco-Roman past, he compared his own "silence" to the work of historical and cultural rediscovery that was a central element of contemporary cultural politics in France.

> And I, who was born on burning shores, a child of the Nile . . . shall I stay silent? . . .
> Shall I, a slave to my enjoyments . . . lead upon on these shores only a life of idleness
> and weak desires?[49]

The conventions of classicizing language allowed Agoub to present a much looser version of his Egyptianness—he called himself a "child of the Nile" and addressed himself to Egypt as "one of your children." Many of his liberal contemporaries were preoccupied with Greek independence; he therefore insisted that Egypt, as the *teacher* of Greece and Rome, deserved even greater efforts for its liberation. But the image of Egypt was continually accompanied by words such as "troubled," "unworthy," and "weak." The second half of the poem broke out into a vision of something lost and destroyed, by a "horde of vile Tartars" who had mutilated the immortal ruins. Joseph angrily rejected the Muslim history of modern Egypt as an enslavement and vandalization of Egypt's antique heritage. "Thunder on these scoundrels, you ghostly liberators!" he wrote. "With a breath knock down their frightened regiments!"[50]

Agoub's more famous poem, *La lyre brisée*, another "dithyrambe," continued this meditation of a troubled soul in a more intensely personal mode. He evoked an early love that conflicted with his desire for glory and his ambition to contribute to the renaissance of Egypt under its new ruler, Muhammad 'Ali. Drawing a picture of his years patiently studying Egypt's past greatness, he now felt the stirring of a "filial disturbance" that inspired him to draw a common identity from the dispersed peoples of Egypt, by bringing his own sense of *patrie* to his native country:

> Alone, borne up by the power of poetry, I carry Europe to the shores of Africa.
> Egypt, one of your sons will be your benefactor! . . . Would that my lute, performing
> Orpheus's miracles and conquering these happy climes, might create a nation from
> your wandering tribes, and make a law-giving song echo across your burning
> sands![51]

Here Joseph was quite explicitly "imagining" a community through his poetry, one that created a "nation" out of multiple differences. Although this project of national imagining was rhetorically directed toward Egypt, Agoub had never been there, and his experience of it referred only to his reading and to his own experience in France. Indeed, after a long struggle with the abandonment of a passionate love for a woman, addressed as "Thaïre," the narrator concludes that he must direct his poetic energy back to Paris:

> I shall give myself up to the fate that leads me. Let us go then, lyre in hand, to the banks of the Seine. I shall test there the power of my songs. I shall launch my genius into greater flight, and astonish the Louvre's swans with its harmonies![52]

Thus Joseph suggested that it was indeed possible to pursue his self-expression in France, and this seemed to be the answer to his "broken lyre," which he now carried confidently to the heart of Paris. It is notable, however, that the poem made no explicit reference to the mending of this broken instrument, the defining metaphor of the work.

Critical responses to this published work echoed some of those tensions that we have observed in the visual representations of the "Oriental" in Paris. In *Le Mercure du XIXe siècle,* Tissot acknowledged Joseph primarily as "a kind of literary phenomenon" in his mastery of "*our* language and its genius." Tissot praised this "Egyptian" for his elegance and purity in prose, the ability to handle verse skillfully, and a vast erudition in antiquity and Oriental literature: "Assuredly a foreigner who writes such verses *is a Frenchman whom we can adopt;* he has earned in Parnassus his letters of naturalization."[53] Unfortunately, as we shall see, such Parnassian identity documents had little value amid the hard realities of a bureaucratic state.

The identity that was being offered to Joseph was not a Franco-Arab identity, but a "double identity"—both Egyptian and French. For Tissot, Joseph could represent the "universality" of French culture, on the condition of remaining foreign. He could be "naturalized" by his talent, but that adoption would always be ambivalent. As an "Egyptian," he would always remain distinct from the "true" Frenchman. Thus Tissot took Agoub to task for being "false and exaggerated" in the most intimate matters—the question of love. He complained that the recriminations Agoub addressed to his mistress "run the risk of wounding her, and above all of making her turn cold."[54] Tissot pointed out that Joseph was not married, and that if his mistress were to leave him, he might "learn some useful lessons on the dangers of *not speaking fluently* the language one should use with women."[55] Thus Tissot suggested that despite Joseph's perfect fluency in French, he had failed to acquire the underlying and indefinable sensibility that defined French culture, the deeper and more intimate dimension of identity.

Other critics were cruder in remarking the foreignness that they claimed to find in Joseph's writings. J. Saint-Martin in the *Journal asiatique* insisted that the "slight *strangeness* [*étrangeté*] in the expression of his thoughts" was the real merit of Joseph's writing. "It is perhaps from a man of the Orient," wrote Saint-Martin, "familiar with all the resources of the French language, that it falls to teach us this Oriental style of which we hear so much and know so little."[56] The term *étrangeté*

was very close to its cognate *étranger* (foreigner). Even the most sympathetic critics read Joseph's work as that of a "foreigner" and marveled at his ability and fluency. They did not, however, consider him to be a "French" poet, and paid little
serious attention to the actual content of his poetry. Joseph found himself trapped
in a duality of roles that he was never fully able to occupy. By 1825, the "Arab"
who had sought a role in French society in 1821 had succeeded beyond his wildest
dreams, but only as an "Egyptian." While the two identities seemed to be in some
way complementary, Joseph increasingly discovered that they were not. The illustrations from his patroness Adélaïde Dufrénoy's 1814 series *Le tour du monde ou
Tableau géographique et historique de tous les peuples de la terre* (figs. 14a and b)
may give us some sense of how these categories were conceived even by the most
liberal and sympathetic of Joseph's admirers, who, according to Tissot, felt for
him "a tender affection."[57] Madame Dufrénoy, the great champion of Agoub, and
perhaps the "Thaïre" of his poem, described the Egyptians as a mixture of "Copts,
descended from the former indigenous inhabitants, and . . . Romans, Arabs, Turks,
renegades of every nation, and Mamluks."[58] The accompanying illustration provided a kind of idyll of Egyptian life, with a beautiful young man pointing out some
local flora to a young woman. The Egyptian here was clearly coded as civilized
and civilizing. The Arab, too, was imagined by Madame Dufrénoy as a highly ro-
manticized figure, full of generosity and hospitality, but much more warlike, particularly in the illustration provided. But at the edge of these positive identifications was the image of the "Barbaresques," the inverse of the positive image of the
Egyptians; these were predatory North African Arab men uncovering an implicitly European naked female figure—not educating, but enslaving women.

These images are instructive in demonstrating that the cosmopolitanism of the
Restoration, for all its liberal and sometimes sentimental identification with a plural conception of "civilization," also had its limits. It is here, I think, that we must
search for the reasons for Joseph's inexplicable plunge from the height of fame
and success into the backwater of obscurity. The "Egyptian" identity that he adopted
as a mode of exchange with his Frenchness placed him in an exterior position to
both Egypt and France. Alongside the "civilized" Egyptian and the "noble" Arab
lay the "barbarian" threat of Islam associated with North Africa. In the tumultuous last years of the Restoration, as we shall see in the next chapter, these cultural and racial conceptions of the Arab would be reconfigured, with disastrous
consequences for Arab France and for Agoub himself.

The "broken lyre" of Joseph's major poem *La lyre brisée* represented his abandonment of poetry, as well as his decision to remain in France and work in the
role offered to him, churning out prose about Egypt to earn himself a living. He
published a series of prefaces and long articles dealing with Egyptian history and
culture and the Arabic language, and secured an excellent post teaching Arabic at
the Lycée Louis-le-Grand.

FIGURE 14A–B. Illustrations from Adélaïde Dufrénoy, *Le tour du monde, ou Tableau géographique et historique de tous les peuples de la terre* (Paris: Alexis Eymery, 1814). Author's collection.

Barbaresques.

FIGURE 14A–B. (*continued*)

Then, in 1826, Agoub was appointed to teach at the "École Égyptienne" in Paris. For the first time, he encountered a large number of Egyptians who had been raised and educated in Egypt. Among them was the young intellectual Rifa'a al-Tahtawi, who in just six years would leave a powerful imprint on this Arab "generation of 1820." But the convergence of different strands that this encounter offered, the integration of the heritage of Islam by a newly confident second generation of French Arabs and their reconnection to the intellectual and social changes taking place in the Muslim world, was shadowed by both internal and external conditions: a new and more reactionary Restoration regime, and global events that pitted an increasingly concerted Europe against a refigured "Orient" in Constantinople, Egypt, and North Africa, under the sign of a new imperial turn.

7

Remaking Arab France

In a remarkable preface to his final work, published after his death, Joseph Agoub offered an eloquent defense of the Arabic language, placing Egypt for the first time in his works as just one element in a larger Arab world. In this text, Agoub acknowledged his debt to the work of Arab intellectuals like Mikha'il Sabbagh and Ellious Bocthor who had come to Paris before him. But where in his early poetry he had condemned Islam as a barbarian attack on the glories of ancient Egypt, for the first time Agoub acknowledged the Qur'an as one of the inexhaustible sources of the power and vigor of the Arabic language and culture:

> All the nations of Turkey, of Egypt, of Syria, of Persia and the three Arabias, the peoples of Algiers, of Tripoli, of Tunis and the empire of Morocco, those of Ethiopia and the Sahara, of the coasts of Zanzibar and Senegal—in a word, all the Muslims scattered pell-mell across the face of the old world draw from this unique and eternal book not only the dogmas of their religious belief but also the true pattern of their civil laws, the rules of their behavior, the instruction of their duties, and often the precepts of their conduct toward Europe and its agents.[1]

At the beginning of the 1820s, Joseph Agoub had written paeans to ancient Egypt in which Muslims appeared only as intruders and vandals, sabotaging the civilizational transfer from Egypt to France. Here, he spoke with force of a Muslim world as a great civilization in itself, stretching across the "face of the old world," that could speak back to Europe on the basis of its "eternal" religious teaching. In this text, Joseph no longer spoke as the ventriloquist's dummy of Restoration Egyptomania, but as an Arab, proud of the Arabic language and culture and its Islamic heritage. He went on to assert the "superiority" of Arabic and its priority over European languages and cultures:

> The Arabic language, strong in its literary superiority, does not even need this political support to maintain itself in the first rank of European studies. [This] language that gave so many works to history, to geography, to all the arts . . . carelessly tossed the first glimmerings of civilization into the middle of Europe, and can still offer to the highest intellects of modern societies an inexhaustible source of pleasure and knowledge.[2]

This insistence upon Arab culture and history not just as an ancient source to be rediscovered by Europeans, but as both a source of and a challenge to European civilization, was something entirely new. For Agoub, the study of the Arabic language had become a place in which the exile of Egyptians, Syrians, and others in France could be made meaningful, in which their intermediary role would no longer be marginal but rather crucial to the elaboration of new identities. But, as we have seen, that project would be cut cruelly short. As we proceed toward the conclusion of this book it is the genesis of that project as well as its collapse that we must investigate.

What had changed in the Arab Paris of the late 1820s, which led Agoub to reconfigure so radically the conflicting categories that had so troubled him throughout his early career? In 1826 the first group of students from an Egypt in transformation arrived in Paris. They were a mixed group, more than forty young men drawn in large part from the family and associates of the governor of Egypt, Muhammad 'Ali. These *effendis,* as they were known, were the Turkish-speaking ruling elite of Egypt. Most also spoke Arabic, but they did not locate either their culture or their identity in Egypt's Arab heritage, but in their own wider Ottoman connections. Among them, however, was a last-minute addition, the Egyptian Arab intellectual Rifa'a al-Tahtawi, who was destined to become by many accounts the most influential Arab writer and intellectual of the nineteenth-century Arab *nahda,* or renaissance.[3] It is the encounter between this seminal figure and the Arab intellectuals of Restoration Paris that we will explore in this chapter.

Rifa'a al-Tahtawi was born to a family in Upper Egypt that had been impoverished by the taxation reforms introduced by the modernizing program of Muhammad 'Ali's administration. He was educated along traditional lines, from the local mosque through the *madrasa* to the university of al-Azhar, the centuries-old intellectual center of the Muslim world. It was his teacher at al-Azhar, Hassan al-'Attar, who proposed his appointment as imam to the planned educational mission to Europe. Al-'Attar had encountered the French during the occupation of Egypt in 1798; after the evacuation he traveled to Istanbul, where he studied medicine and natural sciences, seeking out the most challenging new currents of thought in the Muslim world.

Tahtawi, although originally appointed as a religious adviser to the mission, took the opportunity to learn French soon after his arrival in France. Within a few years he had reached sufficient proficiency to begin translating important French works into Arabic. He organized his notes and observations on his stay in France into a new kind of *rihla,* a familiar tradition of travel narrative in Arabic literature, which he entitled *Takhlis al-ibriz fi talkhis Bariz* (The Extraction of Refined Gold in the Summary of Paris). This book, though by no means the first account of Europe by an Arabic writer, was the first to be printed in quantity and widely distributed; it was also translated into both French and Turkish within a few years of its publication. Young men had been sent to study in various European countries, particularly Italy, France, and Britain, throughout the previous decade; the mission of 1826, however, was the first large group sent to a single country, and thus opened a place for a pastoral supervisor, as well as a number of servants, bringing the total number of the group to fifty-four.

The story of the École Égyptienne has been recounted in detail by many others, including Anouar Louca, Alain Silvera, and Daniel Newman,[4] and Tahtawi's journey to France has often been imagined as an encounter between two radically different—and radically unequal—cultural traditions. It is a story that many observers have treated as an "iconic moment" of the beginnings of modernization in the Middle East.[5] This is exactly how Louca described Tahtawi's journey: "the intellectual adventure of a young Egyptian, frozen by Arabo-Muslim culture, catapulted out of the Middle Ages—as a result of Ottoman stagnation—into a center of modern civilization."[6] Silvera reproduced the whole range of such markers in his article, projecting Tahtawi's emotions on his arrival in Marseille in terms such as "strange," "startling," "bewildered," "endearingly naïve," and "weird and unfamiliar."[7] These historians have assumed that Tahtawi's journey, and that of the other students, was a movement from the periphery to the center, from the past to the present, from barbarism to civilization.

Peter Gran has suggested that the magnitude of the difference between Egypt and France at this period has been inflated by historians in their quest for the picturesque confrontation of an outsider with European culture. In particular, that difference has been conceived as temporal as well as involving distance. Muhammad 'Ali's Egypt has been imagined as a society rushing to "catch up" with Europe. Khaled Fahmy's work has challenged this thesis, demonstrating conclusively that the reforms applied by the Egyptian viceroy were modeled on the Ottoman *nizam-i-jedid* (new organization) begun half a century earlier.[8] Similarly, we must revise the presentation of Tahtawi as a "blank slate" waiting to be inscribed by European culture. He was an ambitious young scholar, fully schooled in his own traditions, who saw the journey to France as the way to advance a career held back by his poverty and lack of social connections. Juan Cole has shown clearly how deeply Tahtawi's work was imprinted with both the form and content of earlier Islamic thought, particularly that of the Rationalist school. Cole insists that "French culture added to and in some ways displaced the other non-Arab elements of Islamic humanism such as Indian fables and Iranian epics."[9] We may complicate this insight further by recognizing the crucial role of Arab intermediaries in the transmission or translation of these "non-Arab" elements.

Tahtawi's own text suggests that he did not perceive France as alien in every way from the Egypt in which he had lived, but rather conceived the distance in geographical terms. He first described a feeling of "strangeness" not on his arrival in France, but rather in the Egyptian city of Alexandria, which he described as one of the "Frankish cities" of a cosmopolitan Mediterranean and very different from the provincial towns of Upper Egypt or the urban complexity of Cairo. "I was strengthened in my view when we arrived in Marseille," he wrote. "Alexandria is both a sample and a model of Marseille."[10] But Tahtawi's view of Marseille was shaped almost from the moment of his emergence from the lazaret, not simply by the architectural similarity of Alexandria and Marseille, but by the presence of a population that had already crossed the boundaries of familiar and unfamiliar. He reported:

> In the city of Marseille there are many Christians from Egypt and Syria, who accompanied the French during their retreat from Egypt. All of them wear French clothes. It is rare to find a Muslim among those who left with the French: some of them have died, whereas others have converted to Christianity—may God preserve us from that![11]

To Tahtawi's surprise, these people were neither French nor Muslim; their abandonment of Egyptian clothing—which had significance in itself for Tahtawi as a religious observance—raised a key challenge to his interpretation of their presence. He described them primarily as "Christians," adopting the traditional sense of their minority identity in Muslim society. But his distance from this community was complicated by a series of conversions and crossings; Tahtawi discussed General Menou's adoption of Islam, the baptism of his son, and the conversion of his Muslim wife in Europe. Particularly troubling to Tahtawi was the case of 'Abd el-Al, who had remained Muslim for fifteen years before converting to Christianity—a punishable act of apostasy under Islamic law.[12] In a later edition of his book, perhaps to allay negative reactions, he added a paragraph declaring that 'Abd el-Al had returned to his faith on his deathbed. Even more confusing was the presence of a young man, dressed in European clothes, whose name was Muhammad, and who, in spite of having left Egypt at an early age, retained knowledge of the religious formulae of Islam. Tahtawi even identified the young man as possibly a descendant of his own family: "His face truly revealed the marks of the *sharifs* of Asyut."[13] These "marks" of a family resemblance that crossed the division of Christian/Muslim and Arab/European destabilized from the very beginning Tahtawi's mental map of identity and difference.

A dossier in the correspondence of the Ministry of War contains letters written by a certain Jean Louis Jérôme, born in Guadeloupe, ex-soldier of the Ninth
Regiment of the Line. In fact, Jean Louis Jérôme was really Ibrahim Mahomet, a
young Muslim Egyptian born in Cairo and taken to Europe at a very young age by a
French captain. Joining the Ninth Regiment at Autun in 1802, he fought with them
in Italy and at the battle of Wagram. In 1807, he was baptized.[14] Ibrahim did return
to his native land after the change of regime in 1814. According to one testimony,
he obtained a passport "on which he passed himself off as a native of Guadeloupe,
and registered under the names given to him at his baptism, in order to avoid the
punishment inflicted by the people of those regions against those who take up
arms against their own country."[15] Ibrahim found the atmosphere in Egypt difficult
and hostile and could not remain long in the house of his father, so, to "escape the
dangers that threatened him," he returned to France and reenrolled in the Legion of
Hohenlohe (a forerunner of the foreign legion) under his baptismal name. In testifying to his real identity in 1821, in order to seek admission to the pension as an
"Egyptian refugee," he included among his papers a passport issued by the Ottoman consulate in Marseille in 1818, in which his name was registered simply as
Mahomet—the traditional French transcription of the name Muhammad.[16]

The story of Ibrahim Mahomet seems too similar to that recounted by Tahtawi
to be merely a coincidence. If this was the case, the encounter may have been a
trigger for Ibrahim's decision in October 1828 to leave France and return to Egypt,
this time apparently with the intention of remaining there on a permanent basis.
Drawing upon the decree of 1816, which had made provision for Egyptians to return
to their native land, he successfully applied to receive a year's pension in return
for a definitive renunciation of future benefits. But within two years he was back
in France, applying for readmission to the refugees' pension. According to the
Ministry of War, he claimed that "his departure from France was motivated by a
mental illness, for the treatment of which his doctor had advised him to revisit his
native land [le sol natal]."[17] On arriving in Egypt he discovered to his distress that
his father and mother were both dead, and that his fortune had been confiscated
from him by the laws of the country (possibly because of his conversion). He then
"remained there until entirely well" before returning at last to Marseille—and,
one assumes, to a far larger circle of friends and acquaintances.

The series of letters documenting Ibrahim Mahomet's struggle with his identity provides one of the few sources for understanding the profound difficulty experienced by many of those living in France—even those who had come very
young to the country or had been born there—in negotiating their identities. The
correspondence can shed light on the struggle that Joseph Agoub expressed
through his poetry. Moreover, when considered alongside Tahtawi's own writings,
they suggest the impact that an encounter with this extraordinary Egyptian figure
could have on a young man who had adopted a new, "French" identity.

But the story of Ibrahim Mahomet also indicates the complexity of the move-ment between France and the Arab world that already characterized Arab France in the wake of the Napoleonic empire. In describing the conversion of Abd el-Al, Tahtawi commented that he later met three children of the Abd el-Al family, two sons and a daughter, in Egypt. One of them, he noted, became a teacher at the same school of Abu Za'bal where Tahtawi himself taught after his return to Egypt. This medical school was opened at the hospital of Abu Za'bal in Cairo in the same year that Tahtawi was sent to France—and notably it was the first school com-posed of 150 Egyptian native students, identified as "Arabs" rather than Turks or Circassians. The students came from the same Azharite educational background as Tahtawi himself and were selected as part of the "Arabizing" program that Muhammad 'Ali used to foster the distinctiveness of Egypt within the Ottoman world.[18] The European teachers initially hired to staff the school were unable to communicate with the students and required interpreters who could speak French or Italian as well as Arabic.[19] These interpreters were drawn from among the local Christians. Several of those named in accounts are from the same fami-lies that had established themselves in Marseille and Paris: Far'aun (Pharaon), Sakakini, and most prominently, Rufa'il Zakhur, whose career in France as Dom Raphaël de Monachis we followed earlier in this book.

Having left the École des Langues Orientales Vivantes in Paris in 1816, after the reduction of his salary by the Restoration government, Rufa'il found a new patron for his modernizing ideas in Egypt. Muhammad 'Ali commissioned an Italian-Arabic dictionary from Rufa'il, along with translations of useful works such as The Prince by Macchiavelli, a life of Napoleon, and a text on the dyeing of silk. It was in the same spirit of reform that Muhammad 'Ali sent students to study various arts and sciences in Italy, France, and Britain. The negotiation of new realities of international politics and commerce required new techniques and skills: Egypt lacked, for example, government printing works necessary for the ex-pansion of a centralized administration. In 1815, Muhammad 'Ali sent Niqula Massabiki, Rufa'il Massabiki, and Ilyas Sabbagh to Milan for education in the processes of printing.[20] It seems likely that the interpreter Messabki (as the name was written in French), after searching unsuccessfully for employment in Paris in 1806, returned to Egypt and placed his sons in a position to succeed where he had not. The first book to be printed after Massabiki's return to Egypt in 1821 was Ru-fa'il's dictionary. In 1828 Tahtawi's former teacher and sponsor, Hassan al-'Attar was appointed editor of the first officially produced Egyptian newspaper, Waqai'i Misriyya (Egyptian Events); Tahtawi would succeed him as editor of this newspa-per in 1831.[21]

These connections can also be seen in Muhammad 'Ali's reorganization of the Egyptian army, which had proved so little able to resist successive French, British, and Ottoman incursions. In 1811, he had ordered the violent elimination of the

Mamluk elite, who had dominated Egypt's military establishment for centuries as individual warlords, each with their own private following. The governor restructured Egypt as a province more closely integrated into the Ottoman model; but at the same time, like other Ottoman governors, he looked for greater autonomy for his province and an extension of his own rule. He looked to European advisers to ensure the redevelopment of his army; France had a surplus of experienced officers, including some from Arab backgrounds, who made ideal candidates for a career in Egypt.[22] The son of Captain Ibrahim of the Mamelukes, Ibrahim Rochemane, went to Egypt after his education at the Collège de Marseille as instructor to the Second Regiment of Cavalry.[23]

Thus, in the 1820s a space of exchange emerged between France and Egypt, two countries in the process of competitive, capitalist modernization. This space was filled by a group that possessed the necessary mobility and language skills to mediate this overlapping space of French and Egyptian modernities—those families, for the large part Syrian Christian in origin, who now had close networks of family, social connections, and commercial links between the two countries. In this sense, arriving in France, Tahtawi followed a path that was already well traveled in both directions.

But if Tahtawi could identify a clear pattern of differences and similarities between Alexandria and Marseille, two ports engaged in a cosmopolitan exchange across the Mediterranean, his journey to Paris was a different matter. Like the many provincials who took the road from small communities to the capital, Tahtawi discovered in Paris a model of a radically different organization of life.[24] Paris was a paradigm of modernity to all those who arrived in this expanding center of culture and commerce, whether from provincial France, other countries of Europe, or the Arab world. This is evident in the very title of Tahtawi's book, which announced the work as a summary (*takhlis*) of Paris (Bariz); it was not titled, for example, "Journey to France" or "An Account of the Land of the Christians." The word *talkhis* suggested that Tahtawi was attempting to rationalize and simplify the results of his experience, to "refine" them into a more profitable form. In this way, "Bariz" was transformed both linguistically and epistemologically into *ibriz* (refined gold).[25] Tahtawi's response to Bariz was to be a "distillation" of an experience rather than an acquisition of something that was already formulated; it was to be an active process of "refinement" carried out by a modernizing intellectual. The title not only transliterated but reinvented Paris as an Arab name that "rhymed" within the literary structure of sophisticated Arabic poetry.[26]

But "Bariz" was not an invention by Tahtawi; it had existed for more than two decades. From the earliest moments, Tahtawi's "refinement" was aided and accompanied by the presence of French Arabs. The Egyptian students were sent to Paris in small groups, each accompanied by an interpreter chosen from among the Arab community in Marseille: Joseph Awad, Eid al-Bajaly, Mikha'il Halabi, and Joanny Pharaon. The new École Égyptienne appointed several French Arabs as interpreters and teachers, and even as domestic servants at the school, as well as inviting them to supervise the students' examinations.[27] By far the most important of these figures was Joseph Agoub, who, as we have seen, continued to teach at the Egyptian School until its dissolution in 1831.

Unlike most of his fellow students, Tahtawi threw himself headlong into the opportunities and challenges that Paris offered. His first goal was to learn French to the highest level; this was accomplished primarily through the assistance of Joseph Agoub, who was appointed as chief teacher of French but was able to instruct the students in their own language, which made it much easier to encourage their rapid progress. In his book, Tahtawi acknowledged his debt to Agoub, whose name he put into Arabic as al-khawaja Ya'qub al-Misri (the learned scholar Jacob the Egyptian).[28] He included in his book a long excerpt from his own separately published translation into Arabic of Joseph Agoub's poem La Lyre brisée.[29] Thus the first text that Tahtawi chose to translate from French into Arabic was not the work of a French thinker such as Rousseau or Voltaire—or, more appropriate during the Restoration, Bossuet or Fenelon—but rather Joseph Agoub's "Broken Lyre," the poem dealing with his struggle to articulate a belonging to both France and Egypt. Thus, even before he wrote his Takhlis, Tahtawi had invested his own Arabic voice in translating this experience and this vision of Egyptian identity into Arabic. Tahtawi wrote of the difficulty of this translation: "Like other poems in French, the original is of a sophisticated nature, while in translation its eloquence vanishes and the spirit of the author hardly manifests itself."[30] The seriousness with which he treated this difficulty suggests how closely Tahtawi had connected with the "spirit" of Agoub's poetry.

These questions of translation crucially concerned not only language, but also the larger issues of history and identity. Later in the Takhlis, Tahtawi included a long prose passage by Agoub concerning the importance of history. In introducing this second translation, he called Joseph a "French author." The passage Tahtawi chose to include covered several pages and constituted a key element of the structure of ideas that made this book so widely read in the Arab world. The significance of this passage was not in teaching Arab authors like Tahtawi the value of history—Tahtawi already drew upon a long and illustrious tradition of Arab historiography by scholars such as Ibn al-Iyas and Ibn Khaldun, whose Muqaddimah anticipated European historical thought by centuries.[31] Rather, the ideas of Joseph Agoub struck him as new and worthy of inclusion at length. Joseph had observed:

> History is like a public school that attracts every nation that seeks instruction. It is also the repository of experiences of past events that are helpful to the present situation. . . . History opens its treasures for the wise man, in order . . . that his mind will

be diverted from the vicissitudes of the trivialities of human existence . . . revealing the many chains of time, the last link of which is attached to the creation of the world. And do these chains not form a vast field through which one can observe at once all nations, states and times?[32]

The novel idea here was that history was not destined only for princes, but for all those seeking wisdom, "irrespective of their rank or standing." History was not an ethnographic description or a collection of stories, but an analytic vision that linked past and present. But Agoub's vision was also a troubled one, where civilizations rise and fall, virtue and vice succeed one another without determination by a single process, and the dominant emotion is one of wonder and amazement rather than analytic detachment and the search for origins:

> Anyone who takes a truthful look at the wonders of history . . . will climb the peak of observation and will see the world in its entirety at his feet, like an ocean on which ships laden with human hopes and aspirations float aimlessly, exposed to storms.

One is reminded here of the storms that accompanied the ships laden with emigrants from Egypt to France, the hopes and aspirations that had been dashed by the death of General Ya'qub and by the terrible events of 1815. But Tahtawi went on to quote directly from Agoub's radically new vision of what it meant to be Egyptian:

> Today's Egyptians do not constitute a race or a nation, but an amalgamation of heterogeneous elements, whose lineage goes back to a number of different races from Asia and Africa. They are like a mixture in which there is no common measure, and their features do not make up a distinct shape by which it is possible to tell whether a person is Egyptian simply by looking at his face. Truly, it is as if all the nations of the world helped to populate the land of the Nile.[33]

Since Agoub had never traveled to Egypt, his observations could be based only on his own experience of the "Egyptians" in France—Syrians, Armenians, Greeks, Muslims, Copts, Jews, Sudanese, and many others. It is clear that this vision of an ethnically—and implicitly also religiously—plural Egyptian identity deeply impressed Tahtawi, since this is the most extensive translation included anywhere in his book. What was unexpressed here—and perhaps could not be expressed in an Egypt still dominated by a Turkish-speaking elite—was the sense of a common Arab heritage, in which both Agoub and Tahtawi invested deeply, beyond the "Egyptian" national boundaries of identity.

Agoub's newfound respect for Islam, as the foundation and strength of the Arabic language, was a profound legacy of his years at the École Égyptienne. Tahtawi drew from his teacher a new, pluralist conception of Egyptian identity. Both writers came to develop an Arab modernizing vision, which drew upon the French context, articulating it powerfully, not as simple "mimicry," but as an

Arab modernity that drew on both the ancient and the Islamic past. Tellingly, Tahtawi's published Arabic translation of Joseph's most famous poem was entitled *Nazm al-'uqud fi kasr al-'ud*. This was not a direct translation of the title "The Broken Lyre," but an Arabic transformation and rereading of the poem's meaning. Tahtawi was trying to convey *his own* understanding of the "spirit" of the author. The word *nazm* suggested a rearrangement, the stringing of pearls, which was also an expression for poetic creation. The word *'uqud* means "knots"—it is used both for a necklace and for a legal transaction (*'aqd*). Thus Tahtawi's Arabic translation transformed the shattering of Joseph's lyre (*kasr al-'ud*) into an active work of poetic reconstruction and transformation, the remaking of something precious.

Dipesh Chakrabarty has written persuasively of the need to reconfigure historical analysis outside the rigidly historicist terms that consign other societies to an "imaginary waiting room of history," either delayed or regressed to an earlier point in a universal mode of development, and imperfectly capable of receiving the gift of "modernity" through the tutelage of more developed minds.[34] This is exactly how most Western scholars have interpreted Tahtawi's famous book, and the impact it had on the Arab world, from Tunisia to Iraq.[35] Paris and Cairo were very different, as Tahtawi was keen to observe, and this difference was the very substance of his book's attraction. However, that difference was accompanied by a familiarity, a negotiation of identity as well as difference that gave his book far greater significance than any other such travelogue. This transformation could take place only in an Arab France that had reached, in some sense, its maturity after a quarter century of Arab life and thought in the capital.

But shadows were gathering on the horizon: Paris was in the process of transformation by larger forces, as an image from the year 1827 may show. This engraving depicts the giraffe sent from Egypt to Paris by Muhammad 'Ali, the arrival of which unleashed a strange cultural explosion in Restoration Paris. Burlesque acts, songs, hairstyles, caricatures, pamphlets, furniture, porcelain, even the name of a flu epidemic, immortalized the arrival of this tall herbivore. In part, these responses can be ascribed to the conjunction of popular scientific curiosity with the proliferating technology of the public sphere, particularly mass print and visual media. The giraffe's story has usually been told as a chronicle of innocent exoticism and scientific curiosity.[36] However, the animal's geographic origins seemed to overshadow even its anatomical uniqueness. Over and over again, this loping beast was troped as a "foreigner" in Paris, as *l'Etrangère*, *l'Africaine, or l'Égyptienne*. And these associations were often accompanied by strange excurses on other foreigners in Paris, above all Egyptians and North Africans, with whom the giraffe was relentlessly associated in caricatures, pamphlets, and vaudevilles.

Just one of dozens of images produced on the theme of the giraffe, this caricature shows the animal led by its Egyptian keeper, who appears in a turban topped
with a crescent, and baggy pantaloons (fig. 15). Piled on the giraffe's back are an
assortment of half-naked savages, carrying clubs and axes, embraced by bare-
breasted women. Perched improbably and in a confused tangle, the figures broad-
cast their foreignness to the point of exaggeration, clearly dislocated in both time
and space. They are threatening, both in the primitive weapons they are bran-
dishing, and in their menacing sensuality.

Between the giraffe's long legs can be read the caption "Collège Égyptien." At
first this seems to be no more than a floating, satirical caption. But on closer in-
spection the words can be seen to be inscribed on the stone wall behind the animal. The ambiguity seems intentional: no doubt the illustrator was referring to
the real "Egyptian School," which had been in operation for just over a year in the
rue de Clichy. Though it kept a discreet distance from publicity, its impresarios
were too proud of its role in the "diffusion of civilization" not to announce its
existence, and provide regular updates on the students' progress in a number
of widely read journals.[37]

The figures on the giraffe's back are obviously not Egyptian. They appear to refer more directly to the arrival at almost the same moment of a group of American Indians from the Osage people of North America.[38] This cartoon was not the
only satire to play on the supposed competition between the zoological fascination with the giraffe and the anthropological fascination with the Osages.[39] What
was particularly significant in this image was the identification of these visitors
not as "noble savages," but as threatening figures who were out of place in the urban landscape. The boards nearby announced that the "Théâtre français" was
showing British, German, Chinese, and Dutch plays. We may infer that the satirical intent of the cartoon was to draw attention to the excessive cosmopolitanism
of Parisian culture—a kind of foreign "cultural invasion," which was literalized in
the figures of the Osages, as well as in the turbaned young Egyptian who holds the
giraffe's lead rope—who was, in fact, a young "Egyptian" from Marseille, Joseph
Ebed. The arrival of the giraffe clearly marked a discursive shift in the relationship
between Europeans and those who were increasingly understood as "foreign."
But it also indicated a particular tension between "France" on one side of the wall
and the ambiguous space of the "Egyptian School" housing the Egyptian students
on the other. Egypt here was no longer presented as a foundational source of European civilization; instead it was associated with a foreign and implicitly barbarian threat. The liberal cosmopolitan frameworks that had embraced Egyptianness
in the early Restoration were thus transformed into suspicion and hostility toward these threatening foreigners. This new perception of Egypt was intensified
by the war in Greece, which brought the military forces of Muhammad ʿAli to the

FIGURE 15. *Pandore, 1827 (Curiosités contemporaines): Une girafe montée.* Bibliothèque Nationale de France, Estampes.

support of his Ottoman suzerain. The destruction of the Ottoman navy at the battle of Navarino in 1827 confirmed the European grip on power, and the following year France sent an expeditionary force to intervene against the Ottomans in the Morea. The "civilized" image of Egypt was replaced by a new and hostile characterization, most crudely depicted in the cruelly triumphant black male standing behind a weeping white female victim in Delacroix's influential canvas *Greece Expiring on the Ruins of Missolonghi,* which was painted that same year.[40] The "modern Athens" had suddenly become an unfriendly place for those figured as "Egyptians."

These shifts had very significant repercussions for the emergent Arab identity in France, suggesting a radically shrinking repertoire of choices. The cartoon was only one of many representations of the giraffe, which drew not only the Egyptians but other "Arabs" into their ambit. A vaudeville presented only a week after the giraffe's arrival, entitled *La Girafe, ou une journée au Jardin du Roi,* featured a fight between two Egyptians and a couple of French students masquerading in Oriental dress.[41] Reputable writers such as Salvandy and Balzac penned satires on the Restoration government in the voice of the giraffe.[42] A poem by Barthélemy and Méry, entitled *La Bacriade,* melded together all the anxieties relating to the Arabo-Mediterranean world into a byzantine fantasy that linked the students and the giraffe to the contemporaneous naval blockade of Algiers.[43] The poem proposed that the students had been sent by Muhammad 'Ali, at the dey's request, to spy on the activities of Nathan Bacri, a Jewish merchant who was the middleman in the financial transactions that had led to the diplomatic rupture between France and Algiers. The poem suggested a conspiracy between the dey and Muhammad 'Ali to prevent an alliance between rebellious Greeks and Jews led by Bacri—the latter a "new Moses" who would lead 300,000 emigrants to Jerusalem. The giraffe featured in the poem as a "blood price" offered by the dey to the government of Polignac in exchange for Bacri. The intervention of Rothschild, threatening to withdraw from Paris his "cosmopolitan gold" and thus "send the whole of Europe bankrupt," prevents the government from carrying out the exchange, and this is what the poets imagined as provoking the dey to insult the French ambassador and fire on French ships blockading the port of Algiers. Finally, Nathan Bacri, the doyen of the Café Tortoni in Paris, proves himself the "hero" of the poem by agreeing to return to Algiers and face the wrath of the cruel tyrant, Hussein, in this way preventing war between the two kingdoms.

In this fantasy, Barthélemy and Méry, in many ways sympathetic toward the Egyptians (Méry had been one of the national guardsmen who intervened to protect the refugees in Marseille in 1815), nonetheless read very accurately the discursive and political shifts happening around them. As the epigraph to their poem they cited Bossuet's prediction that Algiers would fall under the sword "like a vulture hunted in its rocky nest."[44] The year 1827 marked a key inflectional point in the French turn toward imperialism. In the naval battle at Navarino in October, France found itself suddenly—and rather involuntarily—on the victorious side of a confrontation between European and Ottoman/Egyptian forces, helping destroy the very fleet the French had built for their close ally Muhammad 'Ali in preceding years.[45] At almost the same moment, the nonpayment of French debts by Algiers had culminated in the famous insult to the French ambassador by the dey, Hussein, resulting in a punitive French blockade of the Algerian coast.[46] Given the growing crisis within France—the conflict between the rigid, ultraconservative regime of Charles X, which was losing electoral support, and a growing liberal opposition—the popularity of these interventionist measures among conservatives and liberals alike suggested that imperial expansionism might stabilize a fragile national consensus.[47] Such action would have been unthinkable a few years earlier, when military intervention outside France was associated with Bonapartist aggression and the associated disaster it had brought upon France. Now, however, it was the liberal opposition that called for intervention in Greece, on behalf of "freedom" and the values of ancient democracy, while royalists could equally claim such intervention as a defense of embattled Christians against Muslim "barbarity."[48]

This "liberal volte-face," as Jennifer Pitts has called it, was not simply a spontaneous political shift.[49] The events of the late 1820s functioned to confirm a consensus position that was making itself felt across the intellectual field, understood within the frame of a new historical consciousness that interpreted contemporary French society and its recent past in a much grander way, reaching back into distant epochs and claiming a continuity with societies geographically separate from the territory of modern France. The universalist view of "civilization" returned to the fore in the middle years of the Restoration, encouraging the founding of geographical and Orientalist societies such as the Société Asiatique, and the completion of the *Description de l'Égypte*.[50] In this liberal cosmopolitan milieu, Arab intellectuals in Paris found their skills and contributions welcomed, even championed. But the terms on which they were welcomed already contained the seeds of another, more problematic conception, as we saw in Jomard's response to Ellious Bocthor's oration of 1819. Where Madame Dufrénoy's book had distinguished the "civilized" Egyptians from the "Barbaresque" slave traders and pirates, the giraffe carried all of these images jumbled together on its broad back.

If the giraffe was a sign, and a very mobile one, its reception was also a symptom of the breakdown of the liberal cosmopolitanism that characterized the decade after 1817. As Henry Laurens has observed, the plurality of "civilizations" that had been celebrated by the liberal heirs of the Enlightenment was increasingly under fire at this moment.[51] In the work of Guizot, the most influential historian of his generation, the open idea of civilization was circumscribed by a containing historicist framework dominated by the idea of movement and progress, the inexorable forward track later understood as "modernity," whose roots lay exclusively in the European world. It was this structure of thought—the "triad" of "Europe, civilisation, progress,'" as Stuart Woolf has expressed it—that would dominate imperialist thought in nineteenth-century Europe.[52] The Enlightenment conception of European superiority among a plurality of "civilizations" shifted toward a monolinear conceptualization of "civilization" as a single process of development. The dominance of European culture was explained as the result of a development arising out of Egypt, Greece, and Rome, a heritage rediscovered and consolidated by the Renaissance, the Enlightenment, and the Revolution. A new kind of "Orientalism" drew an absolute and qualitative distinction between European and "Oriental" societies. It was in this atmosphere that the Egyptian students arrived in Paris—a city that had been swept by a romantic wave of identification with the Greek struggle for independence, which was now associated with the European heritage struggling to free itself from Ottoman domination.

On 31 July 1826, the bulletin of the Paris Prefecture of Police reported with palpable relief the results of surveillance undertaken at the Barrière de l'Italie, "for the young Egyptians sent to Paris for their education." The agent reported that "a diligence full of these young men arrived in Paris yesterday at half past ten in the evening, traveled along the boulevard, and continued on to its destination without provoking the slightest gathering."[53] The Egyptians were brought into Paris in small groups, beginning with the notables in charge, and followed after a week or so by the students in groups of ten. The imminent arrival of a group of highly visible Egyptians in the capital had taken the French authorities by surprise. On 25 May, the report of the Ministry of Foreign Affairs, confronting this "completely unexpected decision of the pasha of Egypt," presented a number of alternatives to the minister of the interior for dealing with "the inconveniences and the dangers of this peculiar emigration."[54] The imminent arrival of these Egyptian Muslims presented a challenge for a regime so deeply committed to the Catholic revival. Could France place these students in public or private establishments and thus render service to the pasha and to French commerce in Egypt? "It may be," the report suggested, "that after careful consideration of this alternative, and being convinced of the impossibility of accepting and placing such a large number of foreigners of a religion so different and so inimical to our own, he may formally give a negative response." Far from joyfully welcoming these "Muslims" as guests at the banquet of French civilization, the authorities responded to the pasha's gesture with serious reservations and even a certain level of panic.[55]

The relationship between France and Egypt was not in 1827, and in fact would never be, a colonial relationship. Indeed, Egyptian imperial ambitions had preceded those of France by more than a decade. Napoleon's failed plans to expand his rule over Egypt into Syria, Sudan, and the Arabian Peninsula had been realized by Muhammad ʿAli, who by the mid-1820s possessed an empire of more than five million square kilometers, ten times larger than the territory of France. Paris was the capital of a nation stripped of many colonies and controlling less than five hundred thousand square kilometers in offshore possessions.[56] But Muhammad ʿAli remained in theory an Ottoman vassal, his hard-won empire subject to the suzerainty of the Porte. European powers could offer new sciences and technologies, in printing, administration, and military training, that were equally useful as a counterweight to Ottoman domination. But the Egyptian governor could not refuse the call of his Ottoman suzerains to contribute his rapidly modernizing military forces in the suppression of the Greek uprising, and this threatened to lose him the support of European nations.

Thus the sudden dispatch of the forty-four students, from his own family and from the distinguished families of his court in Alexandria—including several Christians—was certainly at least in part inspired by diplomatic canniness. The creation of the Egyptian School was a long-held project of Bernardino Drovetti and Edmé-François Jomard; it gave a significant fillip to their careers in Egypt and France respectively. But its political valency was demonstrated by the government's refusal, despite the urgings of Jomard, to give the school any official status. The creation of a distinct "Egyptian School" was in part inspired by the French government's refusal to accept the students into French public schools.[57] Some in the government had even suggested the creation of an "Oriental College" in Marseille for the children of the "princes of Barbary and Egypt" and recommended that the students should be accepted as "hostages who will ensure [France] of the good disposition of these princes, for whom we will undertake the education of subjects better capable of serving them."[58] Once again, Marseille was viewed as conveniently distant from the center of French civilization; the presence of these foreigners in Paris was a very different matter. But Muhammad ʿAli remained a powerful international player, and the hesitations of the Ministry of Foreign Affairs were easily overruled by the party of liberal "civilizers."

The École Égyptienne, then, constituted from the very beginning a political transaction. At least in part, the student mission represented an attempt by a powerful Egyptian leader to associate his nation with the discourses of political modernity dominant in France. In return, certain parties in France hoped to advance their own careers by convincing the state of the influence to be gained by entertaining these students, who in the best light might be seen as emissaries of French culture, in the crudest as hostages to ensure Egypt's alliance with French interests in Europe and beyond. The students of the school were certainly not unaware of their political significance, and the school's French organizers soon discovered that the effendis—as these members of princely families in Egypt were known—did not in any sense consider themselves beggars at the feast of French civilization. Members of a powerful Ottoman elite in Egypt, they were rapidly disappointed by what they perceived as the impracticality of the French concept of "universal education," which offered as wide a range of subjects as possible, from history and algebra to natural science and composition. This was an entirely inappropriate method for teaching adult students who were learning French as a foreign language; the effendis quite reasonably felt that they should be provided with intensive instruction in French before proceeding to study a particular specialized field that would help them in their careers. These views quickly developed into a mutiny on the part of the leaders of the student mission. As Jomard wrote to the minister of the Interior in September 1826,

> After this period, Messieurs the effendis first asked for, and then demanded, the suspension of their lessons in geometry and arithmetic, after a debate that lasted for several days. The strongest arguments I posed to them were not able to shift their stubborn resolution. . . . The effendis tried to change the manner of instruction in drawing and French language. . . . If this is how they begin, I fear these difficulties will come up again, even to the choice of methods, books, and the teachers themselves. . . . They have declared their intention to run their own affairs [in terms of discipline and finances] and have decided to ignore the French administrators.[59]

Faced with this revolt, Jomard was forced to call upon the authority of the pasha in Egypt. Muhammad 'Ali, whose intention was at least as much diplomatic as educational, simply instructed the students to obey the will of their French instructors.

The shifting responses of Jomard, a model of "enlightened devotion" in his work at the school, provide an important insight into the changing ways of understanding cultural difference. In 1827, Jomard refused a large financial reward offered by Muhammad 'Ali, because, in his words, "I only consented to direct the studies of the young Egyptians with the approval of a large number of the friends of Enlightenment and humanity, and on the understanding that my work would be voluntary."[60] But his "devotion" in this cause was based on an understanding of the "Arabs" in which he was disappointed. As he wrote to Clot-Bey in Egypt, "Emulation did not produce its effect immediately. . . . The rewards attracted their attention only faintly, and the *stimulus* of self-love remained weaker than I would have liked."[61] Clot-Bey responded that the Arabs were "a people made for civilization, but, in order to make that happen, they must be governed by an enlightened absolutism."[62] He remarked that the French in Egypt, in their "system of liberty and moderation," had left themselves the dupes of the wily inhabitants.

This shift from the model of "emulation" to that of "enlightened absolutism" maps quite well the larger shift toward a colonial mentality. Jomard drew his model of "emulation" from the culture of the Enlightenment and Revolution.[63] Clot-Bey's response significantly shifted these ideas onto a colonialist plane: it was no longer a question of voluntary "emulation" but of "civilization" in the *active* sense of the term, through the "absolute" exercise of the power that seemed

more and more to rest "naturally" in the hands of Europeans.[64] Jomard, an arche-
typal representative of the "civilizing mission" of improvement through modernization, viewed the students as a "blank slate" upon which the benefits of civilization could be inscribed. But facing resistance from his students, which he viewed
as a perverse response to the "natural" advantages they were offered, he increasingly responded with a racial conception of the "Arab" reinforced by his counter-
part in Egypt. If the "Arabs" could not appreciate the opportunity offered to them,
if they could not respond to the model of "emulation" that characterized French
cultural transmission, this was because they needed to be treated differently, not
with consultation and kindness, but with firm rule "for their own good." They
should be divided in order to be more effectively ruled, guarded from "inappropriate" external influences, and denied economic autonomy.

Thus the confrontation between the Egyptian students and their French teachers was linked to the shifting relations of power between "Europeans" and "Arabs"
more widely, which prepared the ground for the "imperial turn" of 1830, which I
will examine in the next chapter. The process of "learning" the intellectual structures of modernity was far more active and contested than most accounts have
suggested.

The École Égyptienne was an anomalous space in a Paris that was rapidly
transforming from a liberal cosmopolitan milieu into one in which racialized representations of Arabs exerted an increasingly powerful force. It was the coincidence of Egyptian and French political interests that resulted in the creation of
this space. But this space also allowed an Arab cultural development in France to
intersect momentarily with the modernizing trajectory of an important Egyptian
Arab intellectual. This encounter, however, would be very short-lived.

On 30 April 1827, Joseph Agoub was scheduled to read an extract from his
planned collection of short Arabic songs, or *maouals,* drawn from the culture of
his Franco-Arab community in Marseille, at the annual meeting of the Société
Asiatique, the foremost institution of Orientalism in Paris—and indeed in Europe. In attendance was the society's president, the powerful duc d'Orléans. In the
event, the lateness of proceedings prevented him from reading his work in this
august assembly. Joseph was at the height of his career, a respected journalist and
widely published writer, a member of several learned societies and a frequent figure in the Parisian salons, professor of Arabic at the prestigious Lycée Louis-le-
Grand and chief teacher at the École Égyptienne. He seemed to have taken up the
trajectory cut short by the early death of Ellious Bocthor, whose dictionary at last
appeared in print shortly afterward.[65] In this new project, however, he departed
from the "Egyptian" frames of his previous work to suggest, if only hesitantly, that
the French muse, weary of an ancient Greece "translated a thousand times, imi-
tated a thousand times" might turn instead to Arabic poetry whose "Oriental
charm . . . offers to rejuvenate our ideas."[66] In presenting the Greek poet Anacreon

as "a joyous old man" and the Arabs as a force of youthful energy, Agoub was certainly swimming against the principal currents of Restoration cultural politics. We cannot tell if this played any part in the cancellation of his reading. But the changes taking place in Agoub's cultural expression were very marked.

During the four years in which he taught at the "Egyptian School," Joseph underwent a significant transformation. Gradually, his early ideas about Egypt had changed. Increasingly, he rediscovered the Arab roots of his childhood. He returned to poetry, no longer writing long and melodramatic poems based in a French, classicizing sensibility, about the conflict between love and ambition. Instead he began to collect the *maouals* he had heard in his youth in Arab Marseille— short Arabic songs filled with desire and longing and featuring simple but powerful images.[67] These poems "at the same time erotic and elegiac" offered a "complete meaning" in a single strophe; they were "miniatures sketched without artifice . . . that breathe[d] with all the naïveté of primitive poetry."[68] In one of the poems, called "Le voile,"

> the beloved comes forward, but her face is covered, and all spirits are ashamed and confused at her gaze. The reed of the Valley of Nakas waxes jealous of her tall and waving frame. All at once her hand draws away the envious veil that covers her, and the people of the village cry out in surprise. "Is this lightning," they ask, "which has flashed out over our houses, or have the Arabs lighted fires in the desert?"[69]

These poems were a surprise to all who read them. At least one critic saw Agoub as the seminal influence on French romantic Orientalism, as "the first who broke with the traditions of the degenerate classicism of the imperial period and brought, around 1820, images and depictions of the Orient into French poetry."[70] Lamartine included selections from Agoub's *maouals* as an appendix to his *Voyage en Orient* of 1835.[71] But if Joseph Agoub's work thus served to inspire a new romantic generation of French writers, this contribution came at a heavy cost.

Just over three years later, the duc d'Orléans, president of the Société Asiatique, became king—but no longer king of France, rather "king of the French"— after a revolution that overthrew the Bourbon dynasty for the third and final time. Within a few months of the change of regime, Joseph Agoub was inexplicably sacked from his position at the Lycée Louis-le-Grand. An account of Agoub's life written in 1835 stated tactfully that "the political commotion turned public attention away from literature."[72] But the biographical dictionary of the Michaud brothers told a different story:

> [Agoub] was dismissed from his post in 1831 and left to survive on a meager pension. Neither the efforts of his friends nor the protest registered in the name of science could shift the decision of the minister of foreign affairs. This disgraceful injustice delivered him a fatal blow: he left Paris with his wife, the daughter of the courageous Colonel Pierre, and a young and sickly child, making his way to Marseille to seek the

support of his brother, a merchant of the town. But he could not withstand the violent despair that gnawed at him, and he died in the first days of October 1832.[73]

The documents revealing the reasons for this injustice have not yet come to light. Agoub's may have been an isolated case, or dependent upon other circumstances. But his fate was tied to that of Arab France. In order to better comprehend his fall, we must investigate another dark chapter of this history of Arab France: an extraordinary year that saw both a revolution and a lurch toward a century of empire. The consequences of 1830 would crush French Arabs inexorably between liberty and oppression, shattering the fragile equilibrium they had achieved at last after three decades.

8

The Cathedral and the Mosque

At noon on 18 December 1832, Joanny Pharaon, the chief interpreter to the military commander of the French army in Algiers, stood on the steps of the Kechaoua Mosque in the Shari' al-Diwan. Before him, the great doors of the mosque were closed and barricaded; four thousand Muslims had locked themselves inside. Behind him, a company of the Fourth Regiment of the Line had installed itself in the street facing the mosque. Joanny stood alongside the other interpreters of the "Commission" appointed by the duc de Rovigo, who had been charged with negotiating the seizure of the most beautiful mosque in Algiers. The French had planned for its transformation into a cathedral, which would serve as the centerpiece of their permanent colonial possession of Algeria.[1]

What profound shift had brought Pharaon, a descendant of the first Arab migrants to France, to this stark choice at the front line, between French and Arab identities? As we shall see in this chapter, Joanny played an intimate part in those encounters of the late 1820s that synthesized the heritage of Muslim Egypt and the experience of French Arabs. The friendship and intellectual exchange between Rifa'a al-Tahtawi and Joseph Agoub marked both men deeply, as we have seen. But this exchange remained in the sphere of Arabic language, poetry, and culture: it did not have an overtly political aspect. The strengthened "cultural Arabism" that emerged from their connection must be clearly distinguished from later formations that articulated more clearly their relationship with the structures of political power in Arab countries and globally. Was such a political element entirely absent from the Arab France of the late 1820s? As this was a period of radical political ferment, it seems strange that these currents should not have touched the Egyptians. In the previous chapter we saw that the Egyptians occupied a highly politically charged space, one that could not escape the changing prisms of racialized representation.

Tahtawi made no overt engagement with politics in his book. He meticulously described the political system in France, the parliament, and the Charter of 1814 while refraining from any political comment of his own. But in the later chapters of his book, he devoted considerable space to a description of the events of the Trois Glorieuses of July 1830 that was far more detailed than any other account of contemporary events related in the book. Tahtawi did not mention the source of his information, and it seems unlikely that his respectable and elderly teachers would have been able to provide him with this information. It is more probable that he learned about these events from another French Arab intellectual, Joanny Pharaon, who took an active role in them and wrote extensively about them. Joanny's story can tell us more about the political dimension of Arab identity in France at this highly charged moment. Joanny was raised as a Parisian, and he belonged to the city in a new way. But in the ferment of the political and imperial transformations after 1830, his unexpected path marked out very clearly the trajectory of the Arab France I have set out to describe in this book, and sheds some light, too, on Joseph Agoub's tragic fall from grace.

In July 1826, Joanny Pharaon was appointed with three other "refugees" to accompany the small groups of Egyptian students who were headed to Paris. This journey was not a novel experience for him: his family had been living in the capital for more than two decades. His father, Elias, the former interpreter of General Bonaparte in Egypt, had been settled in the capital when he tried to adjudicate the conflict between Georges Aïdé and Joubran Mehenna in 1811. Under the Empire he had prospered, and he had benefited from the maintenance of Napoleonic pensions in the Restoration. His son Joanny was educated for a period in Marseille, taking advantage of the Arabic lessons given by Gabriel Taouïl, and then at the École des Langues Orientales in Paris. Like Joseph Agoub, he showed great talent for the Arabic language, mastering it to the highest level. He sought several smaller teaching appointments in Paris before he was recruited for the École Égyptienne in 1826. The other guide-interpreters were sent back to Marseille, but Joanny was retained, by his own account, as "first teacher" in the school. This appointment would not last long, however.

In this early period, the school had appointed several members of the Arab community in France as interpreters and teachers, and even domestic servants at the school, as well as inviting them to the students' examinations. It seems, however, that the school's administrators, among whom was Edmé-François Jomard, began to be troubled by the influence of these French Arabs over their compatriots. Pietro Ruggieri, a former soldier of the Mamelouk corps and inveterate Bonapartist, was a particular concern to Jomard, not so much because of his political persuasion, which Jomard largely shared, but because Ruggieri served as a direct connection between the students and the world of Paris, making their purchases for them and encouraging them to partake of Parisian entertainments (which, according to Jomard, involved "an incredible abuse of hard liquor").[2] Ruggieri was followed by police spies, who reported that on arrival in Paris, he had gone to the rue du Bac "to renew his acquaintances there."[3] Another report insisted that he was an interpreter and not a servant and was "held in some esteem by the young Egyptians, as a result of the usefulness of his services to them."[4] Jomard tried, unsuccessfully to have Ruggieri exiled to Marseille. Instead, he received permission to split the students up and distribute them in various private homes and boardinghouses throughout Paris.

When the central house was broken up, Joanny was dismissed as French teacher to the students. Jomard's actions against Ruggieri give some credence to Joanny's subsequent complaint about the "imperious circumstances" of his dismissal.[5] Publishing his "new" teaching method far away in Marseille in 1827, Joanny took particular care to thank "the Muherdar effendi, Turkish head of the college, and the erudite Sheik el-Réfahi [Tahtawi]: the first for having encouraged me to publish this work, the second for having helped me with his advice."[6] It seems likely that it was because of his close relationship with the rebellious students that the young man was packed off to Marseille. Eventually, in 1828, he was given a position in Toulon supervising the education of three Egyptian students studying shipbuilding there.

Joanny demonstrated some rebellious inclinations of his own. He returned to Paris in 1829, filled with bitterness at the problems occasioned for his family under the increasingly reactionary government of Jules de Polignac, Charles X's unpopular prime minister. Joanny's father, Elias, had been appointed consul-general for the République des Sept-Îles during the Empire, but the pension associated with this position—previously assured by the Restoration government—had now been revoked by the new Ministry. Joanny later described his anger at the "arbitrary actions [by the government that] added further to the general discontent" depriving several "respectable families" of their sole financial resource "by the whim of the minister."[7] In a footnote, he elaborated further on his complaint:

> From that terrible moment to this very day, this elderly invalid with a large family to support has not once been able to gain an audience in which to demand justice; more than twenty-five letters have remained unanswered, and every approach has so far been useless. Let us hope, then, that this crying shame will be redressed and that Mr. Pharaon—who is in no way deserving of such treatment—will be restored to his full rights, despite the continuing refusal offered in the name of Polignac by M. Gernier, chief of division at the Department of Foreign Affairs, today, 14 August 1830.[8]

Certainly, for Joanny, this personal affair had become a burning political issue, one for which he was prepared to risk his future and even his life. In this text, for the first time, a member of the Arab community articulated a clear link between the private bonds of family and the public questions of political commitment and participation. Joanny was angry as a *French citizen,* and his response was to commit himself to political action.

But Joanny's writings of the period also demonstrate that this French identity in no way excluded his identification with his Arab origins. In 1829, he published a book treating the key questions of the "Orient"—the reforms in Turkey and the confrontation between the Ottoman and Russian empires. He wrote:

> Familiar with the language, habits, and customs of the Levant, having had frequent relations with distinguished persons of the Orient, we felt that in publishing the result of our observations, sketching the portraits of the emperors Mahmoud and Nicholas, . . . we might focus public opinion on those political affairs that have occupied and will continue to occupy for a long time yet the debates of the newspapers.[9]

Joanny confidently presented himself as a writer whose Levantine background gave him a special understanding of the affairs of the "Orient," yet who remained a full member of the French sphere of "public opinion" and might work to shape and direct it.

The importance of this text, written on the eve of the transformations wrought by the events of 1830, lies in its suggestion of the possibility of a *politicized* Arab identity in France. Joanny demonstrated a willingness to express an independent view of his subject. Where most texts of the time portrayed the Ottoman sultan as a cruel despot denying the legitimate claims to freedom of "European" Greeks, Joanny described a rational, modernizing leader:

> Mahmoud shows wisdom, a firm will, a solid spirit, which contribute to implementing the great revolution that has transformed his states over the last ten years, exasperating his people, and putting his life in danger at every moment. This revolution, which has cost the lives of two sovereigns, and which none of their predecessors dared to attempt before them, Mahmoud alone has managed to accomplish.[10]

A year before the overthrow of the Restoration, Joanny identified with the "revolution" he saw taking place in the Ottoman world, under the leadership of a reforming sovereign who faced great dangers in order to transform his society. In a France dominated by philhellenism, where "Oriental" rulers were routinely depicted as cruel tyrants seeking power at any cost, Joanny's favorable evaluation of Mahmoud as a moderate, rational, and intelligent reformer was a radical countercurrent.

Joanny's admiration of a Muslim ruler who sought to "give a very different direction to the spirit of the Muslims, and elevate them . . . to the level of the other peoples of Europe" challenged the claims of the Europeans to be the sole actors of "civilization." More than simply expressing a pro-Turkish partisanship, Joanny challenged what Johannes Fabian has called the "denial of coevalness" by placing a Muslim leader not only at the same level but *ahead of* the Europeans in his progress toward enlightenment:[11]

> Although the sovereign of a people reputed to be barbarous, Mahmoud has shown himself in more than one situation to be more just and more enlightened than certain sovereigns in a *civilized* Europe. He protects the arts and sciences in cultivating them himself, he encourages the spread of enlightenment in his empire by attaching to his service men of every kind and of every nation who are capable of teaching others.[12]

Joanny placed the emphasis squarely on exchange, and on the role of intermediaries "of every kind and of every nation" who were the bearers of enlightenment. This was the most political text produced by a member of the Arab diaspora, and it achieved its political aims not through loud rhetorical claims, but rather through its dogged counterdiscursive deployment of civilization, modernity, enlightenment, revolution, progress, and reason—the key terms of the historicist narrative of European superiority—attributing them instead to a Muslim leader.

Joanny's writings revealed a young man who identified himself with the liberal critique of absolutist rule in France, while refusing to project this despotism onto the figure of the "Oriental" or Muslim ruler. Joanny was a Christian Arab and thus had every reason to adopt the conventional negative stereotypes of Muslims. But, like Joseph Agoub, he had interacted closely with Tahtawi at the Egyptian School, and he seems to have drawn from this experience the same capacity to observe the Muslim world with a different and more sympathetic eye.

Tahtawi did not mention Joanny anywhere in his book, in contrast to his respectful deference to *al-khawaja* (the learned) Agoub, nor did he include any translations of Joanny's extensive writings. But it seems unlikely that Tahtawi's long, detailed account of the events of the Revolution of 1830 could have been drawn from any other source. Joanny Pharaon was in Paris during the days of July 1830. According to his own account, published in 1831, he was not only an observer but an active participant in the revolution. He claimed to have personally harangued a detachment of the Fifth Regiment of the Line in the rue Neuve des Petits-Champs. He wrote that "it was because of these exhortations that the regiment fired in the air."[13] This was confirmed by a British traveler of the period, who reported:

> At this moment, according to Mr. Sadler, M. Joanny Pharaon ... advanced to the troops; and was proceeding to address them, when the officers interfered, remarking to the orator, that their soldiers did not need his exhortations, knowing, as they did, that their duty was to obey those under whose orders they were. As the men themselves, however, seemed inclined to listen, M. Pharaon did not suffer himself to be

repulsed by this check; but, borrowing a chair from a neighbouring shop, mounted it, and went on with his harangue. He called upon the soldiers to remember that they were not now going forth to fight against the enemies of France,—in which case, he said, no Frenchman would attempt to stop them, or to damp their ardour,—but to shed the blood of their fellow-countrymen, perhaps of their own relations. Their duty, he implored them to consider, could never be to involve themselves in the guilt of such a crime. If they fired at all, in obedience to the orders of their officers, it ought to be in the air. "Some of the soldiers," continues Mr. Sadler, "immediately cried out that they were not assassins—that they would not fire on the people: the cry ran through the ranks, 'We will not fire, we will not fire.'" They kept their words; and these brave Frenchmen, every time they were ordered to fire, elevated their muskets above the heads of the people, and, as soon as they were able, joined them.[14]

Tahtawi reported a strikingly similar scene in his book: "When the soldiers saw that the people were going to win, and that using their arms on the people of their country and their kinsmen was shameful, most of them refused to fight."[15] This description seems too similar to be a coincidence. Pharaon published another book on the trial of the ministers of Charles X, events that are also given a long and detailed analysis in Tahtawi's text.[16] Tahtawi's perception of these events seems to correspond very closely to Pharaon's perception of the "Glorious Revolution." Tahtawi noted the often insulting comparisons of the pasha of Algiers with Charles X in the satirical press and attributed this willingness to disrespect high authority to the "freedom to express one's opinion both orally and in writing."[17] This was a freedom that Joanny, more than any other figure associated with the École Égyptienne, had fought to defend in his revolutionary action.

This translation of the revolutionary idea of "freedom" was, as Alain Roussillon has argued, the most important and original aspect of Tahtawi's text, and a key reason for its continuing importance long after its descriptions of France had become obsolete. Roussillon suggests that Tahtawi's application of rationality to the political functions of the state made him "the first theoretician of an incontestable modernization of political thought" in Arabic.[18] This thought did not have as an inevitable goal the production of the idea of "nation" or "homeland" (in the classical French sense of *patrie*) that Tahtawi's later writings came to promote. Instead, Roussillon presents Tahtawi's thought in this text as "a missed opportunity for the modernization of a specifically Ottoman form of political thought founded on the *millet* [religious community], of which Rifa'a seems to be at once the last representative and the gravedigger."[19] For Roussillon, the key term Tahtawi "translated" was not the nationalism of *patrie*, but what Tahtawi described as "that which they call Liberty," the assertion of the right of a people to determine the forms of its own sovereignty. Tahtawi certainly interpreted the events of 1830 not as an outbreak of violence and disorder, but as a legitimate protest of the French people against tyranny:

[The king] wanted the ruin of his subjects in that he treated them as if they were his enemies. . . . If only he had graciously granted freedom to a party worthy of this quality, then he would not have found himself in such a predicament, and he would not have lost his throne in the course of these last tribulations. Indeed, the French had become so accustomed to the quality of freedom that it became one of their natural features.[20]

This was a radically new response by an Arab intellectual to the political nature of revolution, which was conventionally rendered in negative terms such as "disorder" (*fitna*) and "chaos."[21] But through the medium of Joanny Pharaon, who could converse fluently on these subjects in Arabic, Tahtawi was able to see the revolution in ways that no Arab observer had ever done before.

Joanny Pharaon was in this sense the first truly French Arab: perfectly fluent in both French and Arabic, he had received a classical French education but retained a clear and independent sense of his connection to the Arab world. From Tahtawi he learned to embrace the Arab dimension of his identity more fully, including the heritage of Islam and the connection to the broader Muslim world. In the crucible of the July days, he participated as a fully political member of the French community, expressing his anger at the tyranny of absolutism and risking his life to call upon the solidarity of his compatriots. Tahtawi "translated" this experience from France into the Arab world of the nineteenth century.

Moreover, Joanny used his "freedom" to break the silence that other Arab intellectuals in France had maintained concerning the crimes committed against Egyptians in 1815, crimes that had so deeply marked his community. In writing his book on the Revolution, Joanny placed this terrible experience within his broader sense of French history:

The Midi saw its prisons filled by denunciations, crimes unpunished; and the bloody days of 1815 produced ferocious imitators of the orgies of 1793. After the evils of a double foreign invasion, when spirits had passed through so many violent emotions, it was difficult for them to resume peaceful feelings all at once: we must therefore credit the terrible disorders that took place at that time to the unusual excitation of spirits under a burning sun. As tranquillity reestablished itself little by little, the massacre of Egyptians was forgotten, as was the assassination of General Brune and so many others.[22]

Joanny invoked this memory against the Restoration's politics of *oubli*, by articulating it as a part of a larger historical movement that he believed had now come to its conclusion through the July Revolution. He may be seen to represent the "coming of age" of his community in a public context, finally confident enough to speak openly about its history, and even to reconcile the terrible violence as part of the "violent emotions" that had been a shared experience of convulsion, collapse, and seismic political shifts. But it was to be a short-lived triumph.

The results of 1830 were to be much more ambivalent for Arabs in France than Joanny might have expected in the heady days of July. Only three months before the July Revolution overthrew the Bourbon Restoration, a French fleet had sailed into the harbor of Algiers. After a relatively brief resistance, the city fell to the invading French forces. The overthrow of the regime of Charles X shortly afterward left this newly acquired conquest in a state of nagging uncertainty. What would the new regime of freedom and equality, of the tricolor flag and the "Marseillaise," do with a land conquered and held by force of arms, against the wishes of its population? The way in which this question was answered can tell us a great deal about the transformation that had taken place across the questions of race and civilization since the early 1820s.

In late 1833, the government of Louis-Philippe appointed a commission to investigate the unresolved question of France's occupation of Algiers and its surrounding region.[23] The rapid conquest of the Regency in 1830 had been followed by a period of extended warfare, costing the French government tens of millions of francs, tying up troops needed for the defense of France, and producing a stream of reports of pillage, massacre, and cultural vandalism perpetrated against the population under French occupation. The Commission d'Afrique of 1833 was intended to report on the current situation and recommend a course of action. The members of the Commission worked assiduously and without prejudice to deliver a damning report on French activity in North Africa: "In a word, we have outdone in barbarity the barbarians we came to civilize, and now we bewail our failure with them!"[24]

This conclusion was almost identical to the argument given by the Comité des Maures, a group of Algerian notables, well acquainted with French language and culture, who had assembled in Paris after their expulsion from Algiers by the duc de Rovigo. Each of these men presented a report to the Commission. One of them, Hamdan ibn Uthman Khodja, published the much longer *Aperçu historique et statistique sur la Régence d'Alger,* which was translated into French by a young Arab from the North African city of Tripoli, Hassuna al-Daghiz, who was also living in Paris.[25] Hamdan hoped to convince the Commission of the benefits of appointing an autonomous Muslim government under French tutelage.[26] His reports of disinterred human bones being recycled by unscrupulous entrepreneurs for the bleaching of sugar, and soldiers returning from subjugated villages with gold earrings still dripping with blood, were confirmed by the Commission's own rapporteurs.

But an increasingly voluble colonial party not only condoned these depredations but called for harsher measures. True colonization of the seized land would require the dispossession of the native inhabitants: in the face of the inevitable resistance that would result, this would necessitate measures of extermination, expelling them "like wild animals . . . into the sands of the Sahara for good," as Armand-

Victor Hain wrote in his *À la nation sur Alger*.[27] Yet despite this overwhelming evidence of atrocity, anarchy, the drain on French finances, British opposition, and thin prospects for ever drawing profit from the colony, the Commission still recommended, seventeen to two, in favor of the maintenance of French domination to preserve "the honor and interest of France."

The indefatigable writings of Hamdan Khodja and Ahmed Bouderba demonstrated a remarkable ability to employ the "civilizing" discourse of French society while making their case on the strength of rational government and universal rights and drawing upon the contributions of other North African intellectuals in Paris. Hamdan commented:

> It astonishes me that the leaders of the French army should be so ignorant of the laws governing war and peace that rule the civilized world. . . . As for me, although I cannot read French, I am well acquainted with the faithful translation into Arabic by Sharif Hassuna d'Ghiez [al-Daghiz] of Vattel's *Traité du Droit des Gens*. . . . Can anyone deny these principles? Are Africans excluded from human society?[28]

But Hamdan had misread the transformation occurring in France: such appeals to the "principles" of national and individual rights would fall on ears deafened by pragmatism and a new sense of the strict boundaries to be applied to such universal notions. Africans were indeed to be excluded from human society and from the universal principles articulated by the Revolution. As the decision of the Commission d'Afrique showed very clearly, the necessity of colonization was a logic that no demonstration of futility, expense, or injustice could unseat. The duc de Rovigo made it clear that the "promises" issued in the Arabic proclamation at the time of the French conquest had been no more than a consciously cynical "ruse of war."[29] The government considered its obligations to Arabs null and void in the light of a greater imperial necessity. The call to natural law, human rights, and the legacy of the Enlightenment would no longer be applied to those categories of human beings whose "civilization" was judged inferior, backward, childlike, and outside the vision of "modernity" shaped within a newly historicist conception of society.

It was during this period of uncertainty that Joseph Agoub, so fêted under the Restoration for his status as an "Egyptian," proud of his double identity as an Arab who had read Virgil and Racine, suddenly found himself discharged from his position at a prestigious Paris Lycée, with no immediate motive provided. His friend and colleague, Jean-Baptiste de Pongerville, an academician, wrote that the Ministry of Foreign Affairs

> did not recall that Agoub was an adoptive child of France, and that France owed a consistent protection to this young scholar: they could see nothing but a foreigner [*étranger*] without resources, and persecuted him without constraint. . . . In a single day he saw the honorable existence he had won by his talents torn away from him, and his glorious future forever closed to him.[30]

For Pongerville, then, the critical term was *étranger*—and it is true that Agoub had never formalized his naturalization, perhaps because of his hesitations about a possible return to Egypt, perhaps because he felt no need of formal recognition for his "Frenchness." Only in 1826, with his future in Paris apparently secure, did he seek naturalization, only to be told that he was ineligible because his country of origin had "never been united to France at any moment."[31] Despite the warmest recommendations of the prefect of the Seine, Gaspard de Chabrol (one of Napoleon's "Old Boys from Egypt"), regarding the "gentleness of his character and the urbanity of his manners," Agoub was told that he would have to wait ten years after his declaration to receive the naturalization he requested.[32] It was this unfortunate circumstance that left him, in Pongerville's words, *sans appui* in the new regime of the July Monarchy. Whatever personal rancor the new minister may have had, it was the fact that he was a "foreigner" that left him so utterly exposed. Even Chabrol referred to "cet étranger" in his reply to the Garde des Sceaux.[33]

The aftermath of the 1830 Revolution, and the parallel revolutions it inspired elsewhere in Europe, had brought a flood of foreigners into Paris. Greg Burgess has described the problems created in the capital by the presence of these "revolutionary" foreigners, including hundreds of Italians, Spaniards, Portuguese, and Poles.[34] In reaction to this influx, ministers such as Casimir Périer and François Guizot argued forcefully that France was "French" and not "Belgian, Italian, and Spanish," and that foreigners could not share the same rights, because their "interests, their affairs, their entire existence," lay elsewhere. Burgess suggests that the *droit d'asile*, the revolutionary sense of a right to French protection through ideological proximity to revolutionary ideals, was reconceived as a government *bienfaisance*—an act of voluntary hospitality that could be withdrawn as arbitrarily as it was conferred. The "Law relating to foreign refugees residing in France" of 21 April 1831 authorized the government to compel refugees to "relocate themselves to whichever city should be designated," and to deport them if they refused to obey these instructions.

In 1831, a royal ordinance of Louis-Philippe created the Légion Étrangère as a depot for foreign soldiers fighting for France at a safe distance from the center of power—in Sidi Bel Abbés near Algiers.[35] This colonial space was deemed appropriate for the containment of foreign elements in the state, whose radical commitments threatened to open up the contradiction of a revolutionary monarchy. Algeria would become a space for the expulsion of French elements considered foreign to the bourgeois state, whether rebellious workers, criminals, or Saint-Simonian freethinkers. The usefulness of this space for emptying the metropole of its foreign and dissident elements was an important factor in the decision to retain and expand the North African colony, which continued to be an enormous drain on the French economy and on military resources.

In 1832, Bernard-Joseph Legat published a treatise that brought together for the first time all the various laws regarding foreigners.[36] The treatise emphasized that foreigners could not hold official appointments within the French state. This law had not been enforced for Joseph Agoub on his appointment to the Lycée Louis-le-Grand in 1824. Although the "Egyptian refugees" were in no immediate sense linked to the influx of foreigners from the European states in revolt, their status in French law was suddenly and irrevocably altered. They no longer drew their pension as a "right," but as an act of governmental generosity. Nor did they have the right to mobility; their location would be determined by the authorities. They could no longer hold government office. But where the European refugees described by Burgess were viewed in terms of contradictory *national* attachments, the Egyptians were associated with a broad *racial* difference that rendered them even more alien to the "Frenchness" articulated by Périer and Guizot, bringing their status closer to those long-established statutes on "people of color" that we examined in earlier chapters. Henceforth, the cosmopolitanism of Paris would be constricted by these new racial boundaries.[37]

In his article on "Man" in the dictionary of natural sciences in 1825, Bory de Saint-Vincent classified Arabs for the first time as a separate "species" from Europeans—he noted that previous classifications had included Arabs as part of a *race caucasique* or *race blanche*, at the head of a hierarchical table of six races. A later table of eleven races still included as its first category the "Celto-Scyth-Arabes," to which Europeans and Arabs both belonged. But now "for some time," he wrote, "we have felt that there are a greater number of species in humankind, with a different nomenclature: we will divide them into fifteen." Henceforth, for Bory, the "Japhetic" European species would be distinguished clearly from the "Arab," which was further divided into two races—the "Atlantic" Arabs of North Africa and the "Adamic" race, which included both Jews and Middle Eastern Arabs.[38] But all of these "Arabs" shared certain "primitive traits," notably "a particular conformation of the upper head that provides the basis . . . for that religious exaltation, that tendency to fanaticism, that seems fundamental to the moral character of this species."[39] It was on the basis of new "scientific" ideas such as this that it became possible to reconcile liberty and conquest in Algeria after 1830.

An image from a popular novel of the period dealing with the conquest of Algiers can give us some sense of the crudity of the representation of Arab racial difference in the early 1830s. An illustration from the flyleaf serving to advertise the book's content, it shows a Georgian woman from the harem, her bodice ripped open, protecting the life of a French soldier against a group of marauding Arabs with guns and flowing Bedouin robes (fig. 16).

The pointed faces and hooked noses of the Arabs emphasize their predatory nature and their "Semitic" racial background. The main figure is bent into a lunging posture, his eyes directed at the breasts of the "white slave." In addition to its value

FIGURE 16. Flyleaf from Eusèbe de Salle, *Ali le Renard, ou La conquête d'Alger, 1830: Roman historique* (Paris: Charles Gosselin, 1832).

as titillation, the image served both to reinforce the legitimation of the attack on Algiers as a way of ending piracy and the trade in "white slaves," and to represent the "Arabs" as ignoble and menacing. The young French man is portrayed as the victim, saved through the love of the devoted woman, rather than as an occupying aggressor.

The effect of this racialization was to constrain the open Arab cultural and political identities articulated in the space of French cosmopolitanism by Joseph Agoub and Joanny Pharaon into a dialectic of mutual exclusiveness. As France embraced coercive imperial domination, the inferior (and dangerous) racial identity of the "Arab" would become the only real basis for legitimating the exercise of power. The very violence of the conquest left little room for imagining its victims as candidates for "civilization" in the way the French occupiers of Egypt had imagined. In Egypt, conceived as a land of ancient science, it was the rebellion in Cairo that had hardened French responses to the occupied. In Algeria, the depiction of the Arabs as vicious pirates and slave traders served to defuse hostility to the costly exercise back in France. In this way, the difference between French and

Arab was overlaid with the dynamic of civilization and barbarity, of center and periphery, of modernity and backwardness, of metropole and colony.

This dynamic could not but transform the structures of Arab identity in France. The language upon which French Arabs had built their strong sense of cultural distinctiveness and their proud connection to an Arabo-Muslim heritage was now becoming instrumentalized as a tool of colonial domination. Two generations of Arab intellectuals had achieved cultural participation in France through their ability to teach Arabic in the context of an Orientalism built on the liberal model of civilization. Now Arabic was to be taught with a practical application to the colonial exploitation of Algeria and the extension of French dominance in the Arab world.[40] Under these conditions, it was no longer suitable that a "foreigner" should occupy the sensitive role of teaching this language, even though that "foreigner" might be a native Arabic-speaker. Indeed, an "Arab" would be the very last person to play such a role at the center of the colonial system. There is little record of the circumstances that led to Joseph Agoub's dismissal from the Lycée Louis-le-Grand, and it is impossible to discount the influence of other factors. But Agoub was later considered as a replacement for Gabriel Taouïl in Marseille or as a professor of Arabic in Algiers after his dismissal from Paris.[41] This suggests that it was primarily his presence in the *capital* that was no longer considered appropriate.

The battle over Arabic-language teaching was also under way in Marseille. The Ministry of Commerce and Public Works wrote from Paris requesting that the prefect of the Bouches-du-Rhône report on the "usefulness" of the Arabic course at the Lycée. The prefect replied in favor of retaining the course, but not its teacher, because he no longer attracted "French students" to his classes. The prefect observed: "The course is of no real use except to some of the children of Egyptian migrants [émigrés] in Marseille, who already know Arabic, since they speak it at home, and learn from M. Taouïl only how to read and write."[42]

The prefect recommended the post be offered to Agoub, who was "known widely to be gifted with great intelligence and a vast erudition." But Agoub did not wish to take the place of his old teacher and did not live long enough to be a candidate. When Taouïl fell sick in 1834, he was replaced temporarily by George Sakakini. Under the new teacher the popularity of the course increased, and more than thirty students enrolled. Three years later, when Taouïl finally resigned, many in the Arab community believed that Sakakini was his natural successor. But Guizot, the minister of public instruction in Paris, one of the chief practitioners of the new cultural politics of the July Monarchy, chose to appoint a more "French" figure in his place: Eusèbe de Salle, a former medical student who had thrown himself into the study of Arabic at the École des Langues Orientales in 1827.

De Salle was a very ambitious young man, who had joined the forces invading Algiers and provided a highly fictionalized account of his experiences in his novel *Ali le Renard,* from which the crudely racist illustration we saw earlier in this chapter was taken. He studied Arabic in the late 1820s, apparently with an eye to the approaching opportunities in Algeria. By his own account, he engaged glee-fully in the pillage of the treasury of Algiers but failed to assure himself of the for-tune he had hoped for.[43] According to Henri Cordier, de Salle was considered "pretentious and quarrelsome, having neither the knowledge, the application, nor the enthusiasm required for a position of any importance."[44] But de Salle had other, more appropriate skills—he could employ very effectively the new perceptions of national identity and its hardening limits. Although largely uninterested in this "measly position" in the provinces, he determined to "content [himself] with the bottom rung while waiting to rise up the ladder."[45] But having never traveled to the Levantine countries with which Marseille conducted much of its trade, he came under attack in an anonymous letter to the *Sémaphore de Marseille* as "a purely theoretical teacher, who could easily write a treatise of Arabic grammar, but who, without doubt, would not know how to read or translate a letter from a merchant in Aleppo, Damascus, or Cairo."[46]

The competition over this position had involved members of the Arab com-munity; now the course became the object of a wider political contestation. The letter to the *Sémaphore* may well have been written by Sakakini himself or by an-other member of the Arab community, which was the chief backer of the petition to employ Sakakini. The letter provided a historical background to the Arab commercial presence in Marseille reaching back more than three decades:

> The Revolution caused enormous changes in our relations with the Levant. Our customs duties became equal for French and foreigner alike. Since then foreigners have traded on their own account; they have become principals, and the commercial houses of Marseille have become mere commissionaires. Some have even observed that these people might play the same role in Europe that the French used to play in their own country, and we often see them establishing in Marseille branches of trading houses whose bases remain in various trading ports of the Levant.[47]

The writer insisted on the importance of spoken Arabic in enabling French merchants to compete successfully in the commercial arena. But the letter made no qualitative distinction between foreign and French identities and made none of the conventional references to the French possession of Algeria. In closing, the letter called for the reinstatement of Sakakini under "a just and enlightened gov-ernment, a government that walks at the head of all civilizations."[48] The author thus presented Marseille as an open space of trade, exchange, and competition, and Europe as just one civilization among others. This preservation of an idea of civilizational plurality, even under hierarchical terms, was necessary to protect the space of Arab particularity in France.

De Salle's response was swift. Writing to the Chamber of Commerce of Marseille, he dismissed these accusations as "too absurd and too contemptible . . .

to be worthy of a response in any detail" and questioned the right of such people to make a complaint at all:

> In any case, the questionable style and the poor language demonstrate nothing but a desire for gain, lacking any title at all, even that of French citizenship. . . . Even less do [my friends] agree that one could attribute ability as an educator to the simple habit of speaking a language. We know perfectly well in France that not everyone who speaks French is therefore capable of teaching French. What if they speak it incorrectly? What if they have only learned it displaced from their homeland, and raised by an ignorant family [*dépaysés et au sein d'une famille ignorante*]![49]

The crucial term here is *dépaysés*—out of place, disoriented, like a fish out of water. Foreigners did not belong in this space: they did not hold the rights of citizenship or the benefits of culture: they were ignorant, cut off both from their own culture and from that in which they were aliens. De Salle's letter was an expert sounding of the whole gamut of exclusivist and racist national assumptions, and their new inflection of the Eurocentric civilizational narrative. Teaching Arabic, he insisted, was a matter of "method" rather than any actual ability to speak the language; instead, speaking Arabic should be taken as an automatic indication of an inferior status. De Salle stated this even more bluntly:

> It is through the rapidity, the certainty of method, above all, that Europe is superior to the old Asia. Struck to the very core by such truths, my friends hoped to prevent the recurrence of a form of teaching that is a scandal that outrages both method and European honor. A course paid for by French money in a French city, and officially designated for French youngsters, is being monopolized by a handful of foreigners.[50]

De Salle's argument here, though inspired by his personal spitefulness and overweening ambition, provides a clear indication of the repertoire of ideas that underlay the often more delicate pronouncements of official policy. His repetition of the word "French" was intended to hammer home the alienness of the Arab population in Marseille. His suggestion that European "honor" was at stake linked his statements here to the crude illustration in his book, and to the preoccupations of early nineteenth-century French masculinity, which have been described by historians such as Robert Nye and William Reddy.[51] The mere suggestion that Arabs could speak Arabic better than Europeans was presented here as an outrageous challenge to the assumption of European superiority in every field of knowledge.

The target of de Salle's attack was not only Sakakini but the Arab community of Marseille. In another letter he wrote: "I think I have given you the whole story of the chair of Arabic in Marseille in a few words: Arabs, Jews, and other Levantines . . . will always want to see one of their own occupying it."[52] Caussin de Perceval, professor of Arabic at the École des Langues Orientales, agreed with his colleague: "The Syrians and Egyptians [*MM les Syriens-Égyptiens*] would obviously have liked to see one of their own occupying your position . . . these gentlemen, who speak their language without having studied it, and without knowing how to analyze what they are saying, have an entirely wrong idea about the course. They think it is a matter of routine, when it is in fact a matter of rules and principles."[53] Here, it was not only the foreignness and the ostensible backwardness of the Arabs that was in question, but their identity, and the threat posed by their collective action as a community.

But despite the more unsavory characteristics displayed by de Salle, we should not see this struggle simply as the result of overweening personal ambition or an idiosyncratic racial intolerance. In 1835, de Salle married the granddaughter of an Indian maharaja, whom he had first met during his medical studies in London. It is not simply a question of De Salle's personal vitriol; what was in play here was a transformation in the terms of Orientalist knowledge, which rendered an "Arab" automatically incapable of the kind of "method" that characterized European modernity. De Salle, on the other hand, a trained medical doctor who contributed his skill during the cholera outbreak of 1835, a member of the "Expedition d'Afrique," and now a landowner in Algeria, a man of letters, and a public educator, could claim an active citizenship of a new, modern France after 1830.

If there was rapidly narrowing room for Arabs in the provincial periphery of Marseille, there was certainly none at all at the center of this radiating civilization. No foreigner could be trusted with so sensitive a matter as the teaching of Arabic in Paris. As the "friends" of Eusèbe de Salle wrote in 1838, "Arabic has acquired a kind of nationality since Algeria became obedient to our laws."[54] But as Paris closed as a possible space for the elaboration of a Franco-Arab identity, Algeria appeared as the only possible locus for its expression. Thus it is toward Algiers and the steps of the Kechaoua Mosque that we must finally turn.

Anne Jean-Marie René Savary, duc de Rovigo, a member of the Egyptian expedition and the inner circle of Napoleon, was the police chief under the Empire who had ordered the surveillance of Ellious Bocthor. His appointment as military governor of Algiers marked a new phase in the occupation, one that made the results of the Commission d'Afrique increasingly a foregone conclusion. One of the first things Rovigo did was to request the appointment of Joanny Pharaon as personal interpreter. Many members of the Arab community in France had already joined the expeditionary force in 1830, including Ya'qub Habaïby, his son Joseph, and his nephew Daoud, Abdallah Hasboun, and many of the former officers of the Mamelouk corps. Charles Zaccar, a Syrian priest at Saint-Roch in Paris, had helped draw up the Arabic proclamation to the Algerians and was employed as an interpreter first-class.[55] Rovigo had already requisitioned the son of the Egyptian notable 'Abd el-Al from Marseille, Louis-Alexandre Désiré Abdelal, having admired his "smart appearance, his martial and military bearing," on passing through

Marseille. However, this young man had hoped for military service rather than employment as "secretary-interpreter." According to his unpublished notes,

> It was not exactly what I had been dreaming of. I was more enamoured of the sword than of the pen; but the opportunity offered to a naturally adventurous spirit was too good to pass over. I accepted with the enthusiasm of a sixteen-year-old.[56]

Louis's father had died only two years earlier, so his situation perhaps determined his willingness to join the expedition. Rovigo seems to have been particularly keen to employ the descendants of the notables from among the "Egyptian refugees" in his colonial project, as Eusèbe de Salle, himself an interpreter in the expedition, noted with some resentment in his potboiler *Ali le Renard:*

> It was a very oddly constituted corps, that of the interpreters of the Armée d'Afrique. All nations were mixed up in a kind of foreign legion: every language; every degree of capacity; every shade of morality, in this new Tower of Babel. At least a third did not know any of the dialects spoken in Algiers: favoritism or begging had procured for them this sinecure while they hoped for better things, or in order to disguise their real ambitions. . . . Among the other two-thirds, the mixture was no less bizarre: a Syrian priest had for his assistant a Tunisian Jew, and an Italian triple renegade . . . was comrade to old Mamelouks.[57]

De Salle's fantastic enumeration continued, listing "Fanariote princes, descendants of the emperors of Byzantium, [and] the brothers of the Syrian primate" among those to be encountered in the train of the French expeditionary force. All of these descriptions fit individual interpreters, many of whom had lived for decades in France or had long experience as interpreters in the Levant. But by exaggerating and exoticizing these attributes, de Salle marked his own "Frenchness" as normative, despite his foreignness and insufficiency in the Arabic language. Algeria quickly became a place of exile for the floating foreign population, and most particularly the floating Oriental population of Jews, Arabs, Turks, and Greeks. Just as Rovigo exiled the Algerian intellectuals, the Comité des Maures, from Algiers, he summoned the descendants of Arab migrants in France to Algiers. His policy in this regard appears to have been an aggressive act of colonial possession through the rapid installation of French culture in the Regency, a kind of cultural blitzkrieg:

> It is at once an act of morality and of good politics. . . . The Regency of Algiers will never be truly a French possession until our language is nationalized, and the arts and sciences that are our glory become acclimatized here.[58]

History, Rovigo wrote, echoing Clot-Bey in Egypt, showed that "the Arabs" did not lack intelligence; in fact, they were "cunning and insightful," but these natural gifts were stifled by "ignorance and fanaticism." Rovigo's description closely paralleled that of Bory de Saint-Vincent. Rovigo announced his intention to establish the teaching of French for the young "Jews" and "Moors" whom he felt would be easier to "civilize" than the Arabs. "In the same location," he wrote to the Ministry of War, "a chair will be established for the teaching of Arabic to Europeans, under the intelligent direction of the military interpreter Joanny Pharaon, in order to make the communication between ourselves and the *indigènes* easier and more rapid." He continued:

> The true marvel will be to replace Arabic gradually with French, which, being the language of the authorities and the administration, cannot fail to become wide-spread among the natives, particularly if the new generation floods into our schools for education. . . . With a little time, I don't despair of seeing together . . . French, Italians, Spaniards, Moors, and Jews. It is in these schools that the fusion that is so desirable must be effected.[59]

The "fusion" that Rovigo imagined here, at the periphery of the nation, and under conditions of imperial domination, was very different from the "confusion" that Joseph Agoub had evoked in his struggle to articulate an identification as both a Frenchman and an Arab in the early 1820s. At that time there had been no category available to resolve this complex interweaving of disparate strands— Egyptian, Arab, Melkite, French, Syrian, Armenian, Greek, Marseillais, Parisian. In Rovigo's picture these complexities were overlaid with the "natural" difference between French and *indigène,* increasingly figured as "Arab." But what was Joanny Pharaon in this new construction—an Arab agent of the French, or a French teacher of the Arabs? As far as Rovigo was concerned, Pharaon was not one of the *indigènes,* like the troublesome Moors he had exiled from Algiers. Yet he could play a role of intermediary, because he was not fully "French."

On 17 December 1831, determined to anchor the French presence permanently in the city, Rovigo ordered that a mosque in Algiers should be converted to a Christian church. He created a "commission" that included Ahmad Bouderba and the muftis of the city to find a way to carry out his wishes. Joanny was instructed to oversee this arrangement. The treaty of capitulation on 4 July 1830 had mandated the respect of the religion of the inhabitants of Algiers, and the Muslim members of the commission resisted this arbitrary rupture of the treaty's conditions. "As you are the stronger," they replied, according to Joanny's son Florian, "you are the masters. Take our houses, our wives, our children, but we will give nothing of our free will."[60] Furious at the Muslims' unwillingness to concede the mosque, Rovigo "wanted to break everything, arrest the muftis, storm the mosque by force, and have all those who stood in his way executed."[61] Baron Pichon, the civil administrator, recognizing the illegal nature of the proceeding, suggested the simple alternative of requesting funds to build a church. But according to Florian Pharaon, the Muslim resistance had already begun to take on a symbolic power. At the final meeting of the commission, a crowd of 10,000 assembled outside as the

muezzin called to prayer. The square was cleared by a French battalion summoned down from the casbah. Finally, the commission located a small mosque
built by a Genoese architect that could be honorably ceded to the French. But
when Rovigo discovered this, he screamed and swore at Joanny: "You've been
duped! They've given you the worst-located and least-venerated mosque in the
city. I don't want it. I want the most beautiful one! We are the masters, the conquerors! I've had enough!"[62]

After learning that a *muqaddam* of the Kechaoua mosque had called for the
population to rise up against the French, Rovigo took this as a pretext to seize the
mosque by force, rolling his artillery into the nearby street. Four thousand Muslims were barricaded inside the mosque but finally agreed to open the doors as the
military sappers hacked at the bolts. Pharaon, Bouderba, and others climbed the
steps to enter the mosque, but shots rang out from the French behind them. A
sudden stampede issued from inside the building, almost killing the interpreters
on the steps. The French troops stormed the oncoming crowd with fixed bayonets, driving them back inside the building. The trapped Algerians were forced to
stream from the side entrances, half-suffocating a number of people and injuring
many others. This act seems to have been a deliberate strike on the part of Rovigo
to nullify the treaty signed by General Bourmont in 1830 and make it clear both
to the population of Algiers and to the doubters at home that the military occupation would remain as a permanent colonial presence.

Inevitably, the mosque was seized, and French colonial occupation in Algiers
was entrenched for the next 130 years. Florian Pharaon commented wryly that
"only the members of the commission had been somewhat bruised." The official
newspaper of the French occupation, *Le moniteur algérien,* insisted that

> the handover of the mosque of the rue du Divan [was] the result, not of force or of
> conquest, but entirely of a negotiation conducted with as much care as convenience,
> inspired by a reciprocally appreciated necessity. . . . Thus, after fourteen centuries
> of exile, it fell to France to bring Christianity back to shores whose peoples it had
> once before enlightened.[63]

In this official account the realities of colonial contestation were erased, and a
vision of a "natural" colonial order put in their place. In this vision it was the "negotiation," not the French army, that was responsible for this violent imperial act.
If the commissioners, including Pharaon most of all, were "bruised" in this transaction, it was not only through the bumps they received in the onslaught of the
crowd, but in their transformation from lawful intermediaries acting under the
treaty of capitulation into colonial functionaries delivering the ultimatum of coercive expropriation and exemplary violence.[64] We owe the detailed account of
this moment to a pamphlet published by Joanny's son Florian. In this short work,
Florian recorded a drama whose consequences would shape both his success in

imperial France and the impossibility of reconstructing the connections between French and Arab that his father seemed briefly to have achieved at the end of the 1820s. In the 1860s Florian became an adviser to Napoleon III on Algerian affairs; then, after the fall of the Second Empire he founded an Arabic newspaper called *As-Sada* (The Echo) that the Interior Ministry agreed to subsidize on the grounds that it was "an eminently *national* publication whose sole aim is to make the Arab population love France."[65] But the paper could offer little more than exhortations to Arab dignitaries to visit the Paris Exhibition of 1878. The following year, the newspaper was closed down; the governor-general of Algeria insisted tellingly that "a newspaper printed in Paris, even in Arabic, will always be suspect in the eyes of the *indigènes* simply because of the location of its publication."[66] The police spies who followed Florian until his death in 1885 took more interest in his Bonapartist sympathies and noted that he "usually frequents foreigners of all nationalities, most of whom are Orientals."[67] That milieu of colonial elites and Ottoman visitors offered few possibilities for the dynamic engagement of the Parisian Arab milieu of the 1820s. It demonstrates, however, that the remnants of an Arab France persisted beyond the colonial turn.

Florian's path in some sense followed the trajectory set by his father in those moments of 1831. Joanny found himself on the Kechaoua steps because he had chosen an Arab path in France, maintaining the language of his family and his community and defending their interests as well as those of liberty in the Revolution of 1830. But he was also there because he was French, because he belonged to the conquerors rather than the vanquished. The violent confrontation that ensued was not the result of an act of will on his part, but it presented him with a stark choice. It was no longer possible to be French and Arab at once. Could he imagine his interests as in any way shared with the Muslims spilling out of the mosque under bullets and bayonets? In this moment of necessity—which, regardless of the words of the *Moniteur algérien*, was hardly "reciprocal"— Joanny Pharaon chose, however reluctantly, the imperial act of expropriation and became French in the face of the Arabs on the other side of the thick walls of the mosque.

It was not only Joanny who had to choose. Both the francophone Arab and the Arab Frenchman were confronted with a choice between the different dimensions of their identity. Ahmad Bouderba, the urbane and well-traveled Muslim Algerian—married to a Frenchwoman and fluent in French—was faced with the same stark contradiction. At first, he believed in the possibility of a kind of relationship with France that would provide the benefits of French education and modernity to Algerians while fostering their independent development—much as the École Égyptienne had done in previous years. He had written in March 1831 to the authorities, suggesting on behalf of his compatriots that ten Arab boys be sent every year to schools and technical colleges in France.[68]

Bouderba was also exiled by Rovigo in 1832 on the vaguest of suspicions. Like Hamdan, he went to Paris to the plead the case of his people against the colonial lobby. Provided with temporary financial support by the French government, he was sent back to Algiers after the confirmation of permanent colonial possession. Finally, Bouderba left the service of the French to join the resistance movement of the Emir Abd El-Kader, which would prevent full French occupation of Algeria for the next decade and more. In 1836, Hamdan Khodja wrote to Bouderba from exile, recognizing that he had misjudged his friend's loyalties: "I regard you as a second self. I was mistaken on your account, and I ask your pardon." In this letter of 1836, Hamdan expressed with characteristic eloquence the experience of most Algerians in his revulsion at the cynicism of the French occupation: "Oppression reigns in Algiers, and now it is certainly worse that it ever was under the Turks. God protect us from the injustice of the Turks and from the justice of the French."[69]

The Algerian resistance would continue for twelve years, and emerge again and again in the century to follow, to be met with violence and repression, the confiscation of land and the deprivation of liberty and rights, further hardening this opposition between "French" and "Arab." Indeed, as Patricia Lorcin has shown, the term "Arab" would be increasingly identified with that hostility to France and the French, while the "Berber" or "Kabyle" was consistently misconceived as naturally more friendly to the colonizers.[70]

Joanny Pharaon was henceforth ranged on the side of the oppressors. He was appointed the first professor of Arabic at the Collège d'Alger and settled in Algeria with his wife and family. He published texts on teaching Arabic to Europeans and on the forms of law in Algeria—European, Muslim, and Jewish.[71] He also produced one of the earliest ethnographic studies of the Kabyles in the region of Bougie (Bejaïa), describing himself in this 1835 volume as a "member of several learned societies and the Société Coloniale of Algiers, secretary-interpreter to the governor-general, seconded to the aga of Arabs, and professor of Arabic at the Collège and in the professorial chair of Algiers."[72] His eight-year-old son Florian, who was growing up among the children of Algiers, provided a "short Franco-Kabylo-Algerian vocabulary" for the volume.

Joanny had not been present for the conquest of Algiers, and his response to the conquest of Bejaïa showed the hesitations of a reluctant imperialist. The conquest, he wrote, had cost "more than ten million [francs] and four or five thousand men."[73] Holding the town would cost only more lives. Joanny tentatively offered another possible course:

In the event that one might be tempted to evacuate this country [pays], we should not, in ridding ourselves of the burden of the occupation, abandon the advantages that Bougie can offer to government and commerce. If the forts were to be maintained, guarded by a small garrison, and the presence of a commercial company authorized, which would, with security and under the surveillance of a French agent, take on all possible trading possibilities, the state would still find quite a considerable advantage in the situation, leaving it no regrets at all in regard to the evacuation.[74]

The passage left ambiguous the interpretation of the word *pays*—did Joanny mean only the region of Bejaïa, or the whole of Algeria? The colony would certainly cost millions more francs and hundreds of thousands of lives in the attempt to forge what Joanny called here—characterizing with some irony the view of those he called the "enthusiasts"—a "new Franco-Algerian people."

But if Joanny was a reluctant imperialist, he was nonetheless unable to articulate a principled opposition to the process into which he had been co-opted not only by the former friend of his father, Rovigo, but by the logic of colonial nationalism. In Paris, he would be, like Joseph Agoub, a foreigner whose loyalties would be too questionable to permit him to exercise the politically sensitive role of teaching Arabic, now a colonial language. In Algiers, his French upbringing, his dress, his manners, and his religion made him part of French colonial society, and he would remain always outside the spheres of Algerian life. In Paris he would be an Arab; in Algiers he would be a Frenchman. "Arab France"—that space in which it was possible to be both French and Arab at once—no longer existed. Once the defender of liberty in the rue Neuve des Petits-Champs, Joanny was now the reluctant chronicler of liberty's demise.

Many other French Arabs joined the French occupation of Algiers. Pushed out of France by an increasingly exclusionary national identity, they were attracted both to the opportunities and the Arab culture of Algeria.[75] Others remained in Marseille, looking henceforth outward into the Mediterranean rather than inward toward the center of French life in Paris. There remains another, equally complex story to recount about Franco-Arab life in Algeria, Marseille, Alexandria, and Beirut, and its impact on France in the mid- and late nineteenth century. But the evidence does not reveal any significant Arab milieu in Paris for another fifty years, until the British occupation of Egypt after 1878 created a new political space for Egyptian exiles in the French capital.[76] There are plenty of signs that an underground presence remained, somewhere beyond the Champs-Elysées, along which visiting Arab dignitaries and suborned Algerian notables were paraded. In 1855, Eugène Daumas encountered in Paris "a group of Arabs, mostly from the Sahara, who have taken up in our midst their wandering and carefree existence."[77] A long list of Arab *répétiteurs* (tutors) taught at the École des Langues Orientales, although they were not permitted to occupy the position of professor.[78] In 1894, J. Homsy, a descendant of General Ya'qub, wrote to the press on behalf of "the Syrian colony settled in Paris" to announce their gift to the widow of the assassinated president, Sadi Carnot.[79] But this was a very different Arab France from that which had existed until 1831. It was a colonial Arab France, in which the Franco-Arab identity that seemed possible for a moment during the late Empire and early Restoration was now definitively unmade. All that remained of that first Arab France was an active process of dissolution and forgetting. It is to that forgetting that I will turn in the conclusion.

Conclusion

Today, when the inhabitants of Marseille take a bus along the boulevard Sakakini, it is unlikely that they have any sense of the history that lies behind the thoroughfare's name. The visitor who strikes across the bridge from Notre Dame in Paris toward the church of Saint-Julien-le-Pauvre is unlikely to know that this is a Melkite church where services are regularly conducted in Arabic, like those Isa Carus once performed in the church of Saint-Roch. The *banlieusards* who take the RER D into Paris from Melun pass the barracks where generations of Arabs served in the French military, but it is doubtful that these commuters are thinking of the Mamelouks Abdallah and Chahine. There is no plaque to record the bloody massacre of Egyptian men, women, and children in the cours Gouffé, near the grand circle of the Place Castellane in Marseille. Nor is there any tribute to Ellious Bocthor and Joseph Agoub, each of whom played an important role in the evolution of Arabic-language teaching in Paris—not even in the imposing boat-shaped edifice of the Institut du Monde Arabe. Wandering through the Louvre, one might see the face of Rufa'il Zakhur, or Dom Raphäel as he was known, and many other now nameless Egyptians and Syrians who posed as models for Napoleonic painters. It is the rare viewer who can peel back the layers of exoticism to discover the lives that lay underneath. Outside the Louvre, the pyramid reveals nothing of the Arab histories that once crossed crowded streets where it now stands, mute and glittering.

On 25 October 1836, to strains of Mozart's *Mysteries of Isis*, a giant slab of rose-colored granite inscribed with hieroglyphics was slowly levered into position atop a heavy socle in the Place de la Concorde, on the right bank of the Seine. King Louis-Philippe waved from the balcony of the Ministry of the Navy as the head engineer, Apollinaire Lebas, gave the order to complete the erection of the monument. Below, a crowd of 200,000 spectators filled the vast square, cheering as the huge wooden apparatus creaked into action. This act, as other historians have observed, finally filled a gaping absence at the center of France's self-representation. No regime since the Revolution had been able to solve the problem of what to place at the point where the guillotine had brought the hereditary monarchy to an end. This dilemma was not resolved by the temporary statue of Liberty, which had peeled and crumbled under the Directory, nor by the shifting pageant of Napoleon's popular *fêtes impériales,* nor by a *monument expiatoire,* which was endlessly discussed under the Restoration but never executed. If the emplacement of the obelisk raised, for contemporary observers, questions of how an Egyptian monument could answer this still-unresolved problem of national history, a century of empire would give a new meaning to this act of cultural appropriation. In Egypt, Rifa'a al-Tahtawi's protest to Muhammad 'Ali against the abrogation of the obelisk marked a decisive moment in Egypt's rediscovery of its ancient heritage: Tahtawi was appointed as the first protector of antiquities in Egypt.

This book has attempted a reading of three decades of French history from the perspective of a population whose existence, I would suggest, was also effaced in the great national act of forgetting that the emplacement of the obelisk served to solemnize. The Arab France that this book has mapped was delocalized and deterritorialized—a space of mobility, exchange, and negotiation; of changing meanings, boundaries, and identities. In retracing the journeys and struggles of a population whose presence within this history has disappeared from view, this work has posed key questions about mobility, community, and identity, and the relationship between these three dimensions of a shared existence. I have concluded that only through a recognition of mobility as a constitutive practice of community, rather than as a force eroding traditional social ties, does it become possible to recognize the extent and complexity of this community, which has been lost to "national" history. Rather than seeking to establish community through the evidence of a fixed population living a settled existence in clustered fashion over a particular period of time, it has been my aim to look to what, at first, might seem the counterevidence of a population scattered across France; repeated displacements; weeks spent on road, river, and even on foot; movement across and between different urban spaces. What might at first appear to indicate a form of transience, a shifting and continually reconstituted population that could never form a meaningful community, must be seen in far more spatially extended terms, as a multilocal network extending across a space unconfined by either the metropolitan limits of a city or the political boundaries of a nation.

But this work has pushed further to ask tricky but important questions about identity: identity as an intersection between practices and ideas, as a space of belonging to which individuals voluntarily adhere, a space that can accommodate the existence of a minority that by choice or circumstance retains a sense of difference yet insists on its place as a constitutive part of a larger polity. But the examination of this identity has concluded also that its "making" was not simply a voluntaristic process driven by the commonalities and traditions of the emigrants from Egypt: this process was surrounded and shaped by powerful forces that took their form both from the reconstruction of French society and from wider global shifts taking place across the revolutionary age. These forces helped to determine the set of choices available to a population whose status in France was confused and fragile and peculiarly dependent upon the state: they could function as positive forms of identification and as menacing threats of exclusion, incarceration, and violence.

Arab France was never a fixed social fact but a process of construction, a search for an "accommodation" in the literal and spatial sense of the term. The question of space was crucial to the struggles of the emigration from their first request for asylum expressed in the language of the Bedouins (fi 'ardak) to the "Harem-Hospice Oriental" proposed by the Legation; from the casern in Melun and the "Egyptian village" in Marseille to the struggle against the imposition of a physical realization of the dépôt; in the public spaces of Paris—its gardens and streets, the Invalides and the École des Langues Orientales, the "rallying points" at the home of Rufa'il, and the pay office in the Place Vendôme. In these spaces those identi-fied as "Egyptian refugees" sought to find a place both within French society and distinct from it, as the members of so many diaspora communities have done be-fore and since. The letters they wrote one another in Arabic, the classes and reli-gious services they held, the investment the second (and even third) generation in the study of Arabic language and culture, brought this Arab commonality more to the fore, so that it is possible by 1830 to describe these heterogeneous in-dividuals as Arabs. They were Arab in the sense that they had, on the whole, cho-sen this commonality over their differences and cultivated a certain distinctive-ness from those around them in the three decades they had lived in France.

Thus we can describe these people as Arab in trajectory, even though this Arab "identity of interests" was something that was formed across the period, rather than existing fully formed from the outset. It was formed not solely as a process of positive self-identification, but also as a set of choices made under specific his-torical circumstances, and in response to the action of the state and to the spaces delimited by the society around them. Yet it was not a passive response to these conditions: the categories provided by the state were adopted, adapted, and some-times entirely subverted. The actions and rhetoric of the state and its agents were often co-opted and turned to different ends from those intended; at many differ-ent levels of society, these people exploited with surprising adeptness the contra-dictions and ideological loopholes of the ruling regime to ensure their survival.

But the action of the state must be seen from a long perspective: despite these evasions and diversions, the patient action of the state in applying and reinforcing its categories, combined with the unusually close link created by the structure of pensions accorded directly from the Ministry of War, consistently encouraged those so categorized to consider their interests as mutually connected. And these official categories were not independent of a wider social context or a cultural politics of difference, particularly that kind of difference coded as "Oriental," that was in transformation from the Revolution through the Napoleonic empire and the Restoration to the July Monarchy. Significant dissonances emerged between the meanings of those categories imposed by the state and the wider society, and the ways in which they were lived by Arabs in France. These dissonances were partially resolved, at least in an intellectual sense, by the members of the second Arab generation in France, and specifically in their reconnections with the transformations taking place in their societies of origin. This dynamic process is what I have called the "making" of Arab France.

But what can be made can also be unmade. The later chapters of this book suggest that the meaning of the category around which these people had gradually formed their sense of belonging in France changed suddenly and violently at the end of the 1820s, in a way that ultimately negated its conditions of possibility as a component of identity. The turn toward colonial empire in North Africa produced a particularly sharp transformation of the status of Arabs in the metropole as well as in the new colonial space, at the same moment that the "foreigner" became an unwelcome category in France's truly "national" Revolution of 1830. What was unmade in that turbulent moment was not so much the Arab self-identification of the population, but the space of possibility for such identifications within the metropole, indeed within France itself. Instead, that space was recast as peripheral, with quite immediate consequences for the leading members of the second Arab generation in France. What was unmade was the possibility of being both French and Arab at once. Henceforth Arabs would only be subjects without rights in relation to "France" but only in relation to local authorities, unless they were to abandon irrevocably their belonging to that category. The choice for those who had come to understand themselves as French Arabs was very stark.

But that rupture of the early 1830s cannot be seen in isolation from the ruptures that had preceded it: indeed, we may see the Napoleonic reconstitution of ancien-régime racial arrangements as a crucial condition for the way the logics of 1830 played themselves out. In 1802, the reestablishment of colonial slavery reconstructed the nature of racial categories in France. The decree's collateral reimposition of the color line in France served literally to police the racial identification of the now depoliticized constituency of "Egyptian refugees." In a post-Brumaire French polity defined by this and so many other ruptures with revolutionary isonomy, the "Egyptians" found themselves compelled to claim a consistorial fraction of the new society of privilege, like Jews or Protestants, lest they be relegated to the category of those denuded of all rights, the *nègre*. The choice to invest this "Egyptian" category with a wider Arab commonality was thus powerfully shaped by the threat of an extreme marginalization—indeed an exclusion from French society—based on racial categories of color associated with slavery. But, of course, accepting the diktat of the state could not make this wildly diverse population homogeneously Egyptian at a stroke. Instead, this category was stretched and redefined to accommodate a wider Arab commonality, a process in which the state effectively collaborated, knowingly or otherwise, by accepting the inclusion on the registers of the depot of Arabic-speakers who had no Egyptian connections at all, and even attributing to them the same privileges and pensions as the other refugees. This contractual arrangement with the central state allowed the community to survive threats of incarceration or expulsion, but it irritated local authorities, favored a self-serving and fractious elite and left the darker-skinned fraction of the population dangerously exposed to the violence of political transition, with its lethal mix of political anathematization and racial stigmatization. The wave of destruction that ensued in 1815—the miserable and bloody deaths dealt to those most marginal in the population, and the devastation of the lives and livelihoods of others—changed the nature of the community. In the wake of these events, there is evidence that members of the elite widened their sense of collective responsibility rather than taking the simpler path of abandoning those most targeted by popular resentment.

This progressive substitution of an Arab commonality for the "Egyptian" category offered by the state was predicated on the depoliticization of the emigration, which had originally set out for France with a political project directly linked to the project of Egyptian independence. In that project, the role of the emigration Muslims in ensuring that this project would receive wide elite and popular support from their "brothers in Egypt" was absolutely central. As that project disintegrated with the death of General Ya'qub and the exclusion of the Egyptian Legation from participation in the conclusion of the tripartite peace between England, France, and the Ottoman Empire, the role of Muslims, and the place of Islam, in the emigration became increasingly marginal. The near-total silence surrounding Muslim religious life—prayer, fasting, festivals, and burials, for example—in the existing documentation reflects both this loss of centrality and the place of Muslims as a rather precarious minority in the emigration, as well as the transformation of the Napoleonic regime's "Islamic policy." While religion took a new role in the corporate forms of governance under Napoleon, the numbers of Muslims in France were not sufficient for them to achieve any consistorial status on their own. With the restoration of a fiercely Catholic monarchy in 1814–15, the place of Islam in France became all the more fragile. While Palestinian Catholic Arabs managed to recast their symbolic allegiances with relative ease, many Muslims, including those most notable in the emigration, chose the path of conversion. We have no way of knowing to what degree these conversions were strategic responses to their precarious situation, like the "crypto-Jews" of earlier centuries.

Certainly, we can observe indications of the maintenance of dual identities, and even the return to Islam in certain cases. It is crucial, however, that despite the appeal to the *parrainage* of important Europeans—in other words, the role of influential figures as godparents—the chief driver of these conversions appears to have been the Arab Melkite church established in Marseille in 1821. Thus we may suspect that it was as *Arabs* rather than as *Catholics* that these Muslims embraced Christianity, or at least its outward forms.

More troublingly, however, the new cultural politics of Islam under the Restoration fostered the reinvigoration of an older set of presumptions about Muslim vengefulness and barbarity that the notables of the Arab community in Marseille, and ordinary refugees, drew upon to enhance the chances of success in their petitions to the authorities. In doing so, they contributed in a small way to the exclusion of Islam and Muslims from the postrevolutionary reconstruction of French society. But their own identifications, whether as Egyptian or Arab, could not so easily be separated from these Muslim associations, coded together in terms of an "Oriental" difference. This entanglement would have serious consequences in the later years of the Restoration. As a second generation of Arabs in France came to recognize their intimate connection with Muslims and the Muslim world through the Islamic heritage of Arabic language and culture, events around them, and particularly the conflict in the Aegean regions of the Ottoman Empire that resulted in the Greek war for independence, were working to widen the distance between Europe and the Muslim world. The events of 1827 would demonstrate the military vulnerability of the Ottoman Empire, and particularly its outlying provinces, thereby weakening the old assurances of reciprocity backed by treaties and trading privileges. The invasion of Algiers in 1830 and the evolution of this adventure into a permanent colonial project in North Africa brought for the first time a very large population of Muslims under French control: an invigorated Arab racial category offered ways of entrenching French power and denying political and religious claims by Algerians.

Thus it was not the violence of 1815 that would bring about the "unmaking" of Arab France. Indeed, those terrible events can rather be said to have accelerated the community's turning toward the heart of France—toward Paris—both as a refuge and as a new space for the articulation of belonging, a more formulated sense of their place and permanence in France. It is difficult to establish definitively how the violence marking the new regime shaped the consciousness of members of the Arab community, since none of them ever spoke directly about these events. This silence must in itself be taken as a salient fact, since other refugee populations sought to represent their experience, both good and ill, and integrate it into the frameworks of their national narratives. It may be that what obstructed the capacity of members of the community to make sense of those events was their trajectory of accommodation rather than national return: their forcible separation from an Egyptian national narrative and their embrace of an Arab particularity, along with their sense of "Frenchness," which connected their ordeal to larger political events. At the same time, that "Frenchness" was extremely precarious for a group whose citizenship was not at all certain if they had been born elsewhere, as Joseph Agoub found to his cost at the end of the 1820s.

The "unmaking" of this first French Arab identity occurred rather in the transformations of the period 1827–33, at that moment labeled the "Imperial Meridian" by C. A. Bayly. In fact, the unmaking was double. If Arab France was unmade in the shock of the colonial turn that separated the two components of an identity into oppositional categories, it was definitively dismantled by the reinforcement of the exclusivist national narratives that accompanied these transformations. It is ironic that as the concrete realities of "Frenchness" expanded ever more widely across the globe, its scope and boundaries narrowed and hardened into a powerful and unitary national story that appeared to resolve the contradictions and complexities thrown up by that difficult period between 1780 and 1870. By the close of that period, the first Arab France was a lost memory, little more than an Oriental footnote of Napoleonic glory, a first glimpse of France's manifest imperial destiny. The "Egyptians" in France were henceforth imagined—if their presence was noted at all—as little more than a contingent by-product of France's civilizing mission, its first, frustrated attempt to bring modernity to the Middle East. It is the assumption that "modernity" is a single, coherent phenomenon restricted to, or modeled upon, the historical development of European societies —an assumption that has underwritten the Western historical tradition—that we must reimagine in order to think the history of Arab France.

Arab life in France did not end after 1830, but it was pushed underground or to the peripheries. The Arab milieu in Paris, which had been the space of sociability, experiment, conflict, and exchange, became a colonial show. Visiting dignitaries of friendly or colonized Arab nations were paraded through the boulevards and at the Opera, the "exotic" customs and urban atmosphere of Cairo and Casablanca were reproduced in the Universal Exhibitions, groups of Tuareg horsemen or Nilotic dancers were exhibited in human zoos, and battalions of *troupes indigènes* were brought to France for display, and later for use as cannon fodder in wars from 1870 to 1945. Colonial Arab Paris was a play of mirrors in which French power and prestige were endlessly reflected, and peoples to be "civilized" were brought to provide a spectacle of their own inferiority for the edification of the "civilizers." Paris was the capital of a new "Arab France" existing at the periphery as colonial possession. Napoleon III would call it his "Royaume Arabe," his Arab Kingdom. The Third Republic would call it "l'Afrique Française," "French Africa." But in both of these conceptions, the Arab was excluded from the "true" France, whether as the inhabitant of another "kingdom" or as an *indigéne* denied rights as citizen.

Arab life in France continued in Marseille, where thousands of Arabs and their descendants continued to live, joined by others from France's new territories and from the farther edge of the Mediterranean. If this life was henceforth directed outward into the Mediterranean, the networks and exchanges it fostered nonetheless played a role in the emergence of a pan-Arab cultural and political identity whose powerful political claims would take the world by surprise in the twentieth century. The end of Arab France meant that this intermediary current never found its true place in French history, nor in the history of the Arab world—which itself became the terrain of nationalist reimaginings. What was lost in that "forgetting" was the cosmopolitan dimension of a shared past, with all its rich possibilities for exchange and plurality. We may be hopeful that today, in the clamor of a diverse present, we are beginning to reexamine the past and to discover in new ways its parallel diversity, its rich multiplicity, with all the problems, questions, and contradictions that these insights may bring. It is to that hope that this book has dedicated itself, to a plural past that is also our global future.

NOTES

Translations are mine unless otherwise indicated.

INTRODUCTION

1. Michel Foucault, "La vie des hommes infâmes," *Dits et écrits* (Paris: Éditions Gallimard, 1994), 3: 237, 240.

2. Alain Corbin, *The Life of an Unknown: The Rediscovered World of a Clog Maker in 19th-Century France* (New York: Columbia University Press, 2001), xii.

3. Ibid., xiv.

4. See Robert Darnton, "Google & the Future of Books," *New York Review of Books* 56 (2009).

5. A note on the transliteration of Arabic names in this book: for the sake of consistency I have chosen commonly used versions of the time, despite the inaccuracies involved, since regional pronunciations of Arabic vary markedly, surnames were frequently invented on arrival in France, and first names were often Gallicized, or new ones invented. By the second generation, these French names were clearly used on almost all occasions and even transliterated back into Arabic, as, for example, "Josef" rather than "Yousef."

6. Georges Aïdé to Ministry of War, July 1811, Archives du Ministère de la Guerre, Vincennes (henceforth AMG), XL 37d.

7. Ibid.

8. Sean Shesgreen, *Images of the Outcast: The Urban Poor in the Cries of London* (Manchester: Manchester University Press, 2002), 180–81.

9. Joseph Agoub to Baron Capelle, 7 November 1821, Archives Nationales, Paris (henceforth AN), F^{17}1102.

10. See Robert Gildea, *The Past in French History* (New Haven, CT: Yale University Press, 1994); Linda Orr, *Headless History: Nineteenth-Century French Historiography of the Revolution* (Ithaca, NY: Cornell University Press, 1990).

11. Peter Gran, *Islamic Roots of Capitalism: Egypt, 1760–1840,* 2nd ed. (Austin: University of Texas Press, 1979); Afaf Lutfi Sayyid-Marsot, *A Short History of Modern Egypt* (Cambridge: Cambridge University Press, 1985); Daniel Crecelius, *The Roots of Modern Egypt: A Study of the Regimes of 'Ali Bey al-Kabir and Muhammad Bey Abu al-Dhahab, 1760–1775* (Minneapolis: Bibliotheca Islamica, 1981).

12. C. A. Bayly, *The Birth of the Modern World, 1780–1914: Global Connections and Comparisons* (London: Blackwell, 2004), 86.

13. William Dalrymple, *White Mughals: Love and Betrayal in Eighteenth-Century India* (London: Harper Collins, 2002); Linda Colley, *Captives: Britain, Empire, and the World, 1600–1850* (London: Jonathan Cape, 2002); Maya Jasanoff, *Edge of Empire: Conquest and Collecting in the East, 1750–1850* (London: Fourth Estate, 2005).

14. Jasanoff, *Edge of Empire,* 321.

15. There were certainly Indian, Egyptian, Turkish, and other "collectors" of European culture. See Carter Findley, "An Ottoman Occidentalist in Europe: Ahmed Midhat Meets Madame Gulnar, 1889," *American Historical Review* 103 (1998): 15–49. There were North African, Native American, and Indian "captives" in Europe, and a number of visiting Indian personages in Britain: see, for example, Mirza Abu Taleb Khan, *Westward Bound: Travels of Mirza Abu Taleb,* trans. Charles Stewart (Delhi: Oxford University Press, 2005); and Nabil Matar, *Turks, Moors, and Englishmen in the Age of Discovery* (New York: Columbia University Press, 1999).

16. For explorations of these questions, see Antoinette Burton, ed., *After the Imperial Turn: Critical Approaches to 'National' Histories and Literatures* (Durham, NC: Duke University Press, 2003); Frederick Cooper and Ann Laura Stoler, eds., *Tensions of Empire: Colonial Cultures in a Bourgeois World* (Berkeley: University of California Press, 1997).

17. Fernand Braudel, *The Mediterranean and the Mediterranean World in the Age of Philip II,* trans. Sian Reynolds (London: HarperCollins, 1992), 168.

18. Edward Said, *Orientalism: Western Conceptions of the Orient* (New York: Pantheon, 1978).

19. Raymond Schwab, *The Oriental Renaissance: Europe's Rediscovery of India and the East, 1680–1880,* trans. Gene Patterson-Black and Victor Reinking (New York: Columbia University Press, 1984).

20. For example, Frances Malino, *A Jew in the French Revolution: The Life of Zalkind Hourwitz* (Oxford: Blackwell Publishers, 1996); Ronald Schechter, *Obstinate Hebrews: Representations of Jews in France, 1715–1815* (Berkeley: University of California Press, 2003); Pierre Birnbaum, *L'aigle et la synagogue: Napoléon, les juifs et l'état* (Paris: Fayard, 2007).

21. Pierre Pluchon, *Nègres et juifs au XVIIIe siècle: Le racisme au siècle des lumières* (Paris: Tallandier, 1984); William B. Cohen, *The French Encounter with Africans: White Response to Blacks, 1530–1880* (Bloomington: Indiana University Press, 1980); Sue Peabody, *There Are No Slaves in France: The Political Culture of Race and Slavery in the Ancien Régime* (Oxford: Oxford University Press, 1996); Erick Noël, *Être noir en France au XVIIIe*

siècle (Paris: Tallandier, 2006); Pierre Boulle, *Race et esclavage dans la France de l'ancien régime* (Paris: Perrin, 2007).

22. Pascal Blanchard, Eric Deroo, Driss El Yazami, Pierre Fournié, and Gilles Manceron, *Le Paris arabe: Deux siècles de présence des Orientaux et des Maghrébins* (Paris: La Découverte, 2003).

23. Pascal Blanchard, Eric Deroo, Gilles Manceron, *Le Paris noir* (Paris: Hazan, 2001); Pascal Blanchard and Eric Deroo, *Le Paris Asie: 150 ans de présence asiatique dans la capitale* (Paris: La Découverte, 2004). A different space is described in Tyler Stovall, *Paris Noir: African Americans in the City of Light* (Boston: Houghton Mifflin, 1996).

24. Anouar Louca, *Voyageurs et écrivains égyptiens en France au XIXe siècle* (Paris: Didier, 1970).

25. These included the emir Abdelkader, a series of "Arab chiefs," and Algerian as well as other African soldiers. See, for example, Susan Gilson Miller, *Disorienting Encounters: Travels of a Moroccan Scholar in France in 1845–1846: The Voyage of Muhammad as-Saffar* (Berkeley: University of California Press, 1992).

26. For further background, see François Charles-Roux, *France et chrétiens d'Orient* (Paris: Flammarion, 1939); Yves Lequin, *La mosaïque, France: Histoire des étrangers et de l'immigration* (Paris: Larousse, 1988); Jean-François Dubost and Peter Sahlins, *Et si on faisait payer les étrangers? Louis XIV, les immigrés et quelques autres* (Paris: Flammarion, 1999).

27. On the twentieth-century Algerian migration, see among others Neil MacMaster, *Colonial Migrants and Racism: Algerians in France, 1900–62* (New York: St. Martin's Press, 1997); Alain Gillette and Abdelmalek Sayad, *L'immigration algérienne en France* (Paris: Éditions Entente, 1984); Benjamin Stora, *Ils venaient d'Algérie: L'immigration algérienne en France, 1912–1992* (Paris: Fayard, 1992); Jacques Simon, *L'immigration algérienne en France des origines à l'indépendance* (Paris: Paris-Méditerranée, 2000).

28. Mohammed Arkoun, *Histoire de l'Islam et des musulmans en France du Moyen Âge à nos jours* (Paris: Albin Michel, 2006).

29. Maxim Silverman, *Deconstructing the Nation: Immigration, Racism, and Citizenship in Modern France* (London: Routledge, 1992), 11. See also Pascal Blanchard and Nicolas Bancel, *De l'indigène à l'immigré* (Paris: Gallimard, 1998).

30. Nick Merriman, *The Peopling of London: Fifteen Thousand Years of Settlement from Overseas* (London: Museum of London/Reaktion Books, 1993).

31. See, for example, Gretchen Gerzina, *Black London: Life before Emancipation* (New Brunswick, NJ: Rutgers University Press, 1995); Rozina Visram, *Ayahs, Lascars, and Princes: Indians in Britain, 1700–1947* (London: Pluto Press, 1986).

32. The most informative texts remain those of the early twentieth century: Jules Mathorez, *Les étrangers en France sous l'ancien régime: Histoire de la formation de la population française*, vol. 1, *Les Orientaux et les extra-Européens dans la population française* (Paris: E. Champion, 1919); and Albert Mathiez's important study of foreigners in revolutionary France, *La Révolution et les étrangers: Cosmopolitisme et défense national* (Paris: La Renaissance du Livre, 1918).

33. Gérard Noiriel, *Le creuset français: Histoire de l'immigration, XIXe-XXe siècles* (Paris: Seuil, 1988); Ralph Schor, *Histoire de l'immigration en France de la fin du XIXe siècle à nos jours* (Paris: A. Colin, 1996).

34. For example, Sue Peabody and Tyler Edward Stovall, eds., *The Color of Liberty: Histories of Race in France* (Durham, NC: Duke University Press, 2003).

35. This proscription was recently challenged by the "Loi Hortefeux," which also proposed voluntary DNA testing of candidates for immigration on family reunion schemes. The Conseil d'État rejected the collection of statistics but upheld the legality of genetic screening.

36. See Laurent Lévy, *Le spectre du communautarisme* (Paris: Éditions Amsterdam, 2005).

37. For the debate over colonization, see Pascal Blanchard et al., *La fracture coloniale: La société française au prisme de l'héritage colonial* (Paris: La Découverte, 2005); Chantal Bordes-Benayoun and Dominique Schnapper, *Diasporas et nations* (Paris: Jacob, 2005).

38. For a useful discussion of migrant groups, see Charles Tilly, "Transplanted Networks," in *Immigration Reconsidered: History, Sociology, and Politics*, ed. Virginia Yans-McLaughlin (New York: Oxford University Press, 1990), 79–95.

39. David Garrioch, *Neighbourhood and Community in Paris, 1740–1790* (Cambridge: Cambridge University Press, 1986), 5–6.

40. James Clifford, *Routes: Travel and Translation in the Late Twentieth Century* (Cambridge, MA: Harvard University Press, 1997), 245.

41. Ibid., 22.

42. Martin W. Lewis and Kären E. Wigen, *The Myth of Continents: A Critique of Metageography* (Berkeley: University of California Press, 1997).

43. Paul Gilroy, *The Black Atlantic: Modernity and Double Consciousness* (London: Verso, 1993).

44. Daniel Roche, *Humeurs vagabondes: De la circulation des hommes et de l'utilité des voyages* (Paris: Fayard, 2003).

45. Frederick Cooper and Rogers Brubaker, "Beyond 'Identity'," *Theory & Society* 29 (2001): 1–47.

46. E. P. Thompson, *The Making of the English Working Class* (Harmondsworth, UK: Penguin, 1980), 11–12.

47. Dipesh Chakrabarty, *Provincializing Europe: Postcolonial Thought and Historical Difference* (Princeton, NJ: Princeton University Press, 2000), 20.

1. A ROUGH CROSSING

1. Egyptian Legation to minister of the interior, 1 vendémiaire an 10, AN F[17] 1100 (Commission d'Égypte).

2. See discussion of the nargileh in the exhibition catalogue *Bonaparte et l'Égypte: Feu et lumières, 14 octobre 2008—19 mars 2009* (Paris: Institut du Monde Arabe, 2008), 56–57.

3. See Thomas Philipp, *The Syrians in Egypt, 1725–1975* (Stuttgart: Steiner, 1985).

4. Abd al-Rahman al-Jabarti, *'Abd al-Rahman al-Jabarti's History of Egypt* [*Aja'ib al-athar fi 'l-tarajim wa-'l-akhbar*], trans. and ed. Thomas Philipp and Moshe Perlmann (Stuttgart: Franz Steiner Verlag, 1994), 288.

5. By far the best history is Juan Cole's *Napoleon's Egypt: Invading the Middle East* (New York: Palgrave Macmillan, 2007). Cole expertly draws out the parallels with the US-led occupation of Iraq of which he has been one of the most influential critics. In its use of

a vast range of primary sources, Cole's is also the most important historical account of the "expedition" in English since J. Christopher Herold's *Bonaparte in Egypt* (London: Hamish Hamilton, 1962).

6. E.g., P. J. Vatikiotis, *The History of Egypt: From Muhammad Ali to Sadat* (Baltimore: The Johns Hopkins University Press, 1980), 46.

7. The most influential defender of this view is Bernard Lewis; see, for example, his *Muslim Discovery of Europe* (London: Phoenix Press, 1982), 53.

8. Darrell Dykstra, "The French Occupation in Egypt," in *The Cambridge History of Egypt*, vol. 2, *Modern Egypt, from 1517 to the End of the Twentieth Century*, ed. M. W. Daly (Cambridge: Cambridge University Press, 1998), 115.

9. Henry Laurens, *Les origines intellectuelles de l'expédition d'Égypte: L'Orientalisme islamisant en France, 1698–1798* (Istanbul: Editions Isis, 1987).

10. Henry Laurens et al., *L'expédition d'Égypte 1798–1801* (Paris: Armand Colin, 1989). For a critical discussion of the term *expedition* and the politics of commemoration, see Leïla Enan, "'Si tu le sais, alors c'est un catastrophe . . .' La commemoration: Pourquoi, pour qui?" *Égypte/Monde arabe* 1 (1999): 13–24.

11. Khaled Fahmy, *All the Pasha's Men: Mehmed Ali, His Army, and the Making of Modern Egypt* (Cambridge: Cambridge University Press, 1997).

12. See the collection of essays in Virginia H. Aksan and Daniel Goffman, eds., *The Early Modern Ottomans: Remapping the Empire* (Cambridge: Cambridge University Press, 2007); also Suraiya Faroqhi, *The Ottoman Empire and the World Around It* (London: I. B. Tauris, 2004).

13. See Virginia Aksan, *Ottoman Wars, 1700–1870: An Empire Besieged* (London: Longman/Pearson, 2007).

14. Karen Barkey, *Empire of Difference: The Ottomans in Comparative Perspective* (Cambridge: Cambridge University Press, 2008), 201.

15. See Diana Rizk Khoury, "The Ottoman Centre versus Provincial Power-Holders: An Analysis of the Historiography," in *The Cambridge History of the Ottoman Empire and Turkey*, ed. Suraiya Faroqhi (Cambridge: Cambridge University Press, 2006), 3: 135–56.

16. Daniel Crecelius, "Egypt in the Eighteenth Century," in *Cambridge History of Egypt*, ed. Daly, 2: 59.

17. See Peter Gran, *Islamic Roots of Capitalism: Egypt, 1760–1840* (Austin: University of Texas Press, 1979); Afaf Lutfi al-Sayyid-Marsot, *A Short History of Modern Egypt* (Cambridge: Cambridge University Press, 1985).

18. Nelly Hanna provides an excellent account of these complex processes in her essay "Ottoman Egypt and the French Expedition," in *Napoleon in Egypt*, ed. Irene A. Bierman (Reading, UK: Ithaca Press, 2003), 5–12.

19. Michael Winter, *Egyptian Society under Ottoman Rule, 1517–1798* (New York: Routledge, 1992), 27–28; for the parallel developments under Zahir al-'Umar in Palestine, see Thomas Philipp, *Acre: The Rise and Fall of a Palestinian City, 1730–1831* (New York: Columbia University Press, 2001), 40.

20. Thomas Phillip and Ulrich Haarmaan, eds., *The Mamluks in Egyptian Politics and Society* (Cambridge: Cambridge University Press, 1998).

21. See Daniel Crecelius, *The Roots of Modern Egypt: A Study of the Regimes of 'Ali Bey al-Kabir and Muhammad Bey Abu al-Dhahab, 1760–1775* (Minneapolis: Bibliotheca Islamica, 1981).

22. Crecelius, "Egypt in the Eighteenth Century," 19.

23. See Paul Masson, *Histoire du commerce français dans le Levant au XVIIe siècle* (Paris, 1896).

24. Henry Laurens points to the importance of the dynamic between a singular conception of "civilization" and a plural conception of distinct civilizational trajectories, in *Le royaume impossible: La France et la genèse du monde arabe* (Paris: Armand Colin, 1990).

25. "Le Nil est aussi familier à beaucoup de gens que la Seine. Les enfants mêmes ont les oreilles rabattus de ses cataractes et ses embouchures. Tout le monde a vu et entendu parler des momies." Benoît de Maillet, *Description de l'Egypte . . . composé sur les mémoires de M. de Maillet, ancien consul au Caire, par l'abbé le Mascrier* (Paris: Genneau & Rollin, 1735), iv.

26. Nicole Dhombres and Jean Dhombres, *Naissance d'un pouvoir: Sciences et savants en France, 1793–1824* (Paris: Payot, 1989), 104.

27. Louis Bergeron, *France under Napoleon,* trans. R. R. Palmer (Princeton, NJ: Princeton University Press, 1981), 53; see also Stuart Woolf, *Napoleon's Integration of Europe* (London: Routledge, 1991), 58.

28. André Raymond, *Égyptiens et Français au Caire, 1798–1801* (Cairo: Institut Français d'Archéologie Orientale, 1998); see also Patrice Bret, *L'Égypte au temps de l'expédition de Bonaparte, 1798–1801* (Paris: Hachette Littératures, 1998). Woolf, *Napoleon's Integration of Europe;* Woolf, "French Civilization and Ethnicity in the Napoleonic Empire," *Past and Present* 124 (1989): 96–120; Michael Broers, "Cultural Imperialism in a European Context? Political Culture and Cultural Politics in Napoleonic Italy," *Past and Present* 170 (2001): 152–80.

29. Edward W. Said, *Orientalism* (New York: Vintage Books, 1979), esp. 80–92.

30. Daniel Roche, *La France des lumières* (Paris: Fayard, 1993).

31. Marie-Noëlle Bourguet, "Science and Memory: The Stakes of the Expedition to Egypt (1798–1801)," in *Taking Liberties: Problems of a New Order from the French Revolution to Napoleon,* ed. Howard G. Brown and Judith A. Miller (Manchester: Manchester University Press, 2003), 103.

32. Carter Vaughan Findlay, "An Ottoman Occidentalist in Europe: Ahmed Midhat Meets Madame Gulnar, 1889," *American Historical Review* 103 (1998): 15–49.

33. Henry Laurens, "La Révolution française et l'Islam: Un essai de perspective historique," in *L'image de la Révolution française,* ed. Michel Vovelle (Paris: Pergamon, 1989), 886–94.

34. Dominique Urvoy, "Le monde musulman selon les idées de la Révolution française," *Revue du monde musulman et de la Méditerranée* 52–53, ⅔ (1989): 35–48.

35. Boulay de la Meurthe, *Documents sur la négociation du Concordat* (Paris, 181), 1: 76–77.

36. Jabarti ridiculed the poor Arabic of the declaration with a play on words: "The word *Muslimin* should be *Muslimun* in the nominative. The point of putting the word in the *nasb* (accusative) has already been mentioned. There is another point namely: that

their Islam is *nasb* (fraud). . . . As for his statement 'and destroyed there the Papal See,' by this deed they have gone against the Christians as has already been pointed out. So those people are opposed to both Christians and Muslims, and do not hold fast to any religion. You see that they are materialists, who deny all God's attributes."Abd al-Rahman al-Jabarti, *Tarikh muddat al-faransis bi misr*, trans. Shmuel Moreh as "Al-Jabartî's Chronicle of the First Seven Months of the French Occupation, June-December, 1798," in *Napoleon in Egypt: Al-Jabartî's Chronicle of the First Seven Months of the French Occupation, 1798*, (Princeton, NJ: M. Wiener, 1993), 32. See also Christian Cherfils, *Bonaparte et l'Islam d'après les documents français et arabes* (Paris: Pedone, 1914).

37. Aly Bahgat, "Acte de mariage du général Menou avec la dame Zobaïdah," *Bulletin de l'Institut d'Égypte* 9 (1898): 221–35.

38. See Mohamed Afifi and André Raymond, *Le Diwan du Caire, 1800–1801* (Cairo: IFAO, 2004).

39. Jabarti, *Napoleon in Egypt*, 60.

40. Qtd. in Laurens, *L'expédition d'Egypte*, 114.

41. André Raymond, "Les Égyptiens et les lumières pendant l'expédition française," in *L'expédition d'Égypte: Une entreprise des lumières, 1798–1801*, ed. Patrice Bret (Paris: Technique et Documentation, 1999), 106.

42. Jabarti called syphilis "the European disease of love" (*Marad al-hubb al faranji*). *Aja'ib al-athar*, 3: 62.

43. Aziz S. Atiya, *A History of Eastern Christianity* (London: Methuen, 1968), 79–98; Albert Hourani, "The Syrians in Egypt in the Eighteenth and Nineteenth Century," in *Colloque international sur l'histoire du Caire, 27 mars–5 avril 1969* (Cairo: Ministry of Culture of the Arab Republic of Egypt, 1972), 221–319. The role of these minorities is also discussed in Anthony D. Smith, *The Ethnic Origins of Nations* (Oxford: Blackwell, 1986), 113.

44. Jabarti, *Aja'ib al-athar*, 3: 69.

45. There is an important comparison to made here with the way the French failed to comprehend the complex structure of family, gender, and class politics in Muslim culture in Egypt: see Afaf Lutfi al-Sayyid Marsot, *Women and Men in Late Eighteenth-Century Egypt* (Austin: University of Texas Press, 1995), 37. For a slightly later discussion of related issues, see Lisa Pollard, *Nurturing the Nation: The Family Politics of Modernizing, Colonizing, and Liberating Egypt, 1805–1923* (Berkeley: University of California Press, 2005), esp. ch. 2.

46. Harald Motzki, "Jirjis al-Jawhari," in *The Coptic Encyclopedia*, ed. Aziz Atiya (New York: Macmillan, 1991), 1332–33.

47. Henry Laurens, "Bonaparte et l'Islam," in *Orientales*, vol. 1, *Autour de l'expédition d'Égypte* (Paris: CNRS Editions, 2004), 154.

48. Jabarti, *Aja'ib al-athar*, 3: 43.

49. For an analysis along these lines, see Jean-Loup Amselle, *Vers un multiculturalisme français: L'empire de la coutume* (Paris: Aubier, 1996), 55–84.

50. Raymond, *Égyptiens et Français*, 223.

51. Laurens, *L'expédition d'Égypte*, 295.

52. Ibid., 294.

53. Bruce Masters, *Christians and Jews in the Ottoman Arab World: The Roots of Sectarianism* (New York: Cambridge University Press, 2001), 60.

54. Antoine Galland, *Tableau de l'Égypte pendant le séjour de l'armée française* (1803), qtd. in Raymond, *Égyptiens et Français*, 308.

55. Masters, *Christians and Jews*, 50.

56. Harald Motzki, "Muhammad al-Muhdi," in *The Coptic Encyclopedia*, ed. Atiya, 1695–96; Mustapha al-Ahnaf, "Cheikh al-Mahdi (1737–1815): Uléma, médiateur et businessman; Éléments pour une biographie," *Égypte/Monde arabe* 1 (1999): 115–50.

57. J.-J. Marcel, *Contes du Chekh al-Mohdy* (1833–35; repr., Paris: Summa Aegyptica, 2003).

58. Robert M. Haddad, *Syrian Christians in Muslim Society: An Interpretation* (Princeton, NJ: Princeton University Press, 1970); Masters, *Christians and Jews*, 12–13; Philipp, *Syrians in Egypt*, 18–19. The term Melkite *(malikiyya)* originally referred to those inhabitants of the region who had remained Christian adherents of the Byzantine emperor (*malik*) rather than joining the Monophysite "heresy."

59. The Melkite Catholics did not become an independent *millet* until 1848, after a long struggle; see Masters, *Christians and Jews*, 108–10.

60. Masters, *Christians and Jews*, 112.

61. Benedict Anderson, *Imagined Communities: Reflections on the Origins and Spread of Nationalism* (London: Verso, 1983); see also Youssef Choueiri, *Arab Nationalism: A History* (Oxford: Blackwell, 2000), esp. ch. 3.

62. Philipp, *Syrians in Egypt*, 19.

63. Ibid., 22.

64. Ibid., 1.

65. Philipp, *Acre*; Amnon Cohen, *Palestine in the 18th Century: Patterns of Government and Administration* (Jerusalem: Magnes Press, 1973).

66. Laurens, *L'expédition d'Egypte*, 180.

67. These events are still being politicized by historians today: for example, Raphael Israeli, *Green Crescent over Nazareth* (London: Routledge, 2002), 10.

68. Philipp, *Syrians in Egypt*, 30.

69. Philipp, *Acre*, 117.

70. Philipp, *Syrians in Egypt*, 40–45.

71. Anwar [Anouar] Louca, "Ya'qub, General," in *The Coptic Encyclopedia*, ed. Atiya, 2350.

72. Laurens, *L'expédition d'Égypte*, 260–62; Raymond, *Égyptiens et Français*, 184–214.

73. Relations between French and Muslims were further embittered by the assassination of Kléber by a young Syrian Muslim, Suleiman al-Halabi; Raymond, *Égyptiens et Français*, 214–19.

74. Jabarti, *Aja'ib al-athar*, 3: 180.

75. Ibid., 3: 254.

76. G. Guémard, "Les auxiliaires de l'armée de Bonaparte en Égypte (1798–1801)," *Bulletin de l'Institut d'Égypte* 9 (1927): 1–17.

77. See the analysis of the Coptic resistance by the Egyptian scholar Nasir Ahmad Ibrahim, "Muqawama tahta as-satah: Al-mubashirun al-aqbat wa-l-hamlat al-faransiyya," in *Mi'ata 'am 'ala-l-hamlat al-faransiyya (ru'iyya masriyya)*, ed. Nasser Ahmed Ibrahim (Cairo: Maktabat ad-Dar al-'Arabiyyat al'Kitab, 2008), 56–106.

78. For the text of the treaty, see Georges Rigault, *Le général Abdallah Menou et la dernière phase de l'expédition d'Égypte*, repr. as vol. 6 of Clément de la Jonquière, *L'expédition d'Égypte, 1798–1801* (Paris: Éditions Historiques Teissèdre, 2003), 345–46.

79. Jabarti, *Aja'ib al-athar*, 3: 303–5.

80. Ibid., 3: 282.

81. Ibid., 3: 288.

82. Ibid., 3: 297.

83. Correspondance de l'Armée d'Orient at Vincennes, qtd. by Anouar Louca, "Quels Mamelouks?" in *L'Orient des Provençaux dans l'histoire* (Marseille: Archives Départementales, 1984), 345.

84. Raymond, *Égyptiens et Français*, 271.

85. Archives Départementales des Bouches-du-Rhône, Marseille, 200 E 892.

86. Shafiq Ghurbal, "Le général Ya'qub, le chevalier Lascaris et le projet de l'indépendance de l'Égypte en 1801," trans. Iman Farag, *Égypte/Monde arabe* 1 (1999): 179–203.

87. See Henry Laurens, "Le chevalier de Lascaris et les origines du *Grand Jeu*," in *Orientales*, 1: 167–83; Auriant, *La vie du chevalier Théodore Lascaris, ou L'imposteur malgré lui* (Paris: Gallimard, 1940).

88. Roussillon also suggested that it was generally thought that Ya'qub had been poisoned by the coffee he drank during this interview, but this was only speculation; see "L'expédition d'Égypte: Fragments des mémoires militaires du colonel Vigo Roussillon (1793–1837)," *Revue des deux mondes* 100 (1890): 748–49.

89. George A. Haddad, "A Project for the Independence of Egypt, 1801," *Journal of the American Oriental Society* 90 (1970): 169–83; Georges Douin, *L'Égypte indépendante, projet de 1801: Documents inédits recueillis aux Archives du Foreign Office à Londres* (Cairo: Société Royale de Géographie d'Égypte, 1924).

90. Theodore Lascaris to Captain Joseph Edmonds, 22 September 1801, reproduced in full in Haddad, "A Project for the Independence of Egypt," 179.

91. Ibid.

92. Ibid.; emphasis in original.

93. "Shaykh al-`Arab, the great emir Humam ibn Yusuf ibn Ahmad al-Hawwari, was a patron of the rich and poor alike. His wealth, generosity and hospitality were without equal. . . . The refugees of the Qasimi Mamluks, whom he sheltered, intermarried with his people and learned to speak Arabic. . . . Humam was a deeply religious man. He extended his hospitality to many important ulama, and also supported ulama in Cairo." Michael Winter, *Egyptian Society under Ottoman Rule*, 105.

94. Notes remitted to Captain Joseph Edmonds: Haddad, "A Project for the Independence of Egypt," 181.

95. Ibid.

96. Nemir Effendi to Napoleon, 1st Vendémiaire, Year X: Haddad, "A Project for the Independence of Egypt," 182.

97. Laurens, *L'expédition d'Égypte*, 321.

98. Lascaris wrote, for example: "If Egypt is declared a French colony, every effort of the metropolitan government must be turned toward getting the most from it, because that is the destiny of all possible colonies, to provide for the needs of the metropole." Lascaris

made it clear that this letter of 26 April 1801 was written without orders from Ya'qub. Auriant, *La vie du chevalier Théodore Lascaris*, 61–62.

99. The widespread acceptance of Egyptian origins for ancient Greek culture until the early nineteenth century has been shown by Martin Bernal in his book *Black Athena: The Afroasiatic Roots of Classical Civilization* (New Brunswick, NJ: Rutgers University Press, 1987). If Bernal's championing of this "ancient model" has remained controversial, his demonstration of how widely this model was accepted in the pre- and early modern period is very instructive.

100. See Dipesh Chakrabarty, *Provincializing Europe: Postcolonial Thought and Historical Difference* (Princeton, NJ: Princeton University Press, 2000), 27–34.

101. Christopher Prendergast, *Napoleon and History Painting: Antoine-Jean Gros's La Bataille D'Eylau* (Oxford: Clarendon Press, 1997), 62–70.

2. PORTS OF CALL

1. Anouar Louca, "Quels Mamelouks?" in *L'Orient des Provençaux dans l'histoire* (Marseille: Archives Départementales, 1984), 346.

2. Georges Spillmann, "Les auxiliaires de l'Armée d'Orient (1798–1801): La création de corps auxiliaires égyptiens et syriens," *Revue du souvenir napoléonien* 304 (1979): 10.

3. Like his uncle, Gabriel Sidarious had served in a high position under the Mamluk beys prior to the French occupation. See Gaston Homsy, "Un égyptien colonel dans les armées de Napoléon 1er," *Bulletin de l'Institut d'Égypte* 10 (1928): 83–96.

4. George Haddad, "A Project for the Independence of Egypt, 1801," *Journal of the American Oriental Society* 90 (1970), 183.

5. Auriant, *La vie du chevalier Théodore Lascaris, ou L'imposteur malgré lui* (Paris: Gallimard, 1940), 72.

6. Ibid., 96.

7. Ibid., 97.

8. See Michel Vovelle, *Les républiques-sœurs sous le regard de la Grande Nation (1795–1803): De l'Italie aux portes de l'Empire ottoman, l'impact du modèle républicain* (Paris: L'Harmattan, 2000).

9. Jacques Godechot, *La Grande Nation: L'expansion révolutionnaire de la France dans le monde de 1789 à 1799* (Paris: Aubier, 1956).

10. M. S. Anderson, *The Eastern Question, 1774–1923: A Study in International Relations* (London: Macmillan, 1966), 33–34.

11. Eventually Lascaris was sent on a mission to make contact with Ibn al-Sa'ud and his Wahhabi followers in Arabia: see George Haddad, "Fathallah al-Sayegh and His Account of a Napoleonic Mission among the Arab Nomads: History or Fiction?" *Studia islamica* 24 (1966): 107–23.

12. Several requests were reported as refused in 1806 and 1808: see the secret police bulletins republished in Ernest d' Hauterive, *La police secrète du Premier Empire: Bulletins quotidiens adressés par Fouché à l'Empereur* (Paris: Perrin, 1908), 2: 339, 3: 380.

13. See Yves Benot and Marcel Dorigny, "Introduction," in *Rétablissement de l'esclavage dans les colonies françaises 1802: Aux origines d'Haïti, Ruptures et continuités de la politique*

coloniale française (1800-1830), ed. Benot and Dorigny (Paris: Maisonneuve et Larose, 2003).

14. Michael Rapport, *Nationality and Citizenship in Revolutionary France: The Treatment of Foreigners, 1789-1799* (Oxford: Clarendon, 2000), 316. Aïdé's name appears in this letter as Aydé; such variations were very common in the often haphazard recording and transliteration of Arabic names into French. To avoid confusion, I have chosen the most frequently used version of each name and retained this spelling across the book, except where noted.

15. Rapport, *Nationality and Citizenship*, 316

16. See the recent work by Greg Burgess, *Refuge in the Land of Liberty: France and Its Refugees, from the Revolution to the End of Asylum, 1787-1939* (New York: Palgrave Macmillan, 2008).

17. See Anna-Maria Rao, *Esuli: L'emigrazione politica italiana in Francia (1792-1802)* (Naples: Guida Editori, 1992), esp. ch. 2, "Fuorusciti e 'pellegrini della libertà' dall''89 al '92," 25-43.

18. Anna-Maria Rao, "Les réfugiés italiens en 1799," *Annales historiques de la Révolution française* 52 (1980): 253.

19. Ibid., 261.

20. Anna-Maria Rao, "Italian Refugees in France" (Paper presented at the XVth Biennial Conference of the Australasian Association for European History, Melbourne July 11-15, 2005).

21. Jean René Aymes, *La déportation sous le Premier Empire. Les Espagnols en France, 1808-1814* (Paris: Publications de la Sorbonne, 1983) esp. ch. 10; see also Aline Vauchelle-Haquet and Gérard Dufour, "Les Espagnols naturalisés français et les Espagnols ayant obtenu l'autorisation de fixer leur domicile en France de 1814 à 1831," in *Exil politique et migration économique: Espagnols et Français aux XIXe-XXe siècles*, ed. Centre national de la recherche scientifique (Paris: Éditions du Centre National de la Recherche Scientifique, 1991), 31-46.

22. Pierre Échinard and Émile Témime, *Histoire des migrations à Marseille*, vol. 1, *La préhistoire de la migration, 1482-1830* (La Calade, Aix-en-Provence: Edisud, 1989).

23. Peter Sahlins, *Boundaries: The Making of France and Spain in the Pyrenees* (Berkeley: University of California Press, 1989).

24. Bruce Masters discusses the family in his book on Christians in the Ottoman world: "The ʿAʾida clan was one of the earliest, and most prominent of the Aleppo Catholic merchant families to emerge into the light of the extant historical record." Bruce Masters, *Christians and Jews in the Ottoman Arab World: The Roots of Sectarianism* (New York: Cambridge University Press, 2001), 76-77. Georges Aïdé's birthplace is given in his dossier of naturalization: AN BB/11/112/1 dossier 1095 B3.

25. Auriant, *La vie du chevalier Théodore Lascaris*, 71-95; Haddad, "A Project for the Independence of Egypt," 182-83.

26. Egyptian Legation to minister of interior, 1 vendémiaire an 10, AN F^{17} 1100 (Commission d'Égypte).

27. Ibid.

28. Ernest d' Hauterive, *La police secrète du Premier Empire: Bulletins quotidiens adressés par Fouché à l'Empereur* (Paris: Perrin, 1922), 3: 255 (7 September 1807).

29. Ernest d' Hauterive, *La police secrète du Premier Empire: Bulletins quotidiens adressés par Fouché à l'Empereur . . . , nouvelle série, 1808–1809* (Paris: Perrin, 1963), 1: 481 (24 December 1808).

30. Régis Bertrand, "Les cimetierès des "esclaves turcs" des arsenaux de Marseille et de Toulon au XVIIIe siècle," *Revue des Mondes Musulmans et de la Méditerranée* 99–100 (2002): 211.

31. Léon Levy-Schneider, *L' application du Concordat par un prélat d'ancien régime: Mgr. Champion de Cicé, archevêque d'Aix et d'Arles* (Paris: F. Rieder, 1921), 245.

32. Ibid., 246.

33. Auguste Boppe, "Le colonel Nicole Papas Oglou et le bataillon des chasseurs d'Orient, 1798–1815," in *Carnets de la Sabretache: Revue militaire retrospective* (Paris: Berger-Levrault, 1900), 8: 13, 112.

34. Abd al-Rahman al-Jabarti, *'Abd al-Rahman al-Jabarti's History of Egypt [Aja'ib al-athar fi 'l-tarajim wa-'l-akhbar]*, trans. Thomas Philipp and Moshe Perlmann, (Stuttgart: Franz Steiner Verlag, 1994), 3: 407.

35. Georges Reynaud, "Les données de l'état civil,"in *L'Orient des Provençaux dans l'histoire* (Marseille: Archives Départementales, 1984), 369.

36. Auriant, *La vie du chevalier Théodore Lascaris*, 76.

37. A descendant of Ya'qub's family, Gaston Homsy, wrote a book describing his family's past, perhaps the only such work by a member of this diaspora. See Gaston Homsy, *Le général Jacob et l'expédition de Bonaparte en Égypte, 1798–1801* (Marseille: Éditions Indépendantes, 1921).

38. Léon Gozlan, "Les refugiés égyptiens à Marseille," *Revue contemporaine* 149 (1866): 33.

39. [Laurent Lautard], *Esquisses historiques: Marseille depuis 1789 jusqu'en 1815, par un vieux Marseillais (L. Lautard)* (Marseille: Marius Olive, 1844), 2: 361.

40. Reynaud, "Les données de l'état civil," 368.

41. Gozlan, "Les réfugiés égyptiens," 34.

42. Auriant, *La vie du chevalier Théodore Lascaris*, 79.

43. Ibid., 78.

44. The Arabic word *mamluk* was rendered into French in a bewildering variety of ways: *Mamelouk, Mameluk, Mameluck,* and *Mamelouck.* I will henceforth use the term "Mamelouk" to refer to soldiers of the French Imperial Guard, to distinguish them from the true *mamluk* ruling caste in Egypt. This is for greater clarity here—contemporaries did not bother to make the distinction.

45. Jean Brunon and Raoul Brunon, *Les Mameluks d'Égypte; Les Mameluks de la Garde Impériale* (Marseille: Collection Raoul & Jean Brunon, 1963), 46. This is evident in a photograph of one of the remaining Mamelouk soldiers, albeit of French origin, in Darcy Grimaldo Grigsby, *Extremities: Painting Empire in Post-Revolutionary France* (London: Yale University Press, 2002), 159. It may have been this "Islamic" reference that so enraged the Spaniards during the campaign of 1808, leading to a massacre of the Mamelouk soldiers in the streets of Madrid, depicted by Goya in his painting *Dos de Mayo* (see chapter 3, note 35).

46. Brunon and Brunon, *Les Mameluks d'Égypte*, 70. From their figures it is possible to estimate that a single basic uniform cost at least three hundred francs in 1805, and probably at least double that figure for all items required, such as sabers, golden braids, fringes, spurs, etc.; the sum was proportionally higher for an officer's uniform.

47. Brunon and Brunon, *Les Mameluks d'Égypte*, 46.

48. Alan Forrest, *Conscripts and Deserters: The Army and French Society during the Revolution and Empire* (New York: Oxford University Press, 1989); Natalie Petiteau, *Lendemains d'empire: Les soldats de Napoléon dans la France du XIXe siècle* (Paris: La Boutique de l'Histoire, 2003).

49. This information is drawn from the list provided in Jean Savant, *Les Mamelouks de Napoléon* (Paris: Calmann-Lévy, 1949), 435–79. For comparative statistics on the mortality of French soldiers across the period, see Jacques Houdaille, "Le problème des pertes de guerre," *Revue d'histoire moderne et contemporaine* 17 (1972): 411–23; the statistics suggest total casualty figures well over 25 percent.

50. Arrêtés, 26 prairial an XI, and 18 nivôse an XII, AMG XL 37l (Généralités).

51. For comparison, a four-pound loaf of bread varied from around fifty centimes to seventy-five or eighty centimes during the recession of 1811–12. See Judith A. Miller, *Mastering the Market: The State and the Grain Trade in Northern France, 1700–1860* (Cambridge: Cambridge University Press, 1998), 205–16.

52. Paul Gaffarel, "Les massacres de Juin 1815," Archives Municipales (henceforth AM), Marseille, 19/I/1, p. 14.

53. Erick Noël, *Être noir en France au XVIIIe siècle* (Paris: Tallandier, 2006), 219.

54. Mme Thiers née Amic to J-B Santi-Lhomaca, 24 messidor an 12, Bibliothèque Municipale, Carcassonne, Fonds Chénier, 319 (11797).

55. See Yvonne Knibiehler, Régine Goutalier, Catherine Marand-Fouquet, and Eliane Richard, *Marseillaises: Les femmes et la ville, des origines à nos jours* (Marseille: Côté-Femmes, 1993), 130.

56. See Ian Coller, "Pratiques de voyage et mobilités arabes dans la France de l'Empire et de la Restauration," in *Voyager en Europe de Humboldt à Stendhal : Contraintes nationales et tentations cosmopolites, 1790–1840*, ed. Nicolas Bourguinat (Paris: Nouveau Monde, 2007), 365–85.

57. Rapp, *Mémoires*, qtd. in *Les clémences de Napoléon: L'image au service du mythe* (Paris: Marmottan/Somogy, 2004), 97. This catalogue cites fourteen versions of the image of *L'Égyptienne*.

58. Maryam to Mikha'il Sabbagh, June 1810, Bibliothèque de Genève, MSS Orientales, 16.

59. Sue Peabody, *There Are No Slaves in France: The Political Culture of Race and Slavery in the Ancien Régime* (New York: Oxford University Press, 2002); Michael D. Sibalis, "Les noirs en France sous Napoléon: L'enquête de 1807," in *Rétablissement de l'esclavage*, ed. Benot and Dorigny, 95–108.

60. Jennifer Heuer, "The One-Drop Rule in Reverse? Interracial Marriages in Napoleonic and Restoration France," *Law and History Review* 27 (2009): 515–48.

61. Police commissioner of Sections 5, 6, 20 & 21 to mayor of Midi, 10 messidor an 10 (1802), AM, Marseille, 2 I 240.

62. A. Perrot and C. Amoudru, *Histoire de l'Ex-Garde: Depuis sa formation jusqu'à son licenciement, comprenant les faits généraux des campagnes de 1805 à 1815* (Paris: Delaunay, 1821), 82–83.

63. AM, Marseille, I 2 240.

64. Mayor to prefect Bouches-du-Rhône, 5 July 1807, AM, Marseille, 2 I 240.

65. Prefect Bouches-du-Rhône to mayor, 12 July 1807, AM, Marseille, 2 I 240.

66. État nominatif des individus reconnus mauvais sujets et perturbateurs du repos public appartenant au dépôt de réfugiés égyptiens, 29 September 1807, AM, Marseille, 2 I 240.

67. Indeed, the Jews of Marseille were similarly summoned to deal with the "Algerian" arrivals in the town and had to pay for their passage to Livorno. For the history of this community, see Zosa Szajkowski, "The Jews of Marseille at the End of the Eighteenth Century," in *Jews and the French Revolutions of 1789, 1830, and 1848* (New York: KTAV Publishing House, 1970), 281–96. For the transformation of Jewish corporatism and citizenship in this period, see Ronald Schechter, "A Festival of the Law: Napoleon's Jewish Assemblies," in *Taking Liberties: Problems of a New Order from the French Revolution to Napoleon,* ed. Howard G. Brown and Judith A. Miller (Manchester: Manchester University Press, 2003) 147–65.

68. I have dealt with this episode and the question of slavery at much greater length elsewhere: see Ian Coller, "Race and Slavery in the Making of Arab France, 1802–1815," in *War, Empire, and Slavery, 1770–1830,* ed. Jane Rendall, Nicholas Guyatt, and Richard Bessel (London: Palgrave Macmillan, 2010).

69. Gabriel Taouïl to Mikha'il Sabbagh, December 1807, Bibliothèque de Genève, MSS Orientales, 16.

70. Bulletin de Police, Jan-Mar 1808, AN F⁷ 3659/6, Bouches-du-Rhône, Police.

71. Report of 1810, Cours public d'arabe à Marseille, AN F¹⁷ 4097.

72. Taouïl to Sabbagh, December 1807, Bibliothèque de Genève, MSS Orientales, 16.

73. Taouïl to Sabbagh, October 1807, Bibliothèque de Genève, MSS Orientales, 16.

74. Report of 17 January 1811, AN F⁷ 8415.

75. Georges Aïdé to Ministry of War, 26 February 1811, AMG XL 37d; emphasis added.

76. Taouïl to Sabbagh, January 1811, Bibliothèque de Genève, MSS Orientales, 16.

77. Bocthor to Sabbagh, 1810, Bibliothèque de Genève, MSS Orientales, 16.

78. Homsy, *Le général Jacob,* 141. The document (8 February 1810) lists as present Marie Namé, Hennin Anna, George Aïdé, Nicolas Sakakini, Farag and Michael Couri [Khouri], Joseph Joubara, and Lotfi Nemr (i.e., Nemir Effendi).

79. François Naydorff to Sabbagh, 30 October 1809, Bibliothèque de Genève, MSS Orientales, 16.

80. Naydorff to Sabbagh, 6 October 1808, Bibliothèque de Genève, MSS Orientales, 16.

81. Naydorff to Sabbagh, 26 January 1810, Bibliothèque de Genève, MSS Orientales, 16.

82. Hawadier to Ministry of War, 1810, AMG XL 37d.

83. See Isa Carus, AMG XL 37j; Behennam, AMG XL 37j.

84. Chammas to Ministry of War, 12 March, 1813, AMG XL 37l.

85. Aïdé to Sabbagh, September 1807, Bibliothèque de Genève, MSS Orientales, 16.

86. Clifford Geertz, *Local Knowledge* (New York: Basic Books, 1986), 56.

87. Haddad, "A Project for the Independence of Egypt," 183.

88. Michael Herzfeld, *Cultural Intimacy: Social Poetics in the Nation-State*, 2nd ed. (New York: Routledge, 2005), 3.

89. For this "self-orientalism," see in particular Shaden Tageldin, "Disarming Words: Reading (Post)Colonial Egypt's Double Bond to Europe" (PhD diss., University of California, Berkeley, 2004); for a different approach, see K. E. Fleming, *The Muslim Bonaparte: Diplomacy and Orientalism in Ali Pasha's Greece* (Princeton, NJ: Princeton University Press, 1999).

90. Benedict Anderson, *Imagined Communities: Reflections on the Origin and Spread of Nationalism*, 2nd ed. (London: Verso, 1991).

91. Rashid Khalidi, *Palestinian Identity: The Construction of Modern National Consciousness* (New York: Columbia University Press, 1997).

92. Gilles Veinstein, "Les Ottomans: Variations sur une identité," in *Valeur et distance: Identités et sociétés en Égypte*, ed. Christian Décobert (Paris: Maisonneuve et Larose, 2000), 114.

93. Haddad, "A Project for the Independence of Egypt," 183.

94. Halim Barakat, *The Arab World: Society, Culture, and State* (Berkeley: University of California Press, 1993), 58.

95. Yasir Suleiman, *The Arabic Language and National Identity: A Study in Ideology* (Edinburgh: Edinburgh University Press, 2003), 34 35; see also Joshua Fishman, *Language and Nationalism: Two Integrative Essays* (Rowley, MA: Newbury House, 1972), 45.

96. Anderson, *Imagined Communities*; Ernest Gellner, *Nations and Nationalism* (Ithaca, NY: Cornell University Press, 1983), 123–24; Fishman, *Language and Nationalism*, 40–44.

3. THE MAKING OF ARAB PARIS

1. Étrangers de passage à Paris, An X-1814, Russes, Turcs, Africains et colons, AN F7 2249.

2. Hermine Hartleben, *Champollion: Sa vie et son oeuvre, 1790–1832* (Paris: Pygmalion, 1983), 81.

3. Ibid.

4. Maximilan Habicht, *Epistolae quaedam arabicae (A Mauris, Aegyptis et Syris / Kitab jina al-fawakih al-atmarfy jami' ba'd makatib al-ajnab)* (Wroclaw: Typis Universitatis Regis, 1824).

5. Paul B. Fenton, "Mardochee Najjar, un juif tunisien à Paris au début du XIXe siècle," in *Entre Orient et Occident: Juifs et musulmans en Tunisie*, ed. Denis Cohen-Tannoudji (Paris: Éditions de l'Éclat, 2008), 85.

6. For Behennam, see Behennam, AMG XL 37j. For Abeid, see État nominatif des réfugiés pensionnés à la suite de la Compagnie des Mamelouks, 13 pluviose an 12, AMG XAB 35. Abeid was exiled from Acre by Djezzar Pacha during the Revolution. For these events, see François Charles-Roux, *Les échelles de Syrie et de Palestine au XVIIIe siècle* (Paris: Paul Geuthner, 1928).

7. Yves Lequin, *La Mosaïque, France: Histoire des étrangers et de l'immigration* (Paris: Larousse, 1988), 299; Chammas, AMG XL 37m.

8. Isa-Carus, *Isa-Carus, prélat du rite grec catholique aux âmes sensibles* (Paris: F. Louis, c. 1804).

9. Dom Raphaël and other Arab intellectual figures will be discussed more fully in chapter 4.

10. Stuart Woolf, "French Civilization and Ethnicity in the Napoleonic Empire," *Past and Present* 124 (1989): 97.

11. Ahmed was the former *mamluk* of the *kachef* (governor) Suleiman, but after a period in France, he took upon himself the title Ahmed Kachef Bey de Soliman, and the members of the Council of Refugees at Marseille supported his claim in 1810: see Ahmed Bey de Soliman, AMG XL 370. See also Daniel Crecelius, "The Mamluk Beylicate of Egypt in the Last Years before Its Destruction by Muhammad 'Ali Pasha in 1811," in *The Mamluks in Egyptian Politics and Society*, ed. Thomas Philipp and Ulrich Haarmann (Cambridge: Cambridge University Press, 1998), 128–49.

12. Ernest d'Hauterive, *La police secrète du Premier Empire: Bulletins quotidiens adressés par Fouché à l'Empereur* (Paris: Perrin, 1908), 2: 371 (27 May 1806), 2: 432 (18 July 1806).

13. Ahmed to Chammas, 8 June 1816, AMG XL 37m. One assumes "Tonin" is Antoine, although according to his father he was known as Ibraïm.

14. Taouïl to Sabbagh, September 1807, Bibliothèque de Genève, MSS Orientales, 16.

15. A. Tadié, "Dom Raphaël de Monachis," in *Langues'O, 1795–1995 Deux siècles d'histoire de l'École Nationale des Langues Orientales*, ed. Pierre Labrousse (Paris: Hervas, 1995), 62.

16. Habicht, *Epistolae arabicae*, letter 14.

17. Ibid.

18. Most Arabs in France during this period transcribed their names in different forms, since surnames were largely nonexistent in the Arabo-Muslim world, and additional names usually represented a simple patronymic (e.g., Abdallah), a place of origin (e.g., Halebi, inhabitant of Aleppo; Massery, Egyptian), a rank or profession (e.g., Odabachi, a military rank), or a nickname (e.g., Serra, Turkish for "black"). Many also adopted French versions of their Christian names (e.g., Girgis/Georges) or family names (Fir'aun/Pharaon).

19. Mehenna, AMG XL 37d. In another letter, Joubran makes it clear that he used this name, signing himself Gubran (Gabriel) Tady. The hard *g* is an Egyptian dialectical pronunciation of the soft *j* in standard Arabic.

20. Mehenna, AMG XL 37d.

21. Napoleon Bonaparte, *Correspondance de Napoléon 1er* (Paris: Henri Plon/J. Dumaine, 1860), 5: 465.

22. État des passagers embarqués à la suite du general Yacoub, 29 fructidor an 9, Archives Départementales des Bouches-du-Rhône, E 876.

23. État nominatif des réfugiés pensionnés à la suite de la Compagnie des Mamelouks, 13 pluviose an 12, AMG XAB 35.

24. Mehenna, 18 February 1807, AMG XL 37d.

25. See Daniel Roche, ed., *La ville promise: Mobilité et accueil à Paris (fin XVIIe-début XIXe siècle)* (Paris: Fayard, 2000).

26. Victor-Joseph-Étienne de Jouy, *L'Hermite de la Chaussée-d'Antin, ou Observations sur les moeurs et les usages parisiens au commencement du XIXe siècle* (Paris: Pillet, 1815), 54-56.

27. Mehenna, 18 February 1807, AMG XL 37d.

28. See Michel de Certeau, Dominique Julia, and Jacques Revel, *Une politique de la langue: La Révolution française et les patois* (Paris: Gallimard, 1975).

29. Stuart Woolf, *Napoléon's Integration of Europe* (London: Routledge, 1991), 223-24.

30. Youhanna Chiftichi, 15 March 1809, AMG XL 37m.

31. Joseph Messabki, An 12, AMG XL 37o.

32. Habicht, *Epistolae arabicae*, letter 15.

33. Antoine Siouphi, 18 February 1809, AMG XL 37k.

34. See Charles J. Esdaile, *Fighting Napoleon: Guerrillas, Bandits, and Adventurers in Spain, 1808-1814* (New Haven, CT: Yale University Press, 2004).

35. Francisco de Goya, *El Dos de Mayo de 1808 en Madrid*, 1808—1814, oil on canvas, Prado Museum, Madrid. The painting is also known as "La carga de los mamelucos en la Puerta del Sol" (The Charge of the Mamelouks at the Puerta del Sol).

36. Joseph Sabba, 1 November 1814, AMG XL 37j.

37. See, e.g., Issa Amouth, AMG XL 37d.

38. See Justine Halimé, Marguerite Halimé, AMG XL 37m.

39. Aly Amette/Hamez, "porteur à la halle," BB 11 352 (2015 X2).

40. Louise Virginie, 16 March 1812, AMG XL 37m.

41. Afaf Lutfi al-Sayyid Marsot, *Egypt in the Reign of Muhammad Ali* (Cambridge: Cambridge University Press, 1984), esp. ch. 3.

42. Ibid., 72-73.

43. Martyn Lyons, *Napoleon Bonaparte and the Legacy of the French Revolution* (Basingstoke: Macmillan, 1994), 211.

44. See Marie Louise Biver, *Le Paris de Napoléon* (Paris, Plon, 1963); Maurice Guerrini, *Napoleon and Paris: Thirty Years of History*, trans. Margery Weiner (London: Cassell, 1970).

45. Woolf, *Napoleon's Integration of Europe*, 43.

46. Basilisse, b. 1805; Marie Adèle, b. 1806; Abraham, b. 1809; his son Louis Abdelal, later to become a general in the French army, was born later. AMG XL 37l (Généralités).

47. Georges Aïdé, 12 February 1816, AMG XL 37l.

48. Michel Aïdé, 1816, AMG XL 37l.

49. See the entries for Lotfi Nemr and his son Gustave-Jean (b. 1822), Naturalisations, déclarations de changement de domicile (1849-1866), 98, Archives de la Ville de Paris, VD⁶ 78.

50. AN BB 11/150/1.

51. Nicolas Sakakini, December 1813, AMG XL 37n.

52. Georges Aïdé, "Dair el-Kamar, the 8th of the month of Chaoual which corresponds to 9 February 1805, translation of the letter of the children of Prince Joseph currently reigning in Mount Lebanon and all its dependencies, to M. Georges Aïdé," AMG XL 37l.

53. Aïdé, 11 February 1809, AMG XL 37l. Léon Gozlan describes the very frequent eye diseases in "Les réfugiés égyptiens à Marseille," *Revue contemporaine* 149 (1866): 34.

54. Aïdé to Sabbagh, September 1807, Bibliothèque de Genève, MSS Orientales, 16.

55. Constantin François de Chasseboeuf, comte de Volney, *Œuvres de C.-F. Volney* (Paris: Parmentier, 1825–26), 2: 186.

56. Thomas Philipp, *The Syrians in Egypt, 1725–1975* (Stuttgart: Steiner, 1985), 44.

57. Jean-Louis Clément, 1 January 1812, AMG XL 37j.

58. Ibid.

59. Aïdé, July 1811, AMG XL 37d.

60. Nigel Rapport, "Community," in *Encyclopedia of Social and Cultural Anthropology,* ed. Alan Barnard and Jonathan Spencer (London: Routledge, 1996), 114.

61. James Clifford, *Routes: Travel and Translation in the Late Twentieth Century* (Cambridge, MA: Harvard University Press, 1997), 245.

62. David Garrioch, *Neighbourhood and Community in Paris, 1740–1790* (Cambridge: Cambridge University Press, 1986), 5–6.

63. Georges Aïdé, birth certificate of Césarine Alexandrine Aïdé, 8 July 1812, AMG XL 37l.

64. Aïdé, 26 February 1811, AMG XL 37l.

65. George Aïdé's daughter Rosine was married in 1819 to George Sakakini: see Abdallah Naaman, *Histoire des Orientaux de France du 1er au XXe siècle* (Paris, 2004), 475.

66. Louise Virginie, 16 March 1812, AMG XL 37.

67. Joubran Mehenna, 5 August 1811, AN F7 6475.

68. Mehenna, 22 April 1812, AMG XL 37o.

69. In 1815, both men's pensions were reduced, making life in Paris for both very difficult. With his wife and young child, Joubran moved to the small village of Montainville in Seine-et-Oise. The death of a child, and later of his wife, appear in the register of deaths: Archives Départementales des Yvelines, État Civil, Table Décennale, 1813–1823. Aïdé returned to Marseille with his family in 1816.

4. POLICING ORIENTALISM

1. Minister of war to duc de Rovigo, 13 August 1811, AN F7 6475.

2. Ibid.

3. Rovigo to prefect of police, 4th arrondissement, 23 August 1811, AN F7 6475.

4. Document reproduced in Nicole Gotteri, ed., *La police secrète du Premier Empire, Bulletins quotidiens adressés par Savary à l'Empereur de juillet à décembre 1811* (Paris: Honoré Champion, 1999), 3: 118.

5. Bocthor, undated (c. 1811), AMG XL 37j.

6. 'Abd el-Al to to duc de Rovigo, 21 July 1811, AN F7 6475. 'Abd el-Al was hoping to have his son admitted on a full rather than a half-pension. It seems from Rovigo's reply that this favor would be granted only if he returned to Marseille. Other documents indicate that Jean-Baptiste 'Abd el-Al entered the Lycée de Marseille on a half-pension only; thus we may infer that his father made this sacrifice in order to remain in Paris. See Registres des Boursiers, Lycées, AN F[17] 318.

7. The best of these studies are Stuart Woolf, *Napoleon's Integration of Europe* (London: Routledge, 1991), and Michael Broers, *Europe under Napoleon, 1799–1815* (London:

Arnold, 1996); see also the essays in Philip Dwyer, ed., *Napoleon and Europe* (London: Longman, 2001). A few studies have looked at particular non-French groups in Paris during this period. See, for example, Jean-René Aymes, *La déportation sous le Premier Empire: Les Espagnols en France, 1808–1814* (Paris: Publications de la Sorbonne, 1983); Anna-Maria Rao, "Paris et les exilés italiens en 1799," in *Paris et la Révolution: Actes du Colloque de Paris I, 14–16 avril 1989*, ed. Michel Vovelle (Paris: Publications de la Sorbonne, 1989), 225–35.

8. See *Étrangers de passage à Paris, An 10-1814*, AN F^7 2231–2258.

9. See James Stevens Curl, *Egyptomania: The Egyptian Revival, a Recurring Theme in the History of Taste*, 2nd ed. (Manchester and New York: Manchester University Press, 1994); Jean-Marcel Humbert, *L'Égyptomanie dans l'art occidental* (Paris: Éditions ACR, 1989); Scott Trafton, *Egypt Land: Race and Nineteenth-Century American Egyptomania* (Durham, NC: Duke University Press, 2004).

10. Edward Said, *Orientalism* (New York: Pantheon, 1978).

11. Anna Piussi, "The Orient of Paris: The Vanishing of Egypt from Early Nineteenth-Century Paris Salons (1800–1827)," in *La France et l'Égypte à l'époque des vice-rois, 1805–1882*, ed. Daniel Panzac and André Raymond (Cairo: IFAO, 2002), 43; emphasis in original.

12. Ibid., 44.

13. Ibid., 45.

14. Marie-Noëlle Bourguet, "Science and Memory: The Stakes of the Expedition to Egypt (1798–1801)," in *Taking Liberties: Problems of a New Order from the French Revolution to Napoleon*, ed. Howard G. Brown and Judith A. Miller (Manchester: Manchester University Press, 2003), 107.

15. Berthollet, president of the Commission, wrote: "By his devotion and his enlightenment, Chiftigy deserves the generosity of your Excellency." Chiftichy, AMG XL 37j.

16. For Mansour, see Gaix de Mansour, AMG XL 37d. A document in the archives of the Commission d'Égypte lists also a member of the Habaïby family under a list of engravers in 1826: Commission d'Égypte, Collaborateurs, 7 February 1826, AN F^{17} 1102.

17. See Michel Abeid's application for employment: undated c. 1802, AN F^{17} 1102; for Chammas see Chammas, AMG XL 37j; for Nemr, see Naturalisations, déclarations de changement de domicile (1849–1866), 98, Archives de la Ville de Paris, VD^6 78.

18. Bocthor, certificate dated 1810, AMG XL 37j.

19. Edmé-François Jomard, "Nécrologie—Ellious Bocthor," *Revue encyclopédique* (1821): 239.

20. Sabbagh, AMG XL 37j; Jean Pierre Louis Humbert, *Anthologie arabe, ou Choix de poésies arabes inédites* (Paris: Treuttel and Würtz, 1819), 291; for an account of the murder of Ibrahim al-Sabbagh, see Mikha'il Mishaqah, *Murder, Mayhem, Pillage, and Plunder: The History of the Lebanon in the 18th and 19th Centuries*, trans. W. M. Thackston (Albany: State University of New York Press, 1988), 17–18.

21. Mishaqah, *Murder, Mayhem, Pillage, and Plunder*, 96–97.

22. Patrice Bret, *L'Égypte au temps de l'expédition de Bonaparte, 1798–1801* (Paris: Hachette, 1998), 213.

23. Bocthor, 12 June 1811, AMG XL 37j.

24. Ibid.

25. L'abbé Bargès, "Nécrologie [Don Gabriel Taouil]," *Journal asiatique* (Sept. 1835): 282. Later, Eusèbe de Salle, would claim that Taouïl taught his course exclusively in Arabic from the first lesson "faute de savoir la langue française" (because he could not speak French). Henri Dehérain, *Orientalistes et antiquaires*, vol. 2, *Silvestre de Sacy, ses contemporains et ses disciples* (Paris: P. Geuthner, 1938), 67.

26. See in particular the role of the non-French *auditeurs* to the Council of State: Broers, *Europe under Napoleon*, 201.

27. Woolf, *Napoleon's Integration of Europe*, 73.

28. Constantin François de Chasseboeuf, comte de Volney, "Vues nouvelles sur l'enseignement des langues orientales," in *Oeuvres de C.-F. Volney* (Paris: Parmentier, 1825–26), 8: 501. Drogman is a European rendering of the Arabic word *turjuman*, meaning "interpreter."

29. See chapter 2 above.

30. Dehérain, *Orientalistes et antiquaires*, 63–64.

31. Ibid. It is notable that Edward Said uses Déherain as a key source on Silvestre de Sacy in his book and cites Sacy's work on the army bulletins and the manifesto without any reference to Gabriel Taouïl's part in this work: Said, *Orientalism*, 124.

32. See George M. Haddad, "A Napoleonic Arabic Fragment of Anti-Russian Propaganda in the Ottoman Empire," *The Muslim World* 71 (1981): 99–103.

33. Dehérain, *Orientalistes et antiquaires*, 67.

34. See the voluminous correspondence on this subject in Cours publique d'arabe à Marseille, AN F17 4097.

35. Anouar Louca and Pierre Santoni, "Histoire de l'enseignement de la langue arabe à Marseille," in *L'Orient des Provençaux dans l'histoire* (Marseille: Archives Départementales, 1984), 117.

36. Gabriel Taouïl to minister of war, 13 February 1811, Cours public d'arabe à Marseille, AN F^{17} 4097.

37. Ibid.

38. Bocthor to Sabbagh, 1810, Bibliothèque de Genève, MSS Orientales, 16.

39. Chiftichy, certificates provided by Marduel, curé of St-Roch, 21 December 1805, 9 March 1809, AMG XL 37j; see also Anouar Louca, "Champollion entre Bartholdi et Chiftichi," in *Rivages et déserts: Hommage à Jacques Berque* (Paris: Sindbad, 1988), 209–25.

40. Bocthor to Sabbagh, November 1809, Bibliothèque de Genève, MSS Orientales, 16.

41. Benedict Anderson, *Imagined Communities: Reflections on the Origins and Spread of Nationalism* (London: Verso, 1983), 74.

42. Bocthor, AMG XL 37j.

43. In fact, Henry Laurens has suggested that this commonly used phrase derives from the Ottoman Empire, specifically from the responses of the semiautonomous pashas in the Balkans who were looking toward France to aid them in their independence struggles against Constantinople: Henry Laurens, "Bonaparte, l'Orient et la Grande Nation," in *Orientales*, vol. 1, *Autour de l'expédition d'Égypte* (Paris: CNRS, 2004), 92.

44. Peter Gran, *Islamic Roots of Capitalism: Egypt, 1760–1840* (Austin: University of Texas Press, 1979), 189–91.

45. Shaden Tageldin, "Disarming Words: Reading (Post)Colonial Egypt's Double Bond to Europe" (PhD diss., University of California, Berkeley, 2004), 59.

46. For a discussion of al-'Attar's journeys to Turkey and Syria, see Gran, *Islamic Roots*, 102–10.

47. Bocthor, 18 October 1817, AMG XL 37j.

48. Gran, *Islamic Roots*, 63–67.

49. Ibid., 152.

50. Ibid., 154.

51. Christian Décobert, "L'Orientalisme, des lumières à la Révolution, selon Silvestre de Sacy," *Revue du monde musulman et de la Méditerranée* 52–53 (1989): 49–62.

52. Said, *Orientalism*, 124–27. In contrast to Said's harnessing of these eminently Foucauldian concepts, Foucault himself identified Sacy with a premodern *episteme* in *The Order of Things: An Archaeology of the Human Sciences* (New York: Random House, 1970), 101.

53. Décobert, "L'Orientalisme, des lumières à la Révolution," 58.

54. Ibid.; emphasis in original.

55. The other influential Orientalist at the Collège Royal, Langlès was summoned by the government to participate in the expedition. According to Antoine Arnault, he refused, insisting: "I have duties to fulfill here, both as curator of the Bibliothèque Nationale, and as professor of Arabic, Turkish, Persian, Syriac, Chinese, Sanskrit, and Manchu." See Antoine Vincent Arnault, *Souvenirs d'un sexagénaire* (Paris: Dufëy, 1833), 33–34.

56. Bourguet, "Science and Memory," 43.

57. Constantin François de Chassebœuf, comte de Volney, "Simplification des langues orientales," in *Oeuvres*, 8: 185–204.

58. "L'alfabet européen appliqué aux langues asiatiques: Épitre dédicatoire à l'honorable Société asiatique séante à Calcuta," in Volney, *Oeuvres*, 8: ix; emphasis added. A European alphabet was eventually introduced into Turkish in place of Arabic characters by Kemal Atatürk in 1923.

59. Ibid.

60. Commission d'Égypte, Collaborateurs, AN F[17] 1102. Abeid wrote to the authorities requesting employment but seems to have gotten nowhere. He was later added to the pension list of refugees in 1804, with the following note: "Syrian merchant from Acre: never in Egypt, forced to leave Naples, as all his goods were confiscated on the suspicion of his being a secret agent of the French government." See AMG X AB 35.

61. Rifa'a Rafi' al-Tahtawi, *An Imam in Paris: Account of a Stay in France by an Egyptian Cleric, 1826–1831,* trans. Daniel L. Newman (London: Saqi, 2004), 186. Tahtawi nonetheless expressed his admiration of Sacy's mastery of literary Arabic.

62. A. Tadié, "Don Raphaël de Monachis," in *Langues'O, 1795–1995: Deux siècles d'histoire de l'École Nationale des Langues Orientales,* ed. Pierre Labrousse (Paris: Hervas, 1995), 62.

63. Jamal al-Din al-Shayyal, *Tarikh al-tarjamah wa-al-harakah al-thaqafiyah fi 'asr Muhammad 'Ali* (Cairo: Dar al-Fikr al-'Arabi, 1951).

64. Charles Bachatly, "Un manuscrit autographe de Don Raphaël," *Bulletin de l'Institut d'Égypte* 13 (1931): 28.

65. Charles Bachatly, "Un membre orientale du Premier Institut d'Égypte, Don Raphaël," *Bulletin de l'Institut d'Égypte* 17 (1935): 237–60.

66. Qtd. in Tadié, "Don Raphaël de Monachis," 61.

67. Jean-Edouard Goby, *Premier Institut d'Égypte: Restitution des comptes rendus des séances* (Quetigny: Imprimerie Darantière, 1987), 11. The almanac was produced over the next three years—a copy is preserved at the Bibliothèque Municipale in Marseille, fonds ancien 25548: [Raphaël de Monachis et al], *Annuaire de la République française, pour l'an VIII (et IX) de l'ère française: Constitution de la république française* (Cairo: Imprimerie nationale, an VIII).

68. The translation was entitled *Descente des Français en Égypte, traduite de l'histoire chronologique de Mohammed ben Isaac* and concerned the Egyptian crusade of the thirteenth-century French king Saint Louis; see Goby, *Premier Institut,* 71.

69. Bachatly, "Un membre orientale," 30. Note, however, that this is Bachatly's translation from the Arabic; he does not provide the original Arabic text.

70. For an analysis of al-Azhar and modernization, see Timothy Mitchell, *Colonising Egypt* (Cambridge: Cambridge University Press, 1988), 80–87.

71. Bachatly, "Un manuscrit autographe," 31–35.

72. See Daniel Roche, *La France des lumières* (Paris: Fayard, 1993).

73. Bachatly, "Un manuscrit autographe," 30. There is no indication of what these letters contained, but it is probable that they concerned the power struggles taking place in Egypt, in which the French government retained a keen interest. According to Jabarti, during this time many Egyptians "regretted the departure of the French." See Muhammad Shafiq Ghurbal, *The Beginnings of the Egyptian Question and the Rise of Mehemet Ali: A Study in the Diplomacy of the Napoleonic Era Based on Researches in the British and French Archives* (London: G. Routledge, 1928), 209.

74. See A. J. O'Connor, "Volney, Bonaparte, and Taine," *French Studies* 3 (1949): 149–51.

75. Jean-Claude Perrot and S. J. Woolf, *State and Statistics in France, 1789–1815* (Chur, Switzerland: Harwood Academic Publishers, 1984), 87–88.

76. Marie-Noëlle Bourguet, *Déchiffrer la France: La statistique départementale à l'époque napoléonienne* (Paris: Éditions des Archives Contemporaines, 1989), 311.

77. Gabriel Taouïl, "Biographies et fables d'Ésope" (1808), Bibliothèque Nationale de France, MS Arabes.

78. The Arabic-Italian dictionary was published at Boulaq in 1822, a translation of Macquer's book on silk dyeing in 1823, and Rufa'il completed a translation of *The Prince* by Macchiavelli for Muhammad 'Ali. For a full list of Rufa'il's unpublished works, see Bachatly, "Un manuscrit autographe," 31–35. The publication of a work based on Rufa'il's notes in 1816, after the Restoration, suggests that he had been working during these years. See F. J. Mayeux, *Bedouins ou Arabes du désert* (Paris: Feux-Delaunay, 1816).

79. See Henry Laurens et al., *L'expédition d'Égypte, 1798–1801* (Paris: Armand Colin, 1989), 233.

80. Humbert, *Anthologie arabe*. Sabbagh's manuscripts exist in libraries in Germany; they have never been translated, although they were published in Arabic in Lebanon in the 1930s.

81. Michel Sabbagh, *La colombe messagère, plus rapide que l'éclair, plus prompte que la nue,* trans. A.-J. Silvestre de Sacy (Paris: Imprimerie Impériale, an XIV-1805).

82. Mikha'il Sabbagh, *Cantique à S. M. Napoléon le Grand à l'occasion de la naissance de son fils Napoléon II, roi de Rome: Allégorie sur le bonheur futur de la France et la paix de l'univers,* trans. Antoine Isaac Silvestre de Sacy (Paris: Imprimerie Impériale: 1811).

83. Humbert, *Anthologie arabe,* 292.

84. Antoine Isaac Silvestre de Sacy, *Chrestomathie arabe* (Paris, 1826; repr., Osnabrück: Biblio Verlag, 1973), 1: 365, 380–81.

85. Thomas Philipp, "Class, Community, and Arab Historiography in the Early Nineteenth Century—The Dawn of a New Era," *International Journal of Middle East Studies* 16 (1984): 161–75.

86. Pamela Ballinger, *History in Exile: Memory and Identity at the Borders of the Balkans* (Princeton, NJ: Princeton University Press, 2003), 33.

87. Anouar Louca, "Ellious Bocthor: Sa vie, son œuvre," *Cahiers d'histoire égyptienne* 5/6 (1953): 313.

88. Ibid., 316. Jomard went on to propose the creation of a course in colloquial Arabic that would attract "young Orientals, particularly Egyptians." He explained the project as follows: "We would shape them in our language, we would teach them our arts. They would carry back to the banks of the Nile a perfect knowledge of our country." The accomplishment of this project, Jomard insisted, would require a "an Egyptian rather than a European," someone who could speak French and write it perfectly. This project came to fruition with the "École Égyptienne" of 1826; see chapter 7 in this book.

89. Ellious Bocthor, *Discours prononcé à l'ouverture du cours d'arabe vulgaire de l'École des Langues Orientales Vivantes, le 8 décembre 1819, par Ellious Bocthor* (Paris: Goujon, 1820), 3.

90. Bocthor, *Discours,* 6.

91. Ibid., 15.

5. MASSACRE AND RESTORATION

1. Pierre Rosanvallon, *La monarchie impossible: Les Chartes de 1814 et de 1830* (Paris: Fayard, 1994).

2. Guillaume de Bertier de Sauvigny, *The Bourbon Restoration,* trans. Lynn M. Case (Philadelphia: University of Pennsylvania Press, 1967), 93–111.

3. "Charter of 1814," reprinted in *Government and Society in France, 1814–1848,* ed. Irene Collins (London: Edward Arnold, 1970), 12. For a brilliant analysis of the "politics of oubli," see Sheryl Kroen, *Politics and Theater: The Crisis of Legitimacy in Restoration France, 1815–1830* (Berkeley: University of California Press, 2000), ch. 1.

4. Alan B. Spitzer, "Malicious Memories: Restoration Politics and a Prosopography of Turncoats," *French Historical Studies,* 24 (2001): 37.

5. César Proisy d'Eppe, *Dictionnaire des girouettes, ou Nos contemporains peints d'après eux-mêmes* (Paris: Alexis Eymery, 1815), frontispiece.

6. Natalie Petiteau, *Lendemains d'empire: Les soldats de Napoléon dans la France du XIXe siècle (*Paris: La Boutique de l'Histoire, 2003), 297.

7. See Geoffrey Wawro, *The Franco-Prussian War* (Cambridge: Cambridge University Press, 2003), 38.

8. Ibrahim, AMG XL 37d.

9. Ruggieri, AN F^7 6475; Séraphin, AMG XL 37g.

10. Jean Savant, *Les Mamelouks de Napoléon* (Paris: Calmann-Lévy, 1949), 333. See also the memoirs written by Roustam himself: Hector Fleischmann, ed., *Roustam, Mameluck de Napoléon: D'après des mémoires et de nombreux documents inédits tirés des Archives Nationales et des Archives du Ministère de la Guerre* (Paris: Albert Méricant, 1910).

11. Jean-René-Pierre, comte de Semallé, *Souvenirs du comte de Semallé, page de Louis XVI* (Paris: A. Picard et Fils, 1898), 171.

12. Hamaouy, AMG XL 37d.

13. See Frédéric Masson, *L'affaire Maubreuil* (Paris: P. Ollendorff, 1907).

14. Hamaouy, 13 August 1814, AMG XL 37d.

15. Document conserved at the Musée de l'Empéri (Salon de Provence), reproduced in *L'Orient des Provençaux dans l'histoire* (Marseille: Archives Départementales, 1984), 337.

16. Extrait des registres, 13 pluviose an 12, AMG X^{AB} 35. These figures were combined with elevated pensions for their wives and dependents, adding several thousand francs to their family income.

17. Georges Reynaud, "Les données de l'état civil," in *L'Orient des Provençaux dans l'histoire* (Marseille: Archives Départementales, 1984), 368.

18. Savant, *Les Mamelouks de Napoléon*, 157.

19. Moussa, 12 August 1816, AMG XL 37k.

20. Ibid.

21. Joseph Méry, *L'assassinat: Scènes méridionales de 1815* (Paris: Urbain Canel et Adolphe Guyot, 1832), 35.

22. Daniel P. Resnick, *The White Terror and the Political Reaction after Waterloo* (Cambridge, MA: Harvard University Press, 1966), 9.

23. Cited in William B. Cohen, *The French Encounter with Africans: White Response to Blacks, 1530–1880* (Bloomington: Indiana University Press, 1980), 111.

24. [Laurent Lautard], *Esquisses historiques: Marseille depuis 1789 jusqu'en 1815, par un vieux Marseillais (L. Lautard)* (Marseille: Marius Olive, 1844), 360.

25. [Charles Durand], *Marseille, Nîmes et ses environs par un témoin oculaire,* vol. 1 (Paris: Les Marchands de Nouveautés, 1818). The author's name did not appear on the first volume. The book was written soon after the Restoration, when even printing the words *Vive l'empereur* might have been seen as seditious.

26. Méry, *L'assassinat,* 37–38.

27. For example, Adda, the wife of Bartolomeo, was denounced to the police for having declared in Arabic that Bonaparte would return with an Austrian and Turkish army and cut off the heads of the royalists. Rapport hebdomadaire, 26 November 1815, AN F7 9002.

28. Léon Gozlan, "Les refugiés égyptiens à Marseille," *Revue contemporaine* 149 (1866): 42.

29. [Durand], *Marseille, Nîmes,* 18.

30. Ibid., 20.

31. Report to Ministry of the Interior, no date, AN F^7 9636.

32. Méry, *L'assassinat*, 39.

33. Chaate, 1816, AMG XL 37m.

34. Ibid. Among her other children was Joseph Ebed, who, in 1827, would become famous in Paris as the young Egyptian who accompanied France's first giraffe to the capital. See chapter 7; and Michael Allin, *Zarafa* (London: Headline, 1998).

35. Méry, *L'assassinat*, 38.

36. Gozlan, "Les refugiés égyptiens," 45.

37. Ibid.

38. Méry, *L'assassinat*, 38.

39. From Lautard's description, it seems that he too participated in one of the companies that went to bring back the Egyptians: "A few moments later, the Oriental group were under the wings of our volunteers. These poor people offered a spectacle of misery and loss that broke one's heart." Lautard, *Esquisses historiques*, 366.

40. Nakacly, 1816, AMG XL 37k.

41. Prefect to minister of the interior, 29 août 1815, AN F^7 9636.

42. Daniel P. Resnick, *The White Terror and the Political Reaction after Waterloo* (Cambridge, MA: Harvard University Press, 1966), 11.

43. Saman lists the following names: I. Tutungi, M. Sidarious, G. Mattar, J. Soliman, S. Elaaraj, G. Baher, J. Makli, J. Gabriel, J. Nazo, Anna Koudsy, Hélène Treca. See Edouard Saman, "L'Église Saint-Nicolas de Myre de Marseille et les collaborateurs orientaux de Bonaparte," *Marseille* 124 (1981): 55.

44. Gozlan, "Les réfugiés égyptiens," 46.

45. Lautard, *Esquisses historiques*, 366.

46. Ibid., 188.

47. Rapport hebdomadaire, Préfecture Bouches-du-Rhône, 26 November 1815, AN F^7 9002.

48. Analyse de la réclamation de la Veuve Aydé, 1834, AMG XL 37l (Généralités).

49. Anouar Louca, "Quels Mamelouks?" in *L'Orient des Provençaux dans l'histoire* (Marseille: Archives Départementales, 1984), 353, n. 15.

50. Bruce McGowan points out that Greek ships had carried three-quarters of the Levant trade during the Napoleonic wars. Bruce McGowan, "The Age of the Ayans, 1699–1812," in *An Economic and Social History of the Ottoman Empire, 1300–1914*, ed. Halil Inalcik and Donald Quataert (Cambridge: Cambridge University Press, 1994), 737. This trade was now open to French and Franco-Arab traders in particular.

51. Polycarpe Kayata, *Monographie de l'église grecque catholique de Marseille* (Marseille: Imprimerie Marseillaise, 1901), 3.

52. Saman, "L'Église Saint-Nicolas de Myre," 54. The number of Greek Catholics was estimated as over five hundred by the prefect of the Bouches-du-Rhône in 1828, commenting that the numbers of Greek Orthodox were much lower, around fifty. However, he may have been underestimating the number of these "schismatics," as he called them, in order to discourage their claim for a church of their own; a letter written on their behalf claimed their number was around three hundred. Report of 1828, AN F^{19} 10933.

53. Saman, "L'Église Saint-Nicolas de Myre," 58.

54. Kroen, *Politics and Theater,* esp. ch. 2; François-René, vicomte de Chateaubriand, *Itinéraire de Paris à Jérusalem* (Paris: Le Normant, 1811).

55. Abdallah Hasboune, article from *Journal de Savoie,* 9 August 1816, AMG XL 37d.

56. Ibid.

57. Abdallah Hasboune, report of 1820, AMG XL 37d.

58. Hamaouy, 13 August 1814, AMG XL 37d.

59. Sabbagh, 4 April, 1814, AMG XL 37j.

60. Ibid.

61. Barthélemy-Joseph-Pierre Méffre, *Quelques recherches sur l'effets du café* (Montpellier: Jean Martel, 1820).

62. Saleh, 7 October 1815, AMG XL 37k.

63. Chamin-Abdallah, 1829, AMG XL 37m. According to her husband's file, she had a two-year-old son, and delivered twins sometime in 1815. Abdallah Chama, 1822, AMG XL 37d.

64. Barouty, 20 June 1816, AMG XL 37l. Barouty later became a servant in the house of the banker and deputy Jacques Lafitte: see Barouty, Jacques Lafitte to Ministry of War, 1819, AMG XL 37l.

65. Angeli, report of Ministry of War, 1815, AMG XL 37o.

66. Natidjé, AMG XL 37n.

67. Malati, report of Ministry of War, 1816, AMG XL 37d.

68. Samanne, report of Ministry of War, 25 January 1817, AMG XL 37d.

69. Ayache, petition of Sara Ayache and Marie-Françoise Louvet, 1817, AMG XL 37d.

70. Koubroussi, 1812, AMG XL 37d; Chilkoury, 1813, AMG XL 37d.

71. Note of Ministry of War, April 1816, AMG XL 37l (Généralités).

72. Samanne, Report of Ministry of War, 17 April 1817, AMG XL 37d.

73. Nakacly, February 1822, AMG XL/37k.

74. Halimé, no. 129, 1822, AMG XL 37m.

75. Zanio (Marie Fatoumé Giovanny, wife of Zanio), 1818, AMG XL 37n.

76. Salem Youdi, AMG XL 37k.

77. Tahtawi, *An Imam in Paris,* 154–55.

78. Petition of February 1818, AMG XL 37l (Généralités).

79. Ibid.

80. Ibid.; emphasis in original.

81. See Jamal al-Din al-Shayyal, *Tarikh al-tarjamah wa-al-harakah al-thaqafiyah fi 'asr Muhammad 'Ali* (Cairo: Dar al-Fikr al-'Arabi, 1951), Mulhaq al-Awwal (after p. 227).

82. Petition of February 1818, AMG XL 37l (Généralités).

6. COSMOPOLITANISM AND CONFUSION

1. See chapter 2, notes 18, 19, and 21.

2. Charles Clément, *Géricault: Étude biographique et critique avec le catalogue raisonné de l'œuvre du maître* (Paris: Didier, 1868), 253–54n. The name "Sussen" given by Girodet in his portrait suggests some connection with the family of Tunisian Jews also living in Paris, and mentioned in al-Najjar's letters, although the name "Mustafa" is markedly Islamic.

3. Barouty, Jacques Lafitte to Ministry of War, 1819, AMG XL 37l.

4. M. Merlin, *Recueil alphabétique des questions de droit* (Paris: H. Tarlier, 1829), 10: 41 ff.

5. Adelaker, 1816, AMG XL 37l.

6. Edmé-François Jomard, "Ouverture du cours d'arabe vulgaire," *Revue encyclopédique* 5 (1820): 39.

7. See Pierre Échinard, *Grecs et philhellènes à Marseille, de la Révolution française à l'independance de la Grèce* (Marseille: Institut Historique de Provence, 1973); Stathis Gourgouris, *Dream Nation: Enlightenment, Colonization, and the Institution of Modern Greece* (Stanford: Stanford University Press, 1996).

8. Victoria E. Thompson, "Telling 'Spatial Stories': Urban Space and Bourgeois Identity in Early Nineteenth-Century Paris," *Journal of Modern History* 75 (2003): 523–56.

9. Boilly painted his original canvas in 1804; the surviving monochrome copy was produced in 1809. See Susan Siegfried, *The Art of Louis-Léopold Boilly: Modern Life in Napoleonic France* (New Haven, CT: Yale University Press, 1995), 63–70.

10. Ibid., 550. See also David Garrioch, *The Making of Revolutionary Paris* (Berkeley: University of California Press, 2002).

11. Albert Lenoir, "Le salon de 1837," *Revue des études historiques* (1837): 113.

12. Victor-Joseph-Étienne de Jouy, "L'Hermite en Provence," in *Oeuvres complètes d'Étienne Jouy* (Paris: J. Didot Aîné, 1823), 321–22.

13. The massacre was mentioned, for example, by Benjamin Constant in *La Minerve française* 7 (1819): 157; Alexandre Dumas, *Crimes célèbres* (Paris: Dondey-Dupré, 1839), 41.

14. Letter to Baron Capelle, 7 November 1821, AN F17/1102.

15. The language of this crucial passage is particularly important, and difficult to translate into English.

16. Letter to Baron Capelle, Ministry of the Interior, 7 November 1821, AN F17/1102.

17. Ibid.

18. Henri Guys, *Notice historique sur la vie et les ouvrages de M. Joseph Agoub* (Marseille: Extrait du Répertoire des Travaux de la Société de Statistique de Marseille, Tome XXIV, 1860), 4.

19. Léon Gozlan, "Les réfugiés égyptiens à Marseille," *Revue contemporaine* 149 (1866): 35.

20. This article was written in 1959, during the brief union of Egypt and Syria in the United Arab Republic under Gamal Abdel Nasser, when these issues were once again extremely divisive: Louca, as a Coptic Egyptian, had little patience for Joseph Agoub's claims to be Egyptian "when we well know his father was Armenian." Anouar Louca, "Joseph Agoub: Sa vie et son œuvre," *Cahiers d'histoire égyptienne* 5 (1959), 187–203.

21. See Albert Hourani, "The Syrians in Egypt in the Eighteenth and Nineteenth Century," in *Colloque international sur l'histoire du Caire, 27 mars-5 avril 1969* (Cairo: Ministry of Culture of the Arab Republic of Egypt, 1972), 221–319.

22. See Michael W. Albin, "Napoleon's *Description de l'Égypte*: Problems of Corporate Authorship," *Publishing History* 8 (1980): 65–85.

23. Todd Porterfield, *The Allure of Empire: Art in the Service of French Imperialism, 1798–1836* (Princeton, NJ: Princeton University Press, 1998), 15.

24. Peter McPhee, *A Social History of France, 1780–1880* (London: Routledge, 1992), 115.

25. Sheryl Kroen, *Politics and Theater: The Crisis of Legitimacy in Restoration France, 1815–1830* (Berkeley: University of California Press, 2000), ch. 1.

26. Douglas T. McGetchin, "Wilting Florists: The Turbulent Early Decades of the Société Asiatique, 1822–1860," *Journal of the History of Ideas* 64 (October 2003): 565–80.

27. For example, the hugely popular *Ourika* (1823) by Claire de Duras recounted the life of a Senegalese woman in France. The lesser-known Zoraïa Tochair, "Comtesse d' Oglou," published her *L'Indien en Europe, ou L'Enthousiasme de la patrie* in 1821.

28. Victor Hugo, *Oeuvres Complètes*, vol. 2, *Poésies* (Paris: Laffont, 1985), 7.

29. Jean-Marcel Humbert, *L'Égypte à Paris* (Paris: Action Artistique de la Ville de Paris, 1998); Robert Solé, *L'Égypte, passion française* (Paris: Seuil, 1997). The "Tombeau Égyptien" closed in 1824: see *Moniteur universel*, 25 February 1824, 221.

30. Gustave Dupont-Ferrier, *Du Collège de Clermont au Lycée Louis-le-Grand, 1563–1920* (Paris: E. de Boccard, 1921), 410–11.

31. "La pauvre petite," set to music by Romagnesi: Guys, *Notice historique*, 24.

32. William Reddy provides a wonderful analysis of this world in "Condottieri of the Pen: Journalists and the Public Sphere in Post-Revolutionary France, 1815–1850," *American Historical Review* 99 (1994): 1546–70.

33. See also the biographical notice by M. de Pongerville in Joseph Agoub, *Mélanges de littérature orientale et française* (Paris: Werdet, 1835).

34. *The Biographical Dictionary of the Society for the Diffusion of Useful Knowledge*, vol.1, pt 2. (London: Longman, Brown, Green, and Longmans, 1842), 472.

35. Esther Agoub to minister of education, 17 March 1833, AN F[17] 3110. Esther was not granted a pension until 1838, despite the support of Orientalists such as Jomard and Grandmaison, and the poet Lamartine. Despite the funds granted for the publication of Agoub's translation of the fables of Bidpaï (apparently the first complete translation in Europe of this highly popular collection), there is no indication in any catalogue of its appearance.

36. Pierre Échinard and George Jessula, *Léon Gozlan, suivi des refugiés égyptiens à Marseille*. Marseille: I.M.M.A.J., 2003, 39.

37. Ibid.

38. Ibid., 42–44.

39. Note from Jomard to Grille, 7 July 1852, attached to copy of letter from Joseph Agoub to Baron Capelle, 7 November 1821, Bibliothèque de la Ville d'Angers, MS 615.

40. Alan B. Spitzer, *The French Generation of 1820* (Princeton, NJ : Princeton University Press, 1987), esp. ch. 1.

41. In total, only 110,000 citizens of 30 million were eligible to vote in 1817, a number gradually trimmed down to only 80,000 by 1829 by excluding inconvenient liberals (although retaining many deceased royalists). See Pamela Pilbeam, *The 1830 Revolution in France* (London: Macmillan, 1991), 13–27.

42. According to Kale, "Haussonville found society to be more tolerant during the Restoration than it was to become in subsequent years. François Guizot praised the Restoration for its 'liberal tolerance for the diversity of origins, situations and ideas.'"

Steven Kale, *French Salons: High Society and Political Sociability from the Old Regime to the Revolution of 1848* (Baltimore: The Johns Hopkins University Press, 2004), 108.

43. P. F. Tissot, review of "La lyre brisée, dithyrambe, dédiée à madame Dufrénoy par M. Agoub," *Mercure du dix-neuvième siècle* (1825): 113.

44. Thomas Walsh, *Journal de l'expédition anglaise en Égypte dans l'année mil huit cent, traduit de l'anglais du capitaine Th. Walls [sic] par M. A. T. [Alfred Thierry.], avec des notes fournies par d'anciens officiers de notre armée d'Égypte et une introduction par M. Agoub* (Paris: Collin de Plancy, 1823), xxxviii–xxxix.

45. Anouar Louca, *Les sources marseillaises de l'Orient romantique* (Paris: Maisonneuve et Larose, 2001); Jean-Jacques Luthi, *Le Français en Égypte: Essai d'anthologie* (Beirut: Maison Naaman, 1981); Alain Messaoudi, "Orientaux orientalistes: Les Pharaon, interprètes du Sud au service du Nord," in *Sud-Nord: Cultures coloniales en France, XIXe–XXe siècle,* ed. Colette Zytnicki and Chantal Bordes-Benayoun (Toulouse: Privat, 2004).

46. For Joseph Habaïby, see Habaïby, AMG XL 37j, and Laurent-Charles Féraud, *Les interprètes de l'armée d'Afrique* (Algiers: A. Jourdan, 1876), 51; for Siouffi, see, e.g., Nicolas Siouffi, *Études sur la religion des Soubbas ou Sabéens, leurs dogmes, leurs moeurs* (Paris: Imprimerie Nationale, 1880); for Bullad, see Sakakini, letter of 12 September 1849, AMG XL 37n, and Smaïl Aouli, Ramdane Redjala, and Philippe Zoumeroff, *Abd el-Kader* (Paris: Fayard, 1994), 444–45; for Abdelal, see René Lemoine de Margon, *Le général Abdelal* (Paris: Calmann Lévy, 1887).

47. Letter to Baron Capelle, 7 November 1821, AN F^{17} 1102.

48. Joseph Agoub, "L'Égypte, dithyrambe," *Revue encyclopédique* 18 (Oct. 1820): 43–47.

49. Ibid., 44.

50. Ibid., 47.

51. Agoub, "La lyre brisée, dithyrambe," in *Mélanges de littérature orientale et française,* 312.

52. Ibid., 314.

53. Tissot, "La lyre brisée," 115–23; emphasis added.

54. Ibid., 116.

55. Ibid.; emphasis added.

56. J. Saint-Martin, "Discours sur l'expédition des Français en Égypte, en 1798, considérée dans ses résultats littéraires; par M. Agoub," *Journal asiatique* 2 (1823): 313. The word *étrangeté* is italicized in the text.

57. Tissot, "La lyre brisée," 122.

58. Adélaïde-Gillette Dufrénoy, *Le tour du monde, ou Tableau géographique et historique de tous les peuples de la terre* (Paris: Alexis Eymery, 1814), 5: 204.

7. REMAKING ARAB FRANCE

1. Joseph Agoub, preface to "Maouals arabes," in *Mélanges de littérature orientale et français* (Paris: Werdet, 1835), 9–10.

2. Ibid., 10–11.

3. Key texts are Gilbert Delanoue, *Moralistes et politiques musulmans dans l'Égypte du XIXe siècle, 1798-1882* (Cairo: Institut Français d'Archéologie Orientale du Caire, 1982), 383-487; Albert Hourani, *Arabic Thought in the Liberal Age, 1798-1939* (London: Oxford University Press, 1962), 67-103; Anouar Abdel-Malek, *Idéologie et renaissance nationale: L'Égypte moderne,* 2nd ed. (Paris: Éditions Anthropos, 1969); and more recently Guy Sorman, *Les enfants de Rifaa: Musulmans et modernes* (Paris: Fayard, 2003).

4. Anouar Louca, *Voyageurs et écrivains égyptiens en France au XIXe siècle* (Paris: Didier, 1970); Alain Silvera, "The First Egyptian Student Mission to France under Muhammad Ali," *Middle Eastern Studies* 16 (1980): 1-22; and more recently Daniel L. Newman, "Introduction," in Rifa'a Rafi' al-Tahtawi, *An Imam in Paris* (London: Saqi, 2002), 15-92. See also Prince 'Umar Tusun, *Ba'that al-'ilmiyah fi 'ahd Muhammad 'Ali, thumma fi 'ahday 'Abbas al-Awwal wa-Sa'id* (Alexandria: Matba'at Salah al-Din, 1934).

5. Peter Gran, "Tahtawi in Paris," *Al-Ahram Weekly On-line* 568 (10-16 Jan. 2002).

6. Anouar Louca, *Voyageurs et écrivains égyptiens en France au XIXe siècle* (Paris: Didier, 1970), 58.

7. Silvera, "The First Egyptian Student Mission," passim.

8. Khaled Fahmy, *All the Pasha's Men: Mehmed Ali, His Army, and the Making of Modern Egypt* (Cambridge: Cambridge University Press, 1997).

9. Juan Cole, "Rifa'a al-Tahtawi and the Revival of Practical Philosophy," *Muslim World* 70 (1980): 29-46.

10. Tahtawi, *An Imam in Paris,* 131.

11. Ibid., 154.

12. Ibid., 154-55.

13. Ibid., 157.

14. He was baptized, according to his own account, "by Monseigneur the Bishop of Udine, today Pope; his godfather was the Baron Pepin, former colonel of the Ninth Regiment of the Line." Ibrahim Mahomet, 1831, AMG XL 37k.

15. Ibrahim Mahomet, testimony of Pierre Antoine Boniface, Jean Baptiste Vertray, and Louis Guillaume Duclos, Mairie d'Autun, 1 March 1821, AMG XL 37k.

16. Ibrahim Mahomet, certificate from Demetrius Capuda, consul general of the Sublime Porte in Marseille and Dependencies, 1 July 1818, AMG XL 37k.

17. Ibrahim Mahomet, report of Ministry of War, 9 May 1831, AMG XL 37k.

18. James Heyworth-Dunne, *An Introduction to the History of Education in Modern Egypt* (London: Frank Cass, 1968), 122-31.

19. See the account by the school's head, the Frenchman Antoine Barthélemy Clot, called Clot-Bey: *Compte rendu des travaux de l'École de médecine d'Abou-Zabel, et de l'examen général des élèves, suivi de l'exposé de la conduite et des travaux de l'auteur lui-même en Égypte, 1825-32* (Paris: Deville Cavellin, 1833).

20. Newman, "Introduction," in Tahtawi, *An Imam in Paris,* 17.

21. Ibid., 23.

22. See Fahmy, *All the Pasha's Men.*

23. Ibrahim Rochemane, 12 December 1830, AMG XL 37d.

24. See David Harvey, *Paris, Capital of Modernity* (New York: Routledge, 2003).

25. Tahtawi discusses this linguistic issue in detail, explaining the French pronunciation with the Persian *p* (which does not exist in Arabic) and the silent *s*. In Arabic, however, this root letter is required for transformations of the word. He quotes a poem he wrote using the final *s* rather than the *z* of the title, which he has used to provide the "rhyme" of Ibrīz / Bārīz: Tahtawi, *An Imam in Paris*, 159.

26. The first Arabic newspaper in Paris, published between 1859 and 1866, took a similar transliteration for the city, this time rhyming it differently against the word for eagle, a Napoleonic symbol: *Birgys-Barys,* the Eagle of Paris. It was published by the abbé Bourgade and edited by a Tunisian, Suliman-al-Haraïrl, and a Lebanese, Rochaid-ed-Dahdah.

27. The most influential member of the Arab elite in Paris, Ya'qub Habaïby (see chapter 4 in this book) was invited to be among the examiners at Tahtawi's final presentation in October 1831. See *Revue encyclopédique* 48 (1831): 522.

28. Tahtawi, *An Imam in Paris,* 189.

29. Joseph Agoub and Rifa'a al-Tahtawi, *Nazm al-uqud fi kasr al-'ud (La lyre brisée), dithyrambe de M. Agoub, traduit en vers arabes par le cheykh Réfaha* (Paris: Dondey-Dupré Père et Fils, 1242 [1827]).

30. Ibid.

31. European writers were also in the process of discovering the work of this extraordinary fourteenth-century North African historian. F. E. Schultz wrote in the *Journal asiatique* that European Orientalists had been excessively dazzled by the glories of Arabic poetry: "To put the public in a position to appreciate their immortal genius, to make known to them the foundations of the spirit of this people [the Arabs], the conqueror of the world and the guardian of science, we need to do more than repeat incessantly the rhymes of its Moallakats and the exaggerations of its Motanabbis." Schultz lauded the work of Ibn Khaldun as "an admirable system built upon the dual basis of reasoning and experience." See F. E. Schultz, "Sur le grand ouvrage historique et critique d'Ibn-Khaldun, appelé Kitab-ol-iber we diwan-ol moubteda wel khaber, etc.," *Journal asiatique* 7 (1825): 213–26, 279–300. For the conflict sparked by Schultz's proposals, see Douglas T. McGetchin, "Wilting Florists: The Turbulent Early Decades of the Société Asiatique, 1822–1860," *Journal of the History of Ideas* 64 (October 2003): 565–80.

32. Tahtawi, *An Imam in Paris,* 352.

33. Ibid., 353.

34. Dipesh Chakrabarty, *Provincializing Europe: Postcolonial Thought and Historical Difference* (Princeton NJ: Princeton University Press, 2000), 8.

35. See Béchir Tlili, *Les rapports culturels et idéologiques entre l'Orient et l'Occident, en Tunisie au XIXe siècle, 1830–1880* (Tunis: Université de Tunis, 1974); Ibrahim Abu-Lughod, *Arab Rediscovery of Europe: A Study in Cultural Encounters* (Princeton, NJ: Princeton University Press, 1963).

36. Gabriel Dardaud, *Une girafe pour le roi* (Creil, France: Dumerchez-Naoum, 1985); Michael Allin, *Zarafa* (London: Headline, 1998).

37. "École Égyptienne de Paris," *Journal asiatique* 2 (1828) 96–116; "Note sur l'établissement d'une école égyptienne, à Paris," *Bulletin de la Société de Géographie* 5 (1826): 673; *Revue encyclopédique* 47 (1830): 521–23.

38. Dominique Kalifa links these representations of the Osages to later attitudes toward urban violence: Dominique Kalifa, "Archéologie de l'apachisme: Les représentations des Peaux-Rouges dans la France du XIXe siècle," *Revue de l'histoire de l'enfance "irrégulière"* 4 (2002), http://rhei.revues.org/document51.html.

39. [Honoré de Balzac], *Discours de la girafe au chef des six Osages (ou Indiens), prononcé le jour de leur visite au Jardin du Roi, traduit de l'arabe par Alibassan, interprète de la girafe* (Paris: Martinet, 1827).

40. For the politics of Delacroix's depiction of the Greek struggle, see Nina M. Athanassoglou-Kallmyer, *French Images from the Greek War of Independence 1821–1830: Art and Politics under the Restoration* (New Haven, CT: Yale University Press, 1989); on Delacroix's "Orientalism," see Elisabeth A. Fraser, *Delacroix, Art, and Patrimony in Post-Revolutionary France* (New York: Cambridge University Press, 2004).

41. Louca, *Voyageurs et écrivains*, 255.

42. Narcisse-Achille de Salvandy, *Lettre de la girafe au pacha d'Égypte pour lui rendre compte de son voyage à Saint-Cloud, et envoyer les rognures de la censure de France au journal qui s'établit à Alexandrie en Afrique* (Paris: A. Sautelet, 1827).

43. Auguste Barthélemy and Joseph Méry, *La bacriade, ou La guerre d'Alger: Poème héroï-comique en cinq chants* (Paris: A. Dupont, 1827), republished in Roland Bacri, *La légende des siestes* (Paris: André Balland, 1973), 132–204. See also Chatelain's satire on the Tunisian ambassador in Paris accusing the French authorities of "nauseating antics" in treating with so much respect "the barbarian envoy of a common pirate" while France was united in wishing well to the Greeks: René-Théophile Chatelain, *Lettres de Sidy-Mahmoud, écrites pendant son séjour en France, en 1825* (Paris: Ladvocat, 1825).

44. Barthélemy et Méry, *La bacriade*, 133.

45. Paul W. Schroeder, *The Transformation of European Politics, 1763–1848* (Oxford: Oxford University Press, 1996), 652–53.

46. Charles-André Julien, *Histoire de l'Algérie contemporaine*, vol. 1, *La conquête et les débuts de la colonisation, 1827–1871* (Paris: PUF, 1964), 21–63.

47. David Pinkney, *The French Revolution of 1830* (Princeton, NJ: Princeton University Press, 1972), 18.

48. Albert Boime provides a particularly fine discussion of this response in relation to salons of 1827–28 in his *Art in an Age of Counterrevolution, 1815–1848* (Chicago: University of Chicago Press, 2004), 220–23. See also Athanassoglou-Kallmyer, *French Images from the Greek War of Independence*.

49. See Jennifer Pitts, *A Turn to Empire: The Rise of Imperial Liberalism in Britain and France* (Princeton, NJ: Princeton University Press, 2005).

50. See Raymond Schwab, *The Oriental Renaissance: Europe's Rediscovery of India and the East, 1680–1880*, trans. Gene Patterson-Black and Victor Reinking (New York: Columbia University Press, 1984); Todd Porterfield, *The Allure of Empire Art in the Service of French Imperialism, 1798–1836* (Princeton, NJ: Princeton University Press, 1998), esp. ch. 3; Lisa Lowe, *Critical Terrains: French and British Orientalisms* (Ithaca, NY: Cornell University Press, 1991).

51. Henry Laurens, *Le royaume impossible: La France et la genèse du monde arabe* (Paris: Armand Colin, 1990), 18–21.

52. Stuart Woolf, "Europe and Its Historians," *Contemporary European History* 12 (2003): 324.

53. Prefecture of police, bulletin of Paris, Monday 31 July, 1826, AN F^7 3880.

54. "École des Égyptiens à Paris, 1826–27," report of chancelleries, 25 May 1826, Archives du Ministère des Affaires Étrangères, Quai d'Orsay (henceforth AMAE), ADP France 8, 191.

55. This panic also had sexual overtones. The prefect of the Bouches-du-Rhône investigated public claims that the Egyptian students were sexually abusing their Greek manservants: Prefect Bouches-du-Rhône to minister of interior, 5 June 1826, AN F^7 6979, doss. 3212. Joseph Massad discusses these confrontations of desire, eroticism, and fear in *Desiring Arabs* (Chicago: University of Chicago Press, 2007), esp. 29–37.

56. Yves Laissus, *Jomard: Le dernier Égyptien (1777–1862)* (Paris: Fayard, 2004), 305.

57. Letter to Ministry of the Interior, 8 May 1826, AMAE, ADP France 8, Doss. 191.

58. Report of Ministry of Foreign Affairs, 25 May 1826, AMAE, ADP France 8, 191.

59. Jomard to minister of interior, 1 September 1826, AMAE, ADP France 8, 191.

60. Laissus, *Jomard,* 318.

61. Ibid., 322.

62. Ibid.

63. See Thomas E. Crow, *Emulation: Making Artists for Revolutionary France* (New Haven, CT: Yale University Press, 1995).

64. See Anthony Pagden, *Lords of All the World: Ideologies of Empire in Spain, Britain, and France, c. 1500–c. 1800* (New Haven, CT: Yale University Press, 1995).

65. Ellious Bocthor, *Dictionnaire français-arabe, revu et augmenté par A. Caussin de Perceval* (Paris: F. Didot Père et Fils, 1828).

66. Joseph Agoub, "Romances vulgaires des Arabes," *Journal Asiatique* 10 (1827): 257–64.

67. Ibid., 258.

68. Agoub notes also that he was aided by Sylvestre de Sacy's communication of an Arabic manuscript from the Bibliothèque that contained further *maouals* beyond those he had collected. Once again this may serve to nuance the picture of Sacy given in Edward Said's *Orientalism* (New York: Vintage Books, 1979). For some brief remarks on the importance of *mawwal* in Egypt, see Peter Gran, *Islamic Roots of Capitalism: Egypt, 1760–1840* (Austin: University of Texas Press, 1979), 67.

69. Agoub, "Romances vulgaires des Arabes," 259.

70. From the summary of a communication by M. Dufeu in "Séance du 8 Avril 1864," *Bulletin de L'Institut d'Égypte* (1864): 64. Elsewhere, Dufeu is quoted as saying: "Hugo and Lamartine, these two great leaders of the poetic renaissance, had not yet laid a single stone in the great edifice they would help to build. . . . Agoub's greatest glory, and his most important entitlement to the recognition of France, is therefore to have served as the forerunner of the modern school." Henri Guys, *Notice historique sur la vie et les ouvrages de M. Joseph Agoub* (Marseille: Extrait du Répertoire des Travaux de la Société de Statistique de Marseille, Tome XXIV, 1860), 16.

71. Alphonse de Lamartine, *Voyage en Orient, 1832–1833* (Paris: Charles Gosselin, 1843), 541–42.

72. Jean-Baptiste Sanson de Pongerville, "Notice," in Agoub, *Mélanges de littérature orientale et française*, vii.

73. Joseph François Michaud and Louis Gabriel Michaud, *Biographie universelle, ancienne et moderne, ou Histoire par ordre alphabétique*, vol. 56 (Supplément) (Paris: Michaud Frères, 1862), 99.

8. THE CATHEDRAL AND THE MOSQUE

1. Florian Pharaon, *Épisodes de la conquête: Cathédrale et mosquée* (Paris: A. Lahure, 1880); Charles-André Julien, *Histoire de l'Algérie contemporaine* , vol. 1, *La conquête et les débuts de la colonisation, 1827–1871* (Paris: PUF, 1964), 89–92.

2. Yves Laissus, *Jomard: Le dernier Égyptien, 1777–1862* (Paris: Fayard, 2004), 316.

3. Report of 12 August 1826, AN F^7 6979, 13, 212.

4. Report of 29 August 1826, AN F^7 6979, 13, 212.

5. Joanny Pharaon, *Premiers éléments de la langue française à l'usage des Orientaux qui veulent apprendre cette langue* (Marseille: Chez Comoin, 1827), i.

6. Ibid. The story of Joanny's experience at the school was apparently recorded by him and is lost except for the title that appears in an earlier manuscript version of this Arabic teaching method from 1823, included as vol. 1 of Pharaon's *Œuvres complètes,* which was to include "Une biographie pittoresque des élèves et des chefs de l'École égyptienne, les Premiers éléments de la langue française à l'usage des Orientaux, des Considérations sur la non-existence de Dieu et un Discours sur la jalousie, la méfiance, la mort et les péchés." I thank Annie de Sainte Maréville at the Bibliothèque Municipale in Épernay for this information.

7. F. Rossignol and J. Pharaon, *Histoire de la Révolution de 1830 et des nouvelles barricades* (Paris: Ch. Vimont, 1830), 18. The title page describes the book as "Ouvrage présenté au roi par F. Rossignol (Avocat à la Cour Royale) et J. Pharaon, de plusieurs académies, des Sociétés asiatiques et de géographies de Paris, Directeur de l'École des Enfants dont les pères sont morts pour la Patrie." I have not been able to find any trace of such a school for children whose fathers had been killed (presumably during the Revolution of 1830), but it is telling that Pharaon so proudly listed this role in the first revolutionary moments after July alongside the more conventional membership of learned societies.

8. Ibid., 18n.

9. Joanny Pharaon, *Esquisse historique et politique sur Mahmoud II et Nicolas Ier, suivie de la Description de Schumla, Varna, Andrinople et Constantinople* (Paris: Lecointe, 1829), 7.

10. Ibid., 10.

11. On the "denial of coevalness" see Johannes Fabian, *Time and the Other: How Anthropology Makes Its Object* (New York: Columbia University Press, 1983), 25–69.

12. Pharaon, *Esquisse historique et politique*, 18; emphasis in original.

13. Rossignol and Pharaon, *Histoire de la Révolution de 1830,* 307.

14. George Lillie Craik, *Paris and Its Historical Scenes* (London: C. Knight, 1831), 2: 151.

15. Rifa'a Rafi' al-Tahtawi, *An Imam in Paris*, trans. Daniel L. Newman (London: Saqi, 2002), 312.

16. Joanny Pharaon, *Biographie des ex-ministres de Charles X, mis en accusation par le peuple* (Paris: Selligué, 1830).

17. Tahtawi, *An Imam in Paris,* 328.

18. Alain Roussillon, "Ce qu'ils nomment 'Liberté' . . . Rif'a al-Tahtawi, ou l'invention (avortée) d'une modernité politique ottomane," *Arabica* 48.2 (2001): 143–85. The French language allows an enumeration of the zones of identity in a more particular way: "Il importera ici de démêler comment [l'authenticité] s'énonce et se met en scène, entre ottomanité, islamité, arabité et égyptianité, et la *"modernité"* en marche" (145). Unfortunately, except for "modernity," the equivalents of these terms do not exist in English.

19. Roussillon, "Ce qu'ils nomment 'Liberté,' " 158.

20. Tahtawi, *An Imam in Paris,* 310–11.

21. See Ra'if Khuri, *Modern Arab Thought: Channels of the French Revolution to the Arab East* (Princeton, NJ: The Kingston Press, 1983).

22. Rossignol and Pharaon, *Histoire de la Révolution de 1830,* 12.

23. The *Commission supérieure* included the former premier Decazes, five deputies (including the anticolonial Hippolyte Passy and Xavier de Sade), the king's aide-de-camp, the prefect of Toulon, and Baron Volland (a supporter of permanent occupation). Julien, *Histoire de l'Algérie contemporaine,* 112.

24. Julien, *Histoire de l'Algérie contemporaine,* 110.

25. Hamdan Khodja, *Le miroir: Aperçu historique et statistique sur la régence d'Alger* (Repr., Paris: Sindbad, 1985). For an analysis, see Jennifer Pitts, "Liberalism and Empire in a Nineteenth-Century Algerian Mirror," *Modern Intellectual History* 6 (2009): 287–313.

26. According to the British Foreign Office, Hamdan was lobbying for the establishment of a government under the rule of Ahmed-Bey of Constantine. Abdeljalil Temimi, "L'activité de Hamdan Khudja à Paris et à Istanbul pour la question algérienne," *Revue d'histoire maghrébine* 7–8 (1977): 234–43. It is reported that Hamdan spoke fluent English, as well as French, Arabic, and Turkish.

27. Julien, *Histoire de l'Algérie contemporaine,* 98.

28. "Mémoire remis par Sidi Hamdan ben Othman Khodja à la commission d'Afrique de 1833," reprinted in Michel Habart, *Histoire d'un parjure* (Paris: Éditions de Minuit, 1960), 229.

29. Habart, *Histoire d'un parjure,* 42.

30. Jean-Baptiste Sanson de Pongerville, "Agoub," *La France littéraire* (1832): 603.

31. Garde de Sceaux to prefect of Seine, 4 July 1826, AN BB/11/253 dossier 5659 B6.

32. Prefect of Seine to Garde de Sceaux, 3 June 1826, AN BB/11/253 dossier 5659 B6.

33. Prefect of Seine to Garde des Sceaux, 10 July 1826, AN BB/11/253 dossier 5659 B6.

34. Greg Burgess, *Refuge in the Land of Liberty: France and Its Refugees from the Revolution to the End of Asylum, 1787–1939* (Basingstoke: Palgrave Macmillan, 2008): 48–70.

35. See Gérard Noiriel, *La tyrannie du national: Le droit d'asile en Europe, 1793–1993* (Paris: Calmann-Lévy, 1991), 67.

36. Bernard-Joseph Legat, *Code des étrangers, ou Traité de la législation française concernant les étrangers* (Paris: Béchet Aîné, 1832).

37. Julie Kalman notes these contradictory associations of "cosmopolitanism" for Jews under the July Monarchy in her work on anti-Semitism in early nineteenth-century

France: Julie Anne Kalman, *Rethinking Antisemitism in Nineteenth-Century France* (New York: Cambridge University Press, 2010).

38. Martin Staum, *Labeling People: French Scholars on Society, Race, and Empire, 1815–1848* (Montreal: McGill-Queen's University Press, 2003), 45. See also Ann Thomson, "Bory de Saint Vincent et l'anthropologie de la Méditerrannée," in *L'invention scientifique de la Méditerranée: Égypte, Morée, Algérie,* ed. Marie-Noëlle Bourguet et al. (Paris: École des Hautes Études en Sciences Sociales, 1998), 273–88.

39. Bory de Saint-Vincent, "L'Homme," in *Dictionnaire classique d'histoire naturelle* (Paris: Baudouin Frères, 1825), 8: 288.

40. A decade later, a petition for the establishment of a new chair of Berber bluntly expressed the political valency of language teaching in France: "By using expressions whose meaning and power they will understand, would we not be taking the surest path toward putting an end to that enmity that only exists between them and us because we haven't yet understood them—or they us? Would we not thus obtain all that the government could wish—their separation from the Arabs, their enemies and ours?" École des Langues Orientales, Delaporte to Ministry of Education, 29 Nov. 1842, AN F[17] 4064. For a comprehensive history of this use of "science" in the service of colonial domination, see Patricia Lorcin, *Imperial Identities: Stereotyping, Prejudice, and Race in Colonial Algeria* (London: I. B. Tauris, 1995).

41. Cours publique d'arabe vulgaire, AN F[17] 4097.

42. Letter from prefect, Bouches-du-Rhône, 21 October 1831, AN F[17] 4097.

43. Julien, *Histoire de l'Algérie contemporaine,* 57.

44. Henri Cordier, *Notes sur Eusèbe de Salle* (Paris: H. Leclerc, 1917), 60.

45. Ibid., 70.

46. Ibid., 77.

47. Ibid., 77.

48. Ibid., 78.

49. Ibid., 85; emphasis added.

50. Cordier, *Notes sur Eusèbe de Salle,* 85.

51. Robert A. Nye, *Masculinity and Male Codes of Honor in Modern France* (New York: Oxford University Press, 1993); William M. Reddy, *The Invisible Code: Honor and Sentiment in Postrevolutionary France, 1814–1848* (Berkeley: University of California Press, 1997).

52. Cordier, *Notes sur Eusèbe de Salle,* 59.

53. Ibid., 67. The conflict continued well into the 1840s, and finally Sakakini was appointed to a separate position at the Collège Royal de Marseille in 1846 by Salvandy, who had been appointed minister. Still, according to Anouar Louca, Jean-Baptiste Reynier, de Salle's replacement, defended his predecessor in a brochure that continued to claim that only a Frenchman could teach Arabic correctly. Anouar Louca and Pierre Santoni, "Histoire de l'enseignement de la langue arabe à Marseille," in *L'Orient des Provençaux dans l'histoire* (Marseille: Archives Départementales, 1984), 119.

54. Cours publique d'arabe vulgaire, merchants of Marseille to Ministry of Education, 5 February 1838, AN F[17] 4097.

55. Laurent-Charles Féraud, *Les interprètes de l'armée d'Afrique: Archives du corps* (Algiers: A. Jourdan, 1876), 182–84.

56. René Lemoine de Margon, *Le général Abdelal* (Paris: Calmann Lévy, 1887), 34.

57. Eusèbe de Salle, *Ali le Renard, ou La conquête d'Alger* (1830; Geneva: Slatkine Reprints, 1973), a facsimile reprint of the 1832 edition, which was published in two volumes in Paris by Gosselin.

58. Letter from the duc de Rovigo, governor of Algiers, 1832, provided by the family of Joanny Pharaon, qtd. in Féraud, *Les interprètes de l'armée d'Afrique*, 230.

59. Féraud, *Les interprètes de l'armée d'Afrique*, 231.

60. Pharaon, *Cathédrale et mosquée*, 31.

61. Julien, *Histoire de l'Algérie contemporaine*, 90.

62. Pharaon, *Cathédrale et mosquée*, 43.

63. Ibid., 58–59.

64. For a very recent exploration of this colonial dynamic, see Olivier Le Cour Grandmaison, *Coloniser exterminer: Sur la guerre et l'état colonial* (Paris: Arthème Fayard, 2004).

65. Minister of the interior to governor-general of Algeria, 1879, AN F[18] 415, dossier of *Le Sada.* Emphasis added.

66. GG Algeria to conseiller d'état, 17 May 1879, AN F[18] 415, dossier of *Le Sada.*

67. Arch pref. police, Paris, BA 1220.

68. Hamdan Khodja to Ahmad Bouderba, 26 May 1836, Archives d'Outre Mer (henceforth AOM), Aix-en-Provence, GGA 1H/1.

69. Hamdan Khodja to Ahmad Bouderba, 26 May 1836, AOM GGA 1H/1.

70. See Lorcin, *Imperial Identities.*

71. Joanny Pharaon, *Grammaire élémentaire d'arabe vulgaire ou algérienne à l'usage des Français* (Paris: Didot, 1832); Pharaon, *De la législation française, musulmane et juive à Alger* (Paris: T. Barrois Fils, 1835).

72. Joanny Pharaon, *Les Cabiles et Boudgie* (Algiers: Chez Philippe, 1835).

73. Ibid., 58.

74. Ibid.

75. In 1832, the Council of Refugees, represented by Gaspard Agoub and Antoine Hamaouy, wrote to the Ministry: "We make use of this opportunity, Superintendent, to inform you that a number of other Egyptians, whose pensions are hardly sufficient for their daily survival, are also asking us for permission to move to Algiers in the hope of finding some amelioration of their misery." Rosetti, 1832, AMG XL 37d. Abd el-Al's son Louis became a provincial governor and eventually a general in Algeria and the Franco-Prussian War: see Margon, *Le général Abdelal.*

76. These exiles included crucial figures such as Ya'qub Sanu'a, Muhammad Abduh, and Jamal al-Din al-Afghani. They mixed with Tunisians such as Muhammad al-Sanussi and Muhammad Bayram V, and even the descendants of the first Arab migrants to France, such as Joanny's son, Florian Pharaon.

77. Etienne Daumas, *Mœurs et coutumes de l'Algérie: Tell—Kabylie—Sahara* (Paris: Hachette, 1853), 120; see also Léon Roches, *Dix ans à travers l'Islam, 1834–1844* (Paris: Didier, 1844).

78. See the correspondence in AN F[17] 4097 and AN F[17] 4064.

79. AN F[19] 5590, dossier Saint-Julien-le-Pauvre. The church of Saint-Julien-le-Pauvre, on the Left Bank opposite the Louvre, was affected to the Melkite Catholic rite in 1889.

SELECTED BIBLIOGRAPHY

ARCHIVAL SOURCES
Archives Départementales des Bouches-du Rhône, Aix
2U.1.403 Correspondances au sujet des marriages des nègres ou mulâtres égyptiens, réfugiés en France, 1817.

Archives Départementales des Bouches-du Rhône, Marseille
200 E 20 K.
200 E 892.

Archives Départementales des Yvelines
État Civil, Table Décennale, 1813–1823.

Archives du Ministère des Affaires Étrangères [AMAE]
ADP France 8, 191, École des Égyptiens à Paris, 1826–27.

Archives du Ministère de la Guerre, Vincennes [AMG]
XL 37d-g Orientaux—Mamelouks, Réfugiés égyptiens.
XL 37j Orientaux—Aumônes, Interprètes.
XL 37k Orientaux servant dans les régiments français.
XAB 35 Chasseurs à Cheval et Mameloucks.
1H 1–12 Expédition d'Alger.
1H 18 doss. 3 Comité Maure.

Archives Municipales, Marseille [AM]

I 2 240 Réfugiés égyptiens.
19 I 1 Gaffarel, Paul. "Les massacres de Juin 1815." Manuscript, c. 1910.

Archives Nationales, Paris [AN]

F^7 2249 Étrangers de passage à Paris, An X-1814, Russes, Turcs, Africains et colons.
F^7 3046/2 État des étrangers loges en garnis à Paris, 1806–1813.
F^7 3505 Passeports, Étrangers, relevés des permissions de séjour à Paris, 1806–7.
F^7 3880 Bulletins de Paris.
F^7 6436 Police dossiers, Ibrahim, Mamelouk.
F^7 6475 Police dossiers, no. 291.
F^7 6979 Jeunes Égyptiens appartenant pour la plupart à des familles distingués du pachalick d'Égypte, arrivés à Marseille le 16 mai 1826, etc.
F^7 6833 Police publique, Affaires politiques 1814–1830.
F^7 8415 Police, Bouches-du-Rhône.
F^{17} 318 Registre des boursiers—Lycées.
F^{17} 1100 Commission d'Égypte.
F^{17} 1102 Commission d'Égypte, Collaborateurs.
F^{17} 3110 Instruction publique, Dossier Esther Agoub.
F^{17} 4054—4104. École des Langues Orientales Vivantes et Cours d'arabe à Marseille et en Algérie, an IV [septembre 1795–septembre 1796]–1898.
F^{19} 10933 Cultes non-Catholiques, Grecs Schismatiques.
BB 11 Naturalisations.

Archives d'Outre Mer, Aix-en-Provence [AOM]

F^{80} 9, 10 Commission d'Afrique.
F^{80} 1603 Étude de la langue arabe, Interprètes 1830–1856.
F^{80} 1670 -9 Algérie, Correspondance.
IE 61–68 Commission d'enquête sur l'Algérie 1833–4.
GGA 1H 1–17 Algérie.

Archives de la Ville de Paris

VD 6 162 Déclarations de domicile, 1806–1838.
VD 6 78 Naturalisations, déclarations de changement de domicile, 1849–1866.

Bibliothèque de Genève, Département des Manuscrits

MS O. 16 Letters to Mikha'il Sabbagh written in Arabic by Ellious Bochtor and others by Aïdé, Barthélemy, Dahhan, Fattalla, Hamaouy, Naydorff, Qubtan, Serra, Chammas, Tahhah, Taouïl, Zidan.

Bibliothèque Municipale, Carcassonne

319 (11797) Documents relatifs à Jean-Baptiste Lhomaca, beau-frère de Louis de Chénier, ancien drogman de l'armée de l'Egypte.

OTHER SOURCES

Abdel-Malek, Anouar. *Idéologie et renaissance nationale: L'Égypte moderne.* 2nd ed. Paris: Éditions Anthropos, 1969.

Aboussouan, Camille, ed. *La Révolution française et l'Orient, 1789–1989.* Paris: Cariscript, 1989.

Abu-Lughod, Ibrahim. *Arab Rediscovery of Europe: A Study in Cultural Encounters.* Princeton, NJ: Princeton University Press, 1963.

Ageron, Charles Robert. *Le gouvernement du général Berthezène à Alger en 1831.* Saint-Denis: Bouchène, 2005.

Agoub, Joseph. *Discours historique sur l'Égypte, par M. Agoub.* Paris: Imprimerie de Rignoux, 1823.

———. *La lyre brisée, dithyrambe dédié à Madame Dufrénoy, par M. Agoub.* Paris: Dondey-Dupré Père et Fils, 1825.

———. *Mélanges de littérature orientale et française.* Paris: Werdet, 1835.

———. *Nazm al-uqud fi kasr al-'ud (La lyre brisée), dithyrambe de M. Agoub, traduit en vers arabes par le cheykh Réfaha.* Paris: Dondey-Dupré Père et Fils, 1242 (1827).

———. "Préface." In *Journal de l'expédition anglaise en Égypte dans l'année mil huit cent, traduit de l'anglais du capitaine Th. Walls [sic] par M. A. T. [Alfred Thierry],* xxxviii–xxxix. Paris: Collin de Plancy, 1823.

———. *La querelle terminée, par M. Agoub.* Paris: J. Didot, 1830.

———. *Remarques sur le vocabulaire d'Audjelah, par M. Agoub.* Paris: F. Didot, c. 1827.

———. "Romances vulgaires des Arabes." *Journal asiatique* 10 (1827): 157–64. Reprinted as *Romances vulgaires des Arabes* (Paris: Dondey-Dupré, 1827).

———. *Le sage Heycar, conte arabe traduit par M. Agoub.* Paris: F. Didot, 1824.

Agulhon, Maurice. "Politics, Images, and Symbols in Post-Revolutionary France." In *Rites of Power: Symbolism, Ritual, and Politics since the Middle Ages,* edited by Sean Wilentz. Philadelphia: University of Pennsylvania Press, 1985.

Albin, Michael W. "Napoleon's *Description de l'Égypte:* Problems of Corporate Authorship." *Publishing History* 8 (1980): 65–85.s

Aldrich, Robert. *Greater France: A History of French Overseas Expansion.* Basingstoke: Macmillan, 1996.

———. *Vestiges of the Colonial Empire in France: Monuments, Museums, and Colonial Memories.* New York: Palgrave Macmillan, 2005.

Allin, Michael. *Zarafa.* London: Headline, 1998.

Alméras, Henri d'. *La vie parisienne sous le Consulat et l'Empire.* Paris: Albin Michel, 1909.

Amini, Iradj. *Napoleon and Persia: Franco-Persian Relations under the First Empire.* Richmond, Surrey: Curzon, 1999.

Amselle, Jean-Loup. *Vers un multiculturalisme français: L'empire de la coutume.* Paris: Aubier, 1996.

Anderson, Benedict. *Imagined Communities: Reflections on the Origins and Spread of Nationalism.* 2nd ed. London: Verso, 1991.

Anderson, M. S. *The Eastern Question, 1774–1923: A Study in International Relations.* London: Macmillan, 1966.

Anderson, Robert, and Ibrahim Fawzy. *Egypt in 1800: Scenes from Napoleon's Description de l'Égypte*. London: Barrie & Jenkins, 1988.

Antonius, George. *The Arab Awakening*. Beirut: Librairie du Liban, 1969.

Aouli, Smaïl, Ramdane Redjala, and Philippe Zoumeroff. *Abd el-Kader*. Paris: Fayard, 1994.

Archives Nationales (France), and Jean-François Dubost. *Les étrangers en France, XVIe siècle-1789: Guide des recherches aux Archives Nationales*. Paris: Archives Nationales, 1993.

Arnault, Antoine Vincent. *Souvenirs d'un sexagénaire*. Paris: Duféy, 1833.

Artin, Yacoub. *L'instruction publique en Égypte*. Paris: E. Leroux, 1890.

Ash, Timothy Garton. "Comment: This Is Not Only a French Crisis—All of Europe Must Heed the Flames." *The Guardian*, 10 November 2005.

Athanassoglou-Kallmyer, Nina M. *Eugène Delacroix: Prints, Politics, and Satire, 1814–1822*. New Haven, CT: Yale University Press, 1991.

———. *French Images from the Greek War of Independence, 1821–1830: Art and Politics under the Restoration*. New Haven, CT: Yale University Press, 1989.

Atiya, Aziz, ed. *The Coptic Encyclopedia*. New York: Macmillan, 1991.

———. *A History of Eastern Christianity*. London: Methuen, 1968.

Auriant. "La véritable histoire du chevalier de Lascaris." *Mercure de France* 172 (1924): 577–607.

———. *La vie du chevalier Théodore Lascaris, ou L'imposteur malgré lui*. Paris: Gallimard, 1940.

Aymes, Jean-René. *La déportation sous le Premier Empire: Les Espagnols en France, 1808–1814*. Paris: Publications de la Sorbonne, 1983.

Bacha, Constantin (Qustantin al-Basha al-Mukhlisi). *Tarikh usrat al Fir'awn bi-u'uliha wa-furu'iha*. Harisa: Matba'at al-Qiddis Bulus, 1932.

Bachatly, Charles. "Un manuscrit autographe de Don Raphaël." *Bulletin de l'Institut d'É-gypte* 13 (1931): 26–35.

———. "Un membre orientale du Premier Institut d'Égypte, Don Raphaël." *Bulletin de l'Institut d'Égypte* 17 (1935): 237–60.

Bacri, Roland. *La légende des siestes*. Paris: André Balland, 1973.

Badir, Magdy Gabriel. "Race et nation au XVIIIe siècle: Étude comparative de la nation juive et arabe par Voltaire." *History of European Ideas* 15.4–6 (1992): 709–15.

Baer, Gabriel. *Studies in the Social History of Modern Egypt*. Chicago: University of Chicago Press, 1969.

Bahgat, Aly. "Acte de mariage du général Menou avec la dame Zobaïdah." *Bulletin de l'In-stitut d'Égypte* 9. 2 (1898): 221–35.

Ballinger, Pamela. *History in Exile: Memory and Identity at the Borders of the Balkans*. Princeton, NJ: Princeton University Press, 2003.

[Balzac, Honoré de.] *Discours de la girafe au chef des six Osages (ou Indiens), prononcé le jour de leur visite au Jardin du Roi, traduit de l'arabe par Alibassan, interprète de la gi-rafe*. Paris: Martinet, 1827.

Blanchard, Pascal, Nicolas Bancel, and Sandrine Lemaire. *La fracture coloniale: La société française au prisme de l'héritage colonial*. Paris: La Découverte, 2005.

Barkey, Karen. *Empire of Difference: The Ottomans in Comparative Perspective.* Cambridge: Cambridge University Press, 2008.

Barnard, Alan, and Jonathan Spencer, eds. *Encyclopedia of Social and Cultural Anthropology.* London: Routledge, 1996.

Barthélemy, Auguste. *L'obélisque de Luxor.* Paris: Everat, 1833.

Barthélemy, Auguste, and Joseph Méry. *Adieux à Sidi Mahmoud.* Paris: Ponthieu, Mongie, 1825.

———. *La bacriade, ou La guerre d'Alger, poème héroï-comique en cinq chants, par Barthélemy et Méry.* Paris: A. Dupont, 1827.

———. *Epître à Sidi Mahmoud.* Paris: Ladvocat, Ponthieu, Peythieu, 1825.

Bayly, C. A. *The Birth of the Modern World, 1780–1914: Global Connections and Comparisons.* Malden, MA: Blackwell, 2004.

———. *Imperial Meridian: The British Empire and the World, 1780–1830.* London: Longman, 1989.

Beau, Nicolas. *Paris, capitale arabe.* Paris: Éditions du Seuil, 1995.

Bell, David A. *The Cult of the Nation in France: Inventing Nationalism, 1680–1800.* Cambridge, MA: Harvard University Press, 2001.

Benhabib, Seyla. *The Claims of Culture: Equality and Diversity in the Global Era.* Princeton, NJ: Princeton University Press, 2002.

Bergeron, Louis. *France under Napoleon.* Translated by R. R. Palmer. Princeton, NJ: Princeton University Press, 1981.

Bernal, Martin. *Black Athena: The Afroasiatic Roots of Classical Civilization.* New Brunswick, NJ: Rutgers University Press, 1987.

Bertier de Sauvigny, Guillaume de. *Nouvelle histoire de Paris: La Restauration, 1815–1830.* Paris: Diffusion Hachette, 1977.

Bertrand, Régis. "Les cimetières des 'esclaves turcs' des arsenaux de Marseille et de Toulon au XVIIIe siécle." *Revue des mondes musulmans et de la Méditerranée* 99–100 (2002): 205–17.

Bierman, Irene A., ed. *Napoleon in Egypt.* Reading, UK: Ithaca Press, 2003.

Birnbaum, Pierre. *L'aigle et la synagogue: Napoléon, les juifs et l'état.* Paris: Fayard, 2007.

Biver, Marie Louise. *Le Paris de Napoléon.* Paris: Plon, 1963.

Blanchard, Pascal, and Nicolas Bancel. *De l'indigène à l'immigré.* Paris: Gallimard, 1998.

Blanchard, Pascal, and Eric Deroo. *Le Paris Asie: 150 ans de présence asiatique dans la capitale.* Paris: La Découverte, 2004.

Blanchard, Pascal, Eric Deroo, and Gilles Manceron. *Le Paris noir.* Paris: Hazan, 2001.

Blanchard, Pascal, Eric Deroo, Gilles Manceron, Driss El Yazami, and Pierre Fournié. *Le Paris arabe: Deux siècles de présence des Orientaux et des Maghrébins.* Paris: La Découverte, 2003.

Bocthor, Ellious. *Dictionnaire français-arabe, revu et augmenté par A. Caussin de Perceval.* Paris: F. Didot Père et Fils, 1828.

———. *Discours prononcé à l'ouverture du cours d'arabe vulgaire de l'École des Langues Orientales Vivantes, le 8 décembre 1819.* Paris: Goujon, 1820.

Boime, Albert. *Art in an Age of Counterrevolution, 1815–1848.* Chicago: University of Chicago Press, 2004.

Boppe, Auguste. "Le colonel Nicole Papas Oglou et le bataillon des chasseurs d'Orient, 1798–1815." In *Carnets de la Sabretache: Revue militaire retrospective*. Vol. 8. Paris: Berger-Levrault, 1900.

Bordes-Benayoun, Chantal, and Dominique Schnapper. *Diasporas et nations*. Paris: Jacob, 2005.

Borel, Petrus. *L'obélisque de Louqsor*. Paris: Les Marchands de Nouveautés, 1836.

Boulle, Pierre. *Race et esclavage dans la France de l'ancien régime*. Paris: Perrin, 2007.

Bourguet, Marie-Noëlle. *Déchiffrer la France: La statistique départementale à l'époque napoléonienne*. Paris: Éditions des Archives Contemporaines, 1989.

———, ed. *L'invention scientifique de la Méditerranée: Égypte, Morée, Algérie*. Paris: École des Hautes Études en Sciences Sociales, 1998.

Bourguet, Marie-Noëlle, Daniel Nordman, Vassilis Panayatopolous, and Maroula Sinarellis. *Enquêtes en Méditerrannée: Les expéditions françaises d'Égypte, de Morée et d'Algérie*. Athens: Institut de Recherches Néohelléniques/FNRS, 1999.

Boustany, Salah el-Din. *Bonaparte's Egypt in Picture and Word, 1798–1801*. Cairo: Arab Bookshop, 1986.

Brahimi, Denise. *Arabes des lumières et bédouins romantiques: Siècle de "Voyages en Orient," 1735–1835*. Paris: Le Sycomore, 1982.

Braudel, Fernand. *The Identity of France*. London: Collins, 1988.

———. *The Mediterranean and the Mediterranean World in the Age of Philip II*. Translated by Sian Reynolds. London: HarperCollins, 1992.

Brégeon, Jean-Joël. *L'Égypte française au jour le jour, 1798–1801*. Paris: Perrin, 1991.

Bret, Patrice. *L'Égypte au temps de l'expédition de Bonaparte, 1798–1801*. Paris: Hachette, 1998.

———, ed. *L'expédition d'Égypte: Une entreprise des lumières, 1798–1801*. Paris: Technique et Documentation, 1999.

Broers, Michael. "Cultural Imperialism in a European Context? Political Culture and Cultural Politics in Napoleonic Italy." *Past and Present* 170 (2001): 152–80.

———. *Europe under Napoleon, 1799–1815*. London: Arnold, 1996.

Brooks, Van Wyck. "On Creating a Usable Past." In *American Literature, American Culture*, edited by Gordon Hutner, 213–16. New York: Oxford University Press, 1999.

Brown, Howard G., and Judith A. Miller. *Taking Liberties: Problems of a New Order from the French Revolution to Napoleon*. Manchester: Manchester University Press, 2003.

Brunon, Jean, and Raoul Brunon. *Les Mameluks d'Égypte; Les Mameluks de la Garde Impériale*. Marseille: Collection Raoul & Jean Brunon, 1963.

Burgess, Greg. "Asylum and Refugee Protection in France, 1831–1939: Exile, the State, and Human Rights." PhD diss., University of Melbourne, 2002.

Calabi, Donatella, and Jacques Bottin. *Les étrangers dans la ville: Minorités et espace urbain du bas Moyen Âge à l'époque moderne*. Paris: Éditions de la Maison des Sciences de l'Homme, 1999.

Caron, Jean-Claude, and Maurice Agulhon. *Générations romantiques: Les étudiants de Paris et le quartier Latin (1814–1851)*. Paris: Armand Colin, 1991.

Carré, Jean Marie. *Voyageurs et écrivains français en Égypte*. 2nd ed. Cairo: L'Institut Français d'Archéologie Orientale, 1956.

Carrière, Charles. *Négociants marseillais au XVIIIe siècle: Contribution à l'étude des économies maritimes.* Marseille: Institut Historique de Provence, 1973.

Carrott, Richard G. *The Egyptian Revival: Its Sources, Monuments, and Meaning, 1808–1858.* Berkeley: University of California Press, 1978.

Certeau, Michel de, Dominique Julia, and Jacques Revel. *Une politique de la langue: La Révolution française et les patois.* Paris: Gallimard, 1975.

Chakrabarty, Dipesh. *Provincializing Europe: Postcolonial Thought and Historical Difference.* Princeton NJ: Princeton University Press, 2000.

Champollion, Jean-François. *Lettres à son frère, 1804–1818.* Paris: L'Asiathèque, 1984.

Charles-Roux, François. *Les échelles de Syrie et de Palestine au XVIIIe siècle.* Paris: Paul Geuthner, 1928.

———. *France et chrétiens d'Orient.* Paris: Flammarion, 1939.

Chateaubriand, François-René, vicomte de. *Itinéraire de Paris à Jérusalem.* Paris: Le Normant, 1811.

Châtelain, Abel. *Les migrants temporaires en France de 1800 à 1914: Histoire économique et sociale des migrants temporaires des campagnes françaises au XIXe siècle et au début du XXe siècle.* Villeneuve-d'Ascq: Université de Lille III, 1976.

Chatelain, René-Théophile. *Lettres de Sidy-Mahmoud, écrites pendant son séjour en France, en 1825.* Paris: Ladvocat, 1825.

Cheikho, Lewis. "Mikha'il al-Sabbagh wa usratuhu." *Al-Mashreq* 8 (1905): 24–34.

Chevalier, Louis. *Classes laborieuses et classes dangereuses à Paris pendant la première moitié du XIXe siècle.* Paris: Plon, 1958.

———. *La formation de la population parisienne au XIXe siècle.* Paris: Presses Universitaires de France, 1950.

Choueiri, Youssef. *Arab Nationalism: A History.* Oxford: Blackwell, 2000.

———. *Modern Arab Historiography: Historical Discourse and the Nation-State.* Rev. ed. New York: RoutledgeCurzon, 2003.

Cleemputte, Paul Adolphe van. *La vie parisienne à travers le XIXe siècle: Paris de 1800 à 1900 d'après les estampes et les mémoires du temps.* Paris: E. Plon, Nourrit et cie, 1900.

Clifford, James. *Routes: Travel and Translation in the Late Twentieth Century.* Cambridge, MA: Harvard University Press, 1997.

Clot, Antoine Barthélemy. *Compte rendu des travaux de l'École de médecine d'Abou-Zabel, et de l'examen général des élèves, suivi de l'exposé de la conduite et des travaux de l'auteur lui-même en Égypte, 1825–32.* Paris: Deville Cavellin, 1833.Cobb, Richard. *The Police and the People: French Popular Protest, 1789–1820.* Oxford: Clarendon Press, 1970.

Cohen, Amnon. *Palestine in the 18th Century: Patterns of Government and Administration.* Jerusalem: Magnes Press, 1973.

Cohen, William B. *The French Encounter with Africans: White Response to Blacks, 1530–1880.* Bloomington: Indiana University Press, 1980.

Cole, Juan. *Napoleon's Egypt: Invading the Middle East.* New York: Palgrave Macmillan, 2007.

———. "Rifa'a al-Tahtawi and the Revival of Practical Philosophy." *Muslim World* 70 (1980): 29–46.

Colla, Elliott. "'Non, non! Si, si!': Commemorating the French Occupation of Egypt (1798–1801)." *MLN* 118 (2003): 1043–69.

Coller, Ian. "Arab France: Mobility and Community in Early Nineteenth-Century Paris and Marseille." Special issue, "Mobility in French History," *French Historical Studies* 28 (2006): 433–56.

Colley, Linda. *Captives: Britain, Empire, and the World, 1600–1850*. London: Jonathan Cape, 2002.

Collingham, H. A. C., and R. Alexander. *The July Monarchy: A Political History of France, 1830–1848*. London: Longman, 1988.

Collins, Irene, ed. *Government and Society in France, 1814–1848*. London: Edward Arnold, 1970.

Cooper, Frederick, and Rogers Brubaker. "Beyond Identity." *Theory & Society* 29 (2000): 1–47.

Cordier, Henri. *Notes sur Eusèbe de Salle*. Paris: H. Leclerc, 1917.

Crabbs, Jack A., Jr. *The Writing of History in Nineteenth-Century Egypt: A Study in National Transformation*. Cairo: The American University in Cairo Press, 1984.

Craik, George Lillie. *Paris and Its Historical Scenes*. 2 vols. London: C. Knight, 1831.

Crecelius, Daniel. *The Roots of Modern Egypt: A Study of the Regimes of 'Ali Bey al-Kabir and Muhammad Bey Abu al-Dhahab, 1760–1775*. Minneapolis: Bibliotheca Islamica, 1981.

Crossley, Ceri. *French Historians and Romanticism: Thierry, Guizot, the Saint-Simonians, Quinet, Michelet*. London: Routledge, 1993.

Crow, Thomas E. *Emulation: Making Artists for Revolutionary France*. New Haven, CT: Yale University Press, 1995.

Curl, James Stevens. *Egyptomania: The Egyptian Revival, a Recurring Theme in the History of Taste*. 2nd ed. Manchester: Manchester University Press, 1994.

Dalrymple, William. *White Mughals: Love and Betrayal in Eighteenth-Century India*. London: Harper Collins, 2002.

Daly, M. W., ed. *The Cambridge History of Egypt*. Vol. 2, *Modern Egypt, from 1517 to the End of the Twentieth Century*. Cambridge: Cambridge University Press, 1998.

Daniel, Norman. *Islam, Europe, and Empire*. Edinburgh: Edinburgh University Press, 1966.

Dardaud, Gabriel. *Une girafe pour le roi*. Creil, France: Dumerchez-Naoum, 1985.

Dawisha, A. I. *Arab Nationalism in the Twentieth Century: From Triumph to Despair*. Princeton, NJ: Princeton University Press, 2003.

Décobert, Christian. "L'Orientalisme, des lumières a la Révolution, selon Silvestre de Sacy." *Revue du monde musulman et de la Méditerranée* 52–53 (1989): 49–62.

———, ed. *Valeur et distance: Identités et sociétés en Égypte*. Paris: Maisonneuve et Larose, 2000.

Dehérain, Henri. *Orientalistes et antiquaires*. Vol. 2, *Silvestre de Sacy, ses contemporains et ses disciples*. Paris: P. Geuthner, 1938.

Delanoue, Gilbert. *Moralistes et politiques musulmans dans l'Égypte du XIXe siècle, 1798–1882*. Cairo: Institut Français d'Archéologie Orientale du Caire, 1982.

d'Eppe, César Proisy. *Dictionnaire des girouettes, ou Nos contemporains peints d'après eux-mêmes*. Paris: Alexis Eymery, 1815.

Derogy, Jacques, and Hesi Carmel. *Bonaparte en terre sainte.* Paris: Fayard, 1992.

Desnoyers, Louis, Jules Janin, Old Nick, and Frédéric Mornand. *Les étrangers à Paris.* Paris: Charles Warée, 1844.

Dhombres, Nicole, and Jean G. Dhombres. *Naissance d'un pouvoir: Sciences et savants en France, 1793–1824.* Paris: Payot, 1989.

Dobie, Madeleine. *Foreign Bodies: Gender, Language, and Culture in French Orientalism.* Stanford, CA: Stanford University Press, 2001.

Doguereau, Jean-Pierre. *Guns in the Desert: General Jean-Pierre Doguereau's Journal of Napoleon's Egyptian Expedition.* Westport, CT: Praeger, 2003.

Douin, Georges. *L'Égypte de 1802 à 1804: Correspondance des consuls de France en Égypte.* Cairo: Institut Français d'Archéologie Orientale, 1925.

———. *L'Égypte indépendante, projet de 1801: Documents inédits recueillis aux Archives du Foreign Office à Londres.* Cairo: Société Royale de Géographie d'Égypte, 1924.

———. *Une mission militaire française auprès de Mohamed Aly: Correspondance des généraux Belliard et Boyer.* Cairo: Institut Français d'Archéologie Orientale, 1923.

———. *Mohamed Aly et l'expédition d'Alger, 1829–1830.* Cairo: Société Royale de Géographie d'Égypte, 1930.

———. *Les premières frégates de Mohamed Aly, 1824–1827.* Cairo: Institut Français d'Archéologie Orientale, 1926.

Driault, Édouard. *La formation de l'empire de Mohamed Aly de l'Arabie au Soudan, 1814–1823: Correspondance des consuls de France en Égypte.* Cairo: Institut Français d'Archéologie Orientale, 1927.

———. *Mohamed Aly et Napoléon, 1807–1814: Correspondance des consuls de France en Égypte.* Cairo: Institut Français d'Archéologie Orientale, 1925.

———. *La politique orientale de Napoléon: Sébastiani et Gardane, 1806–1808.* Paris: F. Alcan, 1904.

Driessen, Henk. "Mediterranean Port Cities: Cosmopolitanism Reconsidered." *History and Anthropology* 16 (2005): 129–41.

Dubost, Jean-François, and Peter Sahlins. *Et si on faisait payer les étrangers? Louis XIV, les immigrés et quelques autres.* Paris: Flammarion, 1999.

Duby, Georges, and Guy Lobrichon. *L'histoire de Paris par la peinture.* Paris: Belfond, 1988.

Dufrénoy, Adélaïde-Gillette. *Le tour du monde, ou Tableau géographique et historique de tous les peuples de la terre.* 6 vols. Paris: Alexis Eymery, 1814.

Dupont-Ferrier, Gustave. *Du Collège de Clermont au Lycée Louis-le-Grand, 1536–1920: La vie quotidienne d'un collège parisien pendant plus de trois cent cinquante ans.* Paris: E. de Boccard, 1921.

———. *Les jeunes de langue à Constantinople (1762–1796),* 1923.

———. *Les jeunes ou "Arméniens" à Louis-le-Grand.* Paris: Paul Guethner, 1923.

Durand, Charles. *Marseille, Nîmes et ses environs par un témoin oculaire.* Paris: Les Marchands de Nouveautés, 1818.

Durdent, R. J. *Promenades de Paris, ou Collection de vues pittoresques de ses jardins publics, accompagnée d'un texte historique et descriptif, gravée et publiée par Schwartz: Premier Cahier—Le Jardin des Tuileries.* Paris: Le Normant, 1812.

Dwyer, Philip, ed. *Napoleon and Europe.* London: Longman, 2001.

Dykstra, Darrell I. "Joseph Hekekyan and the Egyptian School in Paris." *Armenian Review* 35 (1982): 165–82.

Échinard, Pierre. *Grecs et philhellènes à Marseille: De la Révolution française à l'indépendance de la Grèce.* Marseille: Institut Historique de Provence, CNRS, 1973.

———. *Marseille au quotidien.* Marseille: J. Lafitte, 1991.

———. *Migrance: Histoire des migrations à Marseille.* Vol. 2, *L'expansion Marseillaise et "l'invasion italienne," 1830–1918.* La Calade, Aix-en-Provence: Edisud, 1989.

Échinard, Pierre, and George Jessula. *Léon Gozlan, suivi des refugiés égyptiens à Marseille.* Marseille: I.M.M.A.J., 2003.

Échinard, Pierre, and Émile Témime. *Migrance: Histoire des migrations à Marseille.* Vol. 1, *La préhistoire de la migration, 1482–1830.* La Calade, Aix-en-Provence: Edisud, 1989.

Enan, Leïla. "'Si tu le sais, alors c'est un catastrophe . . .' La commemoration: Pourquoi, pour qui?" *Égypte/Monde arabe* 1 (1999): 13–24.

Esdaile, Charles J. *Fighting Napoleon: Guerrillas, Bandits, and Adventurers in Spain, 1808–1814.* New Haven, CT: Yale University Press, 2004.

Evenson, Norma. *Paris: A Century of Change, 1878–1978.* New Haven, CT: Yale University Press, 1979.

Fabian, Johannes. *Time and the Other: How Anthropology Makes Its Object.* New York: Columbia University Press, 1983.

Fagan, Brian M. *The Rape of the Nile: Tomb Robbers, Tourists, and Archaeologists in Egypt.* New York: Scribner, 1975.

Faivre d'Arcier, Amaury. *Les agents de Napoléon en Égypte, 1801–1815.* Levallois, France: Centre d'Études Napoléoniennes, 1990.

Fakkar, Rushdi. *Aux origines des relations culturelles contemporaines entre la France et le monde arabe: L'influence française sur la formation de la presse littéraire en Égypte au XIXe siècle.* Paris: Geuthner, 1972.

Farge, Arlette. *Vivre dans la rue à Paris au XVIIIe siècle.* Paris: Gallimard/Julliard, 1979.

Féraud, Laurent-Charles. *Les interprètes de l'armée d'Afrique.* Algiers: A. Jourdan, 1876.

Findley, C. V. "An Ottoman Occidentalist in Europe: Ahmed Midhat Meets Madame Gulnar, 1889." *American Historical Review* 103 (1998): 15–49.

Finot, L. *Société asiatique: Le livre du centenaire, 1822–1922.* Paris: Paul Guethner, 1922.

Fisher, Michael Herbert. *Counterflows to Colonialism: Indian Travellers and Settlers in Britain, 1600–1857.* Delhi: Permanent Black, 2004.

Fishman, Joshua. *Language and Nationalism: Two Integrative Essays.* Rowley, MA: Newbury House, 1972.

Fleming, K. E. *The Muslim Bonaparte: Diplomacy and Orientalism in Ali Pasha's Greece.* Princeton, NJ: Princeton University Press, 1999.

Forrest, Alan. *Conscripts and Deserters: The Army and French Society during the Revolution and Empire.* New York: Oxford University Press, 1989.

Foucault, Michel. *The Order of Things: An Archaeology of the Human Sciences.* New York: Random House, 1970.

Frémeaux, Jacques. *La France et l'Islam depuis 1789.* Paris: Presses Universitaires de France, 1991.

———. "La France, la Révolution et l'Orient: Aspects diplomatiques." *Revue du monde musulman et de la Méditerranée* 52–53 (1989): 19–28.

Furet, François. *Revolutionary France, 1770–1880.* Oxford: Blackwell, 1992.

Garrioch, David. *The Making of Revolutionary Paris.* Berkeley: University of California Press, 2002.

———. *Neighbourhood and Community in Paris, 1740–1790.* Cambridge: Cambridge University Press, 1986.

Gendzier, Irene L. "James Sanua and Egyptian Nationalism." *Middle East Journal* 15 (1961): 16–28.

Gerzina, Gretchen. *Black London: Life Before Emancipation.* New Brunswick, NJ: Rutgers University Press, 1995.

———. *Black Victorians/Black Victoriana.* New Brunswick, NJ: Rutgers University Press, 2003.

Ghoneim, M. "Antoine-Barthélemy Clot créateur de l'école de médecine." *Cahiers d'histoire égyptienne* 11 (1969): 125–36.

Ghurbal, Muhammad Shafiq. *The Beginnings of the Egyptian Question and the Rise of Mehemet Ali: A Study in the Diplomacy of the Napoleonic Era Based on Researches in the British and French Archives.* London: G. Routledge, 1928.

Gibb, H. A. R. *The Encyclopaedia of Islam.* New ed. Leiden: Brill, 1960.

Gildea, Robert. *The Past in French History.* New Haven, CT: Yale University Press, 1994.

Gillette, Alain, and Abdelmalek Sayad. *L'immigration algérienne en France.* Paris: Éditions Entente, 1984.

Gillispie, Charles Coulston, and Michel Dewachter. *Monuments of Egypt, the Napoleonic Edition: The Complete Archaeological Plates from "La Description de l'Égypte."* Princeton, NJ: Princeton Architectural Press, 1987.

Gilroy, Paul. *The Black Atlantic: Modernity and Double Consciousness.* London: Verso, 1993.

Goby, Jean-Edouard. *Premier Institut d'Égypte: Restitution des comptes rendus des séances.* Quetigny: Imprimerie Darantière, 1987.

Godechot, Jacques. *La Grande Nation: L'expansion révolutionnaire de la France dans le monde de 1789 à 1799.* Paris: Aubier, 1956.

Gordon, David C., L. Carl Brown, and Matthew Gordon. *Franco-Arab Encounters: Studies in Memory of David C. Gordon.* Beirut: American University of Beirut, 1996.

Gotteri, Nicole, ed. *La police secrète du Premier Empire: Bulletins quotidiens adressés par Savary à l'Empereur . . .* 4 vols. Paris: Honoré Champion, 1997–2000.

Gozlan, Léon. "Les réfugiés égyptiens à Marseille." *Revue contemporaine* 149 (1866): 31–47.

Gran, Peter. *Islamic Roots of Capitalism: Egypt, 1760–1840.* Austin: University of Texas Press, 1979.

———. "Tahtawi in Paris." *Al-Ahram Weekly On-line* 568 (10–16 Jan. 2002).

Gran, Peter, Arif Dirlik, and Vinay Bahl. *History after the Three Worlds: Post-Eurocentric Historiographies.* Lanham, MD: Rowman & Littlefield, 2000.

Grandmaison, Olivier Le Cour. *Coloniser, exterminer: Sur la guerre et l'état colonial.* Paris: Arthème Fayard, 2004.

Grigsby, Darcy Grimaldo. *Extremities: Painting Empire in Post-Revolutionary France.* London: Yale University Press, 2002.

Guémard, G. "Les auxiliaires de l'armée de Bonaparte en Égypte (1798–1801)." *Bulletin de l'Institut d'Égypte* 9 (1927): 1–17.

Guys, Henri. *Notice historique sur la vie et les ouvrages de M. Joseph Agoub.* Marseille: Extrait du Répertoire des Travaux de la Société de Statistique de Marseille, Tome XXIV, 1860.

Habart, Michel. *Histoire d'un parjure.* Paris: Éditions de Minuit, 1960.

Habicht, Maximilan. *Epistolae quaedam arabicae (A Mauris, Aegyptis et Syris / Kitab jina al-fawakih al-atmarfy jami' ba'd makatib al-ajnab).* Wroclaw: Typis Universitatis Regis, 1824.

Hackforth-Jones, Jocelyn, and Mary Roberts, eds. *Edges of Empire: Orientalism and Visual Culture.* Malden, MA: Blackwell, 2005.

Haddad, George. "Fathallah al-Sayegh and His Account of a Napoleonic Mission among the Arab Nomads: History or Fiction?" *Studia islamica* 24 (1966): 107–23.

———. "A Napoleonic Arabic Fragment of Anti-Russian Propaganda in the Ottoman Empire." *The Muslim World* 71 (1981): 99–103.

———. "A Project for the Independence of Egypt, 1801." *Journal of the American Oriental Society* 90 (1970): 169–83.

Hajjar, Joseph. *L'Europe et les destinées du Proche-Orient, 1815–1848.* Paris: Bloud et Gay, 1970.

Halbwachs, Maurice. *On Collective Memory.* Translated by Lewis A. Coser. Chicago: University of Chicago Press, 1992.

Hanna, Nelly. *Money, Land, and Trade: An Economic History of the Muslim Mediterranean.* London: I. B. Tauris, 2001.

———. *The State and Its Servants: Administration in Egypt from Ottoman Times to the Present.* Cairo: American University in Cairo Press, 1995.

Hanley, Wayne. *The Genesis of Napoleonic Propaganda, 1796–1799.* New York: Columbia University Press, 2005.

Hargreaves, Alec G. *Immigration, "Race," and Ethnicity in Contemporary France.* London: Routledge, 1995.

Hartleben, Hermine. *Champollion: Sa vie et son oeuvre, 1790–1832.* Paris: Pygmalion, 1983.

Harvey, David. *Paris, Capital of Modernity.* New York: Routledge, 2003.

Hatina, Meir. "Historical Legacy and the Challenge of Modernity in the Middle East: The Case of al-Azhar in Egypt." *The Muslim World* 93 (2003): 51–68.

Hauterive, Ernest d'. *La police secrète du Premier Empire: Bulletins quotidiens adressés par Fouché à l'Empereur . . . publiés par Ernest d'Hauterive, d'après les documents originaux déposés aux Archives nationales, Préface de Louis Madelin.* 3 vols. Paris: Perrin, 1908.

———. *La police secrète du Premier Empire: Bulletins quotidiens adressés par Fouché à l'Empereur . . . , nouvelle série, 1808–1809.* Paris: Perrin, 1963.

Herold, J. Christopher. *Bonaparte in Egypt.* London: Hamish Hamilton, 1962.

Herzfeld, Michael. *Cultural Intimacy: Social Poetics in the Nation-State.* New York: Routledge, 2005.

Hesse, Carla. *The Other Enlightenment: How French Women Became Modern.* Princeton, NJ: Princeton University Press, 2001.

Heuer, Jennifer. *The Family and the Nation: Gender and Citizenship in Revolutionary France, 1789–1830.* Ithaca, NY: Cornell University Press, 2005.

Heyworth-Dunne, James. *An Introduction to the History of Education in Modern Egypt.* London: Frank Cass, 1968.

Higonnet, Patrice L. R. *Paris: Capital of the World.* Cambridge, MA: Belknap Press, 2002.

Hillairet, Jacques. *Connaissance du vieux Paris.* Paris: Gonthier, 1963.

———. *Dictionnaire historique des rues de Paris.* 8th ed. Paris: Éditions de Minuit, 1985.

———. *Évocation du vieux Paris: Vieux quartiers, vieilles rues, vieilles demeures.* Paris: Éditions de Minuit, 1952.

Hoerder, Dirk. *Cultures in Contact: World Migrations in the Second Millennium.* Durham, NC: Duke University Press, 2002.

Hoerder, Dirk, Adrian Shubert, and Christiane Harzig, eds. *The Historical Practice of Diversity: Transcultural Interactions from the Early Modern Mediterranean to the Postcolonial World.* New York: Berghahn Books, 2003.

Holtman, Robert B. *Napoleonic Propaganda.* New York: Greenwood Press, 1969.

Homsy, Gaston. "Un égyptien colonel dans les armées de Napoléon 1er." *Bulletin de l'Institut d'Égypte* 10 (1923): 83–96.

———. *Le général Jacob et l'expédition de Bonaparte en Égypte, 1798–1801.* Marseille: Éditions Indépendantes, 1921.

Houdaille, Jacques. "Le problème des pertes de guerre." *Revue d'histoire moderne et contemporaine* 17 (1972): 411–23.

Hourani, Albert. *Arabic Thought in the Liberal Age, 1798–1939.* London: Oxford University Press, 1962.

———. *A History of the Arab Peoples.* London: Faber and Faber, 1991.

———. "The Syrians in Egypt in the Eighteenth and Nineteenth Century." In *Colloque international sur l'histoire du Caire, 27 mars–5 avril 1969,* 221–319. Cairo: Ministry of Culture of the Arab Republic of Egypt, 1972.

Hugo, Victor. *Oeuvres Complètes.* Vol. 2, *Poésies.* Paris: Laffont, 1985.

Humbert, Jean-Marcel. *L'Égypte à Paris.* Paris: Action Artistique de la Ville de Paris, 1998.

———. *L'Égyptomanie dans l'art occidental.* Paris: Éditions ACR, 1989.

Humbert, Jean Pierre Louis. *Anthologie arabe, ou Choix de poésies arabes inédites, traduites en français, avec le texte en regard, et accompagnées d'une version latine littérale.* Paris: Treuttel et Würtz, 1819.

Husry, Khaldun Sati al-. *Three Reformers: A Study in Modern Arab Political Thought.* Beirut: Khayats, 1966.

Ibrahim, Nasser Ahmed, ed.. *Mi'ata 'am 'ala-l-hamlat al-faransiyya (ru'iyya misriyya).* Cairo: Maktabat ad-Dar al-'Arabiyyat al-Kitab, 2008.

Ilbert, Robert, and Philippe Joutard. *Le miroir égyptien.* Marseille: Éditions du Quai, 1984.

Inalcik, Halil, and Donald Quataert, eds. *An Economic and Social History of the Ottoman Empire, 1300–1914.* Cambridge: Cambridge University Press, 1994.

Isa-Carus. *Isa-Carus, prélat du rite grec catholique aux âmes sensibles.* Paris: F. Louis, c. 1804.

Issawi, Charles. *Cross-Cultural Encounters and Conflicts*. New York: Oxford University Press, 1998.

Jabarti, Abd al-Rahman al-. *'Abd al-Rahman al-Jabarti's History of Egypt [Aja'ib al-athar fi 'l-tarajim wa-'l-akhbar]*. Edited by Thomas Philipp, Moshe Perlmann, and Guido Schwald and translated by Thomas Philipp and Moshe Perlmann. 4 vols. in 2 books and a guide. Stuttgart: Franz Steiner Verlag, 1994.

———. *Tarikh muddat al-faransis bi misr*. Translated by Shmuel Moreh as "Al-Jabarti's Chronicle of the First Seven Months of the French Occupation, June–December, 1798." In *Napoleon in Egypt: Al-Jabarti's Chronicle of the First Seven Months of the French Occupation, 1798*, 17–132. Princeton, NJ: M. Wiener, 1993.

Janin, Jules, M. E. Roch, M. A. Bazin, Auguste Barthélemy, et al. *Paris, ou Le livre des cent-et-un*. Paris: Ladvocat, 1832.

Jankowski, James P., and I. Gershoni. *Rethinking Nationalism in the Arab Middle East*. New York: Columbia University Press, 1997.

Jasanoff, Maya. "Cosmopolitan: A Tale of Identity from Ottoman Alexandria." *Common Knowledge* 11 (2005): 393–409.

———. *Edge of Empire: Conquest and Collecting in the East, 1750–1850*. London: Fourth Estate, 2005.

Jelloun, Tahar Ben. *Hospitalité française: Racisme et immigration maghrébine*. Paris: Seuil, 1984.

Johnson, W. McAllister. *French Lithography: The Restoration Salons, 1817–1824: An Historical Publication Based on the Collections of the Département des Estampes et de la Photographie, Bibliothèque Nationale, Paris*. Kingston, Ont.: Agnes Etherington Art Centre, 1977.

Jones, Colin. *Paris: Biography of a City*. New York: Allen Lane, 2005.

Jones, Proctor. *Napoleon: An Intimate Account of the Years of Supremacy, 1800–1814*. New York: Distributed by Random House, 1992.

Jordan, David P. *Transforming Paris: The Life and Labors of Baron Haussmann*. New York: Free Press, 1995.

Jouy, Victor-Joseph-Étienne de. *L'Hermite de la Chaussée-d'Antin, ou Observations sur les mœurs et les usages parisiens au commencement du XIXe siècle*. Paris: Pillet, 1815.

———. *Oeuvres complètes d'Étienne Jouy*. Paris: J. Didot Aîné, 1823.

Julien, Charles-André. *Histoire de l'Algérie contemporaine*. Vol. 1, *La conquête et les débuts de la colonisation, 1827–1871*. Paris: PUF, 1964.

Kale, Steven. *French Salons: High Society and Political Sociability from the Old Regime to the Revolution of 1848*. Baltimore: The Johns Hopkins University Press, 2004.

Kalifa, Dominique. "Archéologie de l'apachisme: Les représentations des Peaux-Rouges dans la France du XIXe siècle." *Revue de l'histoire de l'enfance "irrégulière"* 4 (2002). http://rhei.revues.org/document51.html.

Kalman, Julie. *Rethinking Antisemitism in Nineteenth-Century France*. New York: Cambridge University Press, 2010. .

Kayata, Polycarpe. *Monographie de l'église grecque catholique de Marseille*. Marseille: Imprimerie Marseillaise, 1901.

Khadar, Hedia, ed. *La Révolution française et le monde arabo-musulman*. Tunis: Alif, 1989.

Khalidi, Rashid. *The Origins of Arab Nationalism*. New York: Columbia University Press, 1991.

———. *Palestinian Identity: The Construction of Modern National Consciousness*. New York: Columbia University Press, 1997.

Khan, Mirza Abu Taleb. *The Travels of Mirza Abu Taleb Khan in Asia, Africa, and Europe during the Years 1799, 1800, 1801, 1802, and 1803*. Translated by Charles Stewart. London: Longman, Hurst, Rees, and Orme, 1810.

———. *Westward Bound: Travels of Mirza Abu Taleb*. Translated by Charles Stewart. Delhi: Oxford University Press, 2005.

Khater, A. *Le régime juridique des fouilles et des antiquités en Égypte*. Cairo: Institut Français d'Archéologie Orientale, 1960.

Khodja, Hamdan. *Le miroir: Aperçu historique et statistique sur la régence d'Alger*. Reprint, Paris: Sindbad, 1985.

Khuri, Ra'if. *Modern Arab Thought: Channels of the French Revolution to the Arab East*. Princeton, NJ: The Kingston Press, 1983.

Klaits, Joseph, and Michael H. Haltzel. *The Global Ramifications of the French Revolution*. Cambridge: Cambridge University Press, 1994.

Kroen, Sheryl. *Politics and Theater: The Crisis of Legitimacy in Restoration France, 1815–1830*. Berkeley: University of California Press, 2000.

Kymlicka, Will. *Multicultural Citizenship: A Liberal Theory of Minority Rights*. New York: Oxford University Press, 1995.

Labrousse, Pierre. *Langues'O, 1795–1995: Deux siècles d'histoire de l'École Nationale des Langues Orientales*. Paris: Hervas, 1995.

Lacouture, Jean. *Champollion: Une vie de lumières*. Paris: B. Grasset, 1988.

Laffont, Robert, ed. *Paris and Its People: An Illustrated History*. London: Methuen, 1958.

Laissus, Yves. *L'Égypte, une aventure savante: Avec Bonaparte, Kléber, Menou, 1798–1801*. Paris: Fayard, 1998.

———. *Jomard: Le dernier Égyptien, 1777–1862*. Paris: Fayard, 2004.

La Jonquière, Charles de. *L'expédition d'Égypte, 1798–1801*. 6 vols. Reprint, Paris: Éditions Historiques Teissèdre, 2003.

Lamartine, Alphonse de. *Voyage en Orient, 1832–1833*. Paris: Charles Gosselin, 1843.

Lambrecht, E. *Catalogue de la bibliothèque de l'École des Langues Orientales Vivantes*. Vol. 1, *Linguistique*. Paris: Imprimerie Nationale, 1897.

Lane, Edward William. *An Account of the Manners and Customs of the Modern Egyptians: Written in Egypt during the Years, 1833–1835*. Reprint, London: Darf, 1986.

Laurens, Henry. *Kléber en Égypte, 1798–1800*. 4 vols. Cairo: Institut Français d'Archéologie Orientale du Caire, 1988.

———. *Orientales*. Vol. 1, *Autour de l'expédition d'Égypte*. Paris: CNRS, 2004.

———. *Les origines intellectuelles de l'expédition d'Égypte: L'Orientalisme islamisant en France, 1698–1798*. Istanbul: Editions Isis, 1987.

———. "La Révolution française et l'Islam: Un essai de perspective historique." In *L'image de la Révolution française*, edited by Michel Vovelle, 886–94. Paris: Pergamon, 1989.

———. *Le royaume impossible: La France et la genèse du monde arabe*. Paris: Armand Colin, 1990.

Laurens, Henry, Jean-Claude Golvin, Claude Traunecker, and Charles Coulston Gillispie. *L'expédition d'Égypte, 1798–1801*. Paris: Armand Colin, 1989.

[Lautard, Laurent.] *Esquisses historiques: Marseille depuis 1789 jusqu'en 1815 par un vieux Marseillais (L. Lautard)*. Marseille: Marius Olive, 1844.

Lavallée, Joseph. *Lettres d'un mameluck, ou Tableau moral et critique de quelques parties des moeurs de Paris*. Paris: Capelle, 1803.

Laven, David, and Lucy Riall. *Napoleon's Legacy: Problems of Government in Restoration Europe*. Oxford: Berg, 2000.

Lebovics, Herman. *Bringing the Empire Back Home: France in the Global Age*. Durham, NC: Duke University Press, 2004.

Legat, Bernard-Joseph. *Code des étrangers, ou Traité de la législation française concernant les étrangers*. Paris: Béchet Aîné, 1832.

Lequin, Yves. *La mosaïque, France: Histoire des étrangers et de l'immigration*. Paris: Larousse, 1988.

Leroy, Gabriel. *Le vieux Melun, supplément à l'histoire de la même ville*. Melun: A. Huguenin, 1904.

Lévy, Laurent. *Le spectre du communautarisme*. Paris: Éditions Amsterdam, 2005.

Levy-Schneider, Léon. *L' application du Concordat par un prélat d'ancien régime: Mgr. Champion de Cicé, archevêque d'Aix et d'Arles*. Paris: F. Rieder, 1921.

Lewis, Bernard. *Islam and the West*. New York: Oxford University Press, 1993.

———. *The Muslim Discovery of Europe*. London: Phoenix Press, 1982.

———. "Watan." *Journal of Contemporary History* 26 (1991): 523–33.

Lewis, Bernard, and Benjamin Braude, eds. *Christians and Jews in the Ottoman Empire: The Functioning of a Plural Society*. New York: Holmes & Meier, 1982.

Lewis, Martin W., and Kären E. Wigen. *The Myth of Continents: A Critique of Metageography*. Berkeley: University of California Press, 1997.

Lewis, Reina. *Rethinking Orientalism: Women, Travel, and the Ottoman Harem*. New Brunswick, NJ: Rutgers University Press, 2004.

Livingston, John W. "Shaykh Bakri and Bonaparte." *Studia islamica* 80 (1994): 125–43.

———. "Western Science and Educational Reform in the Thought of Shaykh Rifa'a Al-Tahtawi." *International Journal of Middle East Studies* 28 (1996): 543–64.

Lockroy, Édouard. *Ahmed le Boucher: La Syrie et l'Égypte au XVIIIe siècle*. 4th ed. Paris: P. Ollendorff, 1888.

Lorcin, Patricia M. E. *Imperial Identities: Stereotyping, Prejudice, and Race in Colonial Algeria*. London: I. B. Tauris, 1995.

———. "Rome and France in Africa: Recovering Colonial Algeria's Latin Past." *French Historical Studies* 25.2 (2002): 295–329.

Louca, Anouar. "Champollion entre Bartholdi et Chiftichi." In *Rivages et déserts: Hommage à Jacques Berque*, 209–25. Paris: Sindbad, 1988.

———. "Ellious Bocthor: Sa vie, son œuvre." *Cahiers d'histoire égyptienne* 5/6 (1953): 309–20.

———. "Joseph Agoub: Sa vie et son œuvre." *Cahiers d'histoire égyptienne* 9 (1959): 187–203.

———. "La renaissance égyptienne et les limites de l'œuvre de Bonaparte." *Cahiers d'histoire égyptienne* 7 (1955): 1–20.

————. *Les sources marseillaises de l'Orient romantique.* Paris: Maisonneuve et Larose, 2001.

————. *Voyageurs et écrivains égyptiens en France au XIXe siècle.* Paris: Didier, 1970.

Lowe, Lisa. *Critical Terrains: French and British Orientalisms.* Ithaca, NY: Cornell University Press, 1991.

Luthi, Jean-Jacques. *Le Français en Égypte: Essai d'anthologie.* Beirut: Maison Naaman, 1981.

Lyons, Martyn. *Napoleon Bonaparte and the Legacy of the French Revolution.* Basingstoke: Macmillan, 1994.

Macfie, A. L. *Orientalism: A Reader.* Edinburgh: Edinburgh University Press, 2000.

MacKenzie, John M. *Orientalism: History, Theory, and the Arts.* Manchester: Manchester University Press, 1995.

MacMaster, Neil. *Colonial Migrants and Racism: Algerians in France, 1900–62.* New York: St. Martin's Press, 1997.

Malino, Frances. *A Jew in the French Revolution: The Life of Zalkind Hourwitz.* Oxford: Blackwell Publishers, 1996.

Mansel, Philip. *Louis XVIII.* 2nd ed. Stroud: Sutton, 1999.

————. *Paris between Empires, 1814–1852.* London: John Murray, 2001.

Marcel, J.-J. *Contes du Chekh ul-Mohdy.* 1833–35. Reprint, Paris: Summa Aegyptica, 2003.

Margon, René Lemoine de. *Le général Abdelal.* Paris: Calmann Lévy, 1887.

Markov, Walter M., and Claude Keisch. *Grand Empire: Virtue and Vice in the Napoleonic Era.* New York: Hippocrene Books, 1990.

Marrinan, Michael. *Painting Politics for Louis-Philippe: Art and Ideology in Orléanist France, 1830–1848.* New Haven, CT: Yale University Press, 1988.

Massad, Joseph. *Desiring Arabs.* Chicago: University of Chicago Press, 2007.

Masson, Frédéric. *L'affaire Maubreuil.* Paris: P. Ollendorff, 1907.

————. *Cavaliers de Napoléon.* Paris: Ollendorff, 1920.

Masters, Bruce. *Christians and Jews in the Ottoman Arab World: The Roots of Sectarianism.* New York: Cambridge University Press, 2001.

————. "The View from the Province: Syrian Chronicles of the Eighteenth Century." *Journal of the American Oriental Society* 114 (1994): 353–62.

Matar, Nabil. *Turks, Moors, and Englishmen in the Age of Discovery.* New York: Columbia University Press, 1999.

Mathiez, Albert. *La Révolution et les étrangers: Cosmopolitisme et défense national.* Paris: La Renaissance du Livre, 1918.

Mathorez, Jules. *Les étrangers en France sous l'ancien régime: Histoire de la formation de la population française.* 2 vols. Paris: E. Champion, 1919.

Mayeux, F. J. *Bédouins ou Arabes du désert.* Paris: Feux-Delaunay, 1816.

McGetchin, Douglas T. "Wilting Florists: The Turbulent Early Decades of the Société Asiatique, 1822–1860." *Journal of the History of Ideas* 64 (October 2003): 565–80.

McPhee, Peter. *A Social History of France, 1780–1880.* London: Routledge, 1992.

Méffre, Barthélemy-Joseph-Pierre. *Quelques recherches sur l'effets du café.* Montpellier: Jean Martel, 1820.

Mengin, Félix. *Histoire de l'Égypte sous le gouvernement de Mohammed-Aly, ou Récit des événements politiques et militaires qui ont eu lieu depuis le départ des Français jusqu'en*

1823, ouvrage enrichi de notes par MM. Langlès et Jomard et précédé d'une introduction historique par M. Agoub. Paris: A. Bertrand, 1823.

Merriman, John M. *The Margins of City Life: Explorations on the French Urban Frontier, 1815–1851.* New York: Oxford University Press, 1991.

Merriman, Nick. *The Peopling of London: Fifteen Thousand Years of Settlement from Overseas.* London: Museum of London/Reaktion Books, 1993.

Méry, Joseph. *L'assassinat: Scènes méridionales de 1815.* Paris: Urbain Canel et Adolphe Guyot, 1832.

Messaoudi, Alain. "Orientaux orientalistes: Les Pharaon, interprètes du Sud au service du Nord." In *Sud-Nord: Cultures colourales en France, XIXe-XXe siècle,* edited by Colette Zytnicki and Chantal Bordes-Benayoun. 243–55. Toulouse: Privat, 2004.

Michaud, Joseph François, and Louis Gabriel Michaud. *Biographie universelle, ancienne et moderne, ou Histoire par ordre alphabétique.* Vol. 56 (Supplement). Paris: Michaud Frères, 1862.

Miller, Judith A. *Mastering the Market: The State and the Grain Trade in Northern France, 1700–1860.* Cambridge: Cambridge University Press, 1998.

Miller, Susan Gilson. *Disorienting Encounters: Travels of a Moroccan Scholar in France in 1845–1846: The Voyage of Muhammad as-Saffar.* Berkeley: University of California Press, 1992.

Milza, Pierre, Laurent Gervereau, Émile Témime, and Jean-Hugues Berrou. *Toute la France: Histoire de l'immigration en France au XXe siècle.* Paris: Somogy, 1998.

Mishaqah, Mikhail. *Murder, Mayhem, Pillage, and Plunder: The History of the Lebanon in the 18th and 19th Centuries.* Translated by W. M. Thackston. Albany: State University of New York Press, 1988.

Mitchell, Timothy. *Colonising Egypt.* Cambridge: Cambridge University Press, 1988.

Moch, Leslie Page. *Paths to the City: Regional Migration in Nineteenth-Century France.* Beverly Hills: Sage Publications, 1983.

Morsy, Magali. *North Africa, 1800–1900: A Survey from the Nile Valley to the Atlantic.* London: Longman, 1984.

Naaman, Abdallah. *Histoire des Orientaux de France du Ier au XXe siècle.* Paris: Ellipses, 2004.

Naff, Thomas, and Roger Owen, eds. *Studies in Eighteenth-Century Islamic History.* Carbondale, IL: Southern Illinois University Press, 1977.

Newman, Daniel. "The European Influence on Arabic during the Nahda: Lexical Borrowing from European Languages (ta'rib) in Nineteenth-Century Literature." *Arabic Language and Literature* 5 (2002): 1–32.

Noël, Erick. *Être noir en France au XVIIIe siècle.* Paris: Tallandier, 2006.

Noiriel, Gérard. *Le creuset français: Histoire de l'immigration, XIXe-XXe siècles.* Paris: Seuil, 1988.

———. "For a Subjectivist Approach to the Social." In *Histories: French Constructions of the Past,* edited by Jacques Revel and Lynn Hunt, translated by Arthur Goldhammer, 579–87. The New Press: New York, 1995.

———. *Population, immigration et identité nationale en France, XIXe-XXe siècle.* Paris: Hachette, 1992.

————. *La tyrannie du national: Le droit d'asile en Europe, 1793–1993.* Paris: Calmann-Lévy, 1991.

Noirot, Paul, and Dominique Feintrenie, eds. *La campagne d'Égypte, 1798–1801: Mythes et réalités.* Paris: Musée de l'armée, 1998.

Nora, Pierre, ed. *Les lieux de mémoire.* 7 vols. Paris: Gallimard, 1984–86.

Nuseibeh, Hazem Zaki. *The Ideas of Arab Nationalism.* Ithaca, NY: Cornell University Press, 1956.

Nye, Robert A. *Masculinity and Male Codes of Honor in Modern France.* New York: Oxford University Press, 1993.

O'Connor, A. J. "Volney, Bonaparte, and Taine." *French Studies* 3 (1949): 149–51.

Ogden, Philip E., and Paul White. *Migrants in Modern France: Population Mobility in the Later Nineteenth and Twentieth Centuries.* London: Unwin Hyman, 1989.

L'Orient des Provençaux dans l'histoire. Marseille: Archives Départementales, 1984.

Orr, Linda. *Headless History: Nineteenth-Century French Historiography of the Revolution.* Ithaca, NY: Cornell University Press, 1990.

Pagden, Anthony. *Lords of All the World: Ideologies of Empire in Spain, Britain, and France, c. 1500–c. 1800.* New Haven, CT: Yale University Press, 1995.

Parry, Kenneth, and John R. Hinnells. *The Blackwell Dictionary of Eastern Christianity.* Oxford: Blackwell Publishers, 2000.

Peabody, Sue. *There Are No Slaves in France: The Political Culture of Race and Slavery in the Ancien Régime.* New York: Oxford University Press, 2002.

Peabody, Sue, and Tyler Edward Stovall. *The Color of Liberty: Histories of Race in France.* Durham, NC: Duke University Press, 2003.

Perrot, Jean-Claude, and S. J. Woolf. *State and Statistics in France, 1789–1815.* Chur, Switzerland: Harwood Academic Publishers, 1984.

Petiteau, Natalie. *Lendemains d'empire: Les soldats de Napoléon dans la France du XIXe siècle.* Paris: La Boutique de l'Histoire, 2003.

Pharaon, Florian. *Épisodes de la conquête: Cathédrale et mosquée.* Paris: A. Lahure, 1880.

Pharaon, Joanny. *Biographie des ex-ministres de Charles X, mis en accusation par le peuple.* Paris: Selligué, 1830.

————. *Les Cabiles et Boudgie, précédé d'un vocabulaire franco-cabile-algérien (extrait de Shaler) par Florian Pharaon.* Algiers: Chez Philippe, 1835.

————. *De la législation française, musulmane et juive à Alger.* Paris: T. Barrois Fils, 1835.

————. *Esquisse historique et politique sur Mahmoud II et Nicolas Ier, suivie de la Description de Schumla, Varna, Andrinople et Constantinople.* Paris: Lecointe, 1829.

————. *Exercices de lecture et de traduction arabe.* Algiers: Imprimerie du Gouvernement, 1835.

————. *Grammaire élémentaire d'arabe vulgaire ou algérienne, à l'usage des Français.* Paris: Didot, 1832.

————. *Notice sur Benjamin Constant.* Paris: Imprimerie de Selligue, 1830.

————. *Premiers éléments de la langue française à l'usage des Orientaux qui veulent apprendre cette langue.* Marseille: Chez Comoin, 1827.

Pharaon, Joanny, and Dr. Goldscheider. "Lettres sur l'état des juifs en Algérie." *Archives israélites de France* 1 (1840): 476–78, 537–45.

Philipp, Thomas. *Acre: The Rise and Fall of a Palestinian City, 1730–1831*. New York: Columbia University Press, 2001.

———. "Class, Community, and Arab Historiography in the Early Nineteenth Century—The Dawn of a New Era." *International Journal of Middle East Studies* 16 (1984): 161–75.

———. *The Syrians in Egypt, 1725–1975*. Stuttgart: Steiner, 1985.

Philipp, Thomas, and Ulrich Haarmaan. *The Mamluks in Egyptian Politics and Society*. Cambridge: Cambridge University Press, 1998.

Pinkney, David. *The French Revolution of 1830*. Princeton, NJ: Princeton University Press, 1972.

Pitts, Jennifer. "Liberalism and Empire in a Nineteenth-Century Algerian Mirror." *Modern Intellectual History* 6 (2009): 287–313.

———. *A Turn to Empire: The Rise of Imperial Liberalism in Britain and France*. Princeton NJ: Princeton University Press, 2005.

Pluchon, Pierre. *Nègres et juifs au XVIIIe siècle: Le racisme au siècle des lumières*. Paris: Tallandier, 1984.

Polk, William R., and Richard L. Chambers. *Beginnings of Modernization in the Middle East: The Nineteenth Century*. Chicago: University of Chicago Press, 1968.

Pollard, Lisa. *Nurturing the Nation: The Family Politics of Modernizing, Colonizing, and Liberating Egypt, 1805–1923*. Berkeley: University of California Press, 2005.

Porterfield, Todd. *The Allure of Empire: Art in the Service of French Imperialism, 1798–1836*. Princeton, NJ: Princeton University Press, 1998.

Prendergast, Christopher. *Napoleon and History Painting: Antoine-Jean Gros's La Bataille D'Eylau*. Oxford: Clarendon Press, 1997.

Rao, Anna-Maria. *Esuli: L'emigrazione politica italiana in Francia (1792–1802)*. Naples: Guida Editori, 1992.

———. "Italian Refugees in France." Paper presented at the XVth Biennial Conference of the Australasian Association for European History, Melbourne, July 11–15, 2005.

———. "Paris et les exilés italiens en 1799." In *Paris et la Révolution: Actes du Colloque de Paris I, 14–16 avril 1989*, edited by Michel Vovelle, 225–35. Paris: Publications de la Sorbonne, 1989.

———. "Les réfugiés italiens en 1799." *Annales historiques de la Révolution française* 52 (1980): 225–61.

[Raphaël de Monachis et al.] *Annuaire de la République française, pour l'an VIII (et IX) de l'ère française: Constitution de la république française*. Cairo: Imprimerie Nationale, an VIII.

Rapport, Michael. *Nationality and Citizenship in Revolutionary France: The Treatment of Foreigners, 1789–1799*. Oxford: Clarendon, 2000.

Raymond, André. *Arab Cities in the Ottoman Period: Cairo, Syria, and the Maghreb*. Aldershot: Ashgate, 2002.

———. *Artisans et commerçants au Caire au XVIIIe siècle*. Damascus: Institut Français de Damas, 1974.

———. *Cairo*. Cambridge, MA: Harvard University Press, 2000.

———. *Égyptiens et Français au Caire, 1798–1801*. Cairo: Institut Français d'Archéologie Orientale, 1998.

Raymond, André, and Daniel Panzac, eds. *La France et l'Égypte à l'époque des vice-rois, 1805–1882.* Cairo: IFAO, 2002.

Reddy, William. "Condottieri of the Pen: Journalists and the Public Sphere in Post-Revolutionary France, 1815–1850." *American Historical Review* 99 (1994): 1546–70.

———. *The Invisible Code: Honor and Sentiment in Postrevolutionary France, 1814–1848.* Berkeley: University of California Press, 1997.

Regnier, Philippe, and A. Abdelnour. *Les Saint-Simoniens en Égypte, 1833–1851.* Cairo: Banque de l'Union Européenne/Amin F. Abdelnour, 1989.

Reid, Donald M. *Whose Pharaohs?: Archaeology, Museums, and Egyptian National Identity from Napoleon to World War I.* Berkeley: University of California Press, 2002.

Reig, Daniel. *Homo orientaliste: La langue arabe en France depuis le XIXe siècle.* Paris: Maisonneuve et Larose, 1988.

Resnick, Daniel P. *The White Terror and the Political Reaction after Waterloo.* Cambridge, MA: Harvard University Press, 1966.

Ridley, Ronald T. *Napoleon's Proconsul in Egypt: The Life and Times of Bernardino Drovetti.* London: Rubicon, 1997.

Robiquet, Jean. *Daily Life in France under Napoleon.* Translated by Violet M. Macdonald. New York: Macmillan, 1963.

Roche, Daniel. *La France des lumières.* Paris: Fayard, 1993.

———. *Humeurs vagabondes: De la circulation des hommes et de l'utilité des voyages.* Paris: Fayard, 2003.

———. *La ville promise: Mobilité et accueil à Paris (fin XVIIe–début XIXe siècle).* Paris: Fayard, 2000.

Rodinson, Maxime. *The Arabs.* Chicago: University of Chicago Press, 1981.

Roper, Geoffrey. "Ahmad Faris Al-Shidyaq and the Libraries of Europe and the Ottoman Empire." *Libraries and Culture* 33 (1998): 233–48.

Rosanvallon, Pierre. *La monarchie impossible: Les Chartes de 1814 et de 1830.* Paris: Fayard, 1994.

Rossignol, F., and J. Pharaon. *Histoire de la Révolution de 1830 et des nouvelles barricades.* Paris: P. Vimont, 1830.

Roussillon, Alain. "'Ce qu'ils nomment 'Liberté' . . . Rif'a al-Tahtawi, ou l'invention (avortée) d'une modernité politique ottomane." *Arabica* 48.2 (2001): 143–85.

Roussillon, Vigo. "L'expédition d'Égypte: Fragments des mémoires militaires du colonel Vigo Roussillon (1793–1837)." *Revue des deux mondes* 100 (1890): 576–609, 721–50.

Roustam. *Souvenirs de Roustam, mamelouck de Napoléon Ier.* Paris: P. Ollendorf, 1911.

Russell, Terence M. *The Napoleonic Survey of Egypt: Description de l'Égypte, the Monuments, and Customs of Egypt; Selected Engravings and Texts.* Aldershot: Ashgate, 2001.

Sabbagh, Mikha'il. *Cantique à S. M. Napoléon le Grand à l'occasion de la naissance de son fils Napoléon II, roi de Rome: Allégorie sur le bonheur futur de la France et la paix de l'univers.* Translated by Antoine Isaac Silvestre de Sacy. Paris: Imprimerie Impériale, 1811.

———. *Cantique de félicitation à sa majesté très-chrétienne, Louis le Désiré, roi de France et de Navarre.* Paris: Imprimerie Royale, 1814.

———. *Kitab Musabaqat al-barq wa-al-ghamam fi su'at al-hamam (La colombe messagère, plus rapide que l'éclair, plus prompte que la nue), par Michel Sabbagh, Traduit de l'arabe en françois, par M. A.-J. Silvestre de Sacy.* Paris: Imprimerie Impériale, an XIV-1805.

———. *Tarikh al-Shaykh Dahir al-'Umar al-Zaydani hakim 'Akka wa bilad Safd.* Edited by Qustantin al-Basha al-Mukhalasi. (Harisa: Matba'at al Qiddis Bulus, 1935).

Sacy, Antoine Isaac Silvestre de. *Chrestomathie arabe.* 2 vols. Paris, 1826; reprint, Osnabrück: Biblio Verlag, 1973.

Sahlins, Peter. *Boundaries: The Making of France and Spain in the Pyrenees.* Berkeley: University of California Press, 1989.

———. *Unnaturally French: Foreign Citizens in the Old Regime and After.* Ithaca, NY: Cornell University Press, 2004.

Said, Edward W. "Orientalism and After." In *A Critical Sense: Interviews with Intellectuals,* edited by Peter Osborne, 65–88. New York: Routledge, 1996.

———. *Orientalism: Western Conceptions of the Orient.* New York: Pantheon, 1978.

Saint-Vincent, Jean Baptiste Geneviève Marcellin Bory de. "L'Homme." In *Dictionnaire classique d'histoire naturelle,* 269–346. Paris: Baudouin Frères, 1825..

Salvandy, Narcisse-Achille de. *Lettre de la girafe au pacha d'Égypte pour lui rendre compte de son voyage à Saint-Cloud, et envoyer les rognures de la censure de France au journal qui s'établit à Alexandrie en Afrique.* Paris: A. Sautelet, 1827.

Saman, Edouard. "L'Église Saint-Nicolas de Myre de Marseille et les collaborateurs orientaux de Bonaparte." *Marseille* 124 (1981): 50–59.

Sand, George. *Histoire de ma vie.* Paris: M. Lévy Frères, 1856.

Sauvigny, Guillaume de Bertier de. *The Bourbon Restoration.* Translated by Lynn M. Case. Philadelphia: University of Pennsylvania Press, 1967.

Savant, Jean. *Les Mamelouks de Napoléon.* Paris: Calmann-Lévy, 1949.

Sayyid-Marsot, Afaf Lutfi al-. *Egypt in the Reign of Muhammad Ali.* Cambridge: Cambridge University Press, 1984.

———. *A Short History of Modern Egypt.* Cambridge: Cambridge University Press, 1985.

———. *Women and Men in Late Eighteenth-Century Egypt.* Austin: University of Texas Press, 1995.

Schechter, Ronald. *Obstinate Hebrews: Representations of Jews in France, 1715–1815.* Berkeley: University of California Press, 2003.

Schroeder, Paul W. *The Transformation of European Politics, 1763–1848.* Oxford: Oxford University Press, 1996.

Schur, Nathan. *Napoleon in the Holy Land.* London: Greenhill Books, 1999.

Schwab, Raymond. *The Oriental Renaissance: Europe's Rediscovery of India and the East, 1680–1880.* Translated by Gene Patterson-Black and Victor Reinking. New York: Columbia University Press, 1984.

Semallé, Jean-René-Pierre, comte de. *Souvenirs du comte de Semallé, page de Louis XVI.* Paris: A. Picard et Fils, 1898.

Sharabi, Hisham. *Arab Intellectuals and the West: The Formative Years, 1875–1914.* Baltimore: The Johns Hopkins University Press, 1970.

Shaw, Stanford A. *Ottoman Egypt in the Age of the French Revolution.* Cambridge, MA: Harvard University Press, 1966.

Shayyal, Jamal al-Din al-. *Rifa'ah Rafi' al-Tahtawi, 1801–1873.* Cairo: Dar al-Maarif, 1958.

———. *Tarikh al-tarjamah wa-al-harakah al-thaqafiyah fi 'asr Muhammad 'Ali.* Cairo: Dar al-Fikr al-'Arabi, 1951.

Sheehi, Stephen. *Foundations of Modern Arab Identity.* Gainesville: University Press of Florida, 2004.

Siegfried, Susan L. *The Art of Louis-Léopold Boilly: Modern Life in Napoleonic France.* New Haven, CT: Yale University Press, 1995.

Silvera, Alain. "Egypt and the French Revolution, 1798–1801." *Revue française d'histoire d'outre-mer* 69 (1982): 307–22.

———. "The First Egyptian Student Mission to France under Muhammad Ali." *Middle Eastern Studies* 16 (1980): 1–22.

Silverstein, Paul A. *Algeria in France: Transpolitics, Race, and Nation.* Bloomington: Indiana University Press, 2004.

Simon, Jacques. *L'immigration algérienne en France des origines à l'indépendance.* Paris: Paris-Méditerranée, 2000.

Sinoué, Gilbert. *Le dernier pharaon: Méhémet-Ali, 1770–1849.* Paris: Pygmalion/G. Watelet, 1997.

Siouffi, Nicolas. *Études sur la religion des Soubbas ou Subéens, leurs dogmes, leurs moeurs.* Paris: Imprimerie Nationale, 1880.

Smith, Anthony D. *The Ethnic Origins of Nations.* Oxford: Blackwell, 1986.

Spitzer, Alan B. *The French Generation of 1820.* Princeton, NJ: Princeton University Press, 1987.

———. "Malicious Memories: Restoration Politics and a Prosopography of Turncoats." *French Historical Studies* 24 (2001): 37–61.

Sponza, Lucio. *Italian Immigrants in Nineteenth-Century Britain: Realities and Images.* Leicester: Leicester University Press, 1988.

Staum, Martin. *Labeling People: French Scholars on Society, Race, and Empire, 1815–1848.* Montreal: McGill-Queen's University Press, 2003.

———. "Paris Ethnology and the Perfectibility of 'Races.'" *Canadian Journal of History* 35 (2000): 453–72.

Stora, Benjamin. *Algeria, 1830–2000: A Short History.* Ithaca, NY: Cornell University Press, 2001.

———. *Ils venaient d'Algérie: L'immigration algérienne en France, 1912–1992.* Paris: Fayard, 1992.

Stovall, Tyler Edward. *Paris Noir: African Americans in the City of Light.* Boston: Houghton Mifflin, 1996.

Suleiman, Yasir. *The Arabic Language and National Identity: A Study in Ideology.* Edinburgh: Edinburgh University Press, 2003.

Tageldin, Shaden. "Disarming Words: Reading (Post)Colonial Egypt's Double Bond to Europe." PhD diss., University of California, Berkeley, 2004.

Tagher, J. "Ordres supérieurs relatifs à la conservation des antiquités et à la création d'un musée au Caire." *Cahiers d'histoire égyptienne* 3 (1950): 13–26.

Taguieff, Pierre-André. *La République enlisée: Pluralisme, communautarisme et citoyenneté.* Paris: Syrtes, 2005.

Tahtawi, Rifa'a Rafi' al-. *An Imam in Paris: Account of a Stay in France by an Egyptian Cleric, 1826–1831.* Translated by Daniel L. Newman. London: Saqi, 2004.

———. *Takhlis al-ibriz fy talkhis bariz.* Cairo: Dar Ibn Zaydun, n.d.

Taouïl, Gabriel. "Biographies et fables d'Ésope." Bibliothèque Nationale de France, MS Arabes, 1808.

Tavakoli-Targhi, Mohamad. *Refashioning Iran: Orientalism, Occidentalism, and Historiography.* New York: Palgrave, 2001.

Temimi, Abdeljalil. "L'activité de Hamdan Khudja à Paris et à Istanbul pour la question algérienne." *Revue d'histoire maghrébine* 7–8 (1977): 234–43.

———. *Recherches et documents d'histoire maghrébine: L'Algérie, la Tunisie et la Tripolitaine.* Tunis: Revue d'Histoire Maghrébine, 1980.

Thompson, Victoria E. "Telling 'Spatial Stories': Urban Space and Bourgeois Identity in Early Nineteenth-Century Paris." *Journal of Modern History* 75 (2003): 523–56.

Thomson, Ann. *Barbary and Enlightenment: European Attitudes Towards the Maghreb in the 18th Century.* Leiden: Brill, 1987.

Thornton, Thomas. *A Sporting Tour through Various Parts of France, in the Year 1802.* London: Longman, 1806.

Tibi, Bassam. *Arab Nationalism: Between Islam and the Nation-State.* 3rd ed. New York: St. Martin's Press, 1997.

Tilly, Charles. "Transplanted Networks." In *Immigration Reconsidered: History, Sociology, and Politics,* edited by Virginia Yans-McLaughlin, 79–95. New York: Oxford University Press, 1990.

Tlili, Béchir. *Les rapports culturels et idéologiques entre l'Orient et l'Occident, en Tunisie au XIXème siècle, 1830–1880.* Tunis: Université de Tunis, 1974.

Troupeau, Gérard. "Deux cents ans d'enseignement de l'arabe a l'École des Langues Orientales Vivantes." *Chroniques Yéménites* 6 (1997): 61–68.

Tulard, Jean, ed. *Almanach de Paris.* Vol. 2, *De 1789 à nos jours.* Paris: Encyclopédia Universalis, 1990.

———, ed. *Dictionnaire Napoléon.* Paris: Fayard, 1987.

———. *Le Grand Empire, 1804–1815.* Paris: A. Michel, 1982.

———. *Nouvelle histoire de Paris: Le Consulat et l'Empire, 1800–1815.* Paris: Hachette, 1970.

———. *Paris et son administration, 1800–1830.* Paris: Ville de Paris, Commission des Travaux Historiques, 1976.

Turk, Nakoula el-. *Histoire de l'expédition des Français en Égypte.* Translated by Desgranges Aîné. Paris: Imprimerie Royale, 1839.

Tusun, Prince 'Umar. *Ba'that al-'ilmiyah fi 'ahd Muhammad 'Ali, thumma fi 'ahday 'Abbas al-Awwal wa-Sa'id.* Alexandria: Matba'at Salah al-Din, 1934.

Urvoy, Dominique. "Le monde musulman selon les idées de la Révolution française." *Revue du monde musulman et de la Méditerranée* 52–53, ⅔ (1989): 35–48.

Valensi, Lucette. *On the Eve of Colonialism: North Africa before the French Conquest.* New York: Africana, 1977.

Vauchelle-Haquet, Aline, and Gérard Dufour. "Les Espagnols naturalisés français et les Espagnols ayant obtenu l'autorisation de fixer leur domicile en France de 1814 à 1831." In

Exil politique et migration économique: Espagnols et Français aux XIXe-XXe siècles, edited by Centre national de la recherche scientifique, 31–46. Paris: Éditions du Centre National de la Recherche Scientifique, 1991.

Vidal, Dominique, and Karim Bourtel. *Le mal-être arabe: Enfants de la colonisation.* Marseille: Agone, 2005.

Visram, Rozina. *Ayahs, Lascars, and Princes: Indians in Britain, 1700–1947.* London: Pluto Press, 1986.

Volney, Constantin François de Chasseboeuf, comte de. *Œuvres de C.-F. Volney.* 8 vols. Paris: Parmentier, 1825–26.

Vovelle, Michel. *Les républiques-sœurs sous le regard de la Grande Nation, 1795–1803: De l'Italie aux portes de l'Empire ottoman, l'impact du modèle républicain.* Paris: L'Harmattan, 2000.

Watenpaugh, Keith David. *Being Modern in the Middle East: Revolution, Nationalism, Colonialism, and the Arab Middle Class.* Princeton, NJ: Princeton University Press, 2006.

Weil, Patrick. *La République et sa diversité: Immigration, intégration, discriminations.* Paris: Seuil, 2005.

Wendell, Charles. *The Evolution of the Egyptian National Image: From Its Origins to Ahmad Lutfi al-Sayyid.* Berkeley: University of California Press, 1972.

Werbner, Pnina. *Imagined Diasporas among Manchester Muslims: The Public Performance of Pakistani Transnational Identity Politics.* Oxford: James Currey, 2002.

Wieviorka, Michel, and Philippe Bataille. *La France raciste.* Paris: Seuil, 1992.

Wilder, Gary. "Unthinking French History. Colonial Studies beyond National Identity." In *After the Imperial Turn: Critical Approaches to 'National' Histories and Literatures,* edited by Antoinette Burton. 125–43. Durham, NC: Duke University Press, 2003.

Willms, Johannes. *Paris, Capital of Europe: From the Revolution to the Belle Époque.* New York: Holmes & Meier, 1997.

Winter, Michael. *Egyptian Society under Ottoman Rule, 1517–1798.* New York: Routledge, 1992.

Woloch, Isser. *Napoleon and His Collaborators: The Making of a Dictatorship.* New York: W. W. Norton, 2001.

———. *The New Regime: Transformations of the French Civic Order, 1789–1820s.* New York: W. W. Norton, 1994.

Woolf, Stuart. "The Construction of a European World-View in the Revolutionary-Napoleonic Years." *Past and Present* 137 (1992): 72–101.

———. "Europe and Its Historians." *Contemporary European History* 12 (2003): 323–37.

———. "French Civilization and Ethnicity in the Napoleonic Empire." *Past and Present* 124 (1989): 96–120.

———. *Napoleon's Integration of Europe.* London: Routledge, 1991.

Zachs, Fruma. "Mikha'il Mishaqa—The First Historian of Modern Syria." *British Journal of Middle Eastern Studies* 28 (2001): 67–87.

Zeine, Zeine N. *Arab-Turkish Relations and the Emergence of Arab Nationalism.* Westport, CT: Greenwood Press, 1981.

INDEX

283

TEXT	10/12/5 Minion Pro
DISPLAY	Minion Pro
COMPOSITOR	Westchester Book Group
PRINTER AND BINDER	Sheridan Books, Inc.